Praise for *The Invisible Line*

"An astonishingly detailed rendering ⟨...⟩ ⟨...⟩ial experience in an evolving national cul⟨...⟩ ga-tion to civil rights." ⟨...⟩*iew*

"In this meticulously researched history, Sharfstein's ace-in-the-hole is his ability to re-create dramatic events and build flesh-and-blood characters. . . . He sets out to change the way we think about race, and he succeeds brilliantly. . . . A must-read." —*Financial Times*

"A spellbinding chronicle of racial passing in America . . . Sharfstein . . . approaches his subject with a storyteller's verve and a novelist's gift for telling detail. *The Invisible Line* is not only a work of serious scholarship based on exhaustive archival research but an immensely satisfying read." —*The Boston Globe*

"Everyone knows when slavery ended, but few know how Slavery Lite con-tinued under the oppressive sharecropper system. The persistence of such amnesia long after the triumphs of the civil rights movement makes *The Invisible Line* must reading. With dogged research, lawyer and journalist Daniel J. Sharfstein has stitched together the stories of three families toeing America's racial trip wire across several generations. Woven into a novelistic narrative, *The Invisible Line* presents a primer on the hypocrisies that con-fronted everyday Americans from the Revolution through to the 1960s. . . . *The Invisible Line* contains unforgettable struggles that should be recounted not just during Black History Month but year-round." —*San Francisco Chronicle*

"[This] sweeping history of three black families in the U.S. was impeccably researched. Only a writer who lived and breathed his subject matter for more than six years could write with such authority . . . crafted in an immensely readable style . . . Sharfstein breathes life into his long-deceased characters and their stories." —*Associated Press*

"Enhanced by its almost lyrical prose, [*The Invisible Line*] explores ques-tions of elective identity, usually based on wealth, behavior, and reputation, rather than color, as well as the often tumultuous events that led to historical and personal compromises. American social history scholars, genealogists, and general readers who wish to learn through vivid case studies will be interested." —*Library Journal*

"Drawing on archival material, Sharfstein constructs an absorbing history, demonstrating the fluidity and arbitrariness of racial classification."
—*Booklist* (starred review)

"*The Invisible Line* is a detailed and instructive look at America's tortured history and still-evolving attitudes toward race."   —*BookPage*

"*The Invisible Line* shines light on one of the most important, but too often hidden, aspects of American history and culture. Sharfstein's narrative of three families negotiating America's punishing racial terrain is a must-read for all who are interested in the construction of race in the United States."
—Annette Gordon-Reed, Pulitzer Prize–winning author of *The Hemingses of Monticello*

"*The Invisible Line* offers a trilogy of remarkable tales brimming with risk taking, camouflage, irony, narrow escapes, misgivings, regret, delight, and full-scale human drama. Excellent histories have been published about the Great Migration of twentieth-century African Americans from the rural South to the urban North, but, until now, no authoritative and cumulative work has looked at this preceding and overlapping social movement of race changing. This book overthrows nearly everything Americans thought they knew about race."
—Melissa Fay Greene, author of *Praying for Sheetrock* and *There Is No Me Without You*

"An original and often startling look at the vagaries of the 'color line.' Sharfstein shows definitively that it was not a doctrinaire belief in racial purity that gave the South stability but rather a fluid understanding by its people and its institutions of racial difference and its multiple permutations."
—Henry Louis Gates Jr., Alphonse Fletcher University Professor, Harvard University

"Sharfstein brings his original research alive with a novelist's eye for vivid detail and narrative. A groundbreaking work that will stir reflection and debate."   —Matthew Pearl, author of *The Dante Club*

"With lively prose and remarkable research, Sharfstein creates a fresh and stirring epic of American life. He weaves the vexing problem of race into the very fabric of national life and shows just how unsteady and complicated racial identity can be."
—Martha A. Sandweiss, author of *Passing Strange: A Gilded Age Tale of Love and Deception Across the Color Line*

"A tremendous contribution to our understanding of the role of race in American history . . . One of those rare books that makes history come alive."
—Lawrence M. Friedman, Marion Rice Kirkwood Professor, Stanford Law School, and author of *A History of American Law*

"Deeply intertwined in the American story of race are these stories of camouflaged families and their passages across the color line. Daniel Sharfstein disentangles them with eloquence and compassion."
—David K. Shipler, Pulitzer Prize–winning author of *A Country of Strangers: Blacks and Whites in America*

"A beautifully written book that reveals not only how the law has shaped American ideas about race but also how the complexity of human experience has pushed against the rigid boundaries of our legal categories."
—Mark S. Weiner, professor of law, Rutgers-Newark School of Law, and author of *Black Trials*

"Brilliant . . . a true American story. Its consequences pervade the American past and shadow its future."
—Ira Berlin, professor of history, University of Maryland, and author of *The Making of African America*

"A must-read for all serious students of the race line in American life, written with care, verve, sophistication, and enormous learning."
—Randall Kennedy, Michael R. Klein Professor of Law, Harvard University

"A powerful indictment of one of America's most enduring myths. Written with a novelist's eye for fascinating characters and rich sense of place and a scholar's precision and panoramic perspective, *The Invisible Line* makes visible the shifting artificial nature of the 'color line' and its dire, life-changing consequences. Read this book if you want to understand the roots of our knotted racial history. Read this book if you hope to untangle it."
—Bliss Broyard, author of *One Drop*

ABOUT THE AUTHOR

Daniel J. Sharfstein is an associate professor of law at Vanderbilt University. A graduate of Harvard College and Yale Law School, he has been awarded fellowships in legal history from Harvard, New York University, and the National Endowment for the Humanities. He has written for *The Yale Law Journal*, *The New York Times*, *The Economist*, *The Washington Post*, and other publications. He lives with his family in Nashville, Tennessee.

The
INVISIBLE LINE

A Secret History

of Race in America

DANIEL J. SHARFSTEIN

PENGUIN BOOKS

PENGUIN BOOKS

Published by the Penguin Group

Penguin Group (USA) Inc., 375 Hudson Street, New York, New York 10014, U.S.A. • Penguin Group (Canada), 90 Eglinton Avenue East, Suite 700, Toronto, Ontario, Canada M4P 2Y3 (a division of Pearson Penguin Canada Inc.) • Penguin Books Ltd, 80 Strand, London WC2R 0RL, England • Penguin Ireland, 25 St. Stephen's Green, Dublin 2, Ireland (a division of Penguin Books Ltd) • Penguin Group Australia Ltd, 250 Camberwell Road, Camberwell, Victoria 3124, Australia (a division of Pearson Australia Group Pty Ltd) • Penguin Books India Pvt Ltd, 11 Community Centre, Panchsheel Park, New Delhi–110 017, India • Penguin Group (NZ), 67 Apollo Drive, Rosedale, Auckland 0632, New Zealand (a division of Pearson New Zealand Ltd) • Penguin Books (South Africa) (Pty) Ltd, 24 Sturdee Avenue, Rosebank, Johannesburg 2196, South Africa

Penguin Books Ltd, Registered Offices: 80 Strand, London WC2R 0RL, England

First published in the United States of America by The Penguin Press, a member of Penguin Group (USA) Inc. 2011
Published in Penguin Books 2012

10 9 8 7 6 5 4 3 2 1

THE LIBRARY OF CONGRESS HAS CATALOGED THE HARDCOVER EDITION AS FOLLOWS:
Sharfstein, Daniel J.
The invisible line : three American families and the secret journey from Black to white / Daniel J. Sharfstein
p. cm.
Includes bibliographical references and index.
ISBN 978-1-59420-282-7 (hc.)
ISBN 978-0-14-312063-6 (pbk.)
1. Racially mixed people—Race identity—United States—Case studies. 2. Miscegenation—Social aspects—United States—Case studies. 3. Passing (Identity)—United States—Case studies. 4. Race—Social aspects—United States—Case studies. 5. Race awareness—United States—Case studies. 6. United States—Race relations—Case studies. 7. Gibson family 8. Spencer family. 9. Wall family. I. Title.
E184.A1S5724   2011
305.800973—dc21
2010029647

Printed in the United States of America
Designed by Stephanie Huntwork

For Ann

CONTENTS

AUTHOR'S NOTE

The Invisible Line is a work of history. It tells the stories of real people who left traces of their lives in census and military records, wills and property deeds, the occasional memoir, and stories in the back pages of newspapers. In the course of my research, I drew upon the resources of courthouses, manuscript libraries, government archives, and private collections in eighteen states and the District of Columbia. I found that I was able to reconstruct the lives and worlds of the book's main figures in considerable detail—their neighborhoods down to the siding on the homes, the day-to-day routines of their jobs, even the size of the collars they wore on their shirts. Above all, their individual characters emerged with remarkable clarity in private letters, newspaper interviews, and testimony in court and before Congress.

Many of the people I chronicle left behind a voluminous record of their thoughts, aspirations, and agonies. To convey the richness of their stories, I have written the book from their perspectives whenever possible. I have set scenes and described individuals and places as clearly and vividly as the sources allow, consistent with what I know about the time, locations, people, and events. Often the descriptions are based on letters, interviews, and court testimony. In the absence of these personal expressions, I have relied on other material, including documented sources from contemporaneous observers, local histories, and my own observations. Like every historian, I have made inferences in interpreting primary sources, but these inferences—my interpretations of history—are always rooted in fact.

Because *The Invisible Line* is a history of race told largely from the perspective of people who lived in the eighteenth, nineteenth, and early twentieth centuries, I have made every effort to preserve their individual voices by retaining the original spelling, capitalization, and punctuation in direct quotations. I also use a number of archaic terms to refer to African Americans. These are the terms that the subjects of this book used in order to think about racial categories and to define themselves and others.

"Now measure ten drops into the paint . . . There, that's it, not too goddam fast. Now. You want no more than ten, and no less."

Slowly, I measured the glistening black drops, seeing them settle upon the surface and become blacker still, spreading suddenly out to the edges.

"That's it. That's all you have to do," he said. "Never mind how it looks. That's my worry. You just do what you're told and don't try to think about it. When you've done five or six buckets, come back and see if the samples are dry . . . And hurry, we've got to get this batch back off to Washington by 11:30 . . .

"Let's see," he said, selecting a sample and running his thumb across the board. "That's it, as white as George Washington's Sunday-go-to-meetin' wig and as sound as the all-mighty dollar! That's paint!" he said proudly. "That's paint that'll cover just about anything!"

He looked as though I had expressed a doubt and I hurried to say, "It's certainly white all right."

"White! It's the purest white that can be found. Nobody makes a paint any whiter. This batch right here is heading for a national monument!"

RALPH ELLISON, *Invisible Man* (1952)

"Where is the blood of me? Where is my color? My blood is covered over the cornfield among these hills . . . Blood and sweat of mine is on the bare hills where they ain't no timber—where there is old corn rows. That's where my blood is and my color is."

JESSE STUART, "Battle Keaton Dies," in *Head o' W-Hollow* (1936)

WALL FAMILY TREE

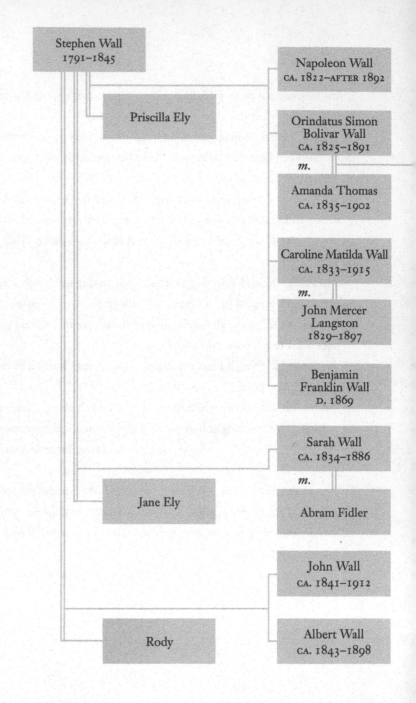

Stephen Wall
1791–1845

Priscilla Ely

Napoleon Wall
CA. 1822–AFTER 1892

Orindatus Simon
Bolivar Wall
CA. 1825–1891
m.

Amanda Thomas
CA. 1835–1902

Caroline Matilda Wall
CA. 1833–1915
m.

John Mercer
Langston
1829–1897

Benjamin
Franklin Wall
D. 1869

Jane Ely

Sarah Wall
CA. 1834–1886
m.

Abram Fidler

Rody

John Wall
CA. 1841–1912

Albert Wall
CA. 1843–1898

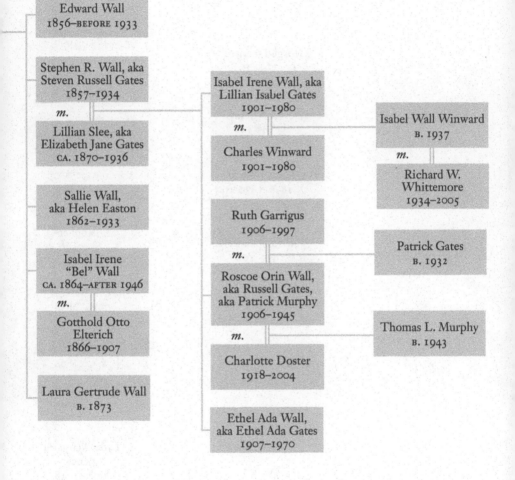

Edward Wall
1856–BEFORE 1933

Stephen R. Wall, aka
Steven Russell Gates
1857–1934

m.

Lillian Slee, aka
Elizabeth Jane Gates
CA. 1870–1936

Sallie Wall,
aka Helen Easton
1862–1933

Isabel Irene
"Bel" Wall
CA. 1864–AFTER 1946

m.

Gotthold Otto
Elterich
1866–1907

Laura Gertrude Wall
B. 1873

Isabel Irene Wall, aka
Lillian Isabel Gates
1901–1980

m.

Charles Winward
1901–1980

Ruth Garrigus
1906–1997

m.

Roscoe Orin Wall,
aka Russell Gates,
aka Patrick Murphy
1906–1945

m.

Charlotte Doster
1918–2004

Ethel Ada Wall,
aka Ethel Ada Gates
1907–1970

Isabel Wall Winward
B. 1937

m.

Richard W.
Whittemore
1934–2005

Patrick Gates
B. 1932

Thomas L. Murphy
B. 1943

*For reasons of space and clarity, the family trees depict only
those branches that are featured in this book. Each family
can claim dozens—even hundreds—of living descendants.*

Spencer Family Tree

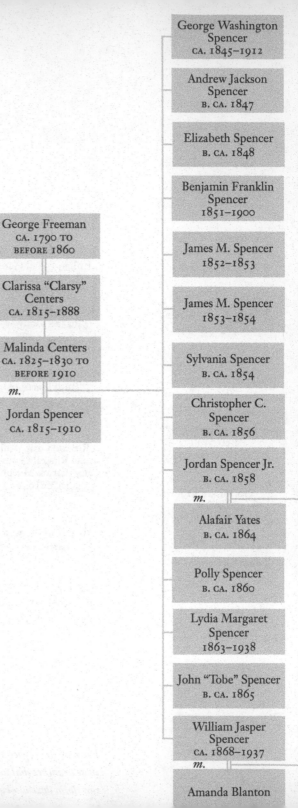

George Freeman
CA. 1790 TO
BEFORE 1860

Clarissa "Clarsy"
Centers
CA. 1815–1888

Malinda Centers
CA. 1825–1830 TO
BEFORE 1910

m.

Jordan Spencer
CA. 1815–1910

George Washington
Spencer
CA. 1845–1912

Andrew Jackson
Spencer
B. CA. 1847

Elizabeth Spencer
B. CA. 1848

Benjamin Franklin
Spencer
1851–1900

James M. Spencer
1852–1853

James M. Spencer
1853–1854

Sylvania Spencer
B. CA. 1854

Christopher C.
Spencer
B. CA. 1856

Jordan Spencer Jr.
B. CA. 1858

m.

Alafair Yates
B. CA. 1864

Polly Spencer
B. CA. 1860

Lydia Margaret
Spencer
1863–1938

John "Tobe" Spencer
B. CA. 1865

William Jasper
Spencer
CA. 1868–1937

m.

Amanda Blanton

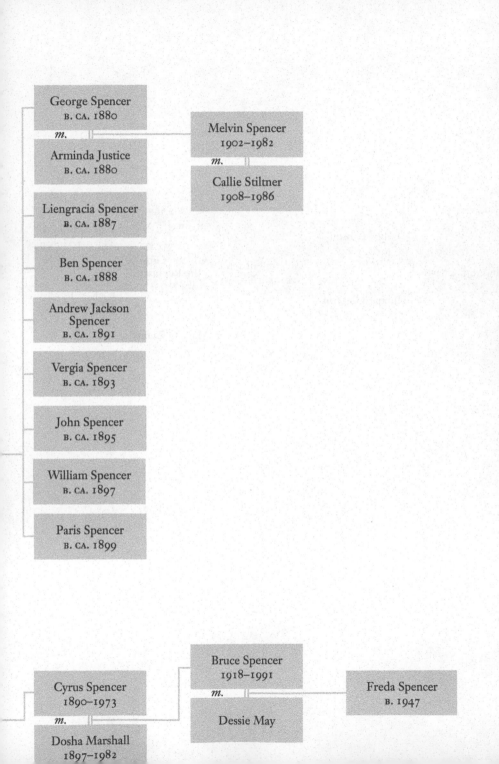

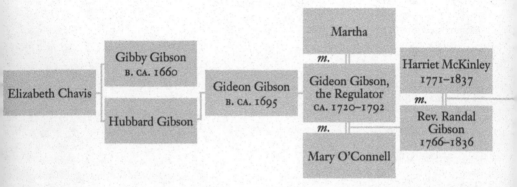

Elizabeth Chavis

Gibby Gibson
B. CA. 1660

Hubbard Gibson

Gideon Gibson
B. CA. 1695

Martha

m.

Gideon Gibson,
the Regulator
CA. 1720–1792

m.

Mary O'Connell

Harriet McKinley
1771–1837

m.

Rev. Randal
Gibson
1766–1836

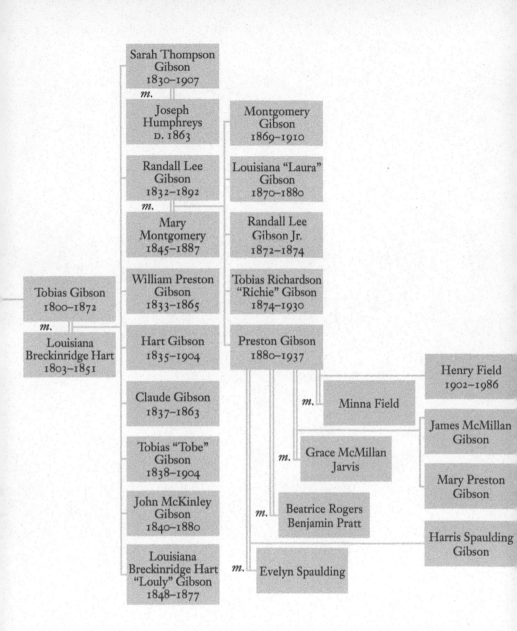

The House Behind the Cedars

THOMAS MURPHY GREETED ME on a warm autumn day in 2005 wearing a baseball cap with a bald eagle staring fiercely across an American flag. He lived twenty-five miles south of Atlanta in an area that was neither country nor city. His house was shrouded by woods yet stood only blocks from a busy commercial strip. It was close enough to the Atlanta Motor Speedway that he could hear the engines revving on NASCAR race days.[1]

Murphy was in his mid-sixties but looked years younger. He had recently retired from his job driving travelers from the Atlanta airport to a rent-a-car lot; soon he would find work baking biscuits for Chick-fil-A. He spoke quickly and was full of ideas. He was buying up property with the help of adjustable-rate mortgages. An enormous pickup truck and towing rig sat in his driveway, part of a plan to start a business hauling cars interstate.

The house that Murphy shared with his roommate was hidden from the road by a copse of cedars and other trees. One could drive past and never guess that it was there. He called it Murphy Manor. It was a spacious contemporary home, although piles of paper and a baroque tangle of computer equipment made it feel cramped inside. A lifelong bachelor, Murphy explained to me that he never married because for the past thirty-five years he had been too busy researching his family's genealogy, devoting his spare hours to tracing his mother's roots back to medieval England. In the mid-1990s he established a connection to the royal house of Lancaster. Since then he has called himself Sir Thomas.

Thomas loved his hobby, all the more because it offered a break from an unhappy work environment. At the rent-a-car company, he could not get along with his co-workers, most of whom were black. He challenged them on the way they dressed and talked, and they frequently called him a racist. After years of arguing, he stopped disputing the accusation.

Having finished his mother's genealogy, Thomas turned to the pedigree of his father, Patrick. Almost immediately he hit a wall. Patrick had died when Thomas was a baby, and his mother had never met anyone from that side of the family. All she seemed to know was that the Murphys came from New York. But after searching birth, death, marriage, census, and probate records, Thomas could not find a single mention of their existence.

Online Thomas found new paths to pursue. He explored some of the dozens of ancestry Web sites that offer searchable databases and connect hundreds of thousands of family-history enthusiasts. He posted inquiries in genealogy chat rooms. He had little luck at first, but then his mother remembered that when she and Patrick first married, he had mentioned a few aliases that he used in case he was ever arrested. About ten years ago Thomas posted this information on the Web. The responses he received changed the way that he looked at himself in the mirror.

A woman in Mississippi wrote in, recognizing the aliases and identifying herself as the granddaughter of one of Patrick's sisters. The Murphys, she informed him, were not from New York. Nor were they Irish—they were not even known as the Murphys until the 1930s. The family name was Wall. Thomas's father had changed his first name, too, the woman wrote. She knew him as Uncle Russell, but he was born Roscoe Orin Wall. Roscoe's grandparents—Thomas's great-grandparents—were named Amanda and Orindatus Wall. Amanda Wall was an Oberlin graduate and civil rights activist who after the Civil War taught newly freed slaves to read and marched for a woman's right to vote. Her husband had been born a slave, but when he died in 1891, he was one of the most politically connected African Americans in Washington, D.C. The Walls were buried together in Arlington National Cemetery. If Sir Thomas Murphy's mother descended from English royalty, his father's ancestors were late-nineteenth-century "colored aristocrats."[2]

THOMAS MURPHY'S STORY IS shared by millions, most of whom do not know it. From the colonial era to the present, people of African ancestry have crossed the color line and faded into the world around them. They have lived among white people, identified themselves as white, and been regarded by others—neighbors, strangers, government officials—as white. On a daily basis, in ways large and small, they asserted their new racial status. On vacation they posed for pictures in front of the "whites only" sign at the beach. At night they told their children and grandchildren tales of the horrors of Sherman's March to the Sea. Their descendants had no reason to imagine that they were anything but white. Like most Americans, they were taught to believe that the line between white and black is and always has been a natural barrier supported by science and religion and fortified by politics and law. Slavery and freedom, segregation and civil rights, whippings and lynchings, discrimination overt and subtle—the history of race in the United States had little to do with them. But all the while, a different story has been hiding in plain sight.[3]

African Americans began to migrate from black to white as soon as slaves arrived on American shores. In seventeenth-century Virginia, social distinctions such as class and race were fluid, but the consequences of being black or white were enormous. It often meant the difference between slavery and freedom, poverty and prosperity, persecution and power. Even so, dozens of European women had children by African men, and together they established the first free black communities in the colonies. With every incentive to become white—it would give them better land and jobs, lower taxes, and less risk of being enslaved—many free blacks assimilated into white communities over time. In response, colonial lawmakers attempted to fix and regulate the status of slaves and free people of color. In 1705 the Virginia legislature defined a person of color as anyone with more than one-eighth African ancestry—a black great-grandparent. Eighty years later the rule was relaxed to one-fourth. Such fractions were a crude proxy for people with recognizably dark skin. To insist on a stricter rule would have been dangerous to the social order, as it would have risked reclassifying an unsettling number of people. The lawmakers were too late—the line between black and white was already porous and would remain so.[4]

The American experience of race continued to oscillate between moments flush with the prospect of racial equality and crackdowns that reaffirmed the categories of black and white, but the migration from black to white never stopped. In the Revolution's wake, nearly all Northern states outlawed slavery, and many Southerners freed their slaves. But during the first half of the nineteenth century, states north and south enacted strict Black Codes, and the common justifications for treating blacks and whites differently began to assume recognizably modern forms. After the Civil War, a decade of Reconstruction promised full citizenship for African Americans. By 1900, however, white supremacy and racial purity had become articles of civic faith, and Southern states were enacting Jim Crow laws that attempted to create entirely separate worlds for blacks and whites, from the maternity ward to the cemetery. Whether the political climate favored or disfavored blacks, the color line did not hold firm. People continued to walk the path from black to white. If anything, rigid rules about race only increased the number of people making the move.[5]

This centuries-long migration fundamentally challenges how Americans have understood and experienced race, yet it is a history that is largely forgotten. According to just about anyone who has considered the question, the migration is impossible to reconstruct. Historians have told us that "passing for white" entailed a radical change of identity, forcing people to abandon their families, alter their names, move far from home, and live in constant fear that their secret would be betrayed. Implicit to this narrative is the assumption that any evidence of passing would always be destroyed.[6]

But traces of the migration have survived. Some of the evidence is relatively well known to those who have gone looking. For centuries African Americans circulated rumors of whites with black ancestry. Occasional news items described moments when the color line bent and broke: a nosy spouse jimmied open a drawer, only to find photographs of a dark-skinned family; an army recruit cut his throat after military doctors assigned him to a colored unit. Memoirs recounted family members who crossed the color line—an aunt who became Italian, a father who was French until he revealed his true origins on his deathbed. During slavery and segregation, judges and juries regularly puzzled over the boundary between black and white. Plaintiffs in freedom suits alleged that they were whites mistakenly held as slaves. Individuals challenged being assigned to black schools and railroad cars. Husbands sought annulments by arguing they had unwittingly married black women. At best, such evidence is scattered across local archives and county courthouses, in library stacks and microfilm reels. Beyond the isolated anecdotes, there seems to be only silence. The assumption that racial passing always entailed secrecy and denial has inspired dozens of novels, plays, and movies over the last two hundred years. But the idea that becoming white required a tragic masquerade has pushed the subject to the margins of history.[7]

In recent years, however, long-buried stories of migration and assimilation across the color line have begun to surface. Thanks to technological advances of the past decade, extraordinary amounts of genealogical material have been digitized, and companies have marketed DNA tests to determine a person's racial background. Millions of Americans are swabbing their cheeks, watching television shows about celebrity genealogies, posting family trees on popular ancestry Web sites—and stumbling across family secrets. The abundant historical resources on the Internet have enabled people to learn names of long-dead ancestors and bare genealogical facts— age, place of residence, occupation, a designation of "mulatto" in the 1850 Census. They have also found clues for understanding how individuals and communities lived, thought, and acted. With every personal account that is recovered, a much bigger story—a new history of what it means to be American—is being revealed.

THE INVISIBLE LINE TELLS the stories of three families that made the journey from black to white at different points in American history. The first family, the Gibsons, were sugar planters in Louisiana and horse breeders in the bluegrass region of central Kentucky. They descended from some of the leading families of the South, yet from generation to generation they also passed down vague stories to explain why some of them had dark skin. Avid genealogists, they traced the family line to a wealthy landowner in colonial South Carolina. But unknown to them, this man hailed from a free family of color that had moved from Virginia in the early 1700s, assimilated into a Welsh and Scots-Irish farming community, and prospered. After the Revolution a branch of the family headed south and west. Becoming white was an early step in their rise to new levels of wealth, power, and influence that enabled the Gibsons to play key roles in shaping how Americans thought about race.

The second family, the Spencers, settled in a community of subsistence farmers in the Appalachian mountains of eastern Kentucky about a decade before the Civil War. In the hills a person could live a long life without ever meeting anyone who identified himself as a person of color. Given the daily struggle to survive and the overriding value of good neighbors in what amounted to a permanent frontier, caring about race was more trouble than it was worth. It was much easier to embrace the idea that everyone was white, and if some of the local white people happened to have dark skin, few seemed to give it a second thought. The Spencers remained poor and lived in the shadow of the color line for decades. Being white was the most valuable thing they had.

The third family, the Walls, established themselves as white in Washington, D.C., between 1890 and 1910, the decades when Jim Crow took root. As Thomas Murphy would discover in the course of his genealogical research, his great-grandparents journeyed from slavery to freedom and from North Carolina to Ohio and eventually to the District of Columbia. After years of fighting for their rights as citizens, they traded a tradition of activism for an insistence on being white. It was a downwardly mobile move, a willing exile from the heights of African American achievement to anonymous lives as whites on the bare edge of the middle class.

THE GIBSONS, SPENCERS, AND WALLS reflect the diversity of Southern life: they were aristocratic planters, hardscrabble farmers, and educated professionals. They lived in colonnaded mansions and in log cabins sealed with mud—in bayou country, steep mountain hollows, and big cities. Taken together, they tell a singularly American story. They were pioneers settling the wilderness, first along the coast and then inland. They endured revolution, fought in the Civil War, and crossed paths with central figures in American history. As the nation cycled through boom times and depression, they earned and lost and recouped their fortunes. They witnessed and participated in the rise of the plantation economy, the coming of the railroad and industry, and the country's transformation into a modern, urban society. And they experienced America's wrenching transition from slavery to freedom to segregation.

As the nineteenth century progressed, the three families viewed the color line from different vantage points. The Gibsons regarded themselves as white with little sense that they could be anything else. The Spencers had a foot on each side of the line. And the Walls cultivated a strong black identity. Their migration stories speak to the development of American ideas about race. Crossing the color line provided occasions for articulating what it meant to be black and what it meant to be white. Before making the journey, many people spent their days insisting that they were black despite appearances to the contrary. After crossing over, they asserted themselves as white so their new status would go unquestioned. They continued to do so even as—or precisely because—memories of an ambiguous racial past had a tendency to linger. Americans have felt compelled to talk and write about race—and act on their beliefs—in part because its meaning has been so mutable. Racial migration was not just the province of the small group of people of African descent who could make the physical claim to be white. It touched the lives of men and women and entire communities who made every effort to epitomize what black and white were supposed to be.

With time the families gained distance from their roots, but they did not escape the nation's collective belief in a line separating black from white. The frontiers the families confronted were never just physical, and their stories draw a tight connection between the evolution of American society and the shifting dynamics of race. In the process, their stories reveal cruel ironies at the heart of American history. On the broadest level, they show the vexed connection between liberty and equality. The Revolution and the Civil War were crucibles of freedom, but they both forged new inequalities, as the palpable prospect of black emancipation yielded to insistent beliefs in the permanent inferiority of people of color. For African Americans, each advance toward full citizenship seemed to create more struggle, a new degree of racial hostility, and a persistently elusive goal.[8]

On a more intimate level, the stories of the Gibsons, Spencers, and Walls suggest a paradoxical relationship between tolerance and intolerance in American life. The conventional understanding of racial passing as masquerade does not begin to approach the broad range of individuals' experiences as they migrated from black to white. They were not invariably forced to leave home and cover their tracks. There were entirely different ways of becoming white. Often Southern communities knew that certain of their members had ambiguous ancestry but still accepted them, even at times of great racial polarization and violence. These communities repeatedly displayed a wealth of humanity and pragmatism with respect to race, but they remained committed to slavery, segregation, and white supremacy. So did their newest members—for racial migrants, and for the communities who accepted them, one of the surest ways to deflect outside scrutiny was to hate black people. White Southerners were amply capable of being tolerant in their daily lives but chose intolerance as a guiding ideology.

This defining contradiction of American life illuminates how Southerners integrated codes of racial conduct into their daily lives. Their attitudes and actions compel us to consider race in a new light. Race is fundamentally a series of rules with different—and sometimes competing—sources of authority. Some of these rules are formally enacted by legislatures. Others are devised by judges or determined by jury verdicts. Many more are developed informally over the course of each day. African American history is infused with the dual knowledge that the Constitution and the courts were both a pathway and an impediment to freedom and equality—justice could be blind, but legal processes and decision making often reinforced society's pervasive unfairness. Throughout American history, formal and informal rules have insinuated themselves into the way people thought about, acted on, and experienced race. The existence of this legal consciousness does not simply mean that people knew what the law was and followed or broke it accordingly. Rather, individuals and communities have always played an active role in interpreting these rules for themselves and pushing hard against opposing interpretations.[9]

The law's language could be confident with respect to race, but reality was more complex. A statute might draw a "bright line"—defining, as many state legislatures eventually did, anyone with any African ancestry as black. In practice, however, such laws were never crystal clear. Enforcing a color line to its logical extreme was impossible—it would classify as black people who by all appearances were white. In most of the South there were no reliable birth records until the twentieth century. Drawing the line with the strictness that slavery, segregation, and white supremacy seemed to demand would have left very few people free of the fear that someone or some agency of the state could attempt to reclassify them. As a result, individuals and communities drew lines for themselves and for their neighbors in ways that suited them best, often allowing racially ambiguous people to become white.

While racial line-drawing was mostly local and informal, dozens of disputes found their way into court. Interpreting the statutory definitions of the color line, judges often showed independence from the unforgiving politics of racial purity. Courts repeatedly classified people as white even when there was ample evidence that they had black ancestry. For example, when the governing law mandated that one-eighth African ancestry made a person legally black, some courts required that a great-grandparent be "a negro of pure African blood"—a formalism that was almost impossible to satisfy with the evidence available in the nineteenth and early twentieth centuries. What mattered to these courts was whether the people at issue had been accepted by their communities as white.[10]

Impossible standards of proof and a host of other rules allowed courts to defer to a community's judgment. They reflected the courts' fundamental conservatism, a tendency to preserve existing social relationships and discourage overzealous policing of the color line. Such rulings allowed the color line to remain porous and at the same time kept people who were living as white secure in their racial status. In fact, white Southerners were secure enough that they could support racial politics and policies that grew increasingly extreme as the nineteenth century turned to the twentieth— politics and policies that might have had a natural stopping point if they had adversely affected established members of white communities. Judicial tolerance of racial ambiguity existed alongside and even enabled an insistence on absolute racial purity and the belief that blacks carried inferiority in their blood.

Regardless of what courts decided, trials provided occasions for public airings of community gossip that had otherwise never risen above a whisper. Neighbors had to testify that they knew or suspected that families were part black, and local juries had to weigh the evidence and reach verdicts. In effect, the legal process itself had the potential to accomplish what judges were reluctant to do—reclassify whites as black. But individuals and communities listened to trial testimony and understood jury verdicts in the same way that they thought about statutes. They interpreted the evidence for themselves, contested what they did not agree with, and reached accommodations that could seem far afield from the language of a judicial mandate. Damaging testimony and unfavorable verdicts did not make the color line any more concrete. After all, the people who were held to be black were the same as they had been before their trials. They were still light enough to become white and remained able to do so. After a trial, racial knowledge that had been uttered aloud for the world to hear could once again become a matter of winks and nods and stories purposely forgotten.

AS THE LIVES OF the Gibson, Spencer, and Wall families unfold over the course of the book, they show that race is not just a set of rules. It is also a set of stories that people have told themselves and one another over and over again. Some are rooted in day-to-day living and hard-won experience, while others derive from fear and fantasy, hope and despair. Some of these stories are built into more formal legal rules. Others attempt to work around legal enactments and decisions. Some gain the authority of law over time.[11]

The Invisible Line proceeds with the conviction that we cannot understand the tragic ironies of race in American history without paying sustained attention to individual stories. If it were possible to catalog everyone who had ever migrated from black to white, the aggregate picture might demolish the idea that the races are separate and distinct and that the line between black and white has been impregnable. But it would fail to grasp the ultimate significance of becoming white: what such migrations meant to the men and women who made the journey, the communities they left behind, and the communities they joined; how people perceived an invisible line that was repeatedly crossed; and how, living with such ambiguity, they continued to believe in racial difference and order their worlds around it. The histories of the Gibsons, Spencers, and Walls help make sense of liberty and equality, tolerance and intolerance, and race and racism in the United States. And they provide a new set of stories for Americans to tell, retell, and understand as their own.

CHAPTER ONE

GIBSON

Mars Bluff, South Carolina, 1768

GIDEON GIBSON RODE ALONE through the perpetual twilight of the woods on a Sunday. In the thick forests of the South Carolina backcountry, light hit the ground scattered and split, filtered through leaves and pine needles as through a cathedral's stained glass. Sunbeams swirled with dust and gnats in the torpid August air. When Gibson reached his destination, one man was waiting for him, as agreed. In the open they would have taken shots at each other. But here they could meet quietly and alone, as equals and gentlemen.[1]

The shadows obscured profound differences between the men. At age fifty-five, George Gabriel Powell was ten years Gibson's elder, one of the most powerful figures in the colony. He held a seat in the colonial Assembly and owned a sprawling plantation called Weymouth at the mouth of the Great Pee Dee River above Georgetown. King George III had given him command of the Pee Dee Militia, which provided protection from Indians and from the threat of rebellion by slaves, who far outnumbered free colonists along the coast. Gideon Gibson, by contrast, was arguably the most dangerous man in South Carolina. He was a leader of a group of backcountry farmers—they called themselves "Regulators"—who in the name of law and order had repudiated the authority of Assembly and Crown. In addition to his treason and violence, what made Gibson a particular menace was the color of his skin—too dark to be white.[2]

For Powell, just meeting Gibson face-to-face was a significant feat. In July 1768 news of Gibson's treachery had hit the distant capital, then called Charlestown, like an inland hurricane. Deluged with accounts of an army of "outcast Mullatoes, Mustee, free Negroes, all Horse-Thieves, &c.," the Assembly tasked George Gabriel Powell with saving South Carolina from Gideon Gibson. His hundred-mile trek from Charlestown was a journey between worlds. There were no roads in the backcountry. Travelers could wander for days through thicket and forest and "deep miry Swamp," along barely marked, overgrown, tick-infested paths. Although it had been settled for nearly forty years, the area was still a frontier, sparsely populated and with almost no political representation. Far from authority and convention, many backcountry colonists appeared utterly alien to recent arrivals from England. An Anglican minister riding circuit in the 1760s described men and women in "dirty smoaky Cabbin[s]" who walked around barefoot and "continually drunk," "swopp[ed] their Wives as Cattel," and ate "[n]o Eggs, Butter, Flour, Milk, or anything, but fat rusty Bacon, and fair Water, with Indian Corn Bread" alongside "exceedingly filthy, and most execrable" meats unknown in Europe. "They delight in their present low, lazy, sluttish, heathenish, hellish Life, and seem not desirous of changing it," the minister reported. "How would the Polite People of London stare."[3]

By August 9, Powell was deep in the backcountry, seventy miles up the Pee Dee River from his plantation, forty miles below the North Carolina border, and within marching distance of Gideon Gibson's home. The rebel lived along the river in a place of rolling hills called Mars Bluff. Powell assumed his command by recruiting a "posse comitatus" twenty-five strong. Thirty-five more from local militia companies made a total of sixty men. But Powell knew the posse was not large enough to arrest Gibson. "By all Accounts," he remembered, "Gibson was Guarded by a large Body of men and could in an hour raise three hundred more." Powell sent orders out to several militia commanders nearby, asking for one hundred additional men in five days' time. With a force of 160, he entertained a "hopefull Expectation" that he could crush Gibson.[4]

At the same time, Powell invited Gibson to negotiate the terms of his surrender. Powell thought meeting with Gibson "might perhaps have a good effect" and was confident that he could talk sense into the rogue. After all, Gibson had not always been a threat to public order. Before the summer of 1768, he had led as honorable a life as a man could lead in the backcountry. Although his holdings were dwarfed by Powell's plantation, Gibson was one of the largest landowners in the Mars Bluff area, with hundreds of acres of fields and cowpens. His family had been one of the first to settle the backcountry in the 1730s. Besides the fact that the Gibsons were free people of color, there was little to distinguish them from other prosperous planters anywhere in South Carolina. They negotiated land deals, rounded up stray horses, loaned money, administered wills, and helped establish a church. They bought and sold slaves and gave them as gifts to family members.[5]

Despite the Gibson family's relative success, South Carolina's backcountry was indisputably wild. In Gideon Gibson's world, the line between civilization and savagery was palpably thin. Life in the wilderness was never secure. In early 1760 thousands of Cherokees had attacked the backcountry, upending thirty years of economic and social ascent for the Gibsons. British and colonial soldiers had battled and starved the tribe into submission by December 1761, but the conflict left a landscape smoldering with torched homes, laid low by pox and hunger, and littered with the mutilated corpses of Indians and settlers. Dazed soldiers and survivors roamed the wilderness, scrounging for food, while the breakdown of civil society attracted debtors and runaway slaves, thieves and poachers, and gangs of "banditti."[6]

Farmers in Gideon Gibson's position found themselves robbed repeatedly of their cattle and horses. Outlaws invaded their homes and stole money and other possessions in brazen, sadistic attacks. They gouged out victims' eyes, stuck their feet into fires, and branded them with glowing pokers. Newspapers reported that bandits were kidnapping and raping women and luring them into lives of crime and vice. With scant law enforcement and no courts in the backcountry, the farmers had to transport criminals more than a hundred miles to Charlestown to bring anyone to justice—a long, difficult, and expensive journey. If a witness could not travel there or arrived late, the defendants went free. "The honest Man is not secure in his Property," landowners complained, "and Villainy becomes rampant with Impunity."[7]

At first, landowners like Gibson implored the Assembly to create new courts in the backcountry, build jails and workhouses, and even establish public schools so that children would not "naturally follow Hunting— Shooting—Racing—Drinking—Gaming, and ev'ry Species of Wickedness." But the Assembly, in Charlestown, was too far removed and too preoccupied with the growing controversies between the colonies and England to make any meaningful response. Moreover, one royal officer, the provost marshal, held the right to exercise law enforcement duties over the entire colony—and collect regular fees for doing so. In charge of running the jail and serving all writs, warrants, and other court documents in the province, the provost marshal earned "bag[s] of dollars and doubloons of gold." The Regulators' insistence on local courts and law enforcement directly threatened the value of the provost marshal's office. The colonial government appeared at best stymied by and at worst indifferent to the backcountry's plight, and farmers increasingly saw themselves as being denied "the Rights and Privileges of British Subjects."[8]

By early 1767, backcountry farmers had resolved to restore order themselves. Their movement would not be a rebellion. Rather, they described it as a "Regulation." Tired of being ignored by Charlestown, troops of Regulators took it upon themselves to enforce the law and spent two years scourging the countryside. They shot and hanged bandits, burned their nomadic settlements, lashed men and women hundreds of times, and banished incorrigibles from the colony. The vigilantes turned on "all idle persons, all that have not a visible way of getting an honest Living"— namely, anyone who chose to survive by hunting and foraging, a short step in the Regulators' eyes to livestock poaching and outright banditry—and forced idlers to work every day except the Sabbath "on pain of Flagellation." All along the Great Pee Dee River, backcountry landowners joined the Regulator movement with what one observer called "indefatigable Ardour." Befitting his relative wealth and power, Gideon Gibson served as their captain.[9]

For a time respectable landowners along the coast had widely sympathized with the Regulators, understanding them to be the "Honest Party," "People of good Principles, and Property, who have assembled . . . professedly with the View of driving all Horse-Thieves, with their Harbourers, Abettors, and Other Vagabonds from amongst them." But in the summer of 1768, the Regulation took a radical turn. Many of its victims had gone to Charlestown, sued or brought criminal charges, and secured judgments against the Regulators. Facing legal actions that were costly and difficult to defend, the Regulators resolved that the court in Charlestown no longer had jurisdiction over them. The colonial government, they wrote, had become "not a Protection but an Oppression." When officers of the court rode into the backcountry to serve Regulators with legal papers, they were pulled off their horses, chained to posts for days, and flogged. Some were forced to eat the papers. Those who escaped or were released fled to Charlestown with a chilling message: the Regulators now ruled the backcountry.[10]

In July 1768, to satisfy judgments levied against local Regulators, Robert Weaver, a Pee Dee merchant who also held the office of magistrate, started issuing warrants seizing their property. Weaver had a long, unhappy history with Gibson—earlier in the decade, in the heat of doing business, Gibson had objected to his prices and shouted, "You are a hog thief!" In an area where livestock thieves were grouped with rapists and murderers, Gibson's words were the height of insult. Weaver sued for slander, seeking thousands of pounds. Despite the plaintiff's political connections, the jury awarded him a mere twenty shillings.[11]

Weaver entrusted a militia lieutenant with serving the property warrants, but vigilantes kidnapped the officer and brought him to Gibson's house. Weaver drew up a demand for the lieutenant's immediate release and charged the militia's sergeant, the local constable, to deliver it. A company of fourteen local men marched on Mars Bluff in the depths of summer. When the militia reached Gibson's fields, they saw, according to one account, a "great number of People." The Regulators were arranged in two lines—a battle formation. They were not going to give up their prisoner. The company kept marching until they could see the vigilantes' faces.

Gibson was leading the mob. Five of the militia approached. The Regulators waited to receive them, then surrounded them and beat them to the ground.[12]

Standing with his men, Gideon Gibson turned his attention to the remaining members of the militia company. He recognized several. They all lived close enough to one another that they had crossed paths before. Three in the company, he saw, were from the same family: William White; his father, James; and his brother Reubin. Gibson likely knew that William White made his living as a cooper—and had a wife and eight children waiting at home. But Gibson casually, even triumphantly, called for his slaughter.

"Shoot down Billey White," Gibson called, "for I have got Reubin, and if you kill Billey we will manage the rest easy enough."[13]

The Regulators advanced. William White drew his sword but was overtaken before he could strike. As fighting raged on all sides, James White pulled his son from the ground, and together they tried to flee the battle. James stumbled, and when William stopped to help him, several guns fired at close range. William felt himself raked, staggered into a run, and collapsed. When he regained consciousness, several men were shading him. His clothes, his skin, were soaked with blood. One ball had grazed his hip, and a second had passed five inches along the bone of his right arm, from near his shoulder to below his elbow. William knew his arm was "totally shattered."

"Shoot him thro' the head at once," said one of Gibson's Regulators.

"No Damn him he can't live long," said another. "Let him feel himself die."

Instead of spilling his brains into the ground, the men picked William White up and dragged him to Gibson's house. They threw him on the floor and left him "weltering in his own blood." All around him was the sound of torment. The Regulators had rounded up the other militiamen and on Gibson's orders were whipping them as many as fifty times. Finally Reubin White, his back bloodied, asked if he could take his brother home, and Gibson's Regulators released the Whites to the swamp and wilderness.[14]

When news of the riot at Mars Bluff reached Charlestown, any remaining sympathy for the Regulation evaporated. In August 1768 the Regulators came to be regarded along the coast as a "desperate Gang," a "Rogues Party" intent on ruining the colony. They were depicted as all the more dastardly because, in William White's words, they included people "of different Colours (viz.) Whites, Blacks and Mulattoes." A colony with a slave majority now faced the specter of blacks whipping whites. If slaves joined the melee, the Regulation could overwhelm South Carolina. The province's rulers devised a conciliatory strategy in response to the incident, proclaiming "a most gracious Pardon" to all "divers[e] dissolute and disorderly persons" who had "daringly resisted the King's process." At the same time, the pardon specifically excluded "Gideon Gibson and others who attacked a Constable and his party . . . near Mar's Bluff." With this policy to divide and conquer, George Gabriel Powell rode inland to isolate and destroy the rebellion's most subversive leader.[15]

GEORGE GABRIEL POWELL RETURNED to camp well pleased with his strategy and powers of persuasion. On Sunday, August 14, 1768, he had talked with Gideon Gibson in the forest for more than an hour. After negotiating terms, the Regulator captain had "solemnly promised to deliver himself up" the next morning. "Indeed I had not the least doubt but that the man would have fulfilled his promise," Powell wrote.[16]

Unlike many of his countrymen, Powell remained unfazed by the Regulation. "I had heard much of the riotous behaviour of the regulators in General," he wrote, "yet as several of them are men of good property I flatter'd myself that they might be . . . induced to admit that the method they were pursuing was not the proper mode to bring about their wis[h]ed for purpose." Powell had endured tougher challenges in his life. As a young man, he had served two years as governor of the bleak South Atlantic island of St. Helena, midway between Brazil and Angola, where he had been born and where his father had made a fortune by marrying a succession of widows. Ousted after a series of scandals, financial and otherwise, Powell had set off for Carolina's green shores, where he found wealth and respect. An observer described him as a "Shrewd cunning subtle Fox." In politics and life he was known to be flexible: "the greatest Mimic in Nature . . . [a] proteus—can transform himself into any Shape or Colour—Can be any thing—Laughs at all Things Civil and Sacred."[17]

Reports of extreme brutality, even of blacks flogging whites, hardly ruffled a man who occupied as lofty a position as Powell. His father had been known on St. Helena for astonishing cruelty to his slaves: he once was fined forty shillings for whipping an eight-year-old boy bloody and then throwing him onto a bed of nettles that slowly stung him to death. When Powell himself was unsatisfied with the quality of a new "wigg of some hair," he had the English wigmaker held down while a "Black boy" administered "fifty lashes upon his bare breach." Regarding all men, black and white, as his inferiors, Powell cared little that Gibson had color in his face, nor did it make sense to treat Gibson differently because of it.[18]

In the backcountry, after all, Gibson was indisputably one of the elite. If the family's race had been a source of alarm, all controversy had been extinguished a generation earlier. Gideon Gibson descended from some of the first free people of color in Virginia. In the seventeenth century the English had had little experience with slavery, and the success of tobacco growing had hardly been assured. For much of the century, the meaning of slavery and the place of Africans in Virginia society remained unsettled. While the English had long imagined that Africans were savage and inferior—even before they encountered people with black skin— slaves who arrived in early Virginia steadily undermined most rationales for being treated as such. They learned to speak a new language, accepted Christ, and were baptized. They turned to courts when they were wronged. They socialized, drank, ran away, and formed families with English men and women. Many, the Gibsons among them, negotiated better terms for themselves: more independence, earnings they could keep, even freedom.[19]

In 1672 near Jamestown a woman named Elizabeth Chavis successfully sued for the freedom of a boy named Gibson Gibson, or Gibby Gibson. Chavis was a free woman, and Gibby was her son. In the previous decade, Virginia's rulers had sought to codify slavery, secure the labor force, and prevent slaves from forming rebellious alliances with servants. Among the enactments was a law mandating that the children of a union between a slave and free person would follow the status of the mother. Although this rule of maternal status—"birth follows the belly"—resulted in widespread rape and generations of light-skinned slaves, it also formed the basis for the first communities of free people of color. English servant women had children with African men in numbers that continually alarmed Virginia's lawmakers. In certain courts, practically the only record that slavery existed consisted of cases of "mulatto bastards" born to English women. In the seventeenth century, thousands of mixed-race people were born into freedom. After Gibby Gibson was set free, he and his brother Hubbard spent half a century amassing land and slaves.[20]

The lives of the Gibsons and other free families of color were not easy. Greatly outnumbered by both the slave and white populations, they went into and out of debt, had trouble holding on to property from one generation to the next, and remained vulnerable to enslavement. As the seventeenth century turned into the eighteenth, Virginia's legislature steadily restricted the rights of free blacks to own property, travel, bear arms, and more. Although such laws were designed to lock free people of color into an inferior status, they paradoxically encouraged blacks to marry Europeans. Whites in the family gave their spouses and children stronger claims to freedom and had immediate economic advantages—while black women were subject to heavy taxes, white women were not. Increasingly harsh laws did not separate Africans and Europeans. To the contrary, they spurred some people of African descent to try to escape their classification.[21]

In the early 1720s Hubbard Gibson and his children left Virginia and bought property in North Carolina along with several other families of color. Virginia's legal restrictions had narrowed the opportunities for free people of color, but also set them in motion, driving them to places where they could experience something approaching liberty. In the mid-eighteenth century hundreds were migrating north into Maryland and Delaware and south into the Carolinas. Their ultimate destinations were places on the frontier that needed settlers. There the Gibsons and others could find land, wealth, status, and acceptance.[22]

Moving to South Carolina in 1731, the Gibsons traveled through the kind of wilderness where many people came to hide. Even so, the family's

arrival managed to attract widespread alarm. At the time the colony consisted primarily of a stretch of rice and indigo plantations along the coast.
Ten thousand free people were living among twenty thousand slaves. For
more than two decades, South Carolina had been majority black, and every
year thousands of new men and women, transported from the West Indies
and directly from West Africa, walked in irons down Charlestown's and
Georgetown's wharves. Most would work on the rice plantations, toiling
in gangs that hardly ever saw a white face, speaking a language mostly of
their own devising. Large numbers of slaves could produce thousands of
barrels of rice; they made plantation owners rich. But by the 1730s, free
colonists were reading regular accounts of slave uprisings in the West Indies, on slave ships—always nearby or drifting closer. Many grew convinced,
as one ship captain wrote upon visiting Charlestown in 1734, that their
slaves lived on a "Foundation of Discontent" and were "watch[ing for] an
Opportunity of revolting against their Masters." Colonists who encountered the Gibsons wondered if their caravan of dark men, pale women, and
children somewhere in between would "be of ill Consequence to this Province," flouting the strict line between slave and free that black and white
had come to represent. Perhaps they were moving through the colony
specifically to foment rebellion.[23]

When word of the Gibsons' arrival reached Charlestown in 1731, the
Assembly convened a committee to investigate, and Governor Robert
Johnson summoned Gideon Gibson's father—also named Gideon
Gibson—for a personal audience. After meeting the man, the governor
reported that the new arrivals were exactly the kind of people the province
needed to settle the frontier. "The account he has given of himself is so
Satisfactory that he is no Vagabond that I have . . . permitted him to Settle
in this Country," Johnson wrote. The elder Gibson was a carpenter who
had owned land and paid taxes in Virginia and North Carolina, and his wife
and others in their clan were "White women Capable of working and being
Serviceable in the Country." If Governor Johnson harbored any worries
as to whether the family—by words, deed, or example—would encourage
slaves to kill their masters, he was reassured that Gibson had come
with "seven negroes of his own." Gibson had a skilled trade, a white wife,

and a personal stake in slavery. His racial designation seemed to lose its meaning. "They are not Negroes nor Slaves but Free people," the governor wrote.[24]

Not only could the Gibsons stay in South Carolina, but they also were granted hundreds of acres in the backcountry. Their land at Mars Bluff was in an area known as the Welsh Tract, where dozens of Welsh Baptists had moved from Pennsylvania intending to grow "Hemp, flax, Wheat, Barley &ca." Other farm families soon joined them in the wilderness, Scottish and Irish and free people of color migrating from Pennsylvania and Virginia and North Carolina. Many were dissenters from the Church of England, Baptists and Presbyterians, receptive to charismatic "New Light" sects whose young, illiterate preachers railed against the Anglican ministry and other authorities tainted by devilment. A century later a Welsh Tract descendant would remember the original settlers as "more jealous of their liberties than even the English, and far more irascible." The Gibsons— reputedly ornery, never content with their station, continually challenging attempts to classify them—fit right in.[25]

The family settled along the bluffs that rolled alongside the Pee Dee River, which offered the best protection from Indian attack, and began the endless task of clearing forests and draining bogs for cowpens and fields. They grew corn and cash crops and drove cattle and hogs to the coast. They endured "bilious fevers," the reek of fermented indigo, and clouds of flies and biting insects. After slave rebels nearly sacked Charlestown in 1739, the province allowed people of color considerably less freedom, but suspicion and surveillance in the low country did not much affect the Gibsons' lives upriver. As the next generation came of age, they married into neighboring families. In 1767, when local landowners resolved to regulate the "Indolent, unsettled, roving Wretches" who threatened their property, it was only natural that Gibson would lead the way.[26]

It was unremarkable that a man of color could be a Regulator captain. Gibson was rich and respected. He conveyed no qualms that many of the people targeted by the Regulators had dark skin. He was secure enough in his status that he could insult a magistrate and coldly order his men to shoot at the local militia—their neighbors—and lash the survivors. By the time Gideon Gibson swore his allegiance to the Regulation, he was not black. He was not white. He was a planter.[27]

POWELL AWOKE ON MONDAY, August 15, 1768, expecting to receive his prisoner. Instead, a messenger arrived with a letter from Gibson "signifying that he had altered his Resolution" and promising to surrender at a later time. Perhaps stung that Gibson had flouted his authority and breached a pact of honor, Powell felt that he had been "egregiously mistaken" in his measure of Gibson and abruptly shifted his strategy. As the day grew hotter, Powell rode out to meet a troop of militia reinforcements, who had halted in the woods half a mile from his camp. He would not need to negotiate with Gibson any longer.[28]

Upon reaching the woods, Powell saw far more men than he had expected—"three hundred men and upwards," by his estimate. Perhaps they would be able to capture Gibson with relative ease. He took three militia captains and two lieutenants aside. He described the "service expected from them" and ordered official proclamations read about Regulator violence that "demand[ed] their aid accordingly." The officers did not hesitate in their reply. To Powell's astonishment, "they absolutely refused . . . Gibson they said was one of them (Regulators)."[29]

The officers then began enumerating typical Regulator gripes about "the want of County Courts and the Exhorbitant expence of the Law as it now stands." Undeterred, Powell invited the men to ride to his camp for "Victuals," convinced that he could bring them around to his position if only he could talk one-on-one with the "leading men," as he had done with Gibson. They agreed, and as the men ate and drank, Powell "took great pains to point out to them the mistakes they were running into." But to his astonishment, he failed to convince them to betray Gideon Gibson. In the late afternoon, he found himself facing three hundred armed men who seemed to delight in the prospect that his party would be "grossly abused."[30]

Powell fled down the Pee Dee River and later that week, after a miserable journey, reached his plantation at Georgetown. Reflecting on his failed expedition, he penned a letter to the lieutenant governor. In shock that the Regulator disturbances had "so dismal a tendency," and galled that

"Turbulent designing persons" had succeeded in turning landowners into rebels, Powell resigned his militia commission and advised "speedy Measures" to end the standoff.[31]

When he returned to the Assembly, Powell suggested a more specific way to cripple the Pee Dee insurrection: make Gideon Gibson subject to provisions of a 1740 law called the Negro Act. Passed by the Assembly after a slave insurrection, the act waived "formal trial and condemnation" for "rebellious negroes" and allowed them to be put to "immediate death." Powell had had no problem meeting Gibson face-to-face and talking to him as an equal. But for Gibson to assert his power at the expense of Powell's lofty status was another matter entirely. Gibson had outfoxed Powell and sent him running for his life. For that inexcusable offense—for giving Powell a glimpse of real equality—Powell would insist that Gibson was a "negro." Almost forty years after the Gibsons had arrived in South Carolina, the Assembly once again found itself discussing whether the Gibsons were black.[32]

The proposition was not simple. In 1731 the Gibsons had escaped classification because they were useful, wealthy, and committed to slavery. In 1768 Gideon Gibson was decidedly less congenial to the colony's interests— but he could also claim many of the Pee Dee's prominent landholders as kin. To classify the Gibsons now as people of color would work to the disadvantage of everyone who had family and business connections with them. Even legislators who could justify any indignity or brutality to suppress a slave rebellion might hesitate to turn the sons and daughters and grandchildren of socially prominent people into blacks. The Gibsons were hardly the only family who were fashioning new identities for themselves. If the colony drew the color line too strictly, large numbers of established whites might be vulnerable to or otherwise touched by reclassification.[33]

When Powell raised the matter in the Assembly, Henry Laurens, a colleague who had made a fortune in slave trading, argued against it. Without a flexible rule, he suggested, few people could make a secure claim of being white. Gibson, he said, had "more Red & White in his face than could be discovered in the faces of half the descendants of the [F]rench Refugees in our House of Assembly." "I challenged them all to the trial," Laurens would remember. "The children of this same Gideon having passed through another state of Whitewash were of fairer complexions than his prosecutor George Gabriel [Powell]." Although Laurens thought that ideally the Gibsons should be classified as black—to "confine them to their original Clothing"—in the end he understood that the realities of life might outstrip the law. "Reasoning from the Colour carries no conviction," Laurens wrote. "By perserverance the black may be blanched & the 'stamp of Providence' effectually effaced."[34]

The Assembly declined to target Gideon Gibson. Instead, for five thousand pounds sterling it bought out the provost marshal's royal monopoly on law enforcement and created a committee, headed by George Gabriel Powell, to draft legislation to establish courts, sheriffs, and jails to serve the backcountry. The provost marshal became the sheriff for Charleston and Beaufort, and Powell served as a judge in one of the new courts. Now that the Regulators' demands for local law enforcement were largely met, the backcountry rebellion disbanded in early 1769, and its participants filed petitions with the Assembly and governor for pardons.[35]

On Mars Bluff, Gibson was no longer a rebel. He resumed his role in the community as a prosperous planter, tending to his crops and cattle, managing his slaves. He enjoyed a few years of peace until a deadlier conflict wound its way up the Pee Dee. It involved a cause distinct from the Regulation but marked a return to the violence that had prompted Gibson's finest and most vulnerable hour. At times it was a small war, neighbors beating and shooting neighbors, stealing their cattle and firing their cabins. Periodically the local brutality blurred into battles between the greatest country in the world and the newest one. An entire people, the Gibsons included, was creating a new identity for itself. At times it seemed an impossible task. But in the South Carolina backcountry, black had become white. Surely, then, English could become American.[36]

CHAPTER TWO

WALL

Rockingham, North Carolina, 1838

W HEN A RIVER FORMS the boundary between two properties, the law draws an invisible line down the middle of the waterway. This line, the river's "thread," is the true property limit, and it has the same legal effect as a fence. Unlike a fenced boundary, however, river channels continually evolve and change course as they cut their way through soil and rock. Most of the time the changes are barely perceptible. Small amounts of soil wash into the river and settle on banks downstream. As this gradual accretion occurs, the law redraws the river's thread along the channel's new center. Few people ever have occasion to notice or care that the property line—a set of property rights—has shifted. There may be winners and losers, but the law recognizes the new realities.[1]

Occasionally, though, a river undergoes what is known as an "avulsion." It rapidly alters course, cuts an entirely new channel, and abandons the old one. The event can alter hundreds of acres of land in the course of mere hours or days. The effect can be profound; in 1775 Thomas Jefferson described America's impending break from England as an "everlasting avulsion." When such a sudden break occurs, however, the law refuses to disrupt settled expectations. The original boundary line remains in effect despite the river's new course. The resulting border may be awkward, even irrational—someone could wind up with a narrow spit of land on the far side of a river—but the law pretends that nothing has changed.[2]

In North Carolina, just above its southern border, the Great Pee Dee River separates Richmond County from Anson County. The river is wide, nearly four hundred yards across, flowing through prime cotton growing land where the sand hills and pine barrens of eastern Carolina yield to red clay. For many decades along one stretch, it was not necessary to determine whether and to what extent the river had changed course. Stephen Wall owned both sides.[3]

To all outward appearances, Wall was a typical gentleman farmer. He was building on traditions set by his father, who had settled in Richmond County before the Revolution, gained a fortune in land and slaves, and served the community as justice of the peace and sheriff, and in other offices held by the best men. Born in 1791, three years before Eli Whitney patented his cotton gin, Stephen Wall came of age as the South embraced large-scale cotton cultivation and built the plantations that came to define the region. Wall became one of the richest growers in the North Carolina interior, with dozens of slaves working fields that stretched for miles. At age thirty, he won an officer's commission in the state cavalry; he would be known as Colonel Wall for the rest of his life. By thirty-five, he had represented Richmond County in the North Carolina Senate for two terms. In his forties, when the county's businessmen periodically attempted to raise money for a railroad and other internal improvements, Wall lent his name to their efforts. When they organized the local Whig Party, Wall helped craft the chorus of indignation at the corruption and tyranny that Jacksonian Democracy represented.[4]

Wall's friends saw a man who embodied the Southern virtues of leadership and mastery. His piercing pale stare projected what they took to be "remarkable energy of character" and "indomitable perseverance." Robust mutton chops supported his "commanding and prepossessing" high cheekbones and bracketed a "strong and discriminating" frown. His hastily tied cravat and the ridge of tangled curls down the middle of his head revealed a man who was too important to bother with his appearance—or perhaps a man without a wife. He drew praise for his generosity and hospitality; "to the distressed always a friend," an admirer wrote, "to the poor ever kind and attentive." To the men, women, and children that he owned, friends supposed, Wall was a "provident and humane master."[5]

Wall's one physical weakness was apparent only to those who watched him closely: he was blind in his right eye, the pupil scarred into a feline crescent. There were some things that he could not see. What he did see he perceived differently from everyone else. His impairment was a mark of the past, perhaps a memento of misfortune or adventure or stoic resolve. It also suggested a tendency to waver from the path in life that had been made for him. According to family rumors passed down for generations, a neighbor had gouged out Wall's eye in a fight—an odd turn for a man reputed to have "a hold upon [his neighbors'] affections that any might envy." The reason for the fight had to do with his slaves.[6]

Although Wall never married, he had many children. Their mothers, at least three of the women who lived on his farm, were lines in Wall's household ledger: Priscilla, Rody, and Jane. Their children bore the irony of great names. The oldest boy was called Napoleon. His half brother was Benjamin Franklin. There was a biblical matriarch, Sarah. Another girl, Caroline Matilda, was named for King George III's sister, a queen of Denmark who scandalized her court when she rode a horse dressed as a man.[7]

Wall's second son shared his father's chin and brow, eyes and cheeks. His mother's influence colored his skin. He had the strangest name of all: Orindatus. Over the course of his life, people were constantly getting it wrong. It was a slave's name through and through. When he was born in 1825, planters like his father had long given their slaves classical names: Caesar. Pompey. Cicero. Datus, which Stephen Wall called his son, was Latin for "given." While "Orin" is Celtic rather than Latin, it made the boy's name even more ornate and fanciful. Yet as much as "Orindatus" signaled slavery, the boy's middle names suggested the opposite: "Simon Bolivar," the great liberator of Latin America who had decreed freedom for slaves and led a movement he described as "closer to a blend of Africa and America than an emanation from Europe." The boy was Orindatus Simon Bolivar Wall.[8]

Perhaps Stephen Wall named his children as a private joke, the ultimate affirmation of his mastery: he owned royalty, and he owned those who would overthrow it. A generation or two earlier such names might have signaled hope for the future. In the Revolution's wake, Northern states had outlawed slavery. Leading Virginians pondered whether to abolish the institution, and their legislature, as in many Southern states, devised procedures in 1782 that allowed owners to free their slaves. Some owners were inspired by the ideals of the new republic to enter deeds of manumission at local courthouses, while others found emancipation to be a rational choice in an era of economic turmoil and exhausted agriculture—it was cheaper to free slaves than to feed them. The wave of emancipations that followed the Revolution exponentially increased the number of free people of color, creating communities that had the potential to embody the promise of a society founded on liberty. In 1808 Congress banned the international slave trade. After the Revolutionary avulsion, freedom was slowly accreting.[9]

By the time Stephen Wall named his children, however, the promise of liberty was waning. Cotton and sugarcane had become white gold, and the rush to turn swamps and forests into plantations in Alabama, Louisiana, southwestern Georgia, and Mississippi created insatiable new markets for forced labor. Far more slaves were marched inland in the early decades of the nineteenth century than had survived the Middle Passage from Africa to the American South. This second mass migration changed the way slaves and their owners lived, and it altered the place of slavery in Southern life. Wealth in slaves became nearly as valuable as wealth in land. Whether people owned one or ten or, like Wall, more than one hundred slaves, the South's economy depended on the continued strength of the institution of slavery.[10]

Driven by fears of revolt—stoked by events from the Haitian Revolution in the 1790s to Nat Turner's gory uprising in Virginia in 1831—powerful Southerners reasserted their support for slavery by means of organized violence and repressive laws. But the prospect that slavery would gradually erode was arguably more real than that of its sudden demise. The immediate presence of freedpeople showed slaves the possibility of a different life, making it harder for masters to dominate them and easier for them to find help in running away. Outside the South, organized groups devoted to slavery's abolition were helping slaves escape to the North and threatening to shift public opinion. In the 1830s the American Anti-Slavery Society sent more than 400,000 petitions to Congress urging it to restrict slavery and mailed thousands of tracts directly to the South, demanding immediate emancipation. To preserve the status quo, support for slavery hardened. Southern postmasters refused to deliver abolitionist tracts, in violation of federal law. State legislators contemplated re-enslaving free people of color, ordered their expulsion, and passed measures that limited their ability to make money, own land, and form communities.[11]

Moreover, slavery's defenders began articulating a series of arguments to justify the institution's continued existence. Some of the defenses were economic, others biblical. Writers from Virginia to Mississippi asserted that slavery was morally superior to the suffering of poor people in the North. Constant was the notion that slaves were unfit for freedom, that blacks were different from whites, an inferior species even. The "amalgamation" of these separate and distinct races would destroy a nation and a civilization: according to reputable men of science, children who blended black with white were sterile, insane, tubercular, enfeebled monstrosities. Slavery would preserve the purity of the white race, while freedom was the road to mixing, madness, and decline.[12]

Wall was a representative man in a community dependent upon and devoted to slavery. At the same time he never married, never formed blood alliances with other powerful families, and never produced legitimate children to continue his legacy into the future. His only natural heirs were slaves. The irony of their names attained a double edge. Perhaps he wanted greater things for them. Perhaps the river would change its course.

A MAN IN HIS PRIME was worth $900. Men older than twenty-five and fertile women could sell for $650. A forty-year-old woman: $400. Small children were worth half that, although by the time a boy reached his teens, he could command a price of $750.[13]

A master would know his slaves well. They cared for him, grew up with him, built his home, plowed and picked his crops, and cooked his food. They were his closest neighbors. Some slept in his house, some in his bed. Many owners worked side by side with slaves in the field; a plantation's success depended on them. But masters were also capable of seeing the same slaves in an entirely different light: as malingerers and layabouts who needed constant discipline lest they become runaways and rebels. They were beasts to be tamed and driven. Boys and girls, men and women, were slapped and whipped, kicked and bloodied, raped and terrorized. Above all, masters could see their property as a set of numbers—low at birth, when surviving the harsh life was unclear, then rising steadily with their strength and fertility, only to decline with age back to a baby's value. Slaves were befriended and beaten and bought and sold.

If slaves experienced the doubleness of being people and property, their masters also had to accommodate themselves to lives of contradiction. Enlightenment and benevolence, the qualities that many Southerners presumed made a person fit to own others, did not coexist easily with everyday violence and sexual assault. Slaveowners and their families had to pretend that men, women, and children whom they saw every day were not related to them. And the robust market for slaves—regular auctions, repeated inquiries by traders, gangs of people in chains marching south—was ever present, reminding masters and slaves alike that lives could change with the shake of a hand.[14]

Year after year Stephen Wall hired out upward of ten slaves when they were not needed on the plantation, supplying them to neighbors and relatives for fifty or one hundred dollars per laborer. While some of the slaves did housework, many people hired slaves to do tasks that they did not want their own servants doing: too dangerous, difficult, or demoralizing. Wall listed his slaves and their renters by name, along with the agreed-upon price. Each year Wall would write in his ledger, "Priscilla & children not hired," or "Priscilla and her children I was compelled to keep as I could not get Hire for them." Such words indicated their special place in his household but also suggested that the next year could be different.[15]

In January 1836 Wall sold twelve people to a Mr. Gunter of Alabama. Perhaps the sale reflected financial distress or worry on Wall's part. As President Jackson was battling banks and soft currency speculators, inflation was spiraling; the following year would see a raft of bank failures and the start of a major economic depression. Maybe Wall needed cash for a large expense. The sale netted him more than six thousand dollars. The strongest worker was a man named Minus, nineteen or twenty years old, followed by a fourteen-year-old named Jim Crow. Bucking the conventional wisdom, Gunter bought older men and women as well as young children. He also kept at least parts of some families intact. Perhaps he had particular tasks for them in mind. An older man might look after the pigs; older women might cook. Maybe he was looking to spend less money and, after examining—inspecting, touching—the slaves' bodies, concluded that he was getting good value. Henry, a thirty-year-old man, was sold with his boys, ages six and three. Milly, also in her thirties, left with her four-year-old son. But Betsy and Comfort, two and five, had no parents to accompany them on the long journey south.[16]

The children might ride in an oxcart, but the adults walked in chains. If their new owner was looking for more slaves to buy, they would take an indirect route, from town to town. He might sell or trade some of his quarry during the journey. Flatboats and steamers may have carried them part of the way—their own Middle Passage, perhaps the only boats they had been on besides ferries across the Pee Dee. Lashed with the cold, they were likely to encounter other shivering gangs: most slaves were marched inland during the winter months.[17]

Exhausted, freezing, and hungry, the slaves reached their destination. Given that Gunter was buying women and children, his piece of wilderness had probably already been logged, burned, grubbed out, cleared, and fenced—that was work for strong men alone. But women and even young children could pick cotton. Instead of tents, they might have rough cabins to sleep in, built by earlier arrivals. If they survived the usual fevers that plagued and often killed new arrivals, they would be plowing and planting cottonseed by early April. All summer they thinned the crop, and by August they were picking the cotton. The harvest could last four or five months.[18]

Unlike men and women sold from tobacco country in Virginia and Maryland, Stephen Wall's slaves had experience tending a cotton crop. They knew how to cope with the work's unrelenting tedium, and the razor-sharp edges of the cotton bolls had already seasoned and calloused their hands into more scar than skin. Unlike North Carolina slaves, though, Alabama cotton hands worked seven days a week, often until they could barely move. After hot days picking, drying, ginning, and baling the crop, they spent nights carding, spinning, and reeling it. While back home a slave might be promoted to foreman, in Alabama they were much more likely to toil under hired overseers, who slaves and masters alike complained were too liberal with the lash and more likely to attack the women. When the slaves were not working, they were crushed with memories of the people and places they would never see again.[19]

Back in North Carolina, the men, women, and children who remained were haunted by memories of the ones who had disappeared—friends and parents, husbands and wives, sons and daughters. Some who went south and west were able to remain in contact with their families, usually in situations in which they were not sold but rather moved with their owners. More often, the lives awaiting slaves in Alabama, Mississippi, and Louisiana were a sickening mystery to the ones left behind. It was all the more sickening because they knew that they could be next.[20]

On Stephen Wall's plantation, the person who knew the most about what the slaves could expect in Alabama was Colonel Wall himself. He had a brother and a sister and nieces and nephews who had moved to northern Mississippi, an area that was preparing to produce more cotton, with more slaves, than just about anywhere else in the world. Wall's kin kept him apprised of their lives on the frontier. They, in turn, followed their family's fortunes back east, whispering among themselves about scandalous goings-on in Stephen Wall's house. Wall was willing to sell twelve of his slaves south even though he knew that he was sentencing them to hardship and misery. Perhaps Wall's enslaved sons and daughters understood what he was capable of doing too.[21]

THE JOURNEY BEGAN like many others. More than two years after his sale of a dozen slaves to Mr. Gunter of Alabama, Stephen Wall watched five more leave the plantation—his own children. He signed the requisite papers, and three boys and their two sisters were put on a wagon heading west with a Mississippi planter named Richmond Love. The children might have taken comfort in the fact that they were traveling out of season—Indian summer instead of winter's depths. Perhaps the older boys—Napoleon, Orindatus—knew their new master, a kinsman and trusted friend of their father who had been visiting his family in Richmond County. Most important, their father probably assured the children that once west, they would turn north to freedom.[22]

Still, much of the way the Wall children followed the ominous route of slaves headed deep into cotton country. They rode through mountain passes and floated downriver to the Ohio. The children, ages two to sixteen, had one another for company, but they had never before left North Carolina, or their mothers. Richmond Love had promised to take care of the children, but no one could stop him from changing direction with the small fortune in slaves that he now owned. Even if he intended to keep his word, the market for slaves was so strong that kidnapping was a constant danger. There were still months of work to do on cotton plantations in Mississippi.[23]

Past Cincinnati, Love and the Wall children finally set foot on free soil. By October, the corn harvest was over. The pale clay fields lay bare, and first frost approached. As they neared their destination, the country roads grew crowded with travelers, including other dark faces. Over the previous fifteen years, the journey from North Carolina to this part of Indiana had become an established route to freedom for people of color. Thousands of Quakers were meeting over several days in a town called Whitewater. It was humble country in the rolling hills just a few miles west of the Ohio line. A visitor would never guess that it was Indiana's highest spot; no hill rose more than thirty feet above its surroundings.[24]

The Quakers received Richmond Love quietly but not coldly. To all appearances, the stranger was a "man of talent, courteous and affable in his manners," yet all the same he was a Mississippi planter traveling with his slaves—children, no less. This made him evil personified, an "unrepenting and obdurate oppressor," a man who bought and sold human beings. Even more than other gatherings of the Society of Friends, the Indiana Yearly Meeting abhorred slavery, declaring that "a just and dreadful retribution" awaited slaveowners in eternity "at that awful tribunal, where sophistry will not prevail to exculpate."[25]

Slavery was the reason many of the meeting's attendees had moved to

Indiana in the first place, forgoing rich inheritances of land and people in
Virginia and the Carolinas in favor of a life of "righteousness and benevolence" and "steady perseverance" in the struggle for universal liberty. Their
ranks included people like Levi Coffin, later described as the "President of
the Underground Railroad," who was already busy helping hundreds of
Kentucky runaways flee north through Indiana. Quakers elsewhere might
talk of gradual emancipation and of sending freedpeople to Liberia and
Haiti, but the Indiana Yearly Meeting rejected colonization and demanded
immediate emancipation. They boycotted Southern cotton, sugar, rice,
and other "slave wrought produce." They hated slavery so much that they
wondered if their feelings were sinful. They had to counsel themselves to
cultivate feelings of sympathy for slaveowners and "pray for these enemies
of humanity."[26]

Richmond Love waited for the meeting to reach consensus on its rules
and discipline. He waited for the Indian Committee to report that it was
having "little success . . . civilizing these sons of the forest." Then the
Committee on the Concerns of the People of Colour convened, and Love
introduced himself and revealed his business with the Society of Friends.
Love informed the committee that he did not see himself as the children's
owner but rather as their guardian. He had traveled so far, and at such
considerable expense, because, as one Quaker reported, "his conscience
would not permit him to hold them any longer as slaves." All he wanted
for them was "that which is just and equal"—the opportunity to be educated, to study agriculture, or to learn a trade. He was hoping the Quakers
would help him find places for the children in good schools and a welcoming community. With money supplied by Stephen Wall, Love offered to
cover any expense.[27]

If Love's words made it seem as if the Quakers' prayers were coming
true, in truth he had experienced no epiphany about bondage and freedom.
He had followed Wall's instructions and freed the children, but it was an
isolated transaction, bound by honor. After he left Indiana, he would return
home to Mississippi, where he owned, and showed no intention of eman-
cipating, many slaves. The Quakers assigned two men the task of finding
new homes and new lives for the children.[28]

———

MAIN STREET in Harveysburg, Ohio, ran several blocks east to west, curving north just before Caesar's Creek. The street was lined with trees, many of them still saplings, and the buildings—wagon maker, blacksmith, tannery, shoemaker—were whitewashed every spring. It was a farming town, about forty-five miles northeast of Cincinnati. The road winding up the hill north of town opened onto a patchwork of green and gold, fields of corn and wheat that stretched for miles to the horizon along the Miami River Valley.[29]

Just before the hill was a plain white-brick building on a quiet street, a single-room schoolhouse. On hard benches the Wall children studied literature, arithmetic, and abolitionism. Not ten years old, the school was the state's first for colored children, founded by Elizabeth and Jesse Harvey. Harvey was a physician and an educator who delivered public lectures on history and science twice a week. But most of all, he was an abolitionist. The town had been named for his family, Quakers who had left North Carolina in protest against slavery. Antislavery ideas flowered and ripened in Harveysburg like the wild plums that local boys and girls feasted on every summer and the blackberries that spread like weeds.[30]

It was one thing to hate slavery; the Wall children could hate slavery in North Carolina. In Harveysburg, however, they were being raised by people who were striving to destroy the institution. Runaways from Kentucky repeatedly made their way north through the town. They had been routed to Harveysburg by people who had harbored them farther south and knew it was "a good anti-slavery neighborhood." It was their second or third stop on free soil. Among Quakers and free blacks, they could begin to shed their fears of capture and imagine life after bondage.[31]

Although Stephen Wall knew that his children were being educated to undo his own way of life, he continued to support them. He gave them enough money to make them some of the richest people in the town and ensured their acceptance in the community. Wall came to regard Jesse Harvey as "my Friend" and became one of the colored school's principal benefactors. When Wall died of a sudden attack of typhus in 1845, he left tens of thousands of dollars and thousands of acres of Ohio land "for the purpose of . . . adeing, defending and securing the just rights of those mulatoe children . . . in a special manner." He left Dr. Harvey another five hundred.[32]

Perhaps Wall acted out of genuine feeling. From Richmond County, his younger brother Mial paid out the bequests faithfully and wrote doting letters to his niece Caroline, offering advice about love, marriage, and life. At the same time, moving the children out of North Carolina allowed Stephen Wall to continue living the way he had always lived. If his slave family had given the neighbors cause for alarm, the children's absence defused it. By being generous with his "mulatoe children," he was proving himself noble enough to continue to own slaves. In gratitude for Richmond Love's honorable behavior in guiding the children to freedom, Wall willed him two men and three boys. Wall gave his children liberty and comfortable lives. At the same time, their mothers stayed in slavery. The course of the river had changed, but the boundary line remained the same.[33]

CHAPTER THREE

SPENCER

Clay County, Kentucky, 1848

T HE MEN SET the spring pole in a muddy clearing along Goose Creek. Projecting diagonally from the earth, the pole—a twenty-foot sapling—looked like a giant fishing rod. Its far end was anchored down, the middle propped by a fulcrum of forked wood. From the near end, high overhead, a taut rope fell straight into a hole in the ground. Instead of a hook, a drill bit was tied to the rope, maybe a hundred, two hundred, or even five hundred feet below the surface. By pulling down on the pole and letting it spring up, a crew of men could generate enough force to bore inch by inch through Kentucky rock.[1]

The drilling never stopped. Night and day a succession of crews operated the spring pole. They sank copper tubing into the well and siphoned sand out. They kept a blacksmith's fire burning in case the bit cracked or grew dull. Some drillers pulled with both hands, and when the pole sprang upward, they looked like they were bound to a whipping post. Other crews tied the ropes to their feet like stirrups, working with an elastic high step, a monotonous, grueling dance.

When the men struck a vein, they rigged a mule to an enormous wooden pump—walking in circles activated its bellows—and drew liquid up through the copper tubing and into a large trough. The liquid was clear but not pure. The men were drilling neither for oil nor for drinking water—they wanted salt.

From the first trough, the liquid ran a short distance through wooden pipes to another trough, and from there it was poured into one-ton iron evaporating kettles set over a blistering furnace. Brine and fire were not the only ingredients. To clarify the evaporate, to give it the proper texture and whiteness, the men would pour a few quarts of beef, pig, or deer blood into the boiling caldrons. By introducing this small impurity, they created the finest salt. In seconds the blood would coagulate and rise, trapping undissolved foreign particles in an albuminous scum easily ladled off the top. It could take several hundred gallons of brine to produce one bushel of salt. In 1840 saltworks up and down Goose Creek and the Collins Fork in the hills of Clay County, Kentucky, produced 196,000 bushels.[2]

Clay County was a place of many borders—where rock met water, water became brine, brine was turned into salt, and salt became gold. It was a wilderness, bounded by Appalachian ridgelines and removed from the great road, blazed by Daniel Boone, that three generations of settlers had followed from Virginia to the rolling meadows of central Kentucky. But because of salt, Clay County was also industrial, dotted with drill sites and smoking furnaces encircled by swaths of clear-cut wasteland. Just up Goose Creek, the county seat was called Manchester, after the great manufacturing city in northern England. Clay County was where the isolation of the highlands met the values and market imperatives of the world beyond. It was Kentucky's biggest producer of salt, at a time when the farmers and livestock men of the bluegrass region around Lexington craved it for their butter and hardtack and animal feed and depended on it for curing the tens of thousands of tons of beef and pork that they were selling down the Ohio and Mississippi rivers.[3]

Clay County also embodied the line between slave and free. Appalachia was too rugged for plantations. Most families that settled the hills of Kentucky, Tennessee, and Virginia neither owned nor needed human property. Whether or not they could afford slaves, many highlanders in the solitude of their mountain hollows viewed liberty—the freedom to be left alone—as their greatest possession, so much so that they believed no one should be owned. But there were more slaves in Clay than anywhere else in the Kentucky mountains, some five hundred out of a population of five thousand.[4]

At the salt furnaces, white crystals were raked and packed by black hands. Most of Clay County's slaves were men bound to the salt makers. In addition to drilling wells and tending the boiling caldrons, slaves made barrels for the salt and tied them onto pack mules and wagons headed down to the Cumberland Gap and the meatpacking concerns of Knoxville, Tennessee. Slaves built and loaded flatboats that escaped Clay County's creeks during spring floods and threaded a series of deadly narrows and rapids before reaching the Kentucky River and the markets of Lexington, Frankfort, and points west. Slaves chopped down thousands of trees to fire the furnaces. As they cleared all the forests within easy distance, they began mining coal for fuel. Every week a young slave would have to clean the furnaces, crawling through the filthy trenches underneath the evaporating pots, shoveling and scraping ash and soot through the tight darkness.[5]

Although Clay County's slaves grew and slaughtered their own food, they were industrial workers. At the drilling rigs and furnaces, chopping down trees and mining coal, they were crushed and suffocated, scalded and broken. During peak production, the owners of the saltworks hired slaves from a hundred miles away in Lexington. Slaves were not just labor. They were a commodity, bought, sold, rented, and borrowed against. Manchester was a tiny settlement, but it had its own auction block. Bidders regularly included slave traders riding a slow circuit down to the plantations in Mississippi and Louisiana.[6]

GEORGE FREEMAN'S NAME ANNOUNCED his status—free man of color—but slavery was always a part of his life. It stretched and receded like shadows through the day. It was almost an invisible presence when he was alone in the hills, girdling trees with an axe, shoeing a horse, or breaking the earth with a bull-tongue plow. The worst he could do was remember the years when he had been someone else's property. But out in the world, anyone encountering him—in the forest, in town, on a mountain path—could presume he was a slave, and Freeman would have to prove otherwise. Only in Louisiana, a place he had never seen, were people of mixed race presumptively free.[7]

Freeman was required to carry papers that established his status beyond doubt. He knew what they said, even if he could not read them. He also knew that a stranger on a lonely road could try to take a match to them and force him back into bondage. It did not worry him much. When he first came into Clay County before 1820, he had no desire to hide. He was young and strong, not yet thirty, relatively tall at five feet ten, and, according to the man who had freed him, "well set." And he was not alone—Clay County had one of the largest concentrations of free people of color in Kentucky. Almost as many blacks were free as were slaves.[8]

Perhaps Freeman had made his way to Clay County because it was both industrial and rugged. The salt makers presented opportunities to earn money that were not available elsewhere, yet Clay's frontier isolation limited the reach of outside authority. In the wilderness no one could tell him who he was or what he could do.

The presence of large numbers of slaves tempered the liberty of life in the hills. Free people of color saw firsthand how fragile their lives were, and whites were continually reminded that people with dark skin were different and that society depended on maintaining that difference. If the everyday experience of slavery were not enough, a series of laws constricted the lives of free blacks like rope around a wrist.

When Kentucky became a state in 1792, its laws were suffused with ideals of the revolutionary age. Like many other states, Kentucky made it relatively easy for owners to free their slaves, and most of Clay County's free blacks had been emancipated there. At least initially there seemed to be no legal distinction between free blacks and every other free person in the commonwealth. Within a decade, however, the legislature had driven a wedge between liberty and equality, as the enthusiasm for revolutionary notions of universal liberty gave way to a society structured around slavery.[9]

In order to justify treating free blacks differently from whites—to rethink the core idea that "all men are created equal"—whites started describing blacks as congenitally inferior. Equality would lead to intermarriage, which in turn would, one South Carolina congressman warned in 1786, "stain the blood of the whites by a mixture of the races." In Kentucky and elsewhere, north and south, advocates for forcibly resettling blacks outside of the country justified their cause in the name of protecting the purity of white blood. The harshness of this emerging understanding of race was unnecessary when most people with dark skin were slaves and the everyday practice of bondage and mastery kept blacks and whites separate. But the prospect of freedom required a new vocabulary of inequality, and a new set of laws followed.[10]

In 1806 Virginia required blacks to leave the state within a year of being freed or else forfeit their liberty. Within two years Kentucky's legislature prohibited free blacks from entering the state, decrying the "very serious evil . . . likely to be produced by the emigration of emancipated slaves from different parts of the Union to this state." Free blacks had to register for certificates of emancipation at county courts. They could not vote. Nor could they "keep or carry any gun, powder, shot, club, or other weapon whatsoever"—an enormous burden in the mountains, where families survived the lean times by eating wild game and where farmers often had to hunt their free-grazing cows and pigs. A black man or woman faced thirty lashes "on his or her bare back" for so much as lifting a hand in self-defense against a white person.[11]

These statutes—and the sentiments that they represented—made freedom resemble slavery. Most of Clay County's free people of color were desperately poor. Some did jobs for the saltworks. Others were laborers or tenant farmers. None of the children went to school. Only one member of the black population was literate. While poor whites could borrow money to buy property, blacks had little access to credit, and the number of black landowners could be counted on one or two hands.[12]

Despite the legal and practical limitations of liberty, blacks in Clay County continued to value their freedom. Slaves negotiated for it over years of working closely with their owners, securing emancipation in their wills. Periodically they ran away, moving deeper into the hills or rafting down the Kentucky River to the Ohio and the North. And in the 1840s nine slaves sued their owner, a salt manufacturer. After years of litigation, they established that they were being unlawfully held in bondage. They retained a lawyer who was a member of another salt-making clan, using the business rivalry to leverage themselves into freedom.[13]

George Freeman's very presence in Clay County embodied the resilience of the idea of liberty. Even though the state legislature had banned free blacks from moving in, Freeman had come through the Cumberland

Mountains from Virginia. Raised in the hills near the Kentucky line, Freeman could appreciate the relative freedom of frontier life. As a slave in the mountains, he would have lived in close quarters with his owner, a man named Joseph Spencer, possibly Freeman's father. They probably worked side by side. Freeman had been born when the Constitution was a year old, and when he was twenty-four, Spencer emancipated him. In 1814 the country had been fighting its second great war with England and rekindling its sense of what liberty and democracy meant. The deed that made Freeman a free man repeated words that were common in the initial wave of emancipations that followed the Revolution. "Freedom," his master declared, "is the natural right of every human being."[14]

By the time he was thirty, Freeman had a wife and four daughters. Their life sprang almost entirely from their own calloused hands. Families in the Clay County hills lived in cabins built from logs that they had hewn and mud that they had quarried. They built their own beds and slept on mattresses that they had sewn and stuffed themselves. They turned forest to farmland, fenced in vegetable and flower gardens, and grew Indian corn and wheat from seed. They sewed their own clothes from wool that they had sheared and spun and with flax that they had woven into stiff linen that softened in time. They could go days without seeing anyone else.[15]

For many mountain families, the outside world did not have to exist. They could survive on what they produced or hunted and could trade corn, eggs, honey, or pelts for just about anything else. The area had little that resembled a cash economy, beyond the wealthy families who controlled the salt industry. When farmers left their hollows to work for salt makers and others, their earnings were usually forfeited to their employers for food and clothes and other necessities of life, things they might have made themselves if they had not been working for someone else.[16]

George Freeman, however, was able to move beyond subsistence in the 1830s. By 1832, with seven children to feed, he had enough money to pay $200 cash for fifty acres of land. Soon other free blacks and even some whites were turning to him for small loans. If the law did not recognize Freeman's equality with whites, the men indebted to him would have to.[17]

Moving upward was a feat that required unyielding health, constant strength, and tireless toil. Undoubtedly Freeman's wife and children had been doing some of the heavy labor on the farm. It was also possible that a young man named Jordan Spencer was living with the family and assisting with their work. Spencer had been born around the time of Freeman's emancipation. Years later some of Spencer's children would remember that he had come from Virginia, while others figured he was from Kentucky. He may have been Freeman's son or brother or other kin. Perhaps, like Freeman, he had been a slave emancipated by the Spencer family, or he may have adopted the last name after hearing Freeman talk about his former owner. Jordan had long hair and shaded his face with a wide-brimmed hat. It was a point of pride that no one worked harder than he did.[18]

Freeman owned his land outright. During the long stretches that he worked without ever seeing anyone who was not his kin, he might have fancied himself the master of his mountain hollow. But he was never truly alone. Under a ten-year-old statute, the justices, sheriffs, and attorneys of Clay County were obliged to give the court monthly reports of the "poor children of colour who are free, and whose parents . . . they shall think are incapable of supporting and bringing them up in honest courses." If the court deemed it "right," the children would be bound out as apprentices to anyone the court chose. Boys would be released from service at age twenty-one, girls at eighteen. Although the law guaranteed apprentices "wholesome meat and drink, suitable cloathing," and instruction "to spell and read, so as to read the New Testament with facility," they lived at the mercy of their masters. The courts and their informants had so much discretion to act that they could take children from just about any black family they wished. Freeman was free, but his children could be enslaved.[19]

Freeman had been working his land for several years when two men took some of his children away. In December 1836 Thomas Strong petitioned the Clay County court to force two of Freeman's sons, Washington and Hiram, to become his apprentices, "to learn the art and mystery of farming." At the same time Strong's brother-in-law Edward Davidson asked the court to bind Freeman's "infant child" Elizabeth to him, "to learn the art and mystery of spinning and weaving." Each petition yielded a one-sentence order from the judge, turning Freeman's children into servants.[20]

The men who petitioned the court for Freeman's children came from farming families that owned thousands of acres of land on the North Fork of the Kentucky River. The Strongs and Davidsons had a long history of feuding with some of the local salt-making clans, starting in 1806 with pitched gun battles over cattle rights and periodically reigniting, generation after generation, for nearly a century afterward. Thomas Strong's father had been a county leader and justice of the peace. They were powerful people—the state worked for them.[21]

Perhaps Freeman had offended Strong and Davidson in routine business dealings, was allied with one of their enemies, or had been too conspicuously successful a free man of color in Clay County. Whatever the reason, Strong's and Davidson's actions were devastating to Freeman. Not only were the apprenticeships a personal affront—taking his children away as if they were on the auction block—but they also threatened his basic aspiration to rise in life. A large family was an economic engine. With sons and daughters working on the farm, Freeman could produce more corn and eggs and wool and timber, raise more cows and sheep and pigs, make more money, and buy more land. By taking his children, Strong and Davidson were turning Freeman's labor force into their own, increasing their wealth and power at his expense.[22]

Kentucky's laws were designed to keep Freeman—and all free blacks—poor, and the local court was actively enriching Clay County's wealthiest citizens. Freeman could easily have deferred to the status that the legislature had fixed for him or shied away from a fight with two men from powerful families who held grudges. Instead, he found a lawyer fifty miles outside the county to appeal the court's ruling.

Freeman's lawyer, James S. Henderson, did not challenge the wisdom or fairness of the apprenticeship law—that would have been a losing proposition, given the general hostility toward free blacks that prevailed in Kentucky. Rather, Henderson focused on the procedures that the county court had followed, arguing that the judge's ruling had been too informal. In order to establish the court's jurisdiction over Freeman, Henderson asserted, the decision would have had to record a series of specific findings, among them that the children were poor, that Freeman and his wife could not care for them, and that Freeman had been given the opportunity to appear in court and contest the apprenticeship petitions. Even if the judges agreed with the substance of the apprenticeship law, they might balk at lax procedure, which could harm whites just as easily as blacks.[23]

A little more than a year later the Kentucky Court of Appeals agreed that "the record is altogether too meagre" to support the decisions to bind out Freeman's children. "These orders," wrote the chief justice, "tested by the record alone, as they must be by this Court, are clearly erroneous." Strong and Davidson did not retain a lawyer to argue their side. Apprentices were supposed to be cheap labor, so it made little sense to spend money on litigation over them. They could always petition the court for custody over other children, children whose families lacked the money or the will to hire an attorney.[24]

Although Kentucky law forbade Freeman to raise a hand in self-defense against a white person, he still found ways to defend himself. He could not challenge the broad injustices he faced because the law classified him as a free man of color, but the simple act of mounting an appeal, however narrow and technical, boosted his status. Just by hiring a lawyer, Freeman showed that he was not too poor to care for his children. The law defined Freeman as something less than a full citizen, but his ability to litigate protected him and his family from the world beyond their fifty acres of hillside. The Kentucky high court's decision was short and crisp. It made no reference to Freeman's color.

WOMEN IN THE HILLS might marry at age twelve and live through ten or even fifteen childbirths, not to mention malaria and dysentery and typhoid. They spun and wove clothes for the family, weeded the cornfields, rooted for ginseng, foraged for herbs, and milked cows that roamed freely in the forest. They cooked and cleaned and carried water from the spring to their cabins. "Only the lowest peasantry of Europe can show anything to parallel it," wrote anthropologist Ellen Churchill Semple at the end of the nineteenth century. "The mountain woman . . . at twenty-five looks forty, and at forty looks twenty years older than her husband."[25]

Travelers marveled at how isolated Appalachian women were from the world outside their mountain hollows. Many never ventured more than a ridgeline or two from home through their entire lives. "They are as rooted as the trees," wrote Semple. But Clarissa Centers had walked and ridden thousands of miles before she was twenty-five. Clarsy had been born in the western hills of South Carolina, but her family soon moved to North Carolina, then eventually up through the Cumberland Gap, where Tennessee, Virginia, and Kentucky meet.[26]

The Centers family was not alone in their journey. In the decades after 1830, exhausted soil, declining tobacco and cotton prices, and financial panics drove tens of thousands of people west—on northern routes stretching from Ohio to Minnesota, along southern routes to Louisiana and Texas, and through mountain passes into Kentucky and Tennessee. From North Carolina and Georgia, an entire nation of dispossessed Cherokees was making its way toward Oklahoma. The routes could be crowded with people, carts and carriages, and horses, cows, pigs, and sheep. Often they were "more like the leading avenue of a great city," wrote one observer, "than a road through rural districts." Families slept under canvas tents on roadsides and in fields. Travelers drank and fought and gambled and conned and killed. Great and small, educated and ignorant, good and wicked—old distinctions mattered little on the road west. Everyone was traveling the same path, in search of new lands, new luck, and new lives.[27]

The Centers family reached Clay County shortly before 1840. Although she was still traveling with her parents and siblings, Clarsy Centers was no longer a girl. She was in her early twenties and had a baby boy on her hip. A child born out of wedlock was hardly uncommon on the frontier. At the very least, the boy showed that Clarsy was fertile, and with only one child, she remained relatively young and strong for her age. If her situation carried any disgrace, she could have devised a story of widowhood, and no one in her new community would have been the wiser.[28]

By 1841, Clarsy and her son had moved into George Freeman's cabin. She was twenty-five and pregnant with his child. George was twice her age. His first wife was probably dead. Eleven people lived with him, some of them his grown daughters—right around Clarsy's age—with children of their own. His family was becoming a clan.[29]

Although Freeman and Centers were not married, that fact in itself would have merited little comment in their hollow. Many others in the wil-

derness had dispensed with such formalities. Having children and struggling through life together made them man and wife. Even if they had
wanted to, however, they could not have married. While George Freeman
was a man of color, Clarsy Centers was white. Kentucky law prohibited
their union.

Freeman and Centers were not the only ones in Clay County breach-
ing the color line. Several free black women were living with white men.
It was less common, however, for black men to have families with white
women, and their relationships were perceived as a far greater threat to the
social and racial order. After all, the mixed-race children of black women
became, more often than not, pieces of property, markers of wealth, for
their owners. But the children of slave men and white women were free
under Kentucky law, and they blurred the physical distinctions that made
racial status conceivable and enforceable. As a result, all such relationships
were subversive, even those involving free men.[30]

Moreover, the control that white men had over their families, something that approached ownership under the law, helped maintain the idea
that all white men were equal citizens in a country increasingly stratified by
wealth, where the salt barons of Clay County could buy and sell the typical
small farmer hundreds of times over. That control was undermined when
white women had children with black men. From seventeenth-century
Virginia onward, politicians, planters, and other groups of white men had
publicly fretted about sexually aggressive blacks and expressed "honest indignation," as ten North Carolina men wrote in 1825, at the prospect of
black men making "any approach towards a connection with a white woman
even by her consent."[31]

At the same time white communities did not always respond to these
relationships with reflexive deadly violence. They were capable of tolerat-
ing difference or pretending it did not exist. Across the South in the early
decades of the nineteenth century, black men and white women were forming families and living in peace.[32]

Clarsy Centers gave birth to a daughter, Elizabeth, in 1841, and would
have nine more children with Freeman over the next dozen years. While
anthropologists years later would dismiss relationships between hus-

bands and wives in the mountains as "very elemental, betray[ing] little of the romantic spirit," Clarsy's situation likely fell closer to that of the woman who would marry Centers's nephew a generation later. Asked why she married him, she responded, "Just like all other people do, because I liked him."[33]

George's rise in the world required strength, intelligence, and will. He offered Clarsy security after a life of wandering. His grown daughters and their children were nearby; Clarsy had women her age to talk to and would not have to raise her babies alone. The fact that Freeman had brown skin or had once been a slave was of little consequence. In Clarsy's home state of South Carolina, the high court ruled in 1835 that a person's status "is not to be determined solely by the distinct and visible mixture of negro blood, but by reputation, by his reception into society, and his having commonly exercised the privileges of a white man . . . [A] man of worth, honesty, industry and respectability should have the rank of a white man." The judge could have been describing Freeman. If his emancipation papers listed him as "mulatto," whites in Clay County were also dark after lives spent working in the sun.[34]

Clarsy Centers's parents left the county soon after she moved into George Freeman's cabin. They may have disapproved of the union or found themselves unwelcome among other whites because of it. But Clarsy's younger sister Malinda stayed behind, suggesting that Freeman's family was better able than her parents to provide for her.[35]

THE JOURNEY WEST WOULD have been the easy one—macadam-paved highways that led to rambling farms for Thoroughbred horses, bustling cities and anonymous crowds, the Ohio River flowing into the horizon. But Jordan Spencer and Malinda Centers chose to head northeast, deeper into the wilderness, through rivers and over hills, along Indian traces, creek beds, and mountain paths, along mud ruts deeper than wagon wheels and steep deadly falls. They had to brave poison snakes, wild animals, and a whole range of human predators—desperate men as well as perfectly respectable people who could choose to give them trouble. They may have had a cart, or they may simply have loaded up a couple of mules or horses with their three babies and everything they owned.

When Clarsy Centers started having George Freeman's children, Malinda had been as young as ten years old. Four years later, in 1845, she was pregnant by Jordan Spencer, who was about a decade her senior. In three years they had three children: George Washington, Andrew Jackson, and Elizabeth. Two presidents and a queen. Proud names.[36]

When Elizabeth was born, there were close to twenty people living on George Freeman's land—three generations, too many for fifty acres to sustain, too many for the neighbors to ignore, in an unsettling progression from dark to light to white. Hot-tempered and fond of whiskey, Spencer may have fought with Freeman or, worse, with someone else in the community. After years of giving Freeman and his family some breathing room, the local authorities again took an interest in them. If Spencer wanted to be left alone, he had to find another hollow in a different set of hills.[37]

In 1852 Freeman was prosecuted for fornication. Because he could not marry Clarsy Centers, having children with her was a crime. Again, he hired an attorney and mounted a vigorous defense. But fighting back cost money. To afford the legal fees, Freeman had to mortgage everything he owned. He paid off his creditors, and when he died soon afterward, he left property to Clarsy and to his daughter Alice. But a few years later Alice was prosecuted for hog stealing, an easy charge to make where pigs ranged freely in the hills. She had to give up her land to pay her lawyer.[38]

Jordan Spencer, Malinda Centers, and their children were gone by then. They made their way north and east through five counties and did not stop until they were a hundred miles away. Malinda managed to stay in contact with Clarsy—no small feat for two illiterate sisters. But they lived in different worlds.

No matter how long or how hard the Freemans worked to find a foothold in Clay County, it could always be taken away in an instant. County officials had near complete authority to make life costly and difficult for the Freemans. Kentucky's laws drew an unambiguous line between white and black. One side was defined by a series of rights, the other by the denial of rights. Free people of color would always constitute a category of people separate from whites and inferior to them. They would be poor. They would be landless. They would be prosecuted for petty offenses. They would have their children taken away.

But the law's reach—the incessant intrusion of authority—did more than keep blacks and whites separate. It pushed Jordan Spencer and Malinda Centers out of Clay County, where they had been an abomination and a threat. As the county disappeared behind them, they became something altogether different: husband and wife. When they finally reached a stopping point, they called themselves Jordan and Malinda Spencer. Their new neighbors welcomed them into their community. As far as they knew, the Spencers were just like them. No matter how hard he fought, Kentucky's laws kept George Freeman in his place. But they turned Jordan Spencer into a white man.[39]

CHAPTER FOUR

GIBSON

New Haven, Connecticut, 1850–55

Fall 1850

T HE TRAIN WHEEZED ITS way north and east along the
Connecticut coast, coughing black smoke. Like a dull
knife, it slowly punched through fields, salt marshes, and fishing villages.
After seven years in operation, the railroad still looked alien alongside the
ancient seascape, indifferent to the tidal lap of Long Island Sound, the gulls
floating high overhead, almost unmoving. Only as it approached its destination did the strange amalgam of wheels and joints, valves and whistles,
appear to have a place in the world. Dozens of smokestacks on the horizon
welcomed the train home to New Haven, a city of coal fire and steam.

Only ten years earlier New Haven had been a sprawling village with
mills and factories scattered on its remote outskirts, fueled by creeks and
rivers. Steam power allowed businesses to move anywhere, but factories
clustered near the port. The central location meant cheap delivery of the
mountains of coal needed to heat the large boilers that made engines run,
and it drastically cut the costs of shipping finished goods. Situated "at the
head of a fine bay," its railroads spidering southwest to New York, northeast to Boston, and straight north to Hartford and Northampton, New
Haven was uniquely positioned to profit from the steam revolution.
By 1855, the city was aswim in cash and teeming with thousands of new

workers. "Nearly every kind of manufactured article known in the market, can here be found and bought direct from the manufactory," wrote the clockmaker Chauncey Jerome, "such as carriages and all kind of carriage goods, firearms, shirts, locks, furniture, clothing, shoes, hardware, iron castings, daguerrotype-cases, machinery, plated goods, &c., &c."[1]

As the train rolled past Long Wharf into the city, as many as fifty ships could be seen steaming and sailing in the harbor beyond. The docks whirled in steady motion like a factory turbine. Thick gangs of stevedores and roustabouts were unloading hundreds of tons of coal, timber, molasses, rum, and oysters out of merchant vessels from points south. Other men were packing ships with equally vast quantities of manufactured goods. Just north of the wharf, the 140-foot clocktower of the New York and New Haven Railroad depot waited, a beacon of calm after a jarring journey. Passengers who had paid the $1.50 or so to travel from New York arrived at a station that still looked new. With its arches and stonework it resembled a Tuscan villa, a graceful counterpoint to the heat, smell, and racket of the train.[2]

In the autumn of 1850, two elegantly appointed young men arrived in New Haven. They were just getting used to being tall and still too young to shave. A well-timed blast of steam could have knocked down the elder of the two. At six feet and 140 pounds, Randall Lee Gibson observed that "there are no hopes of my being a dwarf, but on the contrary, I fear I shall never stop growing." It had been a long journey, but Randall and his brother Hart had taken some time to rest in New York—"a splendid city," thought Hart, "though I should not like to reside in it."[3]

Randall was pleased that his younger brother had maintained a sunny disposition. Hart could easily have spent the journey in tears but instead "st[ood] everything manfully." At fifteen, Hart had never been away from the family for long. Now he found himself nearly a thousand miles away from the family home in Lexington, Kentucky, and even farther from the Gibson sugar plantations in the bayous southwest of New Orleans. He had left behind his beloved mother—"the most attentive, thoughtful + kindest of mothers," in Randall's words—knowing full well that he might never see her again. For more than a year, the family had moved back and forth between Kentucky and Louisiana for her health, even contemplating a voyage to the West Indies, while the best medical minds of the South tried to restore her "sanguine . . . temperament." Although Dr. Samuel Cartwright of New Orleans believed she had fallen prey to a host of ailments due to "the uterus ceasing eliminating function abruptly & at too early a period," it was clear that within months she would die from consumption. Back home, her coughing kept Hart and Randall's older sister Sarah "awake all night," "heart sick" and horrified at their mother's fate.[4]

Far from the impending family tragedy, Hart could focus on the new world around him. Walking with his brother along Chapel Street into downtown, Hart was amazed at the blocks of banks, concert halls, and office buildings. The street was lined with tall lamps recently installed by the New Haven Gas Company. After two blocks Chapel formed the southern side of the New Haven Green, a sixteen-acre fenced preserve where contemplative pathways crisscrossed past a Greek Revival statehouse, two clean brick Congregational chapels, and the Gothic tower of the Trinity Episcopal Church. The Chapel Street side below the Green boasted a series of shops—dry goods, millinery, groceries—leading up to the hundred splendid rooms of the just-built New Haven House at the corner of College Street. East of the Green were the jail, courthouse, and another grand hotel. Bounding the north side was "Quality Row," where New Haven's old families lived in porticoed mansions. Hart was sure to check himself, lest he be too impressed. As grand as the city was, it was nonetheless full of Yankees. In his older brother's experience, they were an unmannered and unpleasant people. They imposed their own views on people instead of engaging them. They worshipped money instead of God. "I must confess that I do not admire the customs of these Northern people," Randall wrote, "and therefore I do not admire them."[5]

Despite the Gibson brothers' distaste for anything "Yankee-like," Hart had come to New Haven to live, just as his brother had two years earlier. Facing the Green from the west was a block of austere dormitories known as Brick Row, veiled by a copse of towering elms. In front of the trees at the corner of Chapel and College streets was a long wooden fence on which dozens of young men sat lounging, laughing, shouting, and singing. Their top hats at jaunty angles, puffing away on long cigars, they resembled a decidedly more leisured version of the smokestacks that filled their city.

In their view New Haven was a town best seen through a cloud of cigar smoke. A nice Connecticut cigar, blending fine Cuban leaf with local South Windsor tobacco, could perfume even the foulest industrial winds. The Gibson brothers had reached their destination, Yale College, where Hart would be prepping for admission and where Randall, at the start of his sophomore year, was already acquitting himself brilliantly.[6]

On the fence at College and Chapel, the Gibsons' schoolmates sat facing away from their "Mecca of the learned." Yale College was supposed to be where the "literary crowd" and "*savans* of science" turned the flower of New England's youth into leaders of men. But every day in class seemed to embody the words inscribed in the brownstone gateway to the cemetery two blocks north on Grove Street: "The Dead Shall Be Raised." The beautiful texts of Xenophon, Cicero, and Tacitus became workaday grist for dull, "gerund-grinding" recitations. During instruction in natural philosophy, students were asked to repeat the assigned reading by rote until it "disgusted the class with the whole subject." History classes consisted solely of memorizing the dates in *The Manual of Ancient History and Geography* by the German scholar Wilhelm Pütz. Even senior coursework with university president Theodore Dwight Woolsey followed the "Yale system" of "hearing men recite the words of a text-book." The students occasionally had "very round expletive[s]," but more usually felt "general indifference . . . toward all this instruction," lamented a member of the class of 1853. "It was listlessly heard, and grievously neglected."[7]

Hart Gibson would soon learn that Yale men saved their energy for the hours outside class. With no formal instruction in literature, students absorbed the great cultural movements of the day from visiting lectures by eminences such as Ralph Waldo Emerson. Exiles from the failed revolutions that had swept Europe in 1848 pushed Yalies to think about the future of democracy and, as one student poet wrote in 1853, "trace / With joy o'er Europe's burning palaces / The path of Freedom." From brass band concerts and book auctions to riding, sailing, and fencing, life in New Haven could be "as stupid and delightful as [the] heart could wish," one student wrote home in 1851. On the green Yale students played brutal football contests as well as a game called "rush," described by a university historian as "football without a ball." Yalies relished a good prank, or "scrape," like the occasional unauthorized "perform[ance] on the college Bell." A professor might enter his classroom to find, much to Randall's delight, "an old grey horse standing on the rostrum with an immense pair of specks on."[8]

Mostly the students educated one another, in dorm room chats and student society debates, on cold walks to their daily six a.m. prayers, and while sitting on the fence at College and Chapel. Every day was a continuing conversation about issues big and small. The debate topics of one student society were typical: Ought legislators to be bound by the will of their constituents? Is the maxim "our country right or wrong" worthy of adoption? Should capital punishment be abolished? Will China probably ever become a commercial nation? Has Chivalry exercised a beneficial effect upon Society? Has the Mohammedan religion exercised an evil effect upon the world? Should the policy of nonintervention in the affairs of other countries be in all cases adhered to by the United States? Is energy or talent more conducive to fame as shown by historical experience? Some of the student arguments were cogent and forceful. Others, in the opinion of one professor, were "ill hung" and "splurgy." Regardless of quality, debates were endless and earnest, as students struggled to figure out the world as it was and their place in it.[9]

By the fall of 1850 Randall Gibson's place at Yale was already assured. As a debater, Gibson made some of the best speeches that his fellow Yalies had "ever heard delivered by anyone"—there was "not a better [speaker] in College," a classmate recorded in a diary. During his first year Gibson's classmates entrusted him with writing the formal challenge and drawing up the rules for the annual freshman-sophomore football game. Later he rowed on Yale's first competitive crew team and was elected to Delta Kappa Epsilon and the Scroll and Key secret society. From his freshman year until he gave the class of 1853's valedictory address, Randall was lionized as a "revelation," wrote a classmate, "the flower of the small company of Southerners" who were following in the footsteps of South Carolina senator John C. Calhoun, class of 1804, and Louisiana senator Judah Benjamin, class of 1828. "We were of an age to be fascinated; of the hero-worshipping age," the classmate wrote, "and a good many of us, boylike, thought Randall Gibson was a hero." He would be a role model and a font of sage, if at times unwanted, advice to his younger brother.[10]

It was no small task for the sons of a wealthy sugar planter to find success at Yale in the 1850s. "Southerner to us meant first of all slaveholder, and then perhaps aristocrat," wrote one member of the class of 1853. "We liked neither in New England." The escalating national crisis over slavery set the differences between Northern and Southern students in stark relief. In 1850 Congress had passed the Fugitive Slave Act, putting the federal government in the service of slaveowners pursuing their runaways. In response, abolitionists moved from debating the morality or legality of slavery to contemplating armed resistance to it. Even as the antislavery position grew more radical, it was entering the mainstream of Northern politics. *Uncle Tom's Cabin*, published in 1852, instilled in countless readers a powerful sympathy for slaves and a visceral disgust for slavery and slaveowners. The drumbeat intensified with the passage of the Kansas-Nebraska Act in 1854, which allowed settlers to vote to determine whether Kansas would be a slave or free state. It promised to cast slavery and antislavery forces in pitched battles.[11]

Of all the subjects that the Yale men liked to debate, the biggest issue by far was "the tremendous political struggle" raging over slavery. Students and professors alike were drawn into controversies over the Fugitive Slave Act and the Kansas question. Although by 1854 several prominent members of the faculty were publicly supporting the abolitionists in Kansas— even raising money to buy rifles—the campus was more moderate regarding slavery than its rival in Cambridge, Massachusetts. Compromise to preserve the Union had long held the middle ground at Yale, but with every passing day it seemed less possible to accede to the "Slave Power." In their formal debate topics, students knew what was at stake: Has a State the right to nullify any Act of Congress? Has a state the right to secede from the Union? Do the present circumstances portend the dissolution of the Union?[12]

Confronted "with the imputation of iniquity and immorality which had begun to fasten on the slaveholder as a class," Southerners parried with insistent defenses of the way things were, marshaling arguments from religion, politics, and law, anthropology, statistics, and medical science. As one Virginian described it, educated Southerners were "rising up to promulgate the philosophical, sociological, and ethnical excellence of slavery." As much as slavery was right, freedom was wrong. The proslavery position increasingly expressed itself as a belief in absolute racial difference, the genetic inferiority of blackness, and the disastrous effects of racial mixing. "The preservation and progress of the race," wrote Henry Hughes in his influential 1854 *Treatise on Sociology*, "is a moral duty of the races. Degeneration is an evil. It is a sin. That sin is extreme. Hybridism is heinous. Impurity of races is against the law of nature. Mulattoes are monsters." At the mere prospect of freedom and equality for blacks, racial loathing began to incubate among privileged Southern whites.[13]

The several dozen students at Yale from slave states tended to stick together and, in the opinion of a schoolmate from Massachusetts, "were slightly haughty in their bearing toward other less favored mortals." They gathered to discuss politics and even examine opposing points of view in the privacy of their own society, the Calliopean, founded after a sectional squabble in 1819. Liberally furnished with spittoons, the society's damask-draped chambers were lined with a ten-thousand-volume library. In 1851, amid fevered debates over the Fugitive Slave Act, the Southern students withdrew from every other club.[14]

Still, Randall Gibson was able to coast above the prejudices that Southern students faced. "I am sure he never gave himself the least trouble to overcome anybody's prepossessions against him," wrote a classmate. "It might not occur to him that there were prepossessions; it certainly would not occur to him that it was his business to remove them. He was quite free from anything like excessive regard for the opinion of others, and from morbid self-consciousness." It did not matter that the Gibson family owned more than a hundred slaves on a sugar plantation southwest of New Orleans, not far from the scene of Uncle Tom's martyrdom at the hands of Simon Legree. Defensiveness on the slavery question was beneath Randall. When his good friend Andrew Dickson White faced opposition for the editorship of the *Yale Literary Magazine* for his strident abolitionist views,

Randall led the push to elect him. In his valedictory oration, Randall viewed himself and his fellow graduates as being the solution to the sectional crisis by virtue of their superior station. "When darkness and gloom gather and settle on the land," he said, "when terror and dismay are depicted in every countenance, and the last resource of conciliation has been appealed to in vain; whither shall the fortunes of the republic turn for light, for hope, for guidance for preservation? . . . [I]t is to educated intellect that we are to look for the preservation of these American institutions."[15]

Randall Gibson's seemingly effortless aristocracy insulated him from suspicion and slight. While his fellow Southerners floundered, Gibson's Yankee classmates could regard him as the quintessential plantation master without dismissing him as immoral, arrogant, and aloof. The secret to Gibson's success was simple. While his manners "betokened ancestry," his outlook and ambitions were decidedly more accessible to Northerners. Gibson was not at Yale to bide time before assuming an inheritance. His father wrote him dozens of letters that described sugar farming as a whipsaw of rising and plunging market prices, drought and flood. "Nothing but superior qualifications will enable a young man to succeed now a days," wrote Tobias Gibson, urging his son to use his education to "rise superior to the mass of those who are content to live and to die as their Fathers did." Randall's father instructed him to economize and keep meticulous records, learn French so that he could succeed in business in Louisiana, and "get and *study* a little book called 'The Pleasant Art of Money Catching.'"[16]

Randall absorbed his father's advice. "I know full well the necessity of fitting myself for the world and I have no hope except in connection with action," the young man wrote. He was resolved to pursue studies that would not "make a young man appear brilliant or interesting in the drawing room" but rather would "strengthen the powers of the mind when developed by rigid training, *preparing it* not only for reading but digesting, for tracing effects to causes, for judging as well as hearing." Randall looked like an aristocrat, but he thought like a Yankee. His classmates could admire him as their hero because they could talk with him as equals.[17]

Randall Gibson's mix of ancient and modern sensibilities—ancestry and ambition—was embodied in his family history. His mother's line, the Harts and Prestons, was Kentucky royalty, founding families who had moved from Virginia during the Revolution and lived on vast bluegrass estates between Lexington and Frankfort, near the aptly named town of Versailles. Their relations were senators and governors. Randall's mother, Louisiana Hart Gibson, was named in honor of the Louisiana Purchase by her cousin John Breckinridge, who had represented Kentucky in the Senate and served as attorney general under Thomas Jefferson.[18]

But the Gibsons were not pure products of the elite. Randall and Hart's father, for one, had a decidedly new spirit. Born in Mississippi, Tobias Gibson made his fortune in the "white gold rush" of sugarcane farming that swept Louisiana in the 1820s and 1830s. Seizing the opportunity presented by favorable tariffs and new sugarcane hybrids, he borrowed heavily to buy dozens of slaves and hundreds of acres of land of "unsurpassed fertility" southwest of New Orleans. Over two decades of intense labor transformed a densely forested wilderness of "alligators[,] musquitoes, snakes [and] frogs" into "large cultivated fields and rich pastures, and improvements, which display taste and energy and wealth, . . . so sudden and yet so substantial." Dividing his time between Louisiana and Kentucky, Tobias built a proud home in the center of Lexington that became a gathering place for supporters of the Whig senator Henry Clay. As befitted Tobias's two lives, the house looked from the front like a Kentucky gentleman's colonnaded manse, but behind the façade it was built around a courtyard in the New Orleans style.[19]

Throughout the Gibson children's youth, the family would periodically steam down the Mississippi River from Louisville to New Orleans, and then take a boat and carriage to Bayou Black near the town of Tigerville, the site of Tobias Gibson's plantation, Live Oak. The Gibson children were educated at Live Oak by private tutors and spent their days mostly outdoors, shooting, riding, fishing, and swimming. But life on the plantation was not entirely an idyll. Tobias invested in the latest technologies, "all the modern improvements of railroads, &c., for expediting the work of sugar making." In the plantation's steam-powered sugar house, the sugarcane was crushed and its juice extracted and evaporated in a violent, recognizably industrial process—in Tobias's words, "the fires of pandemonium were kindled sure enough." The smokestacks of New Haven were hardly the first that Randall and Hart Gibson had encountered.[20]

Even as Southerners were insisting that blacks were biologically inferior and unfit for freedom, Tobias Gibson had a slave working as his overseer and complained, "I am in conscience opposed to slavery—I don't like it, and the older I get the worse it seems—& to entail it upon my children is not very agreeable to think of." Such sentiment provided an easy way for one of the biggest slaveowners in Louisiana to feel virtuous about his way of life—disliking slavery made him a better master. Regardless, his willingness to express distaste for an increasingly inviolable institution was in keeping with his forward-looking character: entrepreneurial, politically savvy, unafraid of technology, pragmatic—a latter-day pioneer.[21]

Tobias Gibson's parents and grandparents had also embraced transformation and the promise of the new. The Gibson family had settled in Natchez, Mississippi, in 1781 and then moved north toward Vicksburg. Randall Gibson never knew the man he had been named for. His father's father had been an early convert to Methodism during the "awakening" of evangelical Christianity that had swept the western territories after the Revolution, and he had ministered to a small congregation that included two slaves. "Brother Gibson" frequently wept while "pouring out the pious breathings of his soul into the ear of God alone." "Many were turned from darkness to light by his ministry," said his eulogist.[22]

In the "Gibson Community" below Vicksburg in Warren County, Mississippi, the family was by and large wealthy and respectable but not above disputing with their neighbors over land and slaves and honor. The Mississippi Gibsons developed a keen sense of tradition—they practiced their penmanship by copying births and deaths out of an old Bible, learning the family tree like a catechism—but the family tree did not extend back past the initial settlement in Mississippi. They handed down a legend about "four Gibson youths" who had sailed for Virginia from England sometime in the seventeenth century, the children of the "younger son of an English lord" and "a Gypsy maid"—which explained the dark features that ran in the family. They knew little about the Gibsons who shortly after the Revolution had moved from the banks of the Great Pee Dee River in the South Carolina backcountry to Mississippi. It was no matter that the Gibson family, most notably represented by Gideon Gibson the Regulator, had hovered on the line between white and black. Within a generation or two, the Gibsons would not think twice about their race. They had become unself-consciously white. Once they reached Mississippi, they were simply pioneers. In Kentucky and Louisiana they were prosperous planters. At Yale, Randall and Hart Gibson would be kings.[23]

Spring 1855

HART GIBSON WALKED past Yale's Brick Row with an air of satisfaction. In March 1855 the weather was crisp and the elms still bare, but the new light of spring promised lovely days ahead. The New Haven winter—the interminable misty rain that insinuated itself into one's bones, not to mention clothes, bedsheets, paper, and tobacco—was already fading into a damp memory. Gibson was confident that the illness and indisposition that had plagued him in the cold months were behind him at last. Soon it would be spring vacation, followed by examinations covering the past two years of courses, and finally graduation.[24]

The Yale senior was making plans to attend the law school at Harvard in the fall. The previous year his fortune had been secured when an uncle named him heir to a Kentucky estate called Hartland. Before he left Yale, however, he had some "hard study" to do during the spring break and would have to ask his father for some extra money. For someone as studious and popular as Gibson, it would be best to leave the city. "New Haven is the worst of all places to study during a vacation," he wrote. "Enough students always remain in town to make idleness *agreeable* and in a measure *necessary* when study is not *compulsory*. Flight is therefore the only alternative if one wishes to accomplish anything."[25]

Gibson was ending his days at Yale well. Although his older brother noted that Hart's Yale career had been less brilliant than his own, Hart had won prizes for debate and declamation and in February 1855 was elected president of the college's large and venerable literary society, Linonia. In his final term Hart could look back on an impressive ascent for someone who started school as a nonentity. "There probably was not a man so little known in our Freshman years or better liked as Seniors," remembered a classmate, "or, when we parted, whose hand was grasped more closely."[26]

During Gibson's years at Yale, life for Southern students had become steadily more contentious. The divide over slavery sharpened and became personal, and Southerners had no place to hide after their Calliopean Society shuttered in 1853, more than a thousand dollars in debt to local booksellers. Many students from slave states bristled with insecurity, confirming everything their Yankee classmates supposed to be true about them. Gibson's younger brother Claude, a freshman in the class of 1858, had already been cast in the part of the "hasty temper[ed]" and "violent defender of his native South," worrying his family with "unfavorable accounts of [his] scholarship & extravagance." Hart, by contrast, flourished in Yale's everyday give-and-take—and not by blending in. He was proudly Southern, matter-of-factly proslavery. If he dressed anything like his cousin William Preston Johnston '53, he "set the fashion" of his class, with splendid cravats, kid gloves, and smartly tailored coats. Hart impressed his classmates as a singular presence with a "peculiar dignity." According to one friend from upstate New York, Hart cultivated a "self contained and self reliant reticence which checked too quick approach, but which, once overcome, held friendships fast."[27]

Hart's "self reliant reticence" hewed to the core of what had made his older brother Randall a leader at Yale. Two years out of college, now reading law at the University of Louisiana at New Orleans, Randall wrote letters to Hart that subtly and not so subtly reinforced the importance of keeping one's ambitions at a higher level than mere social standing at Yale. Randall urged Hart to study law at Yale and Harvard and spend time in Europe. "Don't think as much as we used to about settling in one particular place," Randall opined. "Never think for an instant of marrying in the North," he continued. "I have looked into this matter thoroughly. You can do better here blindfolded than in the North with your eyes open." Above all, Randall wrote, "I would never let others know me as well as I know myself."[28]

While Hart set himself apart as different, he thrived in New England's cultural ferment, responding to Ralph Waldo Emerson's call to "affront and reprimand the smooth mediocrity and squalid contentment of the times." Unlike his fellow Southerners, Hart showed a willingness to criticize the South, a rare candor that intrigued his Northern classmates. "While our Yankee brethren are unable to rival us in statesmanship and popular oratory," he wrote, "we are far, too far, behind them in polite literature and science." When it came to issues of culture and education in the South, Hart tended to express himself like a New England reformer. "Our failure lies in the fact that we have no complete and permanently established system of universal popular education," he wrote, "and the consequence is that knowledge which should be as free as the air we breathe, is conditional upon wealth and is thus placed beyond the reach of the greater part of our people."[29]

Hart's goal—of a culturally enlightened South that could "contend" with the North for "supremacy in History, Poetry, Painting, Sculpture, and the sciences"—was naïvely romantic. Yet he couched his idealism in terms that echoed modern notions of capitalism, the spirit that was making New Haven a rich and powerful city. "Much stress is laid in Political Economy on the law of 'supply & demand,'" he wrote his father. "It will be found I think that this principle operates with perhaps more force and universality in the intellectual than physical world." As he imagined it, public education in the South would create a "permanent demand" that would allow literature to be "pursued and cultivated successfully as a profession." Culture, in Hart's mind, was a commodity to be bought and sold, fostering a regional economy staffed by teachers and professors and sustained by their expertise. It was a vision that more closely resembled New Haven than New Orleans. Whether he was being grandiose or practical, Hart spoke a language that connected with his Northern classmates.[30]

Just beneath the surface of Hart's undergraduate idealism was an appetite for success in the real world. For much of his senior year, he had been attending a series of private lectures by his metaphysics professor on continuing one's education after graduation. It was a subject, Hart wrote, "of vast practical importance to myself, as well as to those who go before and those who are to come after me." The professor urged a course of miscellaneous reading, followed by "the acquisition of Modern languages," training in a profession, and finally travel abroad. The goal was "to make an accomplished scholar and gentleman." But Hart was left dissatisfied—

what he really wanted were lectures that would "enable one to get the upper hand of the bustling activities of our progressive & expanding Republic." Just what he meant by getting the "upper hand" was suggested in an 1854 letter by his older brother Randall, who was traveling at the time down the East Coast. "Washington of all cities attracted my attention," Randall wrote Hart. "There are several very handsome residences in Washington that would suit you very well, but the White House in particular I would recommend."[31]

ON MARCH 21, 1855, Hart Gibson dressed with special excitement for an evening in town. Throughout the winter he had cheerfully attended the "People's Course of Lectures" organized by the New Haven Lyceum, a civic group dedicated to adult education. Even though the talks had been designed "chiefly with a view to aid the anti-slavery agitation," Gibson delighted in the opportunity to see up close some of the great enemies of the South. John Parker Hale of New Hampshire, the first of the new breed of antislavery senators who were roiling the floor debates in the Capitol, did not just talk of abolition—he had served as lawyer for fugitive slaves and vigilantes who had interfered with their recapture. Unitarian minister Theodore Parker railed against the pervasive and corrupting governmental influence of the "Slave Power" and urged Northerners to "annihilate" the "monster" of slavery. The Reverend Henry Ward Beecher, Harriet Beecher Stowe's brother, was a consummate showman who had been raising thousands of dollars to free individual slaves by holding "auctions" that shocked and thrilled his New York congregation. Perhaps most dangerous of all was Cassius Marcellus Clay, a Kentuckian from Gibson's social circle who had been converted to abolitionism as a Yale undergraduate after hearing William Lloyd Garrison speak. Clay proudly remembered being described as someone with a "white skin" but "a very black heart."[32]

While many Southerners responded violently to these abolitionist firebrands—during an 1848 congressional debate, Senator Henry Foote invited Hale to "visit the good state of Mississippi" so that he could "grace one of the tallest trees of the forest, with a rope around his neck . . . [I]f necessary I should myself assist in the operation"—Hart Gibson did not seem remotely threatened. With a light touch he wrote his father that the lectures had been "very edifying and instructive." Just as casually, he refused to be swayed by them. "I need scarcely mention the burden of their song," he said.[33]

On the night of March 21, however, the Lyceum was finally sponsoring a public lecture giving "a 'South Side' view of slavery." The speaker was an introverted, self-taught country lawyer who had never traveled to the North before—indeed, he rarely left his home in the Virginia Tidewater region. Yet George Fitzhugh would be denounced by William Lloyd Garrison in the pages of the *Liberator* as "the Don Quixote of Slavedom—only still more demented." In his physical and intellectual isolation, George Fitzhugh had become a proslavery pamphleteer, cultivating like hothouse flowers original ideas that took root across the South and changed the way people thought about slavery.[34]

Over the previous three decades, in response to abolitionists, Southerners had developed a series of arguments that tended to excuse slavery as a necessary evil, essential for the American economy, sanctioned by the Bible, historically the pathway from savagery to civilization, and regulated by the benevolent self-interest of noble masters. Fitzhugh took such arguments a step further, contrasting slavery with the horrors of free labor and pushing Southerners to "endorse slavery in the abstract." Slavery, to Fitzhugh, "was morally right, . . . as profitable as it was humane." In 1854 Fitzhugh published *Sociology for the South*—named, he wrote, for the new science of sociology that was developed to study the countless "afflictions" of industrial, free society. Fitzhugh's book embraced a radical critique of capitalism, a view that "free competition begets a war of the wits . . . quite as destructive to the weak, simple and guileless, as the war of the sword." As Fitzhugh saw it, in a free society "the negro . . . would be welcome nowhere; meet with thousands of enemies and no friends. If he went North, the white laborers would kick him and cuff him, and drive him out of employment." By contrast, the plantation offered a more stable, just, prosperous, and happy life for blacks and whites alike. "At the slaveholding South all is peace, quiet, plenty and contentment," Fitzhugh wrote. "We have no mobs, no trades unions, no strikes for higher wages, no armed resistance to the law, but little jealousy of the rich by the poor . . . We are wholly exempt from the torrent of pauperism, crime, agrarianism, and infidelity" that was ravaging Europe and the North.[35]

Hart Gibson felt a rush of anticipation at the prospect of seeing this "Mr. Fitzhugh of Va." speak. Perhaps the presentation would help Gibson's Yankee friends understand his position, even sway a few of them, or at the very least give him more ammunition in the daily verbal battles over slavery. Maybe the evening's speaker would show the South's progress in becoming the equal of the North on the intellectual stage. Hart walked straight down Chapel Street, past the Green and through the downtown. It was a Wednesday after sundown. Flickering gas lamps revealed a slow throng of men and women, finished with their shifts at shops, offices, and factories, making their way home—or to bars, social clubs, or even the People's Lectures—in the dusk.[36]

Brewster's Hall, built by New Haven's biggest carriage manufacturer, stood just across the street from the train station, an ornate reminder that culture and ideas followed in industry's wake. The packed auditorium rumbled with excited talk about the night's speaker—the local papers had promised a true novelty, a "philosophical Southern" defense of slavery from "the author of what is claimed to be the most vigorous and consistent work on that side of the controversy." Hart Gibson took his seat among Yale men, professors, and townspeople, rich and poor, young and old. Although he was one of the few Southerners there, he felt comfortable in the crowd. He shared their curiosity, even a certain bemusement at the spectacle.[37]

When the clock struck eight, the auditorium hushed. The evening's speaker took the podium to make what he called "a metaphysical and statistical argument" proving "free society a failure." Hair combed forward and across his high forehead, Fitzhugh looked a touch like Napoleon. He relished the large audience's rapt attention, but he had not prepared a speech for the occasion. Instead, he read directly from *Sociology for the South*. "Men are not 'born entitled to equal rights'!" he proclaimed. In fact, "the weak in mind and body" were better off as Southern slaves than as free people, or rather "under that natural slavery of the weak to the strong, the foolish to the wise and cunning." "It would be far nearer the truth," he said, "to say 'that some were born with saddles on their backs, and others booted and spurred to ride them,' *and the riding does them good*."[38]

Fitzhugh kept reading. Minutes turned to hours, and for a fidgety audience the "profound sensation" of his words gave way to cross-eyed tedium. By ten p.m. Fitzhugh had declared that Thomas Jefferson was little more than an "enthusiastic speculative philosopher" whose ideas "would subvert every government on earth." Benjamin Franklin was "too utilitarian and material in his doctrines, to be relied on in matters of morals or government." The Declaration of Independence was "verbose, new-born, false and unmeaning"—after all, soldiers and sailors, apprentices and wards, and "the wives in all America" had long alienated "both liberty and life." Moreover, "all crimes are notoriously committed in the pursuit of happiness."[39]

Finally, Fitzhugh declared that free society was "theoretically impracticable," "afflicted with disease," and proven a failure "from history and statistics." He stepped back and basked in the applause. If he had expected a hostile reception from an auditorium full of Yankees, he was pleasantly surprised to be "listened to politely throughout." Afterward he received the congratulations of various New Havenites and Yale professors, mostly of the abolitionist stripe. In truth, Fitzhugh had bored the crowd into submission. The next day a local paper offered that "no one was convinced by his attempted arguments; many were amused by their novelty; a few were saddened that a man whom nature evidently intended for a genial gentleman, possessing common sense, and ordinary mental ability, should have the end of his production thwarted by the mere fact of topical location under the influences of slavery."[40]

Hart Gibson watched agog as the slavery question—a struggle that everyone knew portended national tragedy—unraveled into farce. In Gibson's delicate phrasing, Fitzhugh was "a very gentlemanly looking man but it was obvious that neither nature or art intended him for a public speaker." A less secure man might have despaired at Fitzhugh's debacle or felt compelled to defend him. But Gibson, ever the aristocrat, was able to consider the speech with something approaching critical distance. "A more hopeless & enormous failure can not easily be conceived," he wrote.

Fitzhugh's contrast between the free market's horrors and slavery's caring community rang false to the sugar planter's son. Perhaps the slavery Fitzhugh knew in the Virginia Tidewater was different from what Gibson had seen at Bayou Black. More important, the plantation life that Gibson knew was aggressively capitalist. Regardless of whether blacks were economic actors, the Gibsons were constantly competing with whites in markets for land, slaves, and sugar. And they had won. Hart Gibson walked back up Chapel Street to Brick Row, one of many Yalies chuckling over the evening's events.[41]

The next night Gibson returned to Brewster's Hall, joined in the audience by George Fitzhugh, to hear a rebuttal by the eminent abolitionist Wendell Phillips. The Boston lawyer dismissed Fitzhugh's argument with a rhetorical flick of the hand. "He who looks backward upon the past and present of Virginia," Phillips said, "and thinks that her sociality is sound, or that the ulcer eating into her prosperity is Free Trade and not Slavery, is like the old sailor who complaining of the effects of his grog, found the fault not in his rum, but in his water!" Phillips made a fiery call for "all men [to] have their rights—no matter whether the Union goes to pieces or not!" and he attacked the political conservatism of American religion, declaring that "a Church at peace in the presence of oppression is not the Church of Christ."[42]

While Fitzhugh pronounced Phillips's speech to be "flat treason and blasphemy—nothing else," Hart Gibson was enthralled. Part of what made Phillips so appealing was that his brand of antislavery belief did not engage in the wishful thinking, all too common among abolitionists, that the Constitution outlawed slavery. Rather, Phillips relied on blunt realism to explain the stranglehold that the "slave power" had on American politics and life. Like Gibson, he recognized that Americans were a "new people" driven by wealth. "I find no fault with this," he said. "I do not whine over it . . . There is much to be done. There are roads to build; there are hundreds of interests to be provided for, and material prosperity is the mission of the age."

Because slavery had enormous market value—$2 billion at Phillips's count—its legitimacy as an institution naturally followed. "Before that amount of money," he told the New Haven crowd, "the sanguine Yankee's imagination shrinks back." Phillips combined his economic realism with a wickedly cynical assessment of the give-and-take of politics that precluded the adoption of an abolitionist agenda: "A politician serves God so far as that does not offend the Devil."[43]

Phillips's pessimism about the present made his prescriptions for the future all the more radical. Only a true revolution could conquer slavery. "Make way or not," he declared, "justice shall be done here between man and man!" If law and society stood in the way of freedom, then they had to be overthrown. "Men should obey their convictions of duty, without regard to laws and institutions," he said. "Whether the institution is one thing or another, if it be unrighteous, let it be trampled under foot." Let the South secede over slavery, he argued, for the economic reality would ruin them. "Sunder the Union, they could not exist, simply because they could not pay their bills. The free competition of the North would destroy them, as it supports them now."[44]

Phillips's grounding in the economics of slavery and secession—his intuitive grasp of people's motivations in a capitalist world—heightened both the transgressive nature and the seeming rightness of his message. For Gibson, it was a thrilling mix of realism and radicalism, idealism and practicality. He wrote his father that Phillips was "not the man he is reputed to be. A more elegant, polished, scholarly gentleman you will not often find in the South . . . The extent and accuracy of his learning—classical & otherwise is truly wonderful and is only equaled by the ease & elegance with which he delivers himself in public." Gibson remained a proslavery Southerner, but he could appreciate the right kind of opposing perspective. "Boston is a contemptible place and its citizens not much better," he wrote, "but Wendell Phillips is a *splendid* orator and *perhaps* an honest man."[45]

When Fitzhugh boarded the train south the following day, his hosts were convinced that after seeing New Haven in all its prosperity and listening to Phillips, the proslavery author had learned the error of his ways. "Fitzhugh was thunder-stricken," wrote one abolitionist. "He had proved Free Society a failure without ever leaving his State; nobody replied to him, but he went home answered." Yet Fitzhugh returned to Virginia more certain than ever that industrial capitalism and the free market brought temporary wealth and lasting misery, that "a change in the course of trade" would reveal the vanity and impermanence of New England's "fine towns and cities, her mighty factories, her great commerce, her palatial private residences, and her stores and warehouses filled with rich merchandise from every region." Only the South produced "permanent and real" prosperity. If anything, his journey to New Haven convinced Fitzhugh that the slave trade should be revived and slavery extended to the territories.[46]

Hart Gibson was already looking forward to the next month's antislavery lecture at Brewster's Hall. It would feature Charles Sumner, the Massachusetts senator who insisted that "slavery . . . is not mentioned in the Constitution" and denied that Congress had "any *power* to make a Slave or hunt a Slave." Soon Hart would be reading law where Phillips and Sumner had studied. Then he might go to Europe, where his brother Randall was planning to travel. And finally he would settle at Hartland, his Kentucky estate. Once he did, he knew that he could no longer exist above the sectional crisis—the curiosity and independence of mind that so attracted his Northern classmates would become a liability. He would have to embrace his side and fight for it. He could already see that his older brother was losing his critical perspective. "It is a matter of small importance what New England may say or do—she is not the country," Randall warned Hart. "She is but a patch on its surface—a ripple on the deep & wide expanding ocean of our . . . institutions."

After just a couple of years in New Orleans, Randall wrote, "I find my opinions as decided as if I were a member of Congress." The Kansas-Nebraska Act, so stridently opposed in New Haven for potentially expanding slavery beyond the South, was in Randall's view "the enumeration of a just and American principle," an important counterbalance to violations of previous compromises by the North, which were "desecrat[ing] the Constitution" and committing "an unpardonable insult to the people of the South and of the territories." If such views shocked his younger brother, Randall explained, "Y[ou]r opinion of the South + Southerners undergo a great change when you come among them. They are the greatest people on the face of the Earth."[47]

CHAPTER FIVE

SPENCER

Jordan Gap, Johnson County, Kentucky, 1855

T HE ROCK DRAWINGS THAT gave Paint Creek its name
were still visible when Jordan Spencer, Malinda Centers,
and their children built their new home. When they moved one hundred
miles through the mountains from Clay County to Johnson in the late
1840s, they found cliffs adorned with stark lines, some red and some black.
The colors never mixed. Buffalo, deer, turkeys, panthers, and rattlesnakes:
with each winter, each hard rain, and each gouge of a vandal's knife, the
images faded into the sandstone.[1]

The signs that another people had once lived in the hills of Johnson
County, Kentucky, were fleeting. In the course of any hard day, few had a
spare second to think about the past. But just as the land itself influenced
how people lived their lives—what they grew, hunted, built, talked about,
prayed for, and dreamed of—the earlier inhabitants had quietly shaped the
new settlers' worlds. Likely as not, when Jordan Spencer left his cabin for
the three-mile journey to Paintsville, the Johnson County seat, he rode on
Indian trails. Along the way, by Paint Creek, ancient burial mounds produced ceramic shards and arrowheads for burrowing animals and the occasional souvenir hunter.[2]

Old men and women in the area had grown up hearing firsthand tales
of encounters with Native Americans. Around the time of the Revolution,
an Indian raiding party had held a pioneer woman named Jenny Wiley

captive just a short walk from Jordan Spencer's cabin. After nearly a year she escaped south through the hills. In 1850 people were still telling Wiley's story. It was a tale of constant looming threat in the wilderness outside. The world beyond one's mountain hollow was full of things that could kill you or, just as bad, change you. Wiley had almost become an Indian, and it had taken every bit of her strength to return to her husband and remain white. Her escape route was now called Jenny's Creek.[3]

The only thing Spencer painted was his hair. It was long and red, "straight but lay a little in waves," a neighbor reported, "always combed down slick." No one was fooled by the color for long. When Spencer was hot, his sweat ran red down his face. It was something that people tended to remember because Spencer spent most of his days sweating.[4]

Logging, farm labor, construction, in the hills or in town—Spencer worked grueling jobs. He was strong, proud, even ornery, earning him a reputation, by one neighbor's reckoning, as a "very active, keen man." People noticed that he was "particular" about his appearance. He rode a fine horse; "when it galloped," a great-grandson was told, "its legs just about went over its head."[5]

Spencer was not trying to hide. What set him apart was plain to see. Decade after decade, local census-takers eyeballed the man or trusted the local lore and listed him as "mulatto." At most, dyeing his hair seemed to turn his ancestry from something public, his race, into something private— his grooming habits. Neighbors might whisper or scratch their heads, but they did little else. In time his distinctive appearance seemed to fade into the surrounding fields and forests and mountainsides. Like the rock paintings and the burial mounds, it became something people knew was there but had stopped seeing.[6]

TORCHLIGHT CURLED AND STRETCHED in the curve of glass, as the quart bottle passed from one calloused hand to another. Under a star-ticked sky, it looked like the men were drinking flames. Silhouetted in front of them was a mound yards long and higher than their heads. It was not full of Indian treasure—just Indian corn.[7]

The Spencers' lives were made of corn. They grew it in fields so steep that they were best harvested, one of their great-grandsons would joke, by someone with "one leg shorter than the other." Like everyone around them, they mortared corn into meal and baked and fried it into bread. They fed it to the cows and hogs they butchered for meat. Jordan drank corn that had been stilled into whiskey—a corncob made a handy stopper—and he and Malinda smoked tobacco through cobs hollowed out into pipe bowls. Across Appalachia, people sat on chair bottoms and children played with dolls woven from the husks. Piles of corncobs were put by the privy for people to keep themselves clean.[8]

At harvesttime, the mountains were amber and red; spectral cornstalks, hacked low and stripped of leaves, studded the hillsides. Families—men, women, and children—piled their crop in barns and level clearings and invited neighbors to help them shuck and crib the corn. After long days working in their own fields, they came late in the afternoon and worked through sunset and moonrise into the night.[9]

Burning with long pulls of liquor, fueled by outdoor feasts cooked in wash kettles over open fires, men divided into teams and vied to see who could shuck the most corn the fastest. A corn shucking, or husking bee, was an autumn ritual across the South, from tidewater to mountains. In plantation country, slaves from miles around had permission to attend, and shucking became a working holiday, a ritual performance of singing and taunting and joking that made fun of the masters even as they watched. In the hills there were no spectators, and it was hard to tell in the shadow of night what social distinctions might exist between neighbors.[10]

A husking might start slowly, men drinking and chewing tobacco and trading tales, but the roar of competition soon took over. Clouds of dust enveloped the teams as they tore through their piles of corn, and amid accusations of cheating, neighbors often found themselves pummeling each other fist to skull. A fiddler might reel for the boys and girls of courting age, as couples walked away from the lantern light or rejoined the party. After tending the feast, women might work on a quilt; as the night grew darker, they told stories about haints and, according to one observer, "discuss[ed] the signs which, to them, betokened the near approach of the end of the world."[11]

In the summer of 1854, after a few years of living and working on other people's land, Jordan Spencer bought several hundred acres of his own. The land was just west of Jenny's Creek, extending from the Colvin Branch of Barnett's Creek over to Rockhouse Creek and spanning the ridgeline between them. It rose along steep banks to rocky knobs of mountain, broken by a low gap that could be crossed by foot or on horse or mule, a convenient path into town for people deeper in the hills. The property was a forest of black oak, buckeye, beech, dogwood, and poplar. Spencer bought it from a man who changed the color of skin for a living—a tanner, Lewis Todd. Sallow rawhides became mellow browns and reds with chestnut and hickory tanbark from trees on the land. Spencer probably used the bark to dye his hair.[12]

Jordan and Malinda Spencer cleared their land of trees and thicket—the boys, at nine and seven, were old enough to help—split and hoisted fence rails, and broke the hillsides to plant their crop. The boundaries of the Spencers' land ebbed and flowed with its contours, giving the family a community's worth of neighbors. The Spencers would need them to help raise a cabin and shuck their corn. They employed and worked alongside Jordan and traded land and livestock and equipment. They ate and visited with the family regularly and found Malinda to be generous and hospitable—in their words, "clever."[13]

The men along Rockhouse got drunk with Jordan on Saturday nights and prayed with him at church on Sunday. The women would help Malinda through more than twenty years of childbirths and mourned the deaths of at least two babies from scarlet fever. George Washington and Andrew Jackson Spencer were soon joined by Benjamin Franklin, Christopher Columbus, and James Madison. By 1858 the Spencers had either run out of favorite historical figures or felt established enough in the world to name their next-born son Jordan Jr. By decade's end their eldest daughter, Elizabeth, had two new sisters, Sylvania and Polley Ann.[14]

Owning land made the Spencers stand out, but it also enabled the family to blend in. The mere fact of ownership signaled to their neighbors that they were capable of rising in the world and had gained enough acceptance to find someone willing to sell to them. The difficulty of mountain life guaranteed not only that the Spencers would rely on their neighbors but also that their neighbors would come to rely on them. With every cabin raised, every child born, and every ear shucked, it made less sense to ask whether the Spencers were different. By staying in one place, they were creating a cocoon of everyday experience—conversations and business deals and exchanges and debts—strong enough to shut out the rest of the world. In time they became part of the landscape. The farm became known as Spencer's farm. The low gap through the hills—the pass through the land—was the Jordan Gap.

When Jordan Spencer chopped down trees, he used some of the wood for his cabin, some for firewood, and some for furniture and tools. But from the start he was rolling logs down the hillsides and dragging them to Rockhouse Creek with a team of oxen. After a big rain he could float the logs out of Rockhouse and down Paint Creek. Three miles below, just past Paintsville, the creek emptied into the Levisa Fork of the Big Sandy River. Cornfields and marshy bottomland gave way to a boat landing and a small stretch of mills and taverns.[15]

At the mouth of Paint Creek, Spencer sold his timber to Moses Preston. On Preston's land, country silence yielded to the sounds of a larger world—the groans of men hoisting logs out of the water and loading lumber onto barges; the sawing grind of saplings being labored into hoop poles and older trees into barrel staves; the crack and scrape of tanbark chiseled off hemlock and chestnut oaks and stacked like ancient scrolls; and the scream of the first steamboats to make their way up the Levisa Fork. Preston had made a fortune supplying mill men and builders, coopers and tanners. His barges went north and west, 60 miles down the Big Sandy and another 140 down the Ohio to Cincinnati.[16]

Rockhouse Creek was a lonely mountain hollow, but it was fueling the cities and industries and markets of a booming nation. Spencer's trees went down the Ohio, and cash and goods and people and ideas flowed back up the river. It made Moses Preston the county's richest man, someone who, an admirer marveled, "appl[ied] business rules to every department of his extended pursuits." With his lumber wealth he bought several farms, built grand homes in and out of Paintsville, started a large general store in town, and opened one of the first coal yards in the county. Like many Southerners of means, he invested in human beings. In the 1850s Preston owned seven people—two men, two women, two boys, and a girl—more than anyone else in the county, where the slave population topped out at about thirty.[17]

Although the county had few slaves, slavery was never far away. In neighboring Floyd County, slaves were bought and sold and marched in chains, two by two, to markets farther south. Throughout eastern Kentucky, kidnappers worked with slave dealers in Lexington, stealing people for sale to Deep South plantations. During the 1850s the politics of the entire state increasingly revolved around the slavery question. More than 200,000 people were held in bondage in Kentucky, but freedom was within sight. For six hundred miles, the Ohio River was all that separated the state from the free soil of Ohio, Indiana, and Illinois. Slaves had more opportunity to run away than almost anywhere else in the nation. When the river froze, as it did in 1850–51, 1852–53, and 1855–56, slaveowners lived in dread of mass escapes.[18]

A robust antislavery movement had taken root in Kentucky early in its history, and homegrown abolitionists were quietly helping fugitives reach Ohio. As late as 1849 antislavery politicians were confident that they could rewrite the Kentucky Constitution to end slavery, and Cassius Marcellus Clay ran for governor on an emancipationist ticket in 1851. While Jordan Spencer was clearing his land in Johnson County, an abolitionist colony one hundred miles west in Berea was preparing to open a college to educate whites and blacks together.[19]

Kentucky's border fostered some moderation on the slavery question. The Great Compromiser in the United States Senate, Henry Clay, represented Kentucky. It was his conception that averted a national crisis over slavery in 1850 by allowing California to enter the Union as a free state while committing the North to returning fugitive slaves. In his home state, Clay publicly called for freeing all slave men at age twenty-eight and women at twenty-one.[20]

Because of the open support for abolition and the ample opportunities slaves had to escape, Kentucky's advocates of slavery responded all the more aggressively. From the pulpit, ministers like Henry B. Bascom in Lexington defended slavery as God's will and warned that whites would be "butcher[ed]" if slaves were "let loose." Others began grounding their support for slavery in terms not of morality or public safety but something more abstract and scientific. "We hold them in bondage," declared Congressman William Preston, "because we are unwilling to amalgamate with them, and desire to keep our Teutonic blood pure and uncorrupted by any baser admixture." Slavery was necessary because freedom would tear down a crucial barrier separating whites from blacks. "Left without coercion," Preston said, blacks would "pollute our blood and destroy our progress." Beyond words, proslavery Kentuckians used fists, clubs, torches, bowie knives, and pistols to disrupt speeches, destroy abolitionist presses, run activists out of town, and otherwise silence threats to their property and their purity.[21]

Facing violent opposition, antislavery politicians also adopted the rhetoric of racial difference to broaden their appeal. They supported abolition, they said, not because they believed blacks were their equals but because slavery debased whites morally and unfairly competed with free white labor. As far as they were concerned, blacks should leave the state. "I have studied the Negro character," wrote Cassius Clay. "They lack self-reliance—we can make nothing out of them. God has made them for the sun and the banana."[22]

As the Spencer family moved into Johnson County, the politics of slavery hardened year by year. In 1851 the Kentucky legislature required all newly freed slaves to leave the state. The next year Kentucky was on millions of people's minds as Harriet Beecher Stowe published *Uncle Tom's Cabin*, which was largely set in the state and based on her travels there and on interviews she had conducted in Cincinnati with Kentucky runaways. The Democratic Party, which had nearly unanimous support in Johnson County, emerged as the party of slavery. By the terms of Kentucky's debates over slavery, Jordan Spencer represented every side's worst fears: a free man of color expecting equal treatment, marrying a white woman, and having children who were indistinguishable from everyone else—collapsing the divide between white and black and polluting the superior race.[23]

But Jordan Spencer never became a symbol of anything larger. On Rockhouse Creek most people seemed unconcerned with the Spencers' presence in their community. It was more than mere toleration: if anything, the neighbors encouraged the Spencers to move in and stay. When Jordan Spencer bought his land, he handed over $125 for the property, along with a promise to pay the seller an additional $200 over the next couple of years. Even though credit was not typically available to blacks, Spencer repeatedly mortgaged his farm. He lived most of his life in Johnson County in debt, never free and clear, always struggling to keep his land. At the same time he always made good on his loans. By going into debt, he became someone who was worth a risk, someone who had creditors with a stake in his success.[24]

Although Moses Preston was a slaveowner and ardent Democrat, he happily did business with Jordan Spencer. Preston, like everyone else, knew Spencer was different. John Preston, Moses's son, remembered Spencer as "dark complected" and "just about half negro." But Moses Preston bought Spencer's lumber and also lent him hundreds of dollars on multiple occasions. That money—and probably credit at the general store—enabled Spencer to buy supplies, pay off other debts, establish his family, and stay on Rockhouse Creek.[25]

EACH SUNDAY THE SPENCERS worshipped a mile or two from their cabin, in the valley of Rockhouse Creek. The church was a plain room; low windows captured sparse shafts of Sunday-morning sun. The people crowding inside knew one another well, and for hours they cried and testified and fainted together. They listened to parables, situating their everyday struggles within biblical time and experience, and added amens to sermons shouted by weeping preachers. They sang hymns, repeated in call-and-response or committed to heart because few could read. Jordan Spencer's voice rose above the crowd; old men would remember years later that he was a "pretty good singer." Through faith and prayer, through willful transformation, an entire community could find comfort during freeze or flood, hunger or illness.[26]

Moses Preston's son John attended the old-style Methodist meeting at Rockhouse just once in his life. Jordan Spencer did not stand out; to the contrary, John Preston observed, half the congregation "had as much color as the Spencers did." Although Johnson County's churches were, in one neighbor's words, "only what termed themselves white," many of the worshippers at the church on Rockhouse were visibly dark. "Some of them were as dark as Jordan Spencer or darker," Preston reported.[27]

Most of the dark congregants were members of the Collins and Ratliff families. People with the same last names were spread throughout the mountains. For decades they and related families had puzzled neighbors, missionaries, sheriffs, and census-takers. They did not exactly look white. They insisted they were not black. Although the Collins and Ratliff families on Rockhouse Creek described themselves as "Indian," they did not identify with particular tribes. Often families like them described themselves—or were categorized by others—in entirely new terms.

These mountain clans confounded the era's vocabulary of race and racial purity, with its pinched approximations of colors, continents, and "ancestral stock"—white and black and red, European and African and Native American, Anglo-Saxon and Negro. In southwest Virginia they were called Ramps, for the wild leeks that they gathered and ate. In the hills of eastern Tennessee they were called Melungeons, a word that does not exist in any language—perhaps it implied mixture, or derived from a common family name, Mullins. When Johnson County locals were asked to label their dark-skinned neighbors, one thought of them as "East Indians" and another called them "Black Dutch." These "little races" were not confined to Appalachia. In every Southern state and up into Delaware, New Jersey, and New York, in tidewater and backcountry, whites and blacks encountered people called Wesorts, Croatans, Brass Ankles, Turks, Red Legs, Red Bones, Guineas, and more.[28]

Many members of these communities shared last names with the first free people of color in colonial Virginia and Maryland—Goins, Gibson, Chavis, Bunch, Sweat—but they explained their origins in more exotic terms. They were "pure blooded Carthaginians," according to one tradition described by a Chattanooga lawyer who represented a Melungeon woman in 1874, "as much so as was Hannibal or the Moor of Venice and other pure-blooded descendants of the ancient Phoenicians." They descended from the lost English colonists of Roanoke or were Turkish or North African Berbers or Sephardic Jews.

A year after Jordan Spencer bought property on Rockhouse Creek, witnesses in an eastern Tennessee courtroom described a Melungeon man as "Portuguese"—or as it was commonly pronounced, "Porty-gee." On remote mountain ridges, families circulated stories of shipwrecked Portuguese pirates or stranded Spanish explorers who had married Indian women hundreds of years earlier. Although light-skinned blacks had long been described as having a "Portuguese" complexion—and the English had joked about the African "blood" that ran in Iberian veins since the days of the Armada—the Spanish and Portuguese were still Europeans, dark but white. Claims of Mediterranean origin emerged as a way for ambiguous people to assert that they were anything but black. On occasion, these claims also gave white communities a story that allowed them to accept dark people as equals.[29]

In Johnson County and elsewhere, being white did not require exclusively European ancestry. Many whites did not hesitate to claim Native American descent. While Melungeons in Tennessee often lived apart and married among themselves, the Collins and Ratliff families in Johnson County were considerably less isolated. Half of the worshippers at the Rockhouse Methodist meeting had white faces, and light and dark families were neighbors along the nearby creeks. Many of the families themselves were mixed, like Jordan and Malinda Spencer's. Their community offered them a path to assimilation. Although the Spencers were listed as "mulatto" in the 1860 census, dozens of Collins and Ratliff men and women were, at a glance, regarded as white. Jordan Spencer may have been dark, but there was such a thing as a dark white man.[30]

JORDAN SPENCER FOUND HIS WAY to the crowd milling on an open field. At such gatherings, it would have been hard to hear birdsong or creek flow over the din: laughter and cheers and cussing and brawls, political speeches shouted over fife and drum, even "the squealing of pigs, neighing of chargers, barking of dogs, braying of asses." As the day progressed, the noise would be equaled by the smell—sweat and filth, human and animal, fried chicken and roast pork, coffee and gunpowder and the sweet burn of whiskey. If Spencer held a rifle in his hands, it was the most natural thing in the world.[31]

A generation earlier a militia muster had been a serious affair. All able-bodied white men ages eighteen to forty-five regularly practiced the military drills that would enable them to protect the nation from internal and external threat. The Kentucky militia had a proud tradition. They had helped clear the frontier of Indians in the 1790s, and they fought under Andrew Jackson at the Battle of New Orleans. Although Jackson complained of their conduct, people across the country once celebrated their bravery with songs like "The Hunters of Kentucky": "We are a hardy, free-born race, / Each man to fear a stranger; / Whate'er the game we join in chase, / Despoiling time and danger." Johnson County itself was named for Richard Mentor Johnson, Martin Van Buren's vice president, who rose to national prominence during the War of 1812, when he led the Kentucky militia to victory over the Native American chief Tecumseh.[32]

By the 1820s, however, the need for a militia grew less pressing, and the muster was, to one Kentuckian's mind, "more or less a farce." Militia days became "the big to-do," and shambling, tipsy pantomimes of military drills occurred alongside an all-purpose festival of horse trading and races and cockfights. The militia companies assembled with men toting "old shotguns, rusty rifles, long untried fowling-pieces, cornstalks, and hickory sticks."[33]

In the mid-1850s the legislature eventually found no reason to keep requiring the militia to drill six times a year, but until then Jordan Spencer played his part on the muster ground. Someone could have objected to his presence. He was out in the world, publicly claiming a place in the crowd. Carrying a weapon was a serious offense for free people of color, an inevitable precursor, many feared, to claims of equality or outright rebellion.[34]

But in the "pell-mell" of the Johnson County muster, it mattered little that Spencer had dark skin. Even if his appearance raised eyebrows, it was more important that he wanted to be white and acted accordingly. To treat Spencer differently, to police the color line, would have involved a level of time and expense and attention that no one was willing to spend. Even people who cared about racial mixing understood the convenient notion that unless it was impossible to say otherwise, everyone in Johnson County was white. "I always was in sympathy with the man," said a Paintsville businessman about Jordan Spencer, "because he tried to be a good man, and tried to avoid looking like a darkey, and because he wanted to raise himself up instead of lowering himself."[35]

The difference between black and white was less about "blood" or biology or even genealogy than about how people were treated and whether they were allowed to participate fully in community life. Blacks were the people who were slaves, in fact or in all but name; the rest were white. Jordan Spencer's community could accept him as an equal as long as he never forced them to acknowledge his ancestry. As long as he was one of the crowd, people could forget what made his family different.

As the reveling crescendoed, a few men donned sashes or cockaded hats and called their companies to formation. At a typical muster, Jordan Spencer would have stood among a ragged bunch, men of all ages and heights and shapes, some barefoot, some shirtless. Unless they were lining up along a ditch or a corn row, wrote one Kentuckian, the militia's ranks were "motley and ludicrous," "straggling, and crooked." When they paraded, guns on shoulders, through the cheering crowds, "all mingled together in the most beautiful and checkered confusion." Jordan and his brothers in arms would have waited for their officer to coax and prod his troops into straighter lines, then bellow the order: "March!"[36]

CHAPTER SIX

WALL

Oberlin, Ohio, September 1858

A BIG MAN STANDS OUT in a small town. Anderson Jennings was over six feet tall, full bearded, a prime specimen of what was known as a "buffalo bull." When he appeared in the village of Oberlin, people instantly seemed to know who he was and where he was from. Amid the muted tones of Ohio, his Kentucky accent sounded like a fiddle out of tune. Oberlin was a college town and religious settlement, a quiet community of learning and prayer. But Jennings carried two five-shooters, rarely left his room at the tavern by the railroad depot, and kept to the shadows when he did. As he well knew, no town in the United States hated slavery with as much passion as Oberlin. Yet there he was, in his words, "nigger-catching."[1]

Jennings owned a farm and livery stable in Mason County, Kentucky, on the Ohio River's south bank. His slaves were more valuable than his land, and almost every year his human quarry increased. When a young man named Henry disappeared one late summer night in 1858, it was as if $1,500 had fallen out of Jennings's coat. Jennings could guess where Henry was heading. Even though a neighbor described Jennings as someone who did not "follow the business of capturing niggers," he could draw on the decades of experience that Mason County slaveowners had in tracking down runaways. Jennings headed to the river landing at Maysville. In his pockets he carried his guns, a roll of ten- and twenty-dollar bills, and a set of handcuffs. He was ready to recapture a man he thought of as "my boy."[2]

Jennings sensed that if Henry was heading north, sooner or later he would pass through Oberlin. A generation earlier, descendants of New England Puritans had built the college and town in the northern Ohio forest, dedicating themselves to bringing "our perishing world . . . under the entire influence of the blessed gospel of peace." To give themselves time, health, and money to serve the Lord, they renounced "all bad habits, and especially the smoking and chewing of tobacco, unless it is necessary as a medicine," pledged not to drink tea and coffee "as far as practicable," and rejected "all the world's expensive and unwholesome fashions of dress, particularly tight dressing and ornamental attire." They built themselves a simple world: saltbox houses, unadorned brick school buildings, and a village green guarded by a towering elm, like a hand reaching to heaven. They prayed in its shade.[3]

Always the center of the community, the Oberlin Collegiate Institute trained missionaries and teachers "in body, intellect and heart for the service of the Lord." From its beginning in 1832, the school educated both sexes. Within three years it devoted itself to the abolition of slavery, taking the then-radical step of admitting students "irrespective of color." In the decades that followed, blacks and whites studied and worshipped together and spent their vacations lecturing for antislavery societies and teaching in colored schools. Scandalous rumors circulated around the country that white and black Oberliners shared dormitory rooms and were even marrying each other. Hundreds of runaway slaves passed through on their way to Canada, and dozens more put down roots there. It was no secret. Six miles north of town, a sign pointed the way there not with an arrow but with "a full-length picture of a colored man, running with all his might to reach the place."[4]

Jennings did not have to run to Oberlin. He steamed seventy miles up the Ohio to Cincinnati and then took the newly built railroad two hundred miles northeast. It let him off in Wellington, ten miles south of his destination. Sitting in the men's car, watching the muddy expanses of harvested cornfields go by, he had reason to be nervous about his incursion into enemy land. Still, Jennings had the law solidly on his side. In 1850 Congress had passed the Fugitive Slave Act, which allowed slaveowners and their authorized agents to "pursue and reclaim" escapees on free soil. A pursuer could swear out an arrest warrant that a United States marshal was obliged to enforce. The act also permitted slaveowners to kidnap people and force them into federal court. After a short hearing, a commissioner would determine the status of the person in custody. Commissioners were paid ten dollars upon ruling that a person was a slave, but only five dollars if they determined that he or she was free. Anyone interfering with the recapture of a fugitive faced prison and thousands of dollars in fines. Six years later the Supreme Court went one step further than Congress. In the *Dred Scott* decision, the Court ruled that, slave or free, members of the "unhappy black race," "separated from the white by indelible marks," were not citizens of the United States. According to Chief Justice Roger Taney, although the words of the Declaration of Independence "would seem to embrace the whole human family, . . . the enslaved African race were not intended to be included." Jennings knew he had every right to collect what was his.[5]

ALL DAY LONG ORINDATUS Simon Bolivar Wall worked with skin. The Oberlin shoemaker cut it with sharp blades, punched holes in it with awls, pinned it to lasts, and stitched it to soles. He shaped, molded, and manipulated it until it became something else. Every day skin surrendered easily to his hands. It was tanned and dyed, polished black and every shade of brown. In a town where just about everyone was preoccupied with the fine line between slavery and freedom, Wall's expertise in matters of color and skin conferred upon him a certain authority. Asked once whether he "knew the colors by which people of color were classified," the short, stocky man answered simply: "There were black, blacker, blackest."[6]

The day Jennings appeared, the Kentuckian was the talk of Oberlin. The consensus opinion was that he was a slave-catcher. But whom was he after? When would he strike? And what was the best way to resist? His presence was almost certainly topic number one in Wall's shop on East College Street in the center of town. It was cooler than the blacksmith shop, quieter than the sawmill, and less rank than the livery stable—in other words, a congenial place to discuss politics. And amid the workbenches littered with leather scrap, politics for Wall and his partner, David Watson, meant abolitionism. Watson, an Oberlin graduate, was an active member of the Ohio Anti-Slavery Society, and Wall had spent his life walking the line between liberty and bondage.[7]

Freed by their father and sent north, Wall and his brothers and sisters had been raised in comfort by their Quaker guardians in Harveysburg, Ohio, and treated as members of the town's finest family. But they lived with the knowledge that their mothers remained in bondage. As they came of age, Wall's older brother Napoleon used his inheritance to establish himself as a farmer on thirteen hundred acres nearby. A younger sister, Caroline, moved north to enroll at Oberlin.[8]

Orindatus—known as O.S.B. or Datus—decided to learn a trade. With his pick of professions, he settled on shoemaking, a curious choice. By the 1840s shoemaking was not just a lowly line of work; it was a dying craft, rapidly becoming a mechanized industry centered in mill towns like Lynn and Haverhill, Massachusetts. As slaves, the Wall children likely wore cheap shoes mass-produced in New England factories. Yet the trade held a certain allure for Orindatus. It was neither loud nor exhausting nor dangerous and left plenty of time for thinking, reading, and talking. With surprising regularity through the eighteenth and nineteenth centuries, shoemakers turned to radical ideas. The last surviving member of the Boston Tea Party was a shoemaker. A disproportionate number of the mob kicking down the Bastille's doors had stitched their own boots. "Philosophic cobblers" formed the vanguard of English rioters in the 1830s and German revolutionaries in 1848. They wrote political poetry and proudly circulated books with titles such as *Lives of Illustrious Shoemakers*. For Orindatus, perhaps the most illustrious of them all was George Fox, revered in Harveysburg, who started life as a shoemaker's apprentice and went on to found Quakerism.[9]

After the Fugitive Slave Act passed, Wall helped start a local abolitionist society. Across the North slavery's opponents were resolving to do whatever they could to keep runaways free. To their minds, the law of the land had been so corrupted that there was no reason to obey it. The Fugitive Slave Act was little more than "a hideous deformity in the *garb* of law," the

abolitionist orator John Mercer Langston told a convention of black Ohioans in 1851. His brother Charles, a schoolteacher in Columbus who would
be the namesake of his grandson Langston Hughes, called on "every slave,
from Maryland to Texas, to arise and assert their *liberties*, and cut their masters' throats."[10]

O.S.B. Wall would come to know both Langston brothers well. Up in
Oberlin, his sister Caroline started receiving the attentions of a smitten
John Mercer Langston, who had graduated from the college in 1849 and
was studying to be Ohio's first black lawyer. The couple had much in common, from their political ideals to their life stories. Like Caroline, Langston had moved to Ohio as a young child with no mother, freed by his
planter father with a small inheritance. During winter vacation in 1851
Langston visited Caroline in Harveysburg and struck up a friendship with
her older brother.[11]

A little more than a year later O.S.B. Wall moved to Oberlin. Perhaps
he decided to pack his bags after hearing Langston describe Oberlin as "the
most noted Abolition town in America," but he may have had other reasons entirely. In October 1854 Caroline and John were married. The very
next day, Orindatus wed one of Caroline's classmates, seventeen-year-old
Amanda Thomas.[12]

Amanda walked many of the lines that her husband did—between slavery and freedom, black and white. Born in Virginia in 1837 and "quite light"
in appearance, she grew up in Cincinnati well within memory of the time
city officials, aided by murderous mobs, expelled more than a thousand
black residents. Throughout her childhood whites in southern Ohio were
up in arms over the influx of blacks from slave states. Amanda's experience
at Oberlin only reinforced that struggle was part of everyday life. The college's disciplinary board targeted black students disproportionately. The
students had tense run-ins with white locals and classmates. Oberlin's
women of color learned not to back down. When a white student in 1851
shouted "vile epithets" at Caroline Wall when there was not enough room
on the sidewalk for the two of them, Wall responded by reading a pointed
account of the incident in front of the entire class. Caroline's friend Amanda
would be O.S.B. Wall's partner in the fight for freedom and equality.[13]

During the 1850s Wall established himself in the shoe business. He was one of many professionals and tradesmen in a thriving black community, which in a generation had grown to about one fifth of the town's two thousand residents. Oberlin did not just give Wall the opportunity to do business on equal terms with whites—it offered blacks the unheard-of possibility of real political power. In 1857 the town voted John Mercer Langston to be its clerk—a post in which he had recently served for neighboring Brownhelm Township—and appointed him manager of the public schools. He was the first black elected official in the United States.[14]

Having acquired property in town, Wall gave one house to his sister and Langston in exchange for their rambling farm, which was half an hour's ride northwest of Oberlin. With the farm in his name, Wall was no longer just a tradesman. He had become a planter, with cornfields, pastures for sheep and cattle, and graceful orchards leading in neat rows to ancient woods of chestnut and hickory. Like his father, Wall had other people cultivate his land. Though born a slave, he was now the master of a white tenant and laborers. By 1858 O.S.B. and Amanda Wall had two boys and a girl, all light enough to burn in the sun. They named their second son Stephen, for his grandfather the plantation owner, who had given so much to and taken away so much from O.S.B. Wall.[15]

Even as the Wall family prospered in Oberlin, however, their lives were never completely secure. Reports trickled in of court-sanctioned kidnappings in southern and central Ohio. The town reeled with word from Cincinnati of Margaret Garner, who cut her daughter's throat rather than surrender her to slave-catchers. In 1854 Anthony Burns brought his own chilling story to Oberlin, where he was enrolling as a student. That spring he had run away from his master in Virginia, only to be captured in Boston and marched by a military guard past a crowd of tens of thousands to a boat that took him back south. He survived to tell his tale because horrified Bostonians raised $1,300 to redeem him. It was only a matter of time before the slave-catchers reached Oberlin.[16]

They first started arriving in August 1858. In the summer heat Oberliners were besieged from within and without. Upon John Mercer Langston's election as town clerk the year before, the man he defeated switched parties from Republican to Democrat and was appointed deputy U.S. marshal by the proslavery federal administration. Carrying an open grudge against Oberlin's black residents, the new marshal, Anson Dayton, said that he was willing to capture fugitive slaves. He started responding to advertisements and reward notices, sending south descriptions of local blacks and offering to arrest them for money.[17]

In mid-August Dayton tried to seize an entire family, only to be driven away when the father, waving a shotgun, called for help. The next week he and three men dragged a mother and her children from their home in the middle of the night. She wailed so loudly that her neighbors woke up and mobbed the kidnappers; for decades townsfolk would remember her cries. Days later Dayton tried again, timing his move to coincide with the college's commencement exercises. With fire-bells ringing, students rushed out of a graduation speech and thwarted the assault. Soon afterward a local stonecutter named James Smith received a warning that Dayton had offered to kidnap him for someone in North Carolina. Smith met Dayton in the street and thrashed him with a hickory stick. Oberlin's abolitionists decided to spirit Smith out of the area before Dayton could strike back. Flush with victory but wary of a continuing threat, local abolitionists composed nervous lyrics: "Who, bearing his revolvers twain, / Fled from a boy but with a cane, / And bawled for help with might and main? / Our Marshal." A week later, in early September, Anderson Jennings came to town.[18]

BEFORE REACHING OBERLIN, JENNINGS had been told that Wack's Tavern was a hospitable place for a Southern gentleman to conduct Southern business. Although Chauncey Wack had come from Vermont, his politics were deep Dixie. Each Election Day he would haunt Oberlin's polling places, challenging black voters. He could be counted on to connect Jennings with people willing to help him.[19]

Jennings arranged to meet Anson Dayton and told him about his slave Henry. The marshal shook his head. No one in Oberlin answered to that description, but he had ideas about where they could look and a network of local informants to help them. Even though Jennings's slave was not in the area, Dayton took the time to describe all of the town's paupers from the time he was clerk, just in case Jennings recognized anyone. At the mention of one John Price—age about twenty, dark black, five feet eight inches tall, heavyset—Jennings and Dayton found themselves in business.[20]

Jennings thought Price sounded like his neighbor John Bacon's slave. On a January day two years earlier Bacon had left his two slaves alone while visiting with his in-laws. The Ohio River was frozen over, and the slaves had simply walked across the ice, like Eliza in *Uncle Tom's Cabin*. There had been no trace of either one since. Until now.[21]

On Dayton's instruction, Jennings wrote Bacon that night, asking for power of attorney to arrest the fugitive. Wack mailed it the next morning. In the meantime there was still the matter of Jennings's slave Henry. On a tip from one of the marshal's informants, Jennings and Dayton caught a train to Painesville, on the other side of Cleveland, where a person answering to Henry's description had newly turned up. But almost immediately after they started asking townspeople about Henry, fifty armed abolitionists confronted them. "They gave us twenty minutes to leave," the Kentuckian complained, "and then wouldn't allow us that!" It was what abolitionist strongholds such as Painesville had been preparing for since the Fugitive Slave Act's passage eight years earlier. For Jennings and Dayton, the thrill of hot pursuit was doused by sickening fear. When word of the incident got back to Oberlin, the town's abolitionists found themselves with another verse to sing: "Who fled from Painesville on the car, / Because he had no taste for war, / Or more especially for tar? / Our Marshal."[22]

The Kentuckian packed up and left Oberlin as soon as he could. It was Saturday, September 4, 1858. Home again, empty-handed, Jennings may have thought that his career hunting slaves was over before it had even begun. But a visit from John Bacon sent him right back north. Bacon told Jennings that Richard Mitchell, a local slave-catcher who had made multiple incursions into Ohio, had just left for Oberlin with the legal papers authorizing Jennings to capture John Price. Mitchell and Jennings had probably passed each other in steamboats on the Ohio River.[23]

Jennings and Bacon conferred and reached an agreement. If Jennings returned to Oberlin and captured Price, Bacon promised him five hundred dollars or "one half of what the nigger would sell for." It was a generous offer to a man who insisted that he had only notified Bacon about Price "out of pure neighborly regard." "Never made no bargain with him about pay no-ways," Jennings would later insist.[24]

Bacon was a wealthy man—worth at least twice as much as Jennings—but he had never invested his money in slaves. The two he owned were part of an inheritance from his father, and after they ran off, he never bought any others. Perhaps that had to do with the humiliating circumstances under which he lost his slaves—the naïveté, arrogance, or sheer stupidity of leaving them alone. Even worse, the escapes could never be just his own sorry business—because of his neglect, the whole community had reason for alarm. When one slave ran away, others were bound to get ideas and follow. It was as if Bacon had introduced a contagion into his neighbors' homes. Just a few years earlier a distinguished New Orleans physician announced his discovery of *drapetomania*, "the disease causing Negroes to run away." According to Dr. Samuel Cartwright, such cases required one of two treatments: humane living conditions for slaves, or the unrelenting use of the whip.[25]

But a third cure existed for Southerners like Bacon. Nothing would stop the spread of the running-away disease like capturing the fugitives. That was surely worth five hundred dollars, more than twenty times the average reward for a slave. Bacon wanted John Price back in Kentucky. "He is still my property," he said. "Never parted with my interest in him. He is still mine, *bone and flesh*."[26]

IN THE DAYS AFTER Jennings left Oberlin, the town slowly returned to its familiar rhythms. Fall classes were starting at the college, and tradesmen like O.S.B. Wall were catching up on their work. Still, reminders of the evils of slavery were everywhere. Newspapers were reporting that a naval brig, the *Dolphin*, had captured an illegal slave ship bound for Cuba, a mere three hours from port. On East College Street in Oberlin, stories about the *Dolphin* would have been of immediate interest. Generations of shoemakers' apprentices spent their days reading the newspaper aloud while the shoemakers cut, sewed, and lasted. O.S.B. Wall's apprentice, Charles Jones, had himself been born in Africa and most likely been brought illegally to the United States, some forty years after the 1808 ban of the Atlantic slave trade.[27]

When Jennings appeared in Oberlin once again, this time accompanied by a second Southerner, abolitionists like O.S.B. Wall knew that they were facing imminent crisis. In his dustcoat and top hat, Wall did not have to go far to find people to talk to about the slave-catchers. A block down East College Street at the corner with Main was the town's respectable hotel, the Palmer House, and just next to it was a whitewashed wood-frame building where his brother-in-law kept his law office. Just a short way back past the shoe shop, Langston and Wall's sister Caroline lived in the house O.S.B. Wall had traded them, a two-story saltbox with a low veranda across the front, one of Oberlin's finest.[28]

Although Langston was often away on business in early September 1858, Caroline was not alone with their three children, Arthur, Ralph, and baby Chinque, named for the hero of the Amistad slave revolt. Langston's brother Charles was visiting from Columbus, where for years the black community had been feeling constant pressure from slave-catchers. Down in Columbus, rumors circulated that Southern sympathizers were writing up descriptions of the blacks they passed on the streets and swearing fugitive slave warrants out on them, even if they had always been free. Charles Langston was a forty-year-old schoolteacher, slightly built with a meticulous part in his hair that emphasized his fragile features, but he was capable of breathing fire over the threats to liberty. "I have long since adopted as my God, the freedom of the colored people of the United States, and my religion, to do any thing that will effect that object," he declared, "however much it may differ from the precepts taught in the Bible."[29]

Oberlin's blacks braced themselves for the worst. Wall had been raised by Quakers, but the idea that he, his wife, and their children could be kidnapped and taken south—and that the government and courts had every incentive to abet such a crime—was enough to drive him to contemplate violence. Oberlin's blacks started keeping shotguns, rifles, revolvers, and knives at home and at work, in their pockets, over their doors, and by their beds. A local blacksmith kept his firearms within reach, as well as his hammer and a sharpened poker kept searing hot in the forge. "If any one of those men darkens my door, he is a dead man," he said, a sentiment that was widely shared. "Kill a *man*? No. But kill a *man-stealer*? Yes! Quicker'n a dog."[30]

THE SUN DAWNED SLOWLY on the northern edge of Oberlin. Amid the shadows, a young man stood outside a lonely shack stuck between the town and the country, a temporary home for a local charity case. Hungry, coughing, John Price wrapped himself in a blanket but still shivered in the autumn chill. He walked with a limp. A distant sound reached through daybreak's stillness—a horse pulling a cart. As it drew closer, Price recognized the boy at the reins. It was Shakespeare Boynton. In better days Price had worked on the Boynton family farm about three miles outside Oberlin.[31]

The thirteen-year-old asked Price if he wanted to work that morning digging potatoes. At the very least, Shakespeare said, John would get a "good ride" out of it. The man heaved himself into the cart, and together they rode along the dirt roads northeast of Oberlin. Shakespeare drove slowly. Price took a jackknife from his pocket and started picking his teeth.

A mile or so out of town, a small black carriage appeared in the distance, kicking up a high column of dust. By the time Price noticed it minutes later, it was only a few rods away. A man jumped into the cart while it was moving and put his arm around Price. A second man screamed at him to give over his jackknife. He held on to it for an instant but dropped it in the dust when he saw the man reaching for a revolver.

"Bring him along!" cried a third man, holding the reins of the carriage.

"I'll go with you" was all Price could say. In an instant he was in the back of the carriage. One of the men who grabbed him sat to the side, hand in coat pocket. The carriage hurtled forward, while Shakespeare turned his cart around and headed back into Oberlin.

If John had hoped the boy would sound the alarm, he was disappointed. Shakespeare headed straight to Wack's Tavern, where Jennings was waiting. On word that his men had John in their hands, Jennings took out his roll of bills and peeled off a twenty. "Good money," the boy later said.[32]

Five days of planning was all it had taken once Jennings got back to Oberlin. Five days to spring the trap. He had returned to Oberlin in the dark of night on Wednesday, September 8. Richard Mitchell, the man Bacon had sent north, was waiting for him at the tavern. Mitchell handed over the power of attorney papers but warned Jennings that Dayton, the U.S. marshal, would have nothing to do with capturing John Price—no doubt frightened by what had happened in Painesville. The next morning they worked out their plan. Capturing Price at night was too dangerous— someone could take a shot at them and never get caught. It would have to be during the day, and out of town. If they could whisk John away from Oberlin, it would be smooth sailing to Kentucky.[33]

On Friday, Jennings rode the train to Columbus and swore out a warrant for John's arrest as a fugitive slave. Although the federal courthouse in Cleveland was much closer, it was crawling with abolitionists. In Columbus slave warrants were routine, and for years the marshals there had been helping Southerners make arrests. Jennings paid a deputy marshal and a local jailer one hundred dollars to come north to assist him. Back in Oberlin on Saturday, the slave-catchers heard about the Boyntons, active Democrats and supporters of slavery who routinely hired day laborers in town. Jennings rode out to the Boynton farm, met Shakespeare, and brought him on board.[34]

By Sunday, September 12, the plan was set. The next morning the Boynton boy would ask Price to pick some potatoes, and Mitchell and the two men from Columbus would grab their man. Jennings would hang around Wack's to throw the abolitionists off the scent. Upon getting word from Shakespeare that Price had been taken, Jennings would meet his men in Wellington, ten miles south of Oberlin. From there the train would take them to Columbus, where the federal court would formally declare their captive the property of John Bacon. From Columbus, they would ride to Cincinnati, and from Cincinnati, up the Ohio River and back to Kentucky.[35]

The carriage rolled northeast toward Elyria. Perhaps Price had reason for hope. Someone there could turn him loose—there were plenty of friendly souls in Elyria. But after a mile the carriage turned south. They were taking a road that would skirt around Oberlin and get them to the train station at Wellington. Price had already read the warrant for his arrest. He understood that the farmland and forests racing by could be his last glimpses of free soil.

An hour later, at the Pittsfield crossroads south of Oberlin, the carriage slowed down by a quiet country cemetery. Price lunged. The man next to him grabbed him, but he was not trying to escape. His captors did not see what he saw: two young men walking along the road. One of them— enormous, bearded, and dressed in black—may have looked familiar. Price cried out.[36]

The young men did not look up. They just kept walking. Six hard hands pushed, pulled, and punched Price back into his seat.

Minutes later the carriage stopped in the center of Wellington. Where Oberlin had been built to fulfill God's mission on Earth, the town ten miles south was merely a place where farmers sold their crops and shipped them to Columbus. The town square was a muddy void, crisscrossed with wheel ruts. It was bounded by narrow wood-frame and brick storefronts, their whitewash dusted over, a humbly steepled church, and a squat stone town hall. Small trees, planted around the time the railroad came to town a few years earlier, were just beginning to supply a little shade. At the heart of it was Wadsworth's Hotel, a broad brick building with two stories of white-columned verandas across the front. The train depot was a block away.[37]

Farmers, tradesmen, and assorted loafers looked on quietly as the three captors walked John through the street, across the planked sidewalk, and into the hotel. Once inside, they told the hotel owner, Oliver Wadsworth, that they had arrested John and were taking him to Kentucky—but in the meantime they wanted something to eat. All of them, including John, sat down for lunch. Afterward they went upstairs and tossed John into the large room just above the front entrance and shut the door behind them. "That was the first time I ever eat with a nigger," one of the slave-catchers would remember.[38]

BACK IN OBERLIN, summer was returning after a chilly Monday morning. Men were rolling up their shirtsleeves. Most people on the streets were students going to and from class. O.S.B. Wall would not have heard the shouts at first as he reopened the shop after lunch.

Ansel Lyman, a twenty-two-year-old Oberlin College student, told anyone who would listen that he had been walking by the Pittsfield graveyard four miles south of town when he heard a cry for help. Two years earlier he had fought alongside John Brown as a lieutenant in the Kansas Free State Army. The instant John Price's shouts broke the silence of the lonely road, Lyman was back at war.[39]

Knowing he was outnumbered and outgunned, Lyman acted like nothing had happened, waited for the carriage to pass out of sight, and then headed for Oberlin. At first sight of him, his classmates huddled around, then broke to spread the word all over town.[40]

O.S.B. Wall ran into the street. From shops and classrooms, hundreds were gathering in an angry roar—grocers, harness-makers, blacksmiths, students, clerks. Wall worked his way toward an awning where a dozen or so men stood loading their revolvers and rifles. Charles Langston was buckling a holster. His brother John was in Erie County all day on a case—Charles would do the fighting for him.[41]

A few steps farther, and someone grabbed Wall's arm.

It was Simeon Bushnell, a head shorter than Wall. The pale printer's clerk, usually quiet in abolitionist meetings, was hoarse from shouting. He had a cart rigged up and asked if Wall would join him. People were already starting on the journey to Wellington. Riding through cheering crowds, students and townspeople waved their hats and rifles, shouting, "I am going to rescue John Price!"[42]

Bushnell and Wall were part of an armada of buggies, wagons, and hay carts. The two men were conspicuous in the throng, but not because of the contrasts that they represented—skinny and stout, white and black. They attracted notice because Bushnell was driving his horse hard, and Wall was carrying a gun.[43]

WHEN JENNINGS ARRIVED IN Wellington after eating his lunch in Oberlin, he could see groups of people milling around Wadsworth's Hotel. The front entrance and the halls on the first and second floors were packed. Jennings said that he knew where his men were holed up with John Price because fifty or sixty men were "crowding up the steps around the door."

They had guns and were asking for the people who had John. Without saying a word to anyone, Jennings pushed through the throng and knocked on the door.[44]

Thinking back on the day's events, Jennings remembered that he "didn't like the looks of the room, because it was large, and there was folding doors, and there was no fastening to the door." He went looking for Oliver Wadsworth, the hotel owner, and secured a room on the top floor. Armed with pistols and knives, the four slave-catchers walked John Price upstairs. The mob let them by, but Jennings could sense that the calm would not last.[45]

Their new room was lit by the semicircle of a single fantail window. A bare mattress lay sadly in the back corner. Once there had been a stove, but all that remained was a hole in the wall by the door, where the pipe would have gone. Jennings could hear the crowd rumbling below.

Outside the hotel, the town square was filling. Hundreds of people with hundreds of rifles and shotguns were shouting and pushing in the mid-afternoon sun. Time was getting short. A little after five—in a mere two hours—the train for Columbus would be pulling into Wellington station. Another train from Cleveland, rumored to be carrying proslavery federal troops to fight the mob, was scheduled to arrive at four. An onlooker remembered the crowd yelling that they would "'have the boy or pull the house down,' 'pull the roof off,' 'wouldn't leave one brick on another.'" Some were running for ladders to reach the room where John Price was being held captive.[46]

O.S.B. Wall and Charles Langston had ridden into Wellington with guns ready. But as the crowd grew and started calling for blood, the two men pulled back. Resisting the emotional force of the mob, they settled on a different tack. Wall wanted to examine the slave-catchers' legal papers, while Langston and a small group of other Oberlin abolitionists, black and white, sought out a local justice of the peace and swore out an arrest warrant on the slave-catchers for kidnapping. They then found a constable willing to demand that the Kentuckians supply proof of their authority to seize Price.[47]

Why Wall and Langston threw themselves into such a technical and time-consuming process—and why the crowd held back—is not easy to explain. Perhaps they maintained an unshakable faith that the law would favor liberty. But every educated abolitionist understood full well that the Fugitive Slave Act gave John Price and their cause little hope. "I went to Wellington," Langston remembered, "knowing that colored men have no rights in the United States which white men are bound to respect; that the courts had so decided; that Congress had so enacted; that the people had so decreed."[48]

More likely Wall and Langston sensed that resorting to legal arguments could work in their favor even if the arguments were doomed to fail. For one thing, although the legal strategy may have been nonviolent, it was confrontational. Jennings had felt secure in the top-floor room, insulated from the inarticulate mob below. The arrest warrant forced him to talk face-to-face with abolitionists who attacked his fundamental sense that his actions were legitimate. Over and over again in the hours that followed, Jennings found himself admitting groups of three or four men and showing them his legal documents. He offered to free Price for $1,400. One abolitionist cheerfully counteroffered five dollars, and another said he would pay a nickel.[49]

Perhaps for the first time in his life, Jennings was forced to interact with blacks as his equals, or even his social superiors. As John Mercer Langston had long known, the opportunity to make legal arguments admitted blacks into an "aristocracy of eloquence." When Charles Langston entered the hotel room with an abolitionist delegation, he demanded to see the Southerners' papers and gestured out the window, saying, "You might as well give the negro up, as *they* are going to have him any way." Jennings thought he was a lawyer.[50]

The arrest warrant kept the crowd happy, as hundreds eagerly listened to the people who had met with Jennings. The hours were slipping away from the slave-catchers. "There was a great deal of excitement and noise and confusion; didn't take much note of time," one Oberlin abolitionist said. "Didn't hardly know it was night when it was night." The four o'clock Cleveland train came and went, with no troops arriving to disperse the crowd.[51]

Faced with the possibility of missing the train to Columbus, Jennings grew impatient with the arguing and took John Price outside onto a plat-form above the crowd. With Jennings looming behind him, Price stam-mered that the slave-catchers' papers were legal and that he "supposed" he had to go with them back to Kentucky. Rather than calming the crowd, Price's words goaded it into action. "You will have to go back, will you? We'll see about that!" shouted one man. Others waved their arms and called for John to jump. Some trained their rifles on Jennings, who grabbed Price and pulled him inside.[52]

The crowd rushed for the hotel entrance. Jennings hustled Price back to their room, slammed the door, and wrapped a piece of rope around the knob and a wall bracket, pulling as tight as he could. In the excitement, Jennings did not notice that an Oberlin student who had been looking at the Southerners' papers was still in the room. Richard Winsor—twenty-three years old, short, inconspicuous—made his way over to Price and quietly asked him if he wanted to be free. Price said yes.[53]

Like an approaching train, the mob roared its way up the stairs. People slammed into the door, but Jennings and his men held fast, threatening to shoot anyone who crossed the threshold. Winsor told Price to crouch low and hold on to him around the waist. Together they inched toward the door.

For a moment the people on the third-floor landing found themselves at a stalemate. But then Winsor passed a note to them through the hole in the wall where the stovepipe had been. Someone looked through, saw that Jennings was within arm's reach, and punched with all his might.

The blow through the hole in the wall blindsided Jennings. It staggered him, ruined his hat, and left him bloody. The rope slipped through his fingers, and the mob pushed the door open. In an instant Winsor and Price slipped out, and Jennings could only watch as his prize went "a paddlin' down stairs over the heads of the crowd, as it seemed to me."[54]

The current of outstretched arms carried John Price all the way into the Wellington town square. Outside in the cool dusk, the cart that O.S.B. Wall had taken from Oberlin was waiting. Simeon Bushnell covered Price with a blanket, snapped the reins, and headed north, first to Oberlin and eventually to Canada. In the hour that followed, hundreds of men who now called themselves the "Rescuers" traveled the same road, but at a decidedly more leisurely pace.

Wall rode home with Langston. Halfway to town they recognized a man galloping in toward them, shouting. It was John Mercer Langston. He had gone to Oberlin after finishing his business in Erie County, only to find the town virtually empty. Dashing south to Wellington, he passed Sim Bushnell and had the pleasure of congratulating John Price personally on his newfound liberty.[55]

All around them the road was filling up with their neighbors also heading back to Oberlin, singing and laughing and hollering, already telling and retelling their stories. With the Langston brothers at his side, Wall took his place in the victory parade.

CHAPTER SEVEN

CIVIL WAR

Wall, Gibson, and Spencer, 1859–63

Wall: Cleveland, 1859

THE MEN LOCKED ARMS as they marched down the broad hallway outside the courtroom. They were young and old, every shape, size, and color, all formally dressed, holding valises. O.S.B. Wall and Charles Langston took their places among them. Nodding to wives, well-wishers, and newspapermen lining the way, twenty defendants walked two by two into the April rain. It was not much warmer than the day, five months before, when they had been indicted. After a brief walk they stopped outside a shabby building with narrow arched windows and stone guard towers. While the U.S. marshal conferred with the sheriff over the terms of confinement, the men were slowly soaked through as they contemplated their new home, the Cuyahoga County Jail.[1]

Not an hour before, Simeon Bushnell, the Oberlin printer's clerk, had been found guilty of "rescuing" "a certain negro slave called John" at Wellington, Ohio, in violation of the Fugitive Slave Act. It was a result that surprised no one. Every single juror had been a proslavery Democrat. After the judge announced that the same panel would try the remaining defendants, the men known as the Oberlin Rescuers declared in protest that they would no longer accept the terms of their bail. They preferred jail.[2]

Langston would face trial the next Monday, in three days' time. He was already prepared for the worst, convinced that "the courts of this country, that the laws of this country, that the governmental machinery of this country, are so constituted as to oppress and outrage colored men." Wall, by contrast, would soon be released to his family. Because the indictment had listed him as "Oliver S. B. Wall," the judge regarded the document as a fatally flawed "misnomer," and the federal prosecutor was preparing to drop all charges. Throughout his life Wall encountered few people who could spell Orindatus. His slave's name would make him a free man.[3]

Wall had taken the witness stand at Simeon Bushnell's trial, weighing in on a factual dispute. While the slave-catchers had testified that the man they kidnapped was a particular Kentucky runaway well known to them, Bushnell alleged that their captive did not match that runaway's physical description—he had a different height, a different weight, and a different skin color. As a bootmaker accustomed to working with hides, Wall testified on the last issue, drolly cataloging the range of complexions of people of color.

With sly resolve, Wall insisted on such a degree of precision, so far beyond what most whites could imagine—from black to dark and light brown, to "dark, lighter and light mulatto" to "copper color, which is about the color of hemlock tanned sole leather"—that the courtroom erupted repeatedly in laughter. Unintimidated by lawyers or the judge or the majesty of the federal court, Wall was in complete control. Although a guilty verdict seemed preordained, Wall was able to gain some small victory for his people, crafting a performance that invited newspapers to comment that a black man had "show[n] more intelligence, by far, than the Kentucky negro catchers who preceded him."[4]

The air in the jail was damp and hard to breathe, but the prisoners' mood on Saturday and Sunday remained light, even celebratory. Among the Oberlin faithful, the months since their indictment the previous December had been occasions for toasts, militant speeches, and organized gatherings they proudly called Felons' Feasts. Now that the Rescuers were behind bars, men, women, and children visited them from morning to night. Hours passed in discussion and debate, about the Slave Power and Slave Oligarchy, the right to a fair trial, the proper way to respond to the law when it violated God's command. It was the Oberlin College education that Wall had never received. Hundreds joined prayer services in the court-yard, their hymns pushing at the stone walls.[5]

Among the visitors was a tall man with an unblinking stare, hunched into an unnatural posture. Although he had been assured that he would not face arrest, it was never easy for a wanted fugitive to enter a jail. John Brown, the scourge of slavers in Bleeding Kansas, had taken the trouble to tuck his beard into his shirt. He had been watching the trial ever since arriving in Cleveland from Canada. His journey south had not ended. He was look-ing for recruits for a new Provisional Army in order to raid the federal armory at Harpers Ferry, Virginia, inspire thousands of slaves to revolu-tion, and cleanse the nation's sins with fire and blood. More than anyone in the jail, he understood that at some point the speeches would stop, and war would begin.[6]

That Sunday afternoon a local daguerrean gathered the Rescuers in the courtyard for a group portrait. Wall buttoned his waistcoat. As the men gathered, Bushnell and Langston took their places in the center. Wall moved to the edge of the group. Before their image was captured, the Rescuers took off their hats. One man placed his on the ground. Others held them in their hands. Wall looked to his left, stuck out his chest, and kept his top hat high on his head, like a soldier at attention. No one stood taller.[7]

Gibson: Columbus, Kentucky, December 1861

THE MISSISSIPPI RIVER WAS running low; even from the steamer's deck, Randall Gibson had to look up at the banks. As the freezing wind punctured his uniform like canister shot, he could not help but feel exposed. He was outside his regiment's fortified position on high ground, beyond the heavy chain that his general had or-dered extended across the river to Missouri, to render an invisible border impregnable. The white flag that flew overhead was the only thing keeping

Gibson alive. The twenty-five winding miles from Columbus, Kentucky, to Cairo, Illinois, were no less than the distance, in Gibson's mind, between liberty and tyranny.[8]

As the boat steamed north, several officers on board—men from Nashville and Vicksburg and New Orleans, lawyers, planters, and merchants, sugar and cotton men, a fellow Yale alumnus—seemed to be enjoying the excursion. Gibson was not. When one of his colleagues informed him that their guest of honor had requested his presence, the twenty-nine-year-old colonel felt little desire to oblige him. Gibson walked inside to a stateroom, where a man was lying on his back. Henry Dougherty, also a colonel, was ashen from loss of blood; the remains of one of his legs still oozed from three botched amputations. But he was pleased to be heading home and had asked to meet the man among his captors who had spent so many happy years in the North. Gibson could manage a few bare pleasantries and little more. "While I could not help but feel sympathy," he wrote, "I could take no interest in conversation with him & retired quickly."[9]

Even before Abraham Lincoln was elected president in 1860, Randall Gibson had doubted that the Union would survive and was urging the South to "prepare for every emergency." To the young Louisianan, the conflict was less a question of states' rights or of the propriety or necessity of slavery than about the inexorable gulf between whites and blacks, or what he called "the most enlightened race" and "the most degraded of all the races of men." The North, in his view, was committed to the radical dogma of "the political, civil, and social equality of all the races of men." By contrast, "Southern society is based, its life and soul are staked, upon the inequality of the races, not only its aims, its expansion and progress, but its very existence." If the North forced Southern whites to live as equals with the people they owned as slaves, then the South would have to enjoy "independence *out* of the Union."[10]

After the election Gibson's sister Sarah drafted a letter to Lincoln with signatures from the most respectable matrons of Lexington, Kentucky, urging him for the good of the country to resign before taking office. Randall, however, was past any hope of reconciliation, running as a secessionist in the election for delegates to a convention that would determine whether Louisiana remained in or left the Union. The crisis gave his life a purpose that he had not felt since graduating from Yale in 1853. After sitting through a year of law lectures at the University of Louisiana and passing the bar, Gibson sailed for Europe in 1855, traveling with his brother Hart to Paris, London, Heidelberg, St. Petersburg, Rome, and Madrid. Returning after two years, he tried to make a life for himself as a sugar planter. His crop flooded, and he found his neighbors distasteful. While Hart took possession of his vast Kentucky estate and married into one of the state's richest families, Randall had had to sell his land. He started managing one of his father's plantations and dreamed of a life in politics. It seemed impossible, though, for a young man to get elected to office. In the polling for the secession convention, Gibson placed third of four candidates.[11]

In February 1861, two months before Fort Sumter was bombarded and fighting began, Gibson enlisted in Louisiana's army as a private. Hart was commissioned a captain in the Kentucky cavalry, Claude an artillery lieutenant. Of their other brothers, Preston became an army surgeon, and McKinley and Tobe, who had been traveling in Europe, made their way home and joined the army too.[12]

Randall was soon promoted to captain and in September was made colonel of the Thirteenth Louisiana Volunteer Infantry Regiment, ten companies totaling 830 men, mostly from New Orleans. Even though Gibson's faith in the Confederacy was rooted in his desire to preserve the Southern racial order, his troops, according to an aide, were "as cosmopolitan a body of soldiers as there existed upon the face of God's earth. There were Frenchmen, Spaniards, Mexicans, Dagoes, Germans, Chinese, Irishmen, and, in fact, persons of every clime known to geographers or travellers of that day." They wore "jaunty zouave uniform[s]," drilled in English and French, sang songs in their native languages, speculated on their regiment's unlucky number, and lived a continuous "saturnalia" of gambling and drink. Gibson put ideology aside and focused on turning his recruits into soldiers. During the fall of 1861, as he worked with his officers in camp, Gibson did not subscribe to the gentlemanly romance of war— even though many in his regiment predicted a glorious Confederate victory before they had finished their training. Rather, like a Yale man, he devoted himself to the study of military tactics. Without any experience in war, he knew that the army's true weakness was a lack of "military men by education," "scientific officers," and "West Pointers." By November's end, the regiment was leaving Louisiana for the war's western front as a band played "The Girl I Left Behind Me." They reached Kentucky on the last day in November, shrouded in snow and sleet. They camped on frozen ground and waited for the fight.[13]

When the steamer reached the confluence of the Mississippi and Ohio rivers, the Union battery at Fort Holt noted the boat's white flag of truce and fired a shot across the bow. The steamer stopped and waited for another boat, flying an American flag, to approach. After the two were lashed together and turned upstream, the prisoner exchange began. The brigadier general in charge of the Union army at Cairo was short and stooped, his brown beard cascading in waves down to the brass buttons double-breasting his coat. He greeted several rebel officers fondly, having known them from West Point and the Mexican War; a Confederate captain in the party was a kinsman. Officers on both sides shook hands and raised glasses. Although members of the brigadier's staff predicted that they would soon be marching "on to New Orleans," they assured their foes that they "came to save not to destroy." The brigadier declared he would resign his commission "if war should be made against slavery"; he had owned a slave himself just a couple of years earlier in Missouri. Although he freed the man before moving to Illinois, his wife still owned four slaves and was leasing them out.[14]

The outpouring of good feeling unsettled Gibson. "To all appearances," he wrote that week, "there had been a meeting of friends." Just a month earlier the two sides had fought their first major engagement since the rebels occupied Columbus in September 1861. The rebel occupation had violated Kentucky's neutrality, prompting the Union army to move into the commonwealth, and led the legislature to declare its allegiance to the United States. At the Battle of Belmont, more than eleven hundred men had been killed or wounded. In previous meetings to swap prisoners and bury the dead, Union and Confederate officers had recognized each other from the battlefield; they had all been within range of the other side's rifles

The Gibsons

Hart Gibson at Yale, early 1850s. Like his older brother, Hart is wearing his Scroll and Key Society pin. *Image courtesy of Manuscripts & Archives, Yale University.*

Randall Lee Gibson as a Yale undergraduate, early 1850s. *Image courtesy of Manuscripts & Archives, Yale University.*

Yale Class of 1855. *Image courtesy of Manuscripts & Archives, Yale University.*

Sarah Thompson Gibson, Randall and Hart's older sister, ca. 1848. *Courtesy of the Sarah B. Morrison Family Collection.*

Randall Lee Gibson in uniform. *Image courtesy of the Gilder Lehrman Collection, Gilder Lehrman Institute of American History, New York.*

Morgan's Raid—Entry of Morgan's Freebooters into Washington, Ohio, from *Harper's Weekly,* August 15, 1863. Hart Gibson was a captain and an adjutant general in John Hunt Morgan's cavalry during its famous raid into Ohio in July 1863.

Hart Gibson in Confederate cavalry uniform. *Image courtesy of Cowan's Auctions, Inc., Cincinnati, Ohio.*

Hart Gibson with his wife, Mary Duncan, and kin, after the war. *Mrs. William & H. Foster Pettit Family Collection, University of Kentucky Archives.*

Randall Lee Gibson, 1870s, after his election to Congress from Louisiana. *Courtesy of the Library of Congress, Prints & Photographs Division, Washington, D.C.*

Randall Lee Gibson, 1880s. After four terms in the House of Representatives, Gibson served nine years in the U.S. Senate. During that time he helped found Tulane University in New Orleans. *Sarah B. Morrison Family Collection.*

Photograph accompanying Hart Gibson's obituary, 1904. *Mrs. William & H. Foster Pettit Family Collection, University of Kentucky Archives.*

Preston Gibson and his second wife, Grace McMillan, 1909. An iconic member of the "Smart Set" and a fixture on the society pages, Randall Gibson's youngest son married and divorced four times. *Mrs. William & H. Foster Pettit Family Collection, University of Kentucky Archives.*

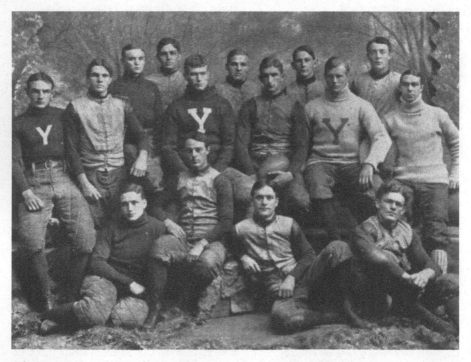

Yale football team, 1899. Preston Gibson is on the far right, middle row. *Photograph courtesy of Manuscripts & Archives, Yale University.*

Henry Field Gibson, Preston's son with his first wife, Marshall Field heiress Minna Field, before 1910. *Mrs. William & H. Foster Pettit Family Collection, University of Kentucky Archives.*

Henry Field, 1928. After dropping his father's name, Field became an internationally known anthropologist and curator at the Chicago natural history museum named for his mother's family. © *1928, The Field Museum, CSA66037.*

Ubangi Woman, sculpture by Malvina Hoffman in the Hall of the Races of Mankind, Field Museum, Chicago. Henry Field discovered the model for this sculpture at the Colonial Exposition in Paris in 1931. Of the sculpture, Field wrote, "The urge to touch her elongated lower lip has proven irresistible to many visitors." © *1933, The Field Museum, MH91.*

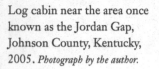

Drilling for Salt Brine with a Spring Pole, in R. B. Woodworth, "The Evolution of Drilling Rigs," *Bulletin of the American Institute of Mining Engineers*, no. 107 (November 1915), p. 2251.

Log cabin near the area once known as the Jordan Gap, Johnson County, Kentucky, 2005. *Photograph by the author.*

A farm in an isolated mountain hollow before coal mining, Wheatfield Branch near Van Lear, Johnson County, about seven miles southeast of the Jordan Gap. *Courtesy of the Van Lear Historical Society, Van Lear, Kentucky.*

Logging in a mountain hollow, Johnson County. Like many farmers in eastern Kentucky, Jordan Spencer and his family spent much of their time clearing their land. Spencer sold his lumber to a Paintsville merchant who made a fortune supplying Appalachian hardwoods to builders in Cincinnati, Ohio. Spencer played poker with the merchant's son. *Image courtesy of Val McKenzie.*

The Spencers

William Jasper Spencer, Jordan Spencer's youngest son, in his casket, Johnson County, 1937. *Courtesy of Freda Spencer Goble.*

Lumber mill, Hurley, Buchanan County, Virginia. Source: W. G. Schwab, *The Forests of Buchanan County, Virginia* (Charlottesville, Va., 1918).

Inside the mines, Johnson County, Kentucky. *Courtesy of the Van Lear Historical Society.*

Mine opening at the Miller's Creek Block Seam, Johnson County, ca. 1885. *Courtesy of the Appalachian Photographic Archive, Alice Lloyd College, Pippa Passes, Kentucky.*

Grundy, Virginia, the site of the slander trial brought by Jordan Spencer's grandson George against his neighbor George Looney in 1912. The Buchanan County Courthouse is in the center foreground, with the tall clock tower. Source: Henry Hinds, *The Geology and Coal Resources of Buchanan County, Virginia* (Charlottesville, Va., 1918).

Main Street, Paintsville, Kentucky, ca. 1912, when depositions in *Spencer v. Looney* took place at the law offices of Howes & Howes. *Image courtesy of Val McKenzie.*

Frona Spencer, Jasper Spencer's daughter, 1930s, Johnson County, Kentucky. *Courtesy of Freda Spencer Goble.*

Freda Spencer Goble, Jordan Spencer's great-great-granddaughter, Paintsville, 2005. *Photograph by the author.*

Orindatus Simon Bolivar Wall, in Joseph T. Wilson, *The Black Phalanx: A History of the Negro Soldiers of the United States* (Hartford, Conn.: American Publishing Co., 1890). *Image courtesy of the the Ohio Historical Society.*

The Walls

Stephen Wall of Rockingham, North Carolina, O.S.B. Wall's father and owner. *Charles Dean Collection, Archives & Special Collections, J. D. Williams Library, University of Mississippi.*

The Oberlin Rescuers, Cuyahoga County Jail, April 1859. From left to right: Jacob Shipherd, O.S.B. Wall, Loring Wadsworth, David Watson, Wilson Evans, Eli Boies, Ralph Plumb, Henry Evans, Simeon Bushnell, John Scott, Matthew Gillet, Charles Langston, Ansel Lyman, James Bartlett, William Lincoln, Richard Winsor, John Watson, James Fitch, Henry Peck, and Daniel Williams. Photograph by T. J. Rice. *Courtesy of the Library of Congress.*

Caroline Wall Langston, O.S.B. Wall's sister, in John Mercer Langston, *From the Virginia Plantation to the National Capitol* (Hartford, Conn.: American Publishing Co., 1894). *Image courtesy of Manuscript, Archives, and Rare Book Library, Emory University, Atlanta, Georgia.*

John Mercer Langston, before 1875. *Brady-Handy Collection, Library of Congress, Prints & Photographs Division, Washington, D.C.*

Significant Election Scene in Washington, June 3, 1867, from *Harper's Weekly*, June 22, 1867. In the first election in which African Americans voted in Washington, D.C., Radical Republicans seized the reins of power. Part of an emerging black political elite, O.S.B. Wall worked in city and territorial government and held elected office. However, over the seven years following that first election, voting rights in the District were steadily reduced. In 1874 Congress established an entirely appointed local government.

Students on campus, Howard University, 1870. *Courtesy of the Moorland-Spingarn Research Center, Howard University Archives, Washington, D.C.*

Stephen R. Wall (O.S.B. and Amanda Wall's son) and Lillie Slee Wall, early 1900s. *Photograph courtesy of Lisa Colby.*

"A pretty little miss about to make her bow to the world": Isabel Irene Wall, Stephen and Lillie Wall's eldest daughter. *Photograph courtesy of Isabel Wall Whittemore.*

Isabel with her siblings, Ethel Ada and Roscoe Orin Wall, in 1909, the year Isabel was expelled from the first grade at the Brookland School for being black. *Photograph courtesy of Lisa Colby.*

Isabel and Charles Winward with their daughter, Cape Cod, mid-1950s. *Photograph courtesy of Lisa Colby.*

Isabel and Charles Winward, mid-1940s or early 1950s. As Lillian Gates McGowan, Isabel met her husband, Charles, in Rhode Island in the 1930s. After marrying, she returned to her original first name and named her daughter Isabel Wall Winward. *Photograph courtesy of Lisa Colby.*

Patrick and Charlotte Murphy, Miami, ca. 1938. Patrick Murphy was the last of many aliases that Roscoe Orin Wall assumed in his life. *Photograph courtesy of Sir Thomas L. Murphy.*

Sir Thomas L. Murphy, 2005.
Photograph by the author.

Isabel Wall Whittemore, New Hampshire, 2008.
Photograph by the author.

but had survived. Their very presence at these parleys seemed a testament to both sides' mercy and good faith. Gibson and his men had arrived three weeks after the fight. Perhaps if the Thirteenth Louisiana had seen action, he would have felt more charitably toward his counterparts.[15]

As it was, Gibson nursed a quiet contempt for his foes throughout the prisoner exchange. "I was thoroughly disgusted with the whole party," he reported. Although he had schoolmates from Maine to Delaware—many of whom were fighting for the Yankees—Gibson made a special effort to resist "any sociability of feeling that may have existed." He refused to be a Southern gallant who treated the war as sport. His ability to kill for the Confederate cause compelled him to loathe the North. He thought the enemy officers were "impudent upstarts . . . [I]t was evident from the whole tenor of their remarks that their purpose individually was subjugation & confiscation." The most Gibson would concede was that the Union army's brigadier general, a man named Ulysses S. Grant, "had somewhat the appearance of a Gentleman."[16]

A few days later, back in Columbus, the Confederate army received reports that the enemy was moving in force just across the river in Missouri, near the site of the battle four weeks earlier. That night Gibson's regiment moved silently upriver and scouted till dawn through cornfields and woods, slowly making their way back to camp. For a moment they heard hoofbeats and assumed that the Yankee cavalry was upon them, but it was only a herd of horses running by. Whatever enemy troops had been there were long gone. Not a weapon was fired.[17]

As morning broke, the regiment moved through the old battlefield at Belmont. For months Gibson had wondered what war would be like. Since arriving in Kentucky, he had been living among officers who had led their men under fire, suffered through the slaughter, and recorded the messages of dying men. Now he saw what awaited him. When the day came, and it would not be long, the field of battle would not be glorious. "I counted as I marched along twelve dead horses and the trees & earth looked scorched & in places torn up," he wrote his father. "It looks like it had been struck by constant streaks of lightning."[18]

Spencer: Paintsville, Kentucky, January 1862

T HE TENTS ON THE HILLSIDE struck newcomers as a "pretty queer" sight, a city where there should only have been a cabin or two. In firelight blurred by sleet and fog, the rows of pale canvas resembled stones in a mountain cemetery. For soldiers in the Fifth Kentucky Infantry, the resemblance did not end there. Hundreds without tents had hacked holes in the hard ground, filled them with leaves and dirt, and slept in them, sometimes huddled together for warmth.[19]

George Washington Spencer was just three miles below Paintsville and a short ride from his family, but he could not have been farther from home. On the Spencer farm he was the oldest of eight boys and girls and had labored many hard years under his father, Jordan. As his brothers got older, and as the farm became more productive, the work and his responsibilities only grew more intense. The war had some effect on the families along Rockhouse Creek. A few of the boys left to fight. Soldiers on both sides took food, and there were more strangers wandering through the hills. Irregular "home guards" of various stripes periodically attacked farms and businesses in Johnson County, but the raids were more like robberies than military actions—victims sued the bushwhackers for damages in the local court. Otherwise, life continued as it always had; every moment of the war, Malinda Spencer was either pregnant or nursing an infant.[20]

Now, instead of being the oldest son, George was among the youngest soldiers in his company, just fourteen or fifteen. He huddled around a fire with five other men. They shared their rations but were still hungry. In January 1862 George Spencer had been a rebel for a little more than two months. His decision to volunteer had hardly been a given. Kentucky was a divided state, and Johnson was a divided county, one of the few places where brother actually fought brother. Even after the commonwealth declared its allegiance to the Union, the county tried to maintain its neutrality. To keep the peace, the local court banned the flying of any flag, United States or Confederate, in a public place. Although the county had long voted by overwhelming margins for Democrats, most of its people remained loyal to the Union. With so few slaves, Johnson County had very little stake in the rebellion; some residents placed *Uncle Tom's Cabin* next to their Bibles.[21]

In the fall of 1861, the rebels started calling for volunteers in the mountain counties. Whether or not George Spencer believed that he was serving "the cause of civil freedom," as Confederate recruiters said, the rebel army provided a change from the daily toil of the farm. As the leaves were turning, he had walked a dozen miles from Rockhouse Creek to Prestonsburg. Volunteers crowded the main road by the Big Sandy River, along with central Kentucky cavaliers riding to Richmond for their officer's commissions. More than a thousand men reached Prestonsburg in October 1861 and organized the Fifth Infantry Regiment. In homespun clothes and bare feet, with so few guns that Robert E. Lee suggested that they be issued pikes, the Fifth Kentucky became known as the Ragamuffins.[22]

George Spencer had two sticks for weapons. Assigned as one of his company's musicians, he woke his comrades every morning with a drumroll. As fall turned to winter, he tapped out orders as the men drilled, tallest to the right, shortest to the left, loading and unloading and aiming their weapons—shotguns, hunting rifles—and fixing bayonets. Issued new boots and a cheap cotton uniform that their brigadier general—Humphrey Marshall, a fat Louisville lawyer and former Whig congressman—had assured the men was wool, Spencer kept the pace as they marched through streaming rain and high mud. In November, when Union forces moved up the Big Sandy River to push the rebels from eastern Kentucky, Spencer survived shelling. At Ivy Mountain, near Prestonsburg, his regiment had fired on the enemy to a fife's whistle and rattling drums, as an officer shouted, "Put it to them, my brave boys!" During and after battle, drummers often served as stretcher bearers and orderlies. It was work for someone who was too young to fight but also for those who did not entirely fit in. His cousin George Centers, the son of George Freeman and Clarissa Centers, served in the Union army, also as a musician. Although he was old enough to be a soldier, Centers assumed a role often reserved to his race, playing music because he was too dark to fight in a white regiment.[23]

In December 1861, after retreating to Pound Gap and the Virginia border, the Ragamuffins marched back down the Big Sandy Valley. They brought the war to their home counties, taking food from local farmers, causing families to flee their cabins for points downriver. The people of Catlettsburg, where the Big Sandy empties into the Ohio River, contemplated a mass removal to southern Ohio. Shortly before Christmas the Ragamuffins set up camp with several cavalry and artillery regiments below Paintsville, dug rifle pits, cut down hundreds of trees to establish clear lines of sight for their artillery, and established pickets around the town. General Marshall attempted to recruit more volunteers and establish rebel governments in eastern Kentucky's mountain counties but was disappointed, finding the locals "perfectly terrified or apparently apathetic. I imagine most of them are Unionists, but so ignorant they do not understand the question at issue." While Marshall complained about their neighbors and kinsmen, the Ragamuffins were waiting to fight Union troops from Kentucky and Ohio who were slowly marching upriver under the command of a thirty-year-old colonel "who had never heard a hostile gun," future president James Abram Garfield.[24]

By the new year, the opposing armies were just a few miles apart. Although outnumbered, Garfield ordered his troops forward. On January 6 a small force of infantry and cavalry attacked rebel pickets near the mouth of Paint Creek at the Big Sandy River. Two hours later a second force attacked a rebel position three miles west at the mouth of Jenny's Creek. And two hours after that a third force attacked down the middle. When the Union soldiers encountered the enemy, the engagements were brief—hills echoing with rifle shot, hoofbeats, and screams, muddy roads littered with overcoats, guns, and equipment dropped by fleeing rebels. Some Union troops paused to look at the few men shot dead or trampled by horses—their first corpses of the war.[25]

The Union cavalry chased the rebels up the narrow rain-swollen creek valleys but could not get far, finding themselves in crossfire from enemy soldiers who had climbed into the hills and were shooting down. As the pickets ran back to camp with reports of the attacks, General Marshall sent a thousand troops to the river, only to order them west two hours later. Convinced that the Union army would outflank his position from Jenny's

Creek and trap his soldiers against the Big Sandy, Marshall ordered the troops to retreat to camp. The next day he decided to abandon it and move upriver to Prestonsburg before Garfield could cut off their path of escape. The Union soldiers swept through Paintsville and up Jenny's Creek, victorious. Within days their Colonel Garfield was promoted to brigadier general. Hailed in the Republican press as a hero, he was elected to Congress that fall, beginning his ascent to the White House.[26]

While Jordan and Malinda Spencer and their children were close enough to hear the gunfire—Garfield had sent some cavalry past their farm on Rockhouse Creek to determine whether the rebels were retreating west—their oldest son was running away with the rest of his regiment. The rebels burned what supplies they could, but the retreat was so frantic that when Garfield and four hundred men reached the abandoned camp on the night of January 7, they found food still bubbling in large kettles. A few days later, just south of Prestonsburg, the Ragamuffins suffered a more decisive defeat and headed for southwestern Virginia; many of the Kentucky volunteers deserted rather than leaving the state. Spencer endured freeze and flood; the civilians whom his regiment encountered in the Virginia hills were starving. For three days in May 1862 the Ragamuffins fought at Princeton Court House, in the western Virginia hills, and finally shouted victorious huzzahs, leading charges and relieving the Union dead of boots, watches, and anything else that turned up in their pockets. That summer the Army of the Mississippi invaded Kentucky from the south. Spencer's regiment spent the month of September marching west with more than four thousand other Confederate troops, all the way to Lexington—the first time the drummer boy had seen the world beyond the mountains. After coming within earshot of a battle west of Lexington that left eight thousand killed or wounded, the regiment turned around and retreated the way they came.[27]

As the Ragamuffins' one-year enlistment was nearing an end, the regiment voted to serve the Confederacy for the rest of the war, on one condition: they wanted to bring their own horses along and fight as mounted infantry. After they had marched until their boots were tattered, the prospect of riding instead of walking had enormous appeal. And for mountaineers who prided themselves on their horsemanship—a feeling shared by Jordan Spencer's son—it may have also been a question of dignity. General Marshall denied the request.[28]

On October 20, the day their term expired, the men were back in eastern Kentucky, within reach of their cabins and hollows. As the drums beat and the sergeant major shouted orders, they woke and refused to line up. Although the Confederate Congress had enacted a statute requiring soldiers to serve an additional two years, the men knew that the law was unenforceable in Kentucky, which had no Confederate government. Seven hundred out of a thousand men stacked their weapons. George Spencer put his drums down, walked into the hills, and left the rebellion behind.[29]

Gibson: Ohio, July 1863

THE HOT SUMMER AIR, the dust of long country roads, blasted Hart Gibson, filled his eyes and lungs, coated his teeth, turned his skin and magnificent black beard brownish red. He could hear nothing, not his heart beating, over the furious shifting rhythm of hoofbeats. With every steady breath, he smelled hundreds of horses—a fog of earth, grass, sweat, and filth. Riding day and night, sleeping on his horse, Gibson had no time to remember even recent events, and it was impossible to think about what awaited him. All that mattered was the ride. As long as he had a horse, as long as he kept moving, there was hope. He could not see the beginning of his column and could only guess how far back it went.[30]

For two weeks, Gibson had been advancing east through Ohio as a captain in Morgan's Cavalry, a brigade of Kentucky horsemen. If Hart's brother Randall had devoted himself to learning the science of war, Morgan's men embraced the dash and honor of the Southern cause. Being a cavalry officer fit Hart's position in Kentucky society. After reading law for a semester at Harvard and studying philosophy and sociology at Heidelberg, he had settled into the life of a gentleman farmer and horse breeder at Hartland, the estate he had inherited in the bluegrass country outside Lexington. In

Morgan's brigade every day promised to be a grand adventure. In fine uniforms, on strong steeds, they covered vast distances, continually surprised the enemy, saved their comrades from death and defeat, turned the tides of battles, and won despite improbable odds. Their leader, John Hunt Morgan, "irresistibly reminded one of the heroes of romance," one of his officers would remember—tall, handsome, and strong, more loyal to his men than to his superiors, able to ride for days without rest, only to gallop another fifty miles to see his ailing wife.[31]

In 1861 and 1862 the Confederacy delighted in the horsemanship and derring-do exhibited by Morgan's men, the raids and mad sprints, the gun- and swordplay. For most of 1863, though, the brigade had been guarding and scouting along a 150-mile front in Middle Tennessee, tedious work, quietly demoralizing. It seemed, according to one officer, that "the glory and the *prestige* began to pass away from the Southern cavalry." Infantry had attained more strategic importance, and as the war ground on in seeming stalemate, the costs of maintaining cavalry had become increasingly daunting to the Confederacy. Cavalrymen were finding themselves short on ammunition and guns, food, tents—they were expected to live off the land, beg and steal from the civilians they encountered, or capture what they needed from the enemy. There was no forage to keep their horses strong; they simply had to take fresh animals where they could find them. They were passed over for promotions. Most galling, even common infantry "webfeet," cannon fodder simply "fattened . . . for the sacrifice," sneered at warriors who did not have to march to battle, dismissing them as "buttermilk rangers."[32]

As the weather grew warm, Morgan sought bolder adventures for his brigade. He asked for and received permission to invade Kentucky and raid Louisville. But he was making far grander plans that he kept to himself. Through the end of June 1863 they cut through Kentucky, skirmishing with federal troops who maneuvered vainly to try to stop them. The raiders burned and plundered towns, destroyed railroads and telegraph wires, and even robbed a train. After General Morgan's adjutant general was murdered trying to discipline a captain for stealing a civilian's watch, Hart Gibson was promoted to the position, with the responsibilities of chief administrator for the brigade.[33]

In early July, as news of General Robert E. Lee's defeat at Gettysburg crushed them, Morgan's men came within sight of the Ohio River at Bradenburg, Kentucky. Instead of turning east to take Louisville, Morgan disobeyed his orders and sent advance parties to the docks to capture steamboats. On July 8 the cavalry crossed the river into Indiana, beginning what became known as the "Great Raid." They dashed across southern Indiana, through villages that still streamed with banners celebrating the Union victory. Entering the homes of people who had fled to nearby limestone caves, they found pots still bubbling and tables set for dinner. Day after day they shot their way through barricades and militia stands. As they rode into southern Ohio, they burned bridges and robbed banks, confiscated fresh horses, and liberally raided local larders. In one officer's words, they "pillaged like boys robbing an orchard," stringing hams and bolts of calico to their saddles, slinging ice skates around their necks, filling their pockets with horn buttons from general stores. Decades later an Ohioan would remember how the raiders "exhibit[ed] abnormal appetites for pound cake and preserves."[34]

Federal cavalry rode in hot pursuit just miles behind. Gunboats patrolled the Ohio River, and tens of thousands of militia volunteers made "every bush an ambush." The rebels' horses wore out and had to be replaced every day. But General Morgan and his men never dreamed that their raid was doomed. They figured they could always outrun the enemy. They rode into the southeastern hills and headed for the West Virginia border, confident they would cross in the shallows near Wheeling. Instead, the river was running high, and on July 19 the brigade found itself facing a flotilla of gunboats with deadly artillery, with ten thousand federal cavalry and infantry closing in. While some men succeeded in crossing into West Virginia, seven hundred were captured. Gibson, General Morgan, and several hundred others escaped the trap and turned north, riding over steep hills to elude their pursuers. A week later, ninety miles south of Lake Erie, Morgan surrendered, nowhere left to ride.[35]

The general and his officers, Hart Gibson among them, rode by steamer to Cincinnati, then by train to Columbus, jeered by crowds along the way. Instead of being sent to a camp for prisoners of war, they were locked up in the state penitentiary. As guards and inmates watched, Morgan's raiders were stripped naked and scrubbed by convicts with horsebrushes, their hair and beards shorn. On behalf of the men, Gibson wrote to Ohio's governor in protest over being "subjected to the ordinary discipline of convicts." The punishment was harsh, particularly the long stretches of solitary confinement, but a gentleman warrior could endure such hardships. What galled Gibson was the notion that other captives were living in much better conditions. Thinking like the lawyer he once had been, he came to believe that equal treatment was the hallmark of fairness. "Who are we," he wrote, "how different from ordinary men, or of what crime are we guilty, that we are put beyond the pale of civilized warfare, the utmost limit of law overleaped to inflict upon us as a punishment at variance with and abhorrent to the moral sense of mankind?"[36]

CHAPTER EIGHT

CIVIL WAR

Wall and Gibson, 1863–66

Wall: Ohio, August 1863

O.S.B. WALL ADVANCED SLOWLY through the heat and dust. The hills of southeastern Ohio were simple country, a rolling progression of farmhouses, barns, orchards, and hedgerows, tens of thousands of sheep grazing on the hillsides, fields swirling with corn, flax, hay, and wheat at their late-summer heights. Wall was far from Oberlin. The area more resembled western Pennsylvania and the western Virginia counties that had opted to remain in the Union at the outset of the war, a border between plains and mountains, east and west, north and south. His brother-in-law John Mercer Langston had grown up in nearby Chillicothe, but Wall was more than a hundred miles away from any place that he knew well. He had to find his way directly from farm to farm and town to town; he could not rely on strangers to guide him.[1]

Just days earlier Morgan's raiders had swept through the area. When Wall began his travels, hundreds of the Confederate cavalrymen had been cornered and captured trying to cross the Ohio River into West Virginia, but General Morgan and a remnant of his men remained at large. The signs of recent terror abounded, from trees felled along the roads to burnt bridges and buildings.[2]

Even without the fighting, the area was torn by conflict. Virginians had settled the Ohio hills and were staunch Democrats. For decades before the war, they had opposed civil rights for blacks, whom they viewed as economic competition and political foes. When the Ohio Supreme Court ruled in 1831 that anyone who was more than half white had all of the rights of a white man, whites in southern Ohio refused to enroll blacks in white schools and stationed themselves at the polls on Election Day to challenge the blood quantum of dark-skinned voters. In court they insisted, despite settled law to the contrary, that one drop of black blood made a person black, that "the term white, as applied to persons, has . . . been . . . applied as expressive of the pure white race." As late as 1851 southern Ohioans at the state's constitutional convention labeled as trespassers the tens of thousands of people of color who lived in their communities, presenting numerous proposals to restrict immigration and send blacks to Africa so that "this should be a State for the white man and the white man only."[3]

When the South seceded, some southern Ohioans joined with Republicans to form a coalition Union Party, but many remained unapologetically opposed to the war. Their primary spokesman, Ohio congressman Clement Vallandigham, supported secession, openly denounced Lincoln, and characterized the war as an illegal invasion that would establish black rule over whites. In 1861 the Ohio legislature banned marriage and sexual relations between the races and entertained petitions to expel black residents. As long as the Union's prospects for victory remained remote, supporters of Vallandigham—known as Copperheads or Butternuts—could find sympathetic ears. President Lincoln regarded them as serious threats to internal order. In May 1863 Vallandigham was tried by a military tribunal, sentenced to two years in prison for disloyalty and sympathy for the enemy, and then exiled across enemy lines on the president's orders. The following year Ohio's Democrats would nominate Vallandigham as their candidate for governor. In the hill counties the Butternuts were unintimidated, even energized, by recent events. Wearing pins that symbolized their political allegiances, they were spending the summer of 1863 breaking up Union Party meetings with fists and pointed pistols.[4]

Riding into unstable, contested country, following in the hot wake of

Morgan's raid, Wall had a delicate task. Although he was not a soldier, his business was war. Where Confederate sympathizers abounded, Wall had come to recruit volunteers for a new Union regiment composed entirely of colored men. His mission represented everything the Butternuts were fighting. They did not simply fear black men with guns—they knew that black men in the military would have an unimpeachable claim to equal rights. From the war's outset, leaders of the race had sought to raise colored regiments for precisely this reason. "Once let the black man . . . get an eagle on his button and a musket on his shoulder and bullets in his pockets," wrote Frederick Douglass, "and there is no power on earth which can deny that he has earned the right to citizenship in the United States."[5]

Northern politicians understood that allowing blacks to enlist in the army would change the debate over civil and political rights forever. Initially, it was too radical a move for states that recognized blacks as free but not equal. Northerners from President Lincoln down suggested that blacks were too cowardly, passive, or feminine to fight—that their presence on the battlefield would undermine army morale and would destroy any prospect of peace with the Confederacy. In Ohio, where Republicans were working to keep Unionist Democrats in their governing coalition, the issue seemed impossible. In 1862 John Mercer Langston offered to raise "a thousand and one" colored men for a regiment. In a face-to-face encounter Ohio's Governor David Tod humiliated him. "Do you not know, Mr. Langston, that this is a *white man's* government; that white men are able to defend and protect it, and that to enlist a negro soldier would be to drive every white man out of the service?" said Governor Tod. "When we want you colored men we will notify you."[6]

By the end of 1862, however, after nearly two years of defeat on the battlefield and with manpower shortages looming, the notion of blacks serving in the military seemed less sinister and preposterous. When Massachusetts sought colored volunteers for its 54th Infantry Regiment in early 1863, Governor Tod asked Langston if he would lead the recruiting effort among black Ohioans. O.S.B. Wall joined him in working for the Massachusetts 54th, and together they enlisted hundreds of men. Wall's two younger half brothers, John and Albert, joined, and at the very moment O.S.B. Wall was heading toward southeastern Ohio, they were charging Fort Wagner in South Carolina.[7]

Not yet forty, Wall left his wife, three small children, and shoemaking business in Oberlin and moved to Columbus, where he coordinated the transportation of the Ohio volunteers to Massachusetts. After the 54th was filled, Langston and Wall recruited troops for the Massachusetts 55th. On June 15, 1863, just after Wall received word that the 55th was full, four dozen recruits appeared at his office. Rather than sending them back to their homes, Wall found beds for them in Columbus. He walked to the statehouse and waited for an audience with Governor Tod, urging him to consider the forty-eight recruits as the first members of an Ohio regiment. Tod telegraphed the War Department, and the next day Secretary of War Stanton authorized the creation of a new regiment, the Fifth United States Colored Troops.[8]

While Wall masterminded the logistics of getting all the recruits to the muster, he also traveled extensively, making direct appeals to black communities across the state and recruiting three hundred men. At the end of July he rode eighty miles southeast to the university town of Athens and by early August was holding meetings along the West Virginia border. Although many in the area supported slavery and secession, had long opposed the war, and blamed blacks for the suffering that it had caused them, Wall kept riding. The threat of violence did not deter him, nor did it intimidate his volunteers. Everywhere he went, he collected commitments to fight for the Union: five men in Jefferson County, two in Harrison County, another six in Belmont County. He shared the stage at large rallies with prominent Ohioans and stood alone at quieter, less public gatherings. His message was unchanged. Joining the fight would "elevat[e] the race from degradation to equality." It was more than a matter of simply "conferring the boon of freedom on their fellow men of the South"; for all blacks, North and South, military service would change the very meaning of freedom. "If the colored citizens of Ohio are such men as they aspire to be," he said, "now is the time to show it."[9]

Gibson: Nashville, December 1864

A T TWILIGHT RANDALL GIBSON could look down from the breastworks at the dark forms in the fields below. They were small, indistinct mounds mostly, but occasionally a hand or leg jutted into the air in agonized silhouette. Just minutes before, in the final light of day, the mounds had been recognizably human, bodies mired in cold mud, snapped, disemboweled, blood running in the hard rain. They were still clothed; Gibson's soldiers had not had time to strip them naked, as many Confederates had done with enemy corpses the night before. It was difficult to make out their individual features, but earlier that afternoon they had been breathing and alive, young men from Indiana charging up the steep rise by the hundreds.[10]

As the light faded on December 16, 1864, Gibson could allow himself a moment of relief: the Army of Tennessee's right flank had held. But his struggle was only beginning. The army's left and center were falling in a sickening cascade. Within moments, it seemed, Union soldiers were behind his position. Confederate soldiers on all sides were dropping their rifles and sprinting "frightened and routed" for the Franklin Pike, their only path of escape.[11]

Three weeks earlier, while the Union army under William Tecumseh Sherman was marching from Atlanta to Savannah, the Army of Tennessee had headed the other way, northward into Union-occupied territory. For months, as Sherman advanced into Georgia, the rebels had been in retreat, their morale battered by the fall of Atlanta and Lincoln's reelection. Instead of continuing to stand in Sherman's way, General John Bell Hood believed it was time for a grand offensive. With forty thousand men, the second-strongest Confederate force aimed to take Nashville, move through Kentucky to Cincinnati, and even threaten Chicago. In the alternative, they would drive east through Tennessee, raise tens of thousands of additional volunteers, cross the Cumberland Gap, and reinforce Robert E. Lee's Army of Northern Virginia. President Jefferson Davis himself had declared the offensive the beginning of a final victory for the Confederacy. Randall Gibson was pleased to be moving forward again. After so much bitter defeat in Georgia, after half his men died in a single charge, 480 in one hour, Gibson described his soldiers as "a defeated army." Perhaps Hood's lofty plans would reverse what seemed an inevitable decline.[12]

At the end of 1864 the Gibsons were all but a defeated family. Randall's brother Hart had just been released after more than a year in captivity. He had lost everything; Union officials confiscated his plantation, Hartland. His main contribution to the war effort had been helping his general escape from the Ohio Penitentiary in November 1863. Hart's wife had sent him boots with a hollow heel stuffed with cash, funds that allowed John Hunt Morgan to flee south and fight another nine months before being ambushed and shot dead. After a brief, undistinguished career as an artillery lieutenant, Claude Gibson, Hart and Randall's brother, had died in 1863 of consumption, the same disease that had killed their mother. That same year their sister Sarah's husband died after a long illness, leaving her a young widow with three children and vast estates in Union-occupied Kentucky that were worse than worthless—they were expensive, overgrown, and unproductive, and she had no means of supporting her family. McKinley Gibson, a younger brother and Randall's aide-de-camp, was also battling consumption; before invading Tennessee, Randall ordered him back to Mississippi for his health.[13]

Their father, Tobias, home on the family plantations in Terrebonne Parish, Louisiana, was also in crisis. In late 1862 the Union army had occupied southern Louisiana and confiscated almost all his horses and mules, wagons, livestock, and corn. Tobias Gibson noticed an immediate change in his labor force. After failing to take Randall's advice to move the best slaves to Texas for safekeeping, he found "many of the negroes led astray by designing persons, believ[ing] that the plantations & everything on them belong to them, the negroes." "They quit work, go & come when they see fit," Tobias and three neighbors wrote the Union commander. "Negroes in numbers from one plantation to an other at all hours night & day—They travel on the railroad—They congregate in large numbers on deserted plantations—All these things are done against the will & in defiance of the orders of their masters . . . In a word we are in a State of anarchy."[14]

Although the Union army insisted that blacks stay on their plantations and work under contract, the Gibson family plantations on Bayou Black were ruined. Levees broke; the sugar crop failed; caterpillars ate the cotton; and many of Tobias's slaves answered the repeated calls for colored soldiers. "The blacks are getting worse every day & at the end of this year I think they will be intolerable," the old man wrote in 1864. On a broader level, he railed against what he saw as the perversion of "American ideas of liberty" in "this Negro War." Where once he had expressed sympathy for his slaves, now he warned his children that a Union victory would mean one thing above all else: equality with blacks. "As far as I know the white children are to grow up in ignorance or mix in the same cabin with the Negro with the same Yankee Marm for the teacher!" he wrote. "With the prevailing tendency to fanaticism at the North I would not be at all surprised if 'miscegenation' became the fashion as well as the Sentiment of those people."[15]

While his family was suffering, Randall Gibson thrived in the war. As colonel of his Louisiana regiment, he had become not only a technically competent officer but a gallant and beloved warrior, someone his men would name their children after. From the Hornet's Nest at Shiloh to Hell's Half Acre at Murfreesboro, to Perryville and Chickamauga, his regiment came to be regarded as some of the Confederacy's most disciplined and fearless fighters. Gibson developed a taste for "a magnificent battle. The country entirely open. The contending hosts plainly to be seen. The fire of batteries + infantry—the wounded + slain—the charge + retreat—the triumphant Confederate yell—the confusion in the enemy's ranks—the flying Regiments—the riderless horses." Under murderous fire he charged ahead, planted flags in the enemy breastworks, rallied and regrouped, and inspired his men to fight again and again. In early 1864, as he was falling back to defend Atlanta, Gibson was promoted to brigadier general.[16]

For years Randall Gibson had complained about incompetent generals. He had fought under Braxton Bragg, his onetime neighbor in Louisiana sugar country, a spiteful, vainglorious fool. During the defense of Atlanta, Joseph Johnston seemed to know only retreat and defeat. For the Nashville campaign, however, John Bell Hood would command the Army of Tennessee. Gibson had thrilled at the prospect of mounting Hood's offensive strategy. When the army decamped from Florence, Alabama, on November 20, 1864, and headed north for Nashville, Gibson had had no doubt that great victories awaited. As his brother McKinley wrote, the soldiers were veterans, well fed and outfitted for winter, amply supplied with "coffee, whiskey and ordnance and ammunition." By contrast, it was an article of faith that Sherman's March to the Sea would be the ruin of the Union army. "We now look forward to his defeat as certain and his surrender as probable. He is harassed night and day," wrote McKinley Gibson. "The fruits of four long years of terrible war will be lost to the Yankees, and the flags of the Confederates will again wave in triumph over the strongholds of '62. How much we have to be thankful for!"[17]

Marching north for nine days through Columbia to Spring Hill, Tennessee, the Confederate army positioned itself to shatter the Union forces below Nashville. On the night of November 29, General Hood ordered an attack, but the order was never communicated. While the army and its officers slept, thousands of Union troops accomplished a silent evacuation that they could only describe as miraculous. The next day, as if to atone for his army's inertia, Hood ordered a frontal assault on a fortified Union position at Franklin, fifteen miles south of Nashville. After five hours of fighting, the Union forces retreated, but Hood's army could not claim victory. Nearly seven thousand Confederate soldiers were dead or wounded, including fifteen generals and fifty-four regimental commanders. Held in reserve at Franklin, Gibson's brigade marched toward Nashville at nearly full strength, but the rest of the Army of Tennessee was in no position to take the city. Arriving on December 1, they formed a series of trenches and fortifications in a three-mile arc in the hills just south of town and waited for the Union army to attack. After two frozen weeks of isolated skirmishes, the Union army advanced with overwhelming force on December 15. After a day of fighting, the Confederate forces retreated two miles and dug in for another pounding.[18]

Rebel soldiers cut down the trees on Peach Orchard Hill and hauled them about forty feet below the Confederate fortifications, to slow the inevitable enemy attack and keep the charging soldiers under fire for as long as possible. All morning on December 16, Union cannons popped and crackled, and shells pushed through the air. By early afternoon, a Union brigade had begun its advance. They marched across open fields and up the hill, but their strong lines grew ragged and pocked as Confederate cannons took out entire clusters of troops. From the hilltop Gibson's men fired their rifles and in ten minutes killed eighty-three men and wounded hundreds. After the first wave broke and ran, a second began. The Union soldiers marched over the bodies of their comrades, only to be slaughtered themselves. Finally a third wave tried climbing the hill. The closest they got was seventy-five yards. Gibson estimated that that afternoon his men killed two hundred outright and wounded between seven and nine hundred more.[19]

Just to Gibson's right, the Union soldiers came within feet of the Confederate line. The rebels had held their fire, waiting until the enemy was close enough to massacre—a deadly reception reserved for black troops. For two weeks these new Yankee soldiers had been skirmishing with the Confederate pickets, and whenever the rebels saw that their foes were black, they had timed their fire to be lethal. The Twelfth and Thirteenth U.S. Colored Troops were composed of former slaves who had never been under fire before. As they marched up in tight formation, Peach Orchard Hill was eerily silent. When they were close enough to talk to, the Confederate line rose and blasted them. A Confederate officer commented that the Negro soldiers "gallantly dashed" forward "but . . . came only to die." Still, the Union troops kept coming. When their color-bearer was killed, a comrade picked up the regimental flag. When he fell, another man took it. Five times the flag went down, and five times another soldier tried to carry the standard up to the Confederate breastworks. Throughout the bloodbath the Confederates displayed "coolness unexampled." Only when the enemy finally retreated, leaving hundreds of corpses behind and a flag that had been presented to them "by the colored ladies of Murfreesboro," did the rebel soldiers begin screaming for more blood. The sight of black soldiers had inspired "the intensest indignation," wrote one soldier from Arkansas, "express[ing] itself in a way peculiarly ominous and yet quite natural for the 'masters.'" The men wanted to charge down the hill and kill them all. "With great difficulty," their commanding officer wrote, "I prevented my line from pursuing."[20]

During the two-day Battle of Nashville, nearly a third of the Union dead and wounded fell on Peach Orchard Hill. But while the Confederates' right flank was busy fighting off the assaults, Union infantry and cavalry smashed the rest of their line. Thousands of rebels surrendered, while thousands more dropped their guns, abandoned cannons and wagons, and ran south. Finding themselves the rear guard of a shattered army column, just steps ahead of the enemy, Gibson and his men retreated from one skirmish after another, a cold, wet, filthy chaos of killing and being killed. A few miles south, on the banks of the Harpeth River, they were charged by five thousand men and surrounded by Union cavalry but shot their way clear. Three weeks later the rebel army reached Mississippi, staggering and starving and blood-soaked, barefoot, ragged, and freezing, about half its original strength.[21]

After one of the worst Confederate defeats in the war, Randall Gibson and his brigade headed south to Mobile, Alabama, as winter turned to spring, to help defend the city from a massive Union attack. Gibson took command of Spanish Fort, east of the city across Mobile Bay. As Union forces twenty thousand strong closed in, Gibson ordered his three thousand soldiers and several hundred black conscripts to dig trenches as quickly as they could—with few spades, picks, and axes at hand, they used any tool they could find. For two weeks they endured constant bombardment. Every day the Union lines neared. By nightfall on April 8, the enemy was beginning to breach Gibson's defenses, and Gibson's scouts reported the situation as hopeless. Without knowing it, the invading army had advanced behind their lines; in the morning they would realize their position and attack. Before they could, Gibson and his men escaped in the dead of night through tall grass and marsh, taking off their shoes and walking slowly so no one would hear them. Although Spanish Fort fell undefended, Gibson could describe the escape as one final victory.[22]

On April 9 Robert E. Lee surrendered to Ulysses Grant at Appomattox. After holding out for another month, the Confederacy's western forces surrendered. General Gibson stood before his men and told them to regret nothing about their "unselfish patriotism" and devotion to what he called the Confederacy's "eventful revolution." As he issued paroles for his men, releasing them to their families, Gibson flatly denied that they had been defeated. Although he urged them to be "law-abiding, peaceable, and industrious" citizens, he did not tell them to forget the previous four years. "Your banners . . . were never lowered save over the bier of a comrade," he said. "You have not surrendered, and will never surrender your self-respect and love of country." Perhaps there were ways to keep fighting, without guns.[23]

Wall: Charleston, 1865–66

T HE SCABBARD FOR O.S.B. Wall's sword bore the words "God Speed the Right," and there were days when they spoke the truth. In late March 1865, before he headed to South Carolina, the people of Oberlin gathered to see him off. A professor from the college addressed the crowd, remembering the day six years earlier when the U.S. government had indicted Wall for his role in the Oberlin-Wellington Rescue. Now the same government was making him a captain in its army, the first regularly commissioned colored captain in the nation's history. The professor presented Wall with the sword—the town's antislavery faithful had raised eighty dollars for the magnificent weapon. Dressed in his officer's uniform, Wall said that he felt humbled by the joy they took in entrusting him with an awesome responsibility. As he looked out at the adoring crowd, black and white, it seemed as if his cause had already triumphed.[24]

Although Wall had been commissioned to help recruit newly freed men for the Union army, he arrived in South Carolina to join the 104th U.S. Colored Troops shortly before the dispatches arrived announcing Lee's surrender. It was a moment of singular joy and emotion—prayer, rejoicing, speeches, music, and fireworks. Many of the officers stationed in Beaufort, South Carolina, headed to Charleston to celebrate. At Fort Sumter the original American flag that had been lowered in the war's first battle exactly four years earlier flew again. "Now for the first time" it was "the black man's as well as the white man's flag," wrote one Union officer. "Let traitors hereafter beware how they rebel against a good government." In Citadel Square in Charleston, thousands of blacks gathered to pray and rejoice on April 15, 1865. Their children marched and sang, "We'll hang Jeff Davis to a sour apple tree."[25]

The victory seemed complete—it was a new day, as inevitable as the rising sun. Word had not reached Charleston that President Lincoln had been assassinated the night before, a devastating reminder that creating a free society would require continuous struggle. With no more recruiting work to do, Wall was detached to the Bureau of Refugees, Freedmen and Abandoned Lands, a new federal agency devoted to integrating former slaves into civil society. His commanding officer, General Rufus Saxton, was a Massachusetts Yankee who earlier in the war had led the effort to give freed slaves in the South Carolina Sea Islands small pieces of land that had been confiscated from Confederates. Wall revered Saxton as "a Christian Patriot," "fearless," "pure hearted," and unfailingly "true to the Negro." With Saxton overseeing affairs relating to freedpeople in South Carolina, Wall felt optimistic that right would prevail.[26]

Based in Charleston, living in a grand home that had been confiscated from a Confederate leader, Wall had the task of convincing freed slaves to work—as salaried employees—for their former masters. The Bureau had begun redistributing thousands of acres of confiscated property to the freedpeople in the summer of 1865, but President Andrew Johnson ordered almost all the land returned to its previous owners, a policy that Wall found dishonorable. Former slaves would not be able to work for themselves as farmers or have any independent source of wealth; they would have to survive as hirelings, dependent on large market forces that determined crop prices, the supply and demand for local labor, and the inclinations of white landowners. All the same, many Northern Republicans, radical abolitionists among them, viewed the ability to enter into employment contracts as the embodiment of freedom. Wall would help free people get "good offers" for work at "fair wages," and when disputes arose on the job, he would keep the peace and "make an adjustment of [the] difficulty between parties." In creating and enforcing new contractual relationships between blacks and whites, Wall was trying to establish a new way for former slaves and masters to relate to each other. His goal was "to do justice to the freedmen" while "do[ing] no injustice to white persons."[27]

In the fall of 1865, Wall was discovering that former slaves took little comfort in their contracts, and that former masters refused to accept that they were now living in a free society. The Union victory, coupled with presidential orders and amnesties that seemed to restore former Confederates to power, made the people Wall called "sympering Rebs" more defiant than ever. "Among nine-tenths of the people . . . there is not Union feeling enough to save their souls from perdition," wrote a Union officer in South Carolina that November. "They are full of the bitterest kind of secession feeling, talk about the d—d nigger, the d—d Yankee, & speak of the Yankee Gov't . . . as if they . . . still belonged to the Confederacy, having no interest or wish in relation to the common good of our country." In December the South Carolina legislature passed a code that forced blacks to make yearlong contracts with white "masters," set the hours of labor from sunup to sundown, forbade workers to leave their plantations, and subjected them to whippings for misconduct. The Union general in charge of the occupation of South Carolina declared the code "null and void," but whites were openly expressing their wish to restore slavery in all but name and were acting accordingly.[28]

What Wall called "the Law of Congress and Policy of the Government" was committed unambiguously to freedom and equality for all, but the Freedmen's Bureau officer learned that changes in the law did not translate neatly into changes in society. Delegations of freedpeople from the interior regularly appeared at Wall's office with stories of lynchings and other suspicious killings, but Wall did not have to leave Charleston to find unfairness, prejudice, and brutality. In Wall's estimation, the city's police were little more than "ex-Rebs" who had "all the hatred they ever had still toward the free negro and the government"; they openly started "rows" and committed "outrages" upon the city's colored people. He spent a morning attending the proceedings in the provost marshal's misdemeanor court, watching helplessly as young blacks were subjected to humiliating punishments for trivial offenses—stripped naked and dragged into the streets "amid the shouts and laughter of the vulgar crowd."[29]

Understaffed and underfunded, Wall relied on private charitable societies such as the American Missionary Association to provide crucial services, such as educating black children, and to pressure Congress to maintain its commitment to the freed men and women of the South. In late November 1865 his wife, Amanda, arrived in Charleston and immediately found herself in a packed classroom teaching dozens of students. Even as the Walls embraced the work of the charitable societies, they felt keenly the casual inequality that pervaded even the most righteous groups. Amanda Wall threw herself into her work and was thrilled by her students' excitement for learning, but the American Missionary Association was paying her less than what they paid other Northern teachers. "I wish to do all the good I can among these poor Freed people," she protested to the head of the association, "but in my circumstance I do not think gratuitous teaching is required of me as to accept less than others get who do precisely the same work."[30]

As 1865 became 1866 Wall watched the promise of freedom and equality fade. Week after week the "commotion & confusion" continued. Blacks complained to him of whites who refused to pay them for honest work. He reluctantly concluded that "whites are not disposed to deal fairly by [freedpeople] but will if forced to." In Washington, however, politicians from the president down seemed indisposed to force white Southerners to do anything. Some of his worst enemies, Wall found, were the "Negro hating union officers (and a majority of them are so)" in the force that was occupying Charleston, men who belittled his authority, battled him for jurisdiction over disputes between whites and blacks, and attempted to take over Freedmen's Bureau buildings, including schools. In January, after white South Carolinians and local army officers had protested for months about Rufus Saxton, Wall's hero was relieved of his Freedmen's Bureau command.[31]

That same month a former slave approached Wall with a depressingly familiar tale. He sold wood to make a living, but recently a white man had taken a load from him without paying. Wall figured out who the man was. Even though the man was rich and well connected, Wall summoned him to appear at the Freedmen's Bureau office, sending an armed guard to deliver the order and escort him back. In front of Wall, the man agreed to pay what he owed and said that he found the settlement fair. But a friend of his, a Philadelphia merchant who had made a fortune supplying boats to the Union navy but was nonetheless a *"rank copperhead,"* complained to the Union army's post commander in Charleston "that it was too bad to have a nigger arrest a gentleman." The commander promptly had Wall arrested.[32]

Sitting in jail for the second time in his life, Wall contemplated the limits of the law. Congress supported his agency and its mission. The Bureau had put him in charge of freedpeople's affairs in Charleston. The law had given him an enormous task. But to the Union army commander, he was a "damned nigger captain," fit only to be snubbed and abused. Appealing to his allies in Washington, Wall vowed to fight on. "We are in Egypt in more senses than one," he wrote, "but we shall still try to do our duty, obeying the orders of our superiors and fearing only God." The law was on Wall's side. But he realized that the freedpeople needed political support, money, and soldiers of their own, and that the Republic would never truly serve them until they had the vote. To serve the righteous cause, Wall needed more than a title and a responsibility, more than the sanction of law. He needed power.[33]

CHAPTER NINE

GIBSON

Mississippi, New Orleans, and New York, 1866–68

Near Vicksburg, February 2, 1866

T HE STEAMER GLIDED THROUGH the cold night, every bend in the river a gentle turn, Louisiana starboard, Mississippi portside, New Orleans just a day ahead. The clean rushing air muffled the churn of engines and smoke. As children, Randall and Hart Gibson had made the journey downriver dozens of times. Though the *W. R. Carter* was one of the newest additions to the Atlantic & Mississippi Steamship fleet, the voyage took the brothers back to more innocent days. It was an island of calm in a troubled world.

The previous May Randall had surrendered his army, relinquished his cause, and fallen in the world. He was no longer a general. Once again he was a failed planter who had studied law. Louisiana was a place of "pinched poverty," its daily life and politics in chaos. "There is no money in the Country," Randall reported to his younger sister Louly, "no sugar, or cotton, or tobacco, or rice—nothing to sell." The Gibsons' plantations were on the brink of failure, flooded from levee breaks and stymied by the transition to free labor. "Most of the negroes have gone off—Father having lost his crops has not the money to hire them," Randall wrote. "We will have enough left I hope to raise corn."[1]

Randall retired to Terrebonne Parish and spent six months depressed and alone, waiting for a pardon from President Johnson and doing little more than thumbing through the books in his father's library—novels, old legal treatises, and the writings of Washington and Jefferson. He declared that "it is a calm, steady persevering patience that is sure to win the fight & carry you through to success in anything," but there were days when it seemed impossible to imagine a future for himself in Terrebonne or anywhere else in the United States. He sent a set of "interrogatories" to M. S. McSwain, asking the former Confederate what life was like for him and the dozens of other Southerners who had moved after the surrender to Paranagua, Brazil, below São Paulo. Although McSwain wrote back extolling cheap lands "that resemble those on Bayou Teche" and saying that sugar grew "larger and much sweeter than Louisiana cane, without any cultivation at all," Gibson remained on his father's settee. He was thirty-three years old, and his life was finished.[2]

When winter came, Randall visited his sisters and brothers in Kentucky. Everyone was in dire financial straits—and his brother McKinley's "hacking cough and hectic flush" suggested "a doomed case of consumption"—but the visit lifted Randall's spirits and "kindled anew my resolutions," he wrote. "It has braced me—for the good fight." Randall and one of his cousins talked about opening a law practice together in New Orleans. And when it was time to return home, Hart, whose lands had been confiscated during the war, agreed to join Randall on the voyage back down to sugar country. They rode to Louisville to buy passage to New Orleans, bringing with them a herd of mules for the plantations.[3]

The journey would take about a week. After a couple of days on the Ohio, the *W. R. Carter* was steaming through the ruins of the Confederacy. On either side of the river, cotton fields were overgrown or flooded. Much of the land that was in cultivation had been confiscated and sold to Northern business interests or, worse, given over to former slaves. Despite the vistas afforded from the decks, the atmosphere on board was cheery. On walks around the boat, at meals, and through hours of reading and leisure, the Gibson brothers found themselves among friends. The passenger list included people they knew from Kentucky and Louisiana, "exceedingly demonstrative" newlyweds, doctors and lawyers and planters, the Confederate brigadier generals Samuel Ferguson and Richard Montgomery Gano, and the wife and three children of the New Orleans physician Tobias Gibson Richardson, named for their father. Everyone was equal, still mourning the loss of friends and sons and brothers, a country and their comfortable place in it. Together they could forget for just a moment the pain and indignity of the previous year. The trip became a floating party, like a weekend gathering on a Kentucky estate before the war.[4]

Days passed "full of gaiety and hope," conversation, and laughter. The ladies on board were "banging away and singing on the Piano—'The sea, the deep sounding sea,' horrible music!" Randall wrote. It had been years since he had experienced such simple joy. "We are a curious people—our Countrypeople!" he mused. "They are just as much at home on this boat as if it belonged to them—not the slightest ceremony is observed and yet great candour and kindness mark their intercourse."[5]

On February 2, as the steamer approached Vicksburg and the ancestral "Gibson neighborhood," Randall could barely sleep. He stayed up until midnight talking with an old friend and then awoke in his stateroom at half past two. Hart was also awake, so they chatted until three. Randall "concluded to make one more effort to sleep," and his brother went outside to smoke. Randall shut his eyes and drifted off. He was returning to Louisiana actually looking forward to the days ahead. "I forecast the future in such cheering colours," he had written Louly from the boat. "I think how energetic and industrious I am going to be, how soon our affairs shall be restored to their wonted prosperity."[6]

Just an hour later Randall was jolted from bed, gasping for air. The doors, windows, and floor planks of his room burst apart in a "tremendous explosion," and the room filled with "scalding steam." The ship's massive boilers had blown, and with "wonderful rapidity," Randall observed, "the flames swallowed up everybody and everything." Suffocating and blind in the "intense smoke and darkness," Randall "made a desperate lunge" to get outside. He could hear nothing but screaming. Two men rushed past him, calling for him to join them as they leaped off the deck. Randall hesitated, and for a moment "a gust of wind blew the steam and smoke aside." To his horror, Randall saw that the men had not jumped overboard—instead they had fallen "into a crater, where many others were vainly struggling, but being rapidly burned to death. They had jumped right on the red-hot boiler." Randall lost his footing but grabbed a rope and swung past what he called the "devouring crater of flames." "I thought the spectacle surpassed any description of Hades I had ever read or seen," he later wrote. "The cries of desperation, of despair . . . were heart-rending." It was worse than what he had seen at Shiloh, Chickamauga, and Spanish Fort.[7]

Just past the crater, a fellow passenger grabbed Randall, yelled, "Is that you, General? God bless you!" and pulled him to the edge of what remained of the ship. With flames at his back, Randall plunged into the Mississippi. In a river "so cold that it burned like fire," pulled by its "irresistible" current, Randall grabbed at a bobbing cotton bale. Although it was four in the morning, the inferno cast a great light that could be seen miles away. Dozens of burning and drowning men and women were shrieking for help, as a deadly barrage of bolts, bars, stovepipes, and planks pierced air and water. Randall saw a half-submerged lifeboat. As he swam toward it, he saw it was holding four scalded men. Randall climbed in, bailed the boat out, and fought the current with a stray plank. Slowly the boat made its way to shore, but it was taking on water. For half an hour Randall paddled as hard as he could, trying to get close enough to the shore that no one would drown when the lifeboat sank. When they finally abandoned the boat, there were roots to grab on to, and people on land soon pulled them to safety.[8]

Soaking wet, dressed only in a flannel nightshirt, Randall watched the *W. R. Carter* burn to the waterline. Everything was gone—clothes, money, watches. He could not find his brother. One instant all had been pleasant, and he could see the path clear to prosperity and happiness. The next, everything was "blown to atoms." "It was like the explosion of a mine, or a stroke of lightning," he thought, "so sudden, so instantaneous, so destructive." There was nothing he could have done—"not by individual effort or agency," he wrote—to stop what had happened or help a single soul. Was he at the mercy of "Providential interposition" or the cold laws of "accident"?[9]

A boat came to shore, carrying people and corpses pulled from the river. Randall climbed on board, looking for Hart among the survivors. Calling his name and asking for help, he was guided to a body among the dead, "wrapped up in a blanket, wholly unconscious and insensible, and in a rigid state." The skin on Hart's hands had been burned off. His feet were bare. Randall knelt by his brother and touched his chest—frozen. If Randall's mind emptied as he felt his loss, he was jolted back by a beat under his hand. And another. Hart lived.[10]

Randall told several men to start rubbing his brother's body, and they covered Hart's feet with hot water bottles. He plied Hart with an all-purpose remedy during the war, brandy and camphor. For an hour Randall knelt over his brother, working, giving orders as if he were still a general. Slowly, he would remember, Hart "came to himself." After feeling utterly powerless, Randall had used his hands—his touch—to bring his brother back from the dead. The two men picked themselves up from the slick wet floor of the boat. They sat side by side as night turned to day.[11]

FROM HIS OFFICE in the business district, where the American Quarter gave way to the French, Randall Lee Gibson could feel the steady push of commerce. New Orleans was ripening into spring, puddled and perspiring, cascading with fronds, flowers, and hanging moss. It was a jungle of merchandise and money and dreams. It swarmed, in one traveler's words, with "merchants, planters, travelers, river-men, army men, (principally Rebels,) manufacturing and jobbing agents, showmen, overseers, idlers, sharpers, gamblers, foreigners, Yankees, Southern men, the well dressed and the prosperous, the rough and the seedy." In Terrebonne Parish, Gibson's father was bemoaning the refusal of his former slaves to work for him as they once had. But in New Orleans people dreamed of inventing new machines—cotton planters and pickers and cane cutters—that would remedy the problem of free labor and bring them untold riches. Streetcars rumbled, and beautiful women promenaded up nearby Canal Street, but Gibson was too busy to take notice.[12]

Just weeks after the *W. R. Carter* explosion, Gibson moved to the city and opened a law office with John Austin, who had commanded a battalion of sharpshooters under Gibson during the war. He advertised his services as a "counselor at law" in the local dailies. One column over, in those same papers, shipping lines promised adventures in New York, Liverpool, Havana, and Le Havre, but Gibson's thoughts did not wander from his new home. He immersed himself in routine contract disputes and debt collection, title searches, insurance matters, and the occasional divorce. Almost immediately after hanging out his shingle, Gibson wrote that he was "overwhelmed—literally overwhelmed with business. I say overwhelmed but you can hardly imagine how little it takes to do this, so slender is my stock of knowledge either of the Law or of practical affairs."[13]

Gibson soon learned that the world of practical affairs seldom fit his idea of how people should act. He had to calm clients who were ready to kill over their legal disputes. One client, describing a man who had defaulted on a debt, wrote Gibson, "I had the utmost difficulty for many days in restraining myself from publicly horse-whipping him . . . I have denounced him very liberally and selected for that purpose the ears of those who I hoped would convey my words to him. In fact [I] have asked persons to tell him that I habitually denounced him as a Thief and Swindler. Which he is." Another client, whose title to a plantation, Gibson assured him, was "beyond dispute," was shot point-blank by a neighbor with a rival claim.[14]

In postwar New Orleans very little hinged on what was right or gentlemanly. Gibson continually encountered people who, despite the politest of protestations, would "never pay a cent [they] can avoid" and thought that "any act not indictable at Law cannot be wrong or dishonorable." Morality foundered in the murky currents of material struggle. A Nashville lawyer contacted Gibson on behalf of an Irish woman whose husband had moved to New Orleans, prospered in business, and married another woman without a divorce; the request for Gibson's services did not involve initiating bigamy charges. Rather, the lawyer explained, "we only want money out of him + don't care to interfere with him in any other way."[15]

Despite the unseemly reality of practical affairs, Gibson found the law to be a "very pleasant occupation." It gave him a living, albeit "not one that holds out very large pecuniary rewards," and after months of depressed isolation, it provided him with colleagues and a community. But more than anything, it offered him a measure of control over the chaos of modern life. The steamboat fire that had nearly killed him and his brother had been the fourth boiler explosion along the Ohio and Mississippi rivers in a single week. Back in sugar country, his father, Tobias, was in "exceedingly low spirits," watching his fields go to ruin and convinced that "history proves that the labor of free negroes can not be made profitable." Gibson knew from hard experience that in the scramble of each day, no one could be certain if he would find life or death, fortune or want.[16]

Beset by disaster and uncertainty, people outside the profession looked to the law for guidance and answers. The legislature, composed largely of former rebels including Tobias Gibson, enacted a series of measures that forced blacks into labor contracts and restricted their ability to quit their jobs. In a society without slavery, the law would be the master. Its new assertive place in people's lives extended to accidents. "Would it not be well to enact a law . . . compelling that the strength and thickness of the boilers be increased, or the maximum pressure of steam reduced?" asked one newspaper after the *W. R. Carter* sank. "Let Congress prescribe safeguards for the future."[17]

Attorneys and judges, by contrast, took comfort in the elaborate internal logic of the law, even when it offered little relief to accident victims, debtors, and others suffering in a calamitous new world. Legal reasoning tethered the ambiguities of the present to the confident wisdom of the past. It could reduce a gory steamboat catastrophe to a technical question about what risks the victims had assumed by buying tickets for the voyage or to a tidy argument about the meaning of a certain clause in an insurance policy. The fact that damages were unavailable to many accident victims somehow became less distressing when given the Latin label *damnum absque injuria*, a wrong without a remedy, a category of cases that treatises assured their readers had always existed, and for good reason. Gibson relished the "solemnity of the Law" and the role of lawyers in filtering the violence of modern life and business through elaborate procedures and forms of argument, notaries and judges and juries. It was an alchemy that turned pain into pleadings, rage into writs, transforming what he called the "rubbish of facts" into something cleaner, morally neutral, guided by principle, natural and right. "I had no idea I should like the profession so much," he wrote a cousin. "I become as much interested in the application of a principle of law—the tracing out [of] some single point . . . across other + apparently conflicting principles—until I find safe ground to base it on."[18]

Gibson soon landed large insurance companies as steady clients. Although all the Gibson plantations were heavily mortgaged and debt was smothering his family—and although he had lived through the devastation of an industrial accident—he was making his living foreclosing on mortgaged properties and defending the denials of insurance claims arising from fires. The neat formality of the law, its position of safe, abstract remove from the real world, not only enabled Gibson to represent his clients well; it also gave him deep satisfaction. "I am charmed with the profession," he wrote.[19]

What Gibson called the "arduous and responsible labors of the Bar"—poring over treatises and Louisiana Civil Code provisions, composing stern letters and meeting face-to-face with opposing counsel, drafting pleadings and arguing in court—took the novice lawyer back to better days. "I enjoy this really more than anything I ever experienced since the days of debating societies," he wrote. When he was giving orations at Yale, Gibson had been part of a national aristocracy. Although a newspaper punned that as a lawyer he "now begins life *de novo*," no longer a gentleman of leisure with a "princely estate," practicing law opened Gibson's eyes to the fact that the fall of the Confederacy had not cost him his status. When he started advertising his services, the dailies announced that Gibson was "an able member of the profession, well versed in the principles of law, and assiduous in his devotion to the interests of his clients." "There is no Louisianian who served in the army of the West but will mention his name with pride and respect," trumpeted the *Daily Crescent.* "We have no doubt [he] will soon rank among the first members of the Louisiana bar." To friend and foe alike, he was "General Gibson."[20]

The continued respect that Gibson commanded was not merely symbolic. Tens of thousands of rebel veterans had flocked to New Orleans and, Gibson wrote, "have from the highest to the lowest, cast their fortunes for better or worse, with the City." That world still organized itself by its wartime memories and allegiances and even by unit. On occasion they rearmed for what were essentially military operations. When Louisiana's governor broke with the legislature and attempted to convene a constitutional convention in July 1866 to disenfranchise former Confederates, armed veterans wearing white handkerchiefs around their necks rampaged through the streets of New Orleans for hours, breaking up the convention and murdering hundreds of blacks.[21]

Although Gibson did not participate in the massacre, many of the rioters had been his men, and his fortunes were intertwined with theirs. He described the former Confederates as "an element of strength to the City," and they made him a public man, revered for his past and respected in the present. As a lawyer, he represented the creditors who cast a continuous pall over the efforts of Southern whites to rebuild their lives. Yet the onetime rebels looked to Gibson to protect their position in the world and lead them back to a better place. A few months after opening his law practice, he was elected president of the Benevolent Association of Gibson's Brigade, charged with "relieving the wants of our needy and destitute, and to preserve sacred and inviolate the last resting places of those who fell, as only brave men die, with the flag of their country floating over them, with their faces to the foe, and paid the price of their devotion with their lives." As their former general, Gibson embodied a time that had promised security, prosperity, and control. He might still lead his people to safety, as he had done at Spanish Fort.[22]

Settling into life in New Orleans meant regularly memorializing the South's glory days, but Gibson's thoughts began to radiate outward, beyond the South, to places and people he had not seen since his youth. After years of convincing himself that he disliked the North and its people, he discovered that not even four years of bloody fighting could come between old friends. "I have watched you through the War, so far as I could through the newspapers," wrote one college classmate in New York, "with anxious good wishes, +, personally, unabashed friendship, though differing totally from you—of course—in political matters." In Gibson's abandonment of the plantation to pursue his new career, his Yankee friends saw a frank acknowledgment of defeat and an earnest attempt to rejoin their world, all on terms that they could understand. "I trust you will be greatly successful in your new path," his classmate wrote, "+ that the rewards of a noble professional career will be in the end an ample compensation for all you have lost by the war."[23]

New York, July 1868

I N THE BEST OF times New York was crowded, but at the start of July 1868 the city was bursting. The streets—the entire city, even—were, in one newspaper's words, a "living mass of seething and sweltering humanity." To join the plodding mob of straw hats and bonnets, waistcoats and full skirts, was to experience immersion, even drowning. It was almost impossible to walk. Going a few blocks uptown on Broadway was more like drifting in a current.[24]

Along with ten thousand weekly arrivals from Europe, New York was packed with country folk there to watch the Fourth of July fireworks, as well as fifty thousand visitors, "refreshed with mighty rivers of lager-beer," attending a German cultural celebration and shooting match, the Schützenfest. On top of everything was a gathering taking place just east of Union Square. At Fourteenth Street the crowd encountered a coterie of police, "as plenty as blackberries." Spanning the street behind them was a fifty-foot archway made of pine branches. It was anchored with American flag bunting to a grand building on the north side of Fourteenth, the tallest on the block, its heavy Italianate cornice crowned with a statue of a proud Indian sachem and the words "Tammany Society."[25]

While the headquarters of New York's fabled Democratic political machine would later appear as if it "lurked, menacing, in dingy red brick," the building gleamed in July 1868. Thousands of people were gathered around, some pausing to admire it, others thinking only of the business taking place inside. The new Tammany Hall—the "Wigwam," as it was known to the party faithful—had opened just in time to host the National Convention of the Democratic Party.[26]

The cavernous hall inside was a riotous drape of red, white, and blue. Behind the stage was a large bust of George Washington and a banner proclaiming "Pro Patria." The wall around it was decked with oil paintings of the seals of the thirty-seven states. The seal of Utah Territory was also included by mistake, prompting one newspaper to write that the Democrats had been "so long exiled from control of the National Government that they have forgotten exactly what communities constitute the several

States of the Union." Enormous bronze statues flanked the stage, Roman gods holding gaslit candelabras, an unwitting symbol of old ideas in a new era. "Will the new edifice be the symbol of a wholly reconstructed Democracy," asked *Harper's Weekly*, "or will the old Tammany organization and the old Democratic party there die together?"[27]

Tammany Hall was filled to capacity, five thousand men. As the convention went through twenty-one ballots to nominate its presidential candidate, it was nearly impossible to hear the speakers on the dais. When Susan B. Anthony took the stage on the first day, her appeal for women's suffrage was lost in a roar of laughter and jeers. Nominating their first presidential candidate since the war's end, the Democrats were a motley assembly—Easterners and Westerners and Southerners, reformers and big-city bosses, Copperheads who had opposed the war and War Democrats who had toed Lincoln's line, advocates for financial interests who favored repaying government bonds with hard money and "greenbackers" who sought to aid farmers and other debtors by printing paper money to inflate the currency. In the upstairs gallery, dozens of "seasoned Wigwam shouters" and Tammany hacks were cheering for the machine's favored candidates.[28]

Amid the noise, press of people, and soggy heat, Randall Lee Gibson was experiencing what felt more like an intimate family reunion or gathering of veterans than a political convention. Inside Tammany Hall the Kentucky and Louisiana delegates were seated next to each other on long wooden benches. Randall, who was representing the Louisiana Democratic Party that he had helped organize earlier in the year, could walk over and shake his brother's hand—Hart, now serving in the Kentucky House of Representatives, was a delegate, as was their cousin William Preston. The Louisiana and Kentucky contingents, along with associated "camp-followers, political bummers, skirmishers, alternates and 'guards,'" were staying down Broadway at the New York Hotel, a meeting place during the war for Confederate spies. Randall and Hart were joined there by their cousins Billy Breckinridge, a Kentucky lawyer, and William Preston Johnston, a Yale classmate and dear friend of Randall's who was teaching history and English literature at Washington College in Lexington, Virginia. Everywhere they went, they saw old friends and comrades—"everybody I know almost," Johnston marveled in a letter home to his wife. "I might have traveled a month without meeting so many people of use to me." Many of the people they saw had been Confederate generals, among them Nathan Bedford Forrest, still notorious for massacring black Union soldiers at the 1864 Battle of Fort Pillow and just elected the first grand dragon of the Ku Klux Klan; Wade Hampton, now leading South Carolina's Democratic Party; Jefferson Davis's nephew Joe, practicing law in Mississippi; Alfred Colquitt, a lawyer in Georgia; and Simon Bolivar Buckner, preparing to return to Kentucky after exile in New Orleans.[29]

Although Johnston wrote that "everybody is very hot about politics," Gibson was uncharacteristically at ease. He entertained little hope that the party of secession would win the first presidential election after the war. "I do not believe it makes much difference whether the South be represented or not," he wrote. "The moral effect will be wholesome but I fear inadequate to beneficial purposes." Nor was he much encouraged by the Senate's recent acquittal of President Johnson on impeachment charges, or for that matter the amnesty proclamation that the president had timed for the convention's first day, clearing every high-ranking Confederate official except Jefferson Davis. Such measures did little to change everyday circumstances in Louisiana: crop failures, economic ruin, and, worst of all, "the installation of the Negro in power *over* the white Race," which Gibson believed would "lead ultimately and inevitably, to the banishment and destruction of the White Race or a war of Races."[30]

INSTEAD OF WORRYING ABOUT bleak days ahead, Gibson enjoyed the company of his friends and comrades. Just seeing them was pleasure enough, but the gathering was even sweeter for being in New York. While Republican newspapers huffed at the attendance of former rebels who, "until now, have not ventured to show their once familiar faces" in the North, Randall Lee Gibson had spent a good deal of the previous year in the city. With his law practice on solid footing, he had allowed himself to do something that he could not before the war—fall in love. In January 1868 he married Mary Montgomery, the daughter of a New Orleans belle and a New England–born banker who had taken fortune and family north before 1860. Gibson had cousins living near the Montgomerys in New York.

Mary was twenty-two, "rather small—nearer a blonde than a brunette," a "very ardent Catholic," just home from years of schooling in Europe. She could speak fluently with her family's French and German maids. Risking a display of "overweening vanity," Randall wrote a cousin that she was "in every way I think entirely too good for me."[31]

Walking to the convention, Randall could look up Fifth Avenue, knowing that ten blocks away, at Madison Square, his wife's family owned a large lot. A couple of miles farther north, Mary was staying with her mother at the Montgomerys' hilltop mansion in Westchester County, High Bridge, where she could gaze across the Harlem River at Manhattan's northern heights. Marrying into New York money meant immediate financial security for Randall as well as considerable amounts of future legal work—he found himself managing the estate of his father-in-law, who had died three months before the wedding. The Montgomerys' support for the Union during the war gave Randall no pause. Mary had idyllic memories of her childhood in New Orleans and was eager to move there and assume the duties of a society hostess. Their marriage did not force Randall to rethink any of his beliefs about the future course of the South and the nation. At the same time their union of North and South carried a symbolic power that was not lost on their friends. "She rendered him inestimable service," a cousin would remember, "in the exceedingly difficult undertaking . . . to knit anew the social ties, public confidence, and personal relations that had been severed by civil war."[32]

For the rebel veterans who had gathered for the convention, the sectional reunion embodied by Randall and Mary Gibson was accompanied by an "exultant" and unapologetic refusal to compromise on Reconstruction. As Fourth of July fireworks flashed over New York like a bombardment that they had never managed to wage, Southern delegates continued to believe that secession had been legal and constitutional and that the United States was a republic of independent states and "not a consolidation of the whole people into a nation." Any preconditions to readmitting Southern states to the Union were illegal, and extending the vote to blacks endangered the nation and the purity of the white race. While they may have realized that they were nominating onetime New York governor Horatio Seymour for the privilege of losing to Ulysses S. Grant in the

November election, the Southern delegates insisted on shaping a party platform that demanded immediate restoration of all states to the Union, amnesty for all past political offenses, full power to the states to regulate who could vote, and "the abolition of the Freedmen's Bureau and all political instrumentalities designed to secure negro supremacy."[33]

Southern delegates also secured the vice-presidential nomination of Francis P. Blair, a former Union army officer from Missouri who, days before the convention, had expressed his desire to void the Reconstruction Acts, "compel the army to undo its usurpations at the South, disperse the carpet-bag State governments, [and] allow the white people to reorganize their own governments and elect senators and representatives." Under the cloak of the Democratic Party, it had become acceptable to advocate restoring Confederates to power. "It was a rather wild boast of the rebel leader four years ago that he would water his horses in the Delaware," wrote one of many newspapers that commented on the conspicuous Southern presence at the convention, "but he has more than made good his promise, by sending his men to New York to nominate a President for 1868. It matters not who the Democratic candidate may be, he is the candidate of the rebellion."[34]

After a week of "hurrahing and hat-swinging and standing on benches," the former rebels retreated south. While their vice-presidential candidate gave speeches describing the Reconstruction governments as "semi-barbarous . . . worshippers of fetishes and poligamists" who would "subject the white women to their unbridled lust," Democrats threatened blacks with firing, loss of credit, and eviction if they voted Republican. Throughout the South whites spent the summer organizing Ku Klux Klan and other paramilitary orders, assassinating opponents, rioting through cities like New Orleans, and beating and massacring dozens, even hundreds, of blacks in rural areas.[35]

Randall and Mary remained in New York, avoiding the heat, cholera, yellow fever, and assorted man-made pathologies of the Louisiana summer. Randall had little need to return home—the courts had closed on July 1 and would not reconvene until the first week of November. New York was almost pleasant after nearly 100,000 visitors cleared out. Ambling along Broadway, shaded by the brim of his boater, Gibson could feel a light wind, as if the streets were sighing. It had grown increasingly rare to enjoy a moment of ease and anonymity and pleasant drift. His days were now crowded with business, political, and social obligations. Gibson did not even have time to read for pleasure. "This city life keeps one always on the run," he reflected. "You glance only at everything."[36]

As Gibson slowly walked, a man coming toward him stopped short and blocked his path. Gibson looked dully for a moment at the slight man with a dark full beard and severe part in his wavy hair. The man grabbed Gibson's hand, triggering a glimmer of recognition. It was Andrew Dickson White, one of Gibson's college classmates. More than a decade had passed, he exclaimed, but "Randall looked not a day older" than when they had worked together on the *Yale Literary Magazine* and wandered around Paris's Left Bank after graduation. Just a year before, he had founded Cornell University and was serving as its first president.[37]

White insisted that they dine together. Over lunch he asked if Gibson had come north to attend Yale's commencement, scheduled for the end of the month. "No," Gibson said, "I have not expected to go; there will be hardly anybody there who will care to see me." The response jolted Gibson. "You are just the man they would wish to see," White said.[38]

THE MOMENT GIBSON STEPPED off the train, he knew that the city of his college days was gone. The station no longer resembled a lovely Tuscan villa—after twenty years of hard use, it was well known as "the Black Hole at New Haven." The enormous elms lining the recently paved streets stared down astonished at what they were shading. New Haven was in full throttle, two and a half times bigger than when Gibson had been a Yalie, well on its way to doubling in size yet again. The war had made the city rich, crisscrossed every few minutes by horse trolleys carrying workers to factories, a never-ending industrial parade.[39]

Although some of its buildings were new, Yale remained recognizable, an island of tradition, continuity, and brotherhood. The students, still spending their idle hours sitting on the fence at College and Chapel, could easily have been mistaken for some of Gibson's old chums. As it happened, his graying classmates were wandering the campus, imagining their younger selves. Just two weeks after the Democratic Convention, Gibson faced another assembly of friends. The events could not have been more different. While the Democrats had been singing anthems like the Seymour and Blair campaign song "The White Man's Banner" ("Let, then, all free-born patriots join, with a brave intent / To vindicate our Father's choice 'A white-man's Government'"), Yale's ceremonies began and ended with Mendelssohn's Overture from *A Midsummer Night's Dream*. Instead of tirades about Reconstruction, college seniors delivered orations on "Henry IV of France" and "Civil Service in the United States."[40]

At the alumni dinner one of Gibson's classmates asked if he would give a speech. Surrounded by Northerners, he appeared to one observer "shy and rather overwhelmed." Standing before people he had written off as "the enemy," Gibson "pledg[ed] his best efforts in the future for the union and harmony of the whole country under the old . . . flag." He then echoed his college valedictory address about the responsibilities of a national elite, declaring that "every educated man in the country ought to consider himself a missionary to spread abroad knowledge." To his audience, the former Confederate general seemed to be giving "a strong and earnest Union speech," showing that he was "wholly, and without one cloud or doubt, back in his old and natural connections." The reaction was emotional, the applause enthusiastic.[41]

Gibson never had to explain that he viewed the end of Reconstruction and the continuation of white rule as essential to the "union and harmony of the whole country"—that the "old national flag" should not wave over everyone. Two years of law practice had taught him that any position could be abstracted out to a principle that had universal support. As a Yalie, he had symbolized the Southern aristocracy. Now he embodied the South's gracious reconciliation with the North. "He spoke and spoke like a man," wrote one classmate of Gibson's address. Specifically, Gibson spoke like a Yale man. He was realizing that his classmates had also lost something in the war. Even if they were not facing immediate poverty or black rule, the modern world—cities teeming with immigrants, an economy dominated by corporations and industry, a social scene flooded with new people—posed a future rife with uncertainty. As long as he resembled one of them, Northerners of his class would look to Gibson as a partner in rebuilding the Republic. "His reception," the classmate wrote, "was just what it should be."[42]

CHAPTER TEN

WALL

Washington, D.C., June 14, 1871

O.S.B. WALL DID NOT see the man enter his office. When the outside door to the building opened, the sounds of Seventh Street momentarily intruded—the streetcar groaning its way into the city, the coughs and curses of people choked by summer dust, a dull duet of hoofbeats and creaking wooden carts. Then the rap and drag of crutches slowly approaching. The sound of steady breath. The click of metal on metal. And the blast, deafening in a small space. An acrid wave of burnt powder washed over the room.[1]

Wall recognized the man who was steadying himself and raising the revolver a second time. He had only recently met James Davenport, once an army captain, now a clerk in the Second Auditor's Office at Treasury. The pale Kentuckian had not shot at anyone in seven years, since the day he led a charge into a rebel trench south of Atlanta and lost his leg in the screaming blur. Wall, in all his time in the Union army, had never come under fire. Now he was at war.[2]

Nowhere to hide, Wall palmed an old door hinge that he kept close by and ran straight at his attacker. With a swift slice through the air, he connected full force with Davenport's head, a thump of scalp and skull. A second blast knocked Wall to the floor. Dazed with pain, his shirt starting to soak with blood, he remained conscious as people rushed into the room. He felt the tight grip of strange hands, the heaving lift into the air, and the

late-afternoon sun, warm in June. Up and down Seventh Street, people
were calling out that Justice O.S.B. Wall had been shot.[3]

WHEN WALL FIRST CAME to the District of Columbia in February 1867,
the Capitol was under construction. The White House looked dingy and
gray in the snow. Winter rains had turned the city's thoroughfares into
fields of stinking muck, in some places ten inches deep. Congressmen complained of "the infinite, abominable nuisance of cows, horses, sheep, and
goats, running through all the streets," regularly knocking down trees.
Much of Washington's garbage was simply fed to "hogs in hog pens in
almost every part of the city." According to John Burroughs, a naturalist
who spent his days as a Treasury Department clerk, turkey buzzards circled
overhead by the dozen, "sweeping low over some common or open space
where, perchance, a dead puppy or pig or fowl ha[d] been thrown."[4]

Wall settled on Seventh Street just above the Boundary, which divided
Washington City from the largely rural section of the District known as
the County. Downtown, Seventh Street passed midway between the White
House and the Capitol. Beyond the Boundary street, it stretched to the
Maryland line, skirting the grand wooded estates of Washington's richest
and most powerful people. Down where Wall lived, the army's Campbell
Barracks housed the District's poorest residents, former slaves who were
arriving from Virginia and Maryland by the thousands. On the hill rising
above the barracks was farmland that was soon to become the Howard
University campus.[5]

The five miles of Seventh Street between the Boundary and the Maryland line were virtually impassable. The road was narrow, steep, pocked
with "murder-holes" and gulleys, and bounded on each side by gutters so
deep and wide that they could swallow up horse and wagon. To get into
the city safely, Washington's elite took elaborate detours over to Fourteenth Street. Farmers who lived just on the Maryland side of the border
preferred to ride their crops to market dozens of miles away in Baltimore rather than take their chances with Seventh Street.[6]

The District remained haunted by four years of mass slaughter and the
murder—still recent—of its most famous resident. The site of the crime,

Ford's Theatre, had been turned into a museum, displaying dozens of "wet specimens" of "injuries done to the human body by shot and shell" during the rebellion—"glass cases of broken bones," wrote one observer, "cracked and smashed and bulbous and exfoliated in every form of distortion, as poor mother nature had tried to glue them together and splice them again." Outside, the District's streets were a living museum of the horrors of war, besieged by a spectral army of shattered veterans. Behind countless desks at every government agency, men were trying to last through a day without remembering their hours in hell. Black-clad widows making pension claims filled their own waiting room in the Senate. Throughout the city "raw and ragged" masses of men, women, and children who had fled slavery were starving, freezing, and dying in plain view.[7]

AT O.S.B. WALL'S HOME, the surgeon's examination was like being slowly bayoneted. The pain turned Wall's dimly lit bedroom into an unrecognizable, awful place. Robert Reyburn and Patrick Glennan inspected the small hole on the right side of Wall's stomach, just above the navel, as they had done too often during their days in the Union army. The lead ball had pierced Wall's gut near his liver, gallbladder, and intestines. Sponging off the blood and flushing the wound with water, they plunged a porcelain-tipped wand into Wall's abdominal cavity. If the probe so much as touched the lead ball, a black mark would stain the white porcelain tip. After a seeming eternity, they pulled it out. Nothing. There would be far worse agonies to come.[8]

Lying in his sickbed, Wall told visitors he had no idea why James Davenport had tried to kill him. Weeks ago a woman named Wright had come to his office complaining that a man had sold her a faulty secondhand stove. Wall visited the man, Davenport, at his desk at Treasury and asked whether he intended to give Wright a refund. Davenport initially said that he would, but then changed his mind. Wall said that he "would have no more to do with the case" and that Wright and Davenport "might fight their own battles." Wall had all but forgotten about Davenport when the man appeared in his doorway, pistol in hand.[9]

There was nothing remarkable about the dispute over the stove or

Wall's role in it. In 1869 President Grant had appointed him the District's first colored justice of the peace, a position that empowered him to hear small claims cases. At the same time, he served as a local police magistrate, the first—and for minor offenders, the only—judicial figure people faced after arrest. For many poor blacks in the District, Wall was the law.

Even before assuming the title of Justice, Wall was used to people seeking his help. It was the reason he had come to the District in the first place. The mud and dust of a half-formed city, the suffering of tens of thousands of its residents—for Wall, these were not causes for despair. The District of Columbia was not simply an unpleasant place to live. It was a problem that needed solving, a project to be finished. So was the Republic itself, just two years after millions of slaves had become citizens through the brutal alchemy of war.

SHORTLY AFTER WALL'S ARRIVAL in the District of Columbia, he rode to Harpers Ferry on behalf of the Freedmen's Bureau. In April 1867 the Potomac River's rumble and roar echoed through the hills, swollen by snowmelt and spring rain. Just sixty miles downstream its bracing current stagnated in the malarial flats of Washington. But on the border separating Maryland from West Virginia, the river gave no hint of the mire ahead. It flowed in a steady rush of progress and escape.

In 1859 John Brown had martyred himself on this spot, attempting to spark a massive slave rebellion by raiding the federal armory at the Ferry; three Oberlin men had died fighting at his side. Eight years later O.S.B. Wall walked into town representing the government that had killed them. The town had been shot up, blasted, and emptied out. The only armory building to survive multiple rebel raids during the war was the one-story brick fire-engine and guard house where Brown had barricaded himself against U.S. Marines commanded by a colonel named Robert E. Lee. Most of Harpers Ferry's three thousand residents before the war had abandoned the place, many to join the rebellion. During the war the Ferry teemed with Union soldiers, guarding this strategic railroad junction and gateway to the Shenandoah Valley. By 1867 the soldiers were gone too. In their place nearly a thousand men, women, and children drifted in from the Shenandoah Valley and the eastern West Virginia panhandle, hoping to find freedom after lives of bondage. Instead, with war's end, what they found was no jobs. Augustus Ferzard Higgs, a twenty-three-year-old army lieutenant working with the Freedmen's Bureau, described the town as a "nest of paupers," a hell of cholera and pox and starving children. Slavery was dead. John Brown's disciples controlled the government. But the fight was not over.[10]

Wall met with Augustus Higgs in April 1867 through his work with the Bureau's District of Columbia office, which had just been given responsibility for West Virginia. In the company of a "few persons here, white and colored, who are most interested in the welfare of the Freedpeople," Wall inspected the wretched conditions. "A very large population of them are either entirely idle, or get only partial employment," he wrote. "There are quite a number of families who are so very degraded they take no interest in the education of their own children."[11]

The night after his arrival hundreds crowded the schoolhouse to hear Wall speak. Responding to the squalid destitution of the freedpeople, Lieutenant Higgs had written that "nothing but a revolution or something similar will change this state of affairs." Looking out at faces flickering with the lantern light, Wall claimed to offer that "something similar": new homes and jobs in the West, with transportation provided by the government. No more cholera, no more hunger, no more idle want, no more fear of violence. Afterward, people emerged from the shadows to give him their names, and he set up another session, "as the entire meeting desired me to talk to them again."[12]

Wall had left the comforts of Oberlin to devote himself to the cause of integrating newly freed men and women into American life. It was the cause of his country and his race. The Freedmen's Bureau head, General Oliver Otis Howard, appealed to triumphant abolitionists across the North and West to redirect their holy fervor to perhaps the one task more difficult than destroying slavery: building a new world from its ashes. Wall's brother-in-law John Mercer Langston, appointed a general inspector in the Bureau, was traveling throughout the South, "arousing, inspiring and encouraging the free people" to educate themselves, save money, build "comfortable necessary homes," and participate constructively in public life so that "they may win the respect and gain the confidence even of those who formerly held them in bondage."[13]

Langston's speeches stressed that with slavery's demise the Constitution guaranteed "our people their rights and privileges" without "any complexional discrimination," but Wall had seen in South Carolina that the bare language of the Constitution was not enough to establish freedom and equality. Citizenship was not simply a function of education, savings, and civic involvement. If anything, Negro gains only strengthened white hatred, a hatred that overwhelmed any obligation to obey mere words on paper. In Wall's experience, the law was neither the Constitution nor the legislature's enactments. It was how people lived every day. Without a grounding in base political authority—without the moral force or brute leverage to make people follow a rule until they believed in it—not even the most soul-stirring appeals to basic American values would stop whites in the South from enslaving blacks in one way or another.[14]

Wall held out little hope that white Southerners would learn to see their erstwhile property as people. Instead he joined the Freedmen's Bureau District of Columbia field office as an employment agent. If the situation in Harpers Ferry was bad, it was immeasurably worse downriver. Some thirty thousand blacks in the District were jobless and destitute, more slave than citizen. They still bore the designation given them by the Army when they fled to the Union lines as fugitive property: "contrabands." One of the first freedoms that former slaves had asserted was the freedom to move off the plantation and away from their masters. It was why Washington was overflowing with new residents, why entire areas of the city were, in one newspaper's words, more "characteristic of Senegambia than of the United States." But with few job prospects awaiting them, the migrants' freedom to move seemed to lead inexorably to slums, starvation, crime, and disease. Across the South Bureau officials were pressuring people to return to their plantations and go back to living, in everything but name, as slaves.[15]

Wall's mission was different. He knew firsthand that geographic mobility could lead to social betterment. Had his father not sent him to Ohio, he would never have become a respected war veteran and government official—he would be just another anonymous Negro in North Carolina whom Freedmen's Bureau field agents discussed in their reports to headquarters. As long as the migrants had a destination, however, their freedom to move could become a solution for the nation, not a problem. Wall would find the freedpeople work in the North. Where there were good jobs, blacks could become part of the free economy, without having to fight sworn enemies every step of the way. Educating their children would not seem like a revolutionary act. They could acquire property, the key to full citizenship. By lining up positions in advance, Wall hoped to disrupt the concentrated poverty that made life in the District miserable for so many and gave ammunition to the enemies of civil rights. He was trying to create a pathway from freedom to equality.

Wall arrived in Washington with a captain's commission and a reputation for abolitionist heroics, due to his role in the Oberlin-Wellington Rescue. He was part of an instant elite. He had friends and family nearby and in positions of power. A short walk up Seventh Street from his home stood the newly created university for Negroes. Although Wall had never sought higher education, he felt a strong connection to Howard. Not only had its namesake, General Howard, appointed Wall to the Freedmen's Bureau, but the general had also asked him to find some "capable young men" in Oberlin to enroll at Howard. Wall recruited all three members of the first graduating class, including James Monroe Gregory, the valedictorian who was then hired to teach Latin and mathematics.[16]

Saddled atop a horse named Splint, Wall trotted down city streets eye to eye with the District's wealthiest denizens. On Sundays he prayed at the First Congregational Church, the moral heart of Reconstruction, alongside Chief Justice Salmon Chase, Senator Samuel Pomeroy, and General Howard. Before Divine Worship, Wall attended the church's Sabbath School, thoroughly integrated thanks to his efforts to attract numerous "esteemed young colored ladies" and men, where teachers were known to "tell a negro that the chair at the White House was not too good for him to sit in." When the minister balked at Wall's application for membership, General Howard and much of the congregation sided with Wall, and the minister resigned.[17]

Despite his elite connections, black and white, Wall spent most of his time among Washington's poorest people. In vast army barracks given over to former slaves, he heard complaints about their living conditions and treatment and passed them along to his boss, the assistant commissioner for the Washington field office. He opened his home to the freedpeople. His wife, Amanda, taught a class of twenty freedpeople there several days a week.[18]

Initially, though, Wall spent his time offering them a way out. He spoke generally of the advantages of moving north and west. He also tried to fill specific openings that people sent him in response to reports that he was seeking "good employment" and "fair contracts" for former slaves. From Oberlin, Sandusky, and elsewhere in Ohio, people were asking Wall to provide "a woman of good moral character," "two men & two women that are *married* & *steady*," "a *reliable* man that will work diligently when I am not with him," "a good washer and ironer," "a good intelligent mulatto boy," "a good strong & willing farm laborer." "I want *honest steady reliable* men & women, and I will do well by them," wrote a probate judge in Toledo seeking help for his farm and orchard. "They shall have the same wages I pay other hands." Wall negotiated pay, recruited people for the jobs, and organized their transportation north and west. A new nation would spring not from the words of the Constitution but from the terms of a contract.[19]

THE SURGEONS WERE CONFERRING, shadows in the dim light of Wall's bedroom. One had the trace of a Scottish accent, the other Irish. Both had moved to the United States as boys before the war. Immediately they had become Americans and, over time, men of consequence. Both had worked with Wall in the Freedmen's Bureau, and they continued to serve the cause of liberty at the Freedmen's Hospital nearby.[20]

The days since Wall was shot had been all fits and starts, black sleep and burning consciousness, whispered prayers, and blood-soaked gauze. The lead ball remained unyielding inside him, posing a grave threat of infection. Newspapers as far away as San Francisco were reporting Justice Wall's condition—small solace for a suffering man.

His doctors stopped talking, approached, and told Wall that he would die. It was a quick pronouncement, barely enough for one sentence in the newspaper: "The physicians have notified the colored justice, shot the other day by Davenport, that he is not likely to recover." A death sentence. Wall was forty-six years old. He had a grieving wife. Their two sons, Edward and Stephen, were schoolboys, just beginning to see the world as men. The girls, Sallie and Bel, were still so young. He had traveled vast distances, from Rockingham to Oberlin to the national capital. He had moved from slavery to freedom, helped others do the same, and then recruited an army to liberate those left behind. He returned to the South a leader of men. He was still fighting the great struggle. There was so much more to do.[21]

TWO YEARS EARLIER, on a Friday afternoon in September 1869, half a dozen boys stood scuffed and silent before O.S.B. Wall. In his makeshift hearing room, the police magistrate listened as the arresting officers cataloged the boys' crimes. Their afternoon had started innocently enough: a baseball game in a field off Boundary Street, shadows long and lean in the low autumn sun. In an instant the game dissolved when a wild fox ran across the field. They chased the animal "helter-skelter, pell-mell" along the northern limit of Washington City, once just farm and wilderness but increasingly the heart of colored life in the District. The Freedmen's Hospital was straight ahead. Howard University's main building was up the hill a few blocks away.[22]

The fox had a head start, but it was sure to be cornered and trapped—something else for the boys' bat to hit. Almost within reach, it ducked inside an open door. Without breaking stride, the boys piled in after it. Through a restaurant and out to the alley. Into another open door, through another building, back to the street. The boys' laughter phased into gruff shouts, as home and business owners tried to end the chase. Gleeful, out of breath, the boys could barely understand what the adults were saying. But the grip of rough hands and a few words hissed with hate stopped the boys cold, saving the fox from an untimely end. The adults were angry. They were white.[23]

The two groups faced each other, the line between them buckling with every shove. "The whites and the blacks bandied epithets which are not for our columns," reported one newspaper, "and at one time it was thought a serious riot would take place." Within minutes, though, shrill whistles and the dull rap of nightsticks cut through the shouts. Metropolitan police officers broke up the scrum, sent people running with a slap and a glare, and made some arrests for good measure. The precinct house was just around the corner, on Seventh beyond the Boundary. For Wall, their arrival broke the relative calm before the nightly tide of drunks, prostitutes, and confidence men, toughs, knife artists, and desperadoes. After a quick hearing, O.S.B. Wall fined the boys one dollar each.[24]

As police magistrate, Wall was no longer trying to convince the District's freedpeople to move north and west and embrace lives as agricultural laborers. Instead, he was trying to build something right where he lived. In his years with the Freedmen's Bureau, he had never helped more than a few dozen people abandon Washington. Even Hell's Bottom—the teeming slum just steps from Wall's house—seemed preferable to Elyria, Ohio. The freedom to move was not just about getting away from slavery and masters. It was about being able to choose a community.

Perhaps Wall's mission to resettle the freedpeople was doomed from the start. Just days before he joined the Bureau, Congress had passed a law over President Johnson's veto conferring the "elective franchise . . . without distinction of race or color." With full voting rights, colored men could cast ballots in municipal elections in Washington and Georgetown, which were two separately chartered cities in the District. While most of the South was wracked by racial violence and governed by onerous Black Codes, Washington was becoming "an experimental garden for radical plants." If there was any place where blacks could make a better world for themselves, it was Washington.[25]

When the Freedmen's Bureau all but folded in 1869, Wall cast his lot with his adopted city and the new world of politics. Voting in the District had been on his mind long before he moved there. Along with John Mercer and Charles Langston, he had been part of a group that petitioned Congress to make the change. Even in his darkest moment in South Carolina in January 1866, he contemplated the prospect of political power in a city that was being remade by former slaves. At the end of a letter detailing his arrest ordered by Charleston's Union army commander, Wall inserted "Think President Johnson will veto the District colored suffrage bill? I hope not." His wife, Amanda, also believed strongly in the ballot, maintaining, as Susan B. Anthony and others did, that the Constitution guaranteed women full equality as citizens. In 1869 and 1871 Amanda marched with a group of woman suffragists, black and white, who attempted to register to vote in the District of Columbia.[26]

Exercising the right to vote meant making a boisterous and public assertion of power. It would be two decades before the secret ballot was adopted in the United States. Voters cast ballots outdoors in full view of one another, with preprinted tickets and separate boxes for each candidate. On Election Day they marched in parades, shouted their candidates' names to the sky, and bare-knuckled their way through opposing mobs. Even Republican ward meetings were shouting, scuffling affairs, held in otherwise decorous churches and schools. Although blacks made up only a third of Washington's population, they voted in numbers nearly equal to whites. In 1868 blacks had succeeded in electing mayor Sayles Jenks Bowen, a Republican so radical that the Democrat he replaced refused to give him the keys to the office. When his predecessor refused to use local taxes to fund colored schools, Bowen had paid the expenses out of his private fortune.[27]

Once asked what his politics were, Wall responded, "I suppose I am a republican, to the best of my knowledge." It was an understatement. He was a committed Republican and, thanks to his brother-in-law, a connected one. Upon his election, Mayor Bowen appointed him police magistrate for the second precinct.[28]

With a world of patronage opening up to capable colored men, Wall had his pick of jobs. But he sought out legal positions, committed to the idea that the law would provide a pathway to equality. In 1870 he started attending night classes at the newly formed Howard University Law Department. John Mercer Langston was the dean. His professor, the aptly named Albert Gallatin Riddle, proclaimed to the class, "I shall not attempt to give you a definition of law . . . [T]he law does not claim to be an actual science, and you will be at liberty to discover or invent a definition of your own." While Riddle described the law as "at once a despot and an embodied democracy," an institution that "does not know that there can be advantage on the side of wealth, or that high position can exist," Wall knew

better. In Ohio before the war, he had seen how legislatures that were corrupted by slavery made unjust rules. In Charleston he had learned that
even when well-intentioned people had the law on their side, they could
accomplish little without the brute strength of a like-minded army, police
force, or electorate. The law required skill within the courtroom; Riddle
urged Howard's law students to "surpass" their "white competitors" because "the world has already decided that a colored man who is no better
than a white man is nobody at all." But the law would be a useful tool for
colored Americans only when accompanied by political activism, organizing, and ultimately power.[29]

Inside the station house, a short walk from home, Wall embodied
Negro equality. He also saw firsthand, every day, how fragile it was. The
prisoners were young and old, male and female, charged with all manner
of misdeed: rape and attempted rape, disorderly conduct, carrying a concealed weapon, assault with intent to kill, death threats, theft of a child's
bank, stealing a pair of boots, running an unlicensed pushcart, and punch-
ing a man named Bean in the head. Colored Washington was desperately
poor and plagued by crime—facts used constantly to justify disenfran-
chising blacks. Although Washington was spared the Klan terror and the
race rioting that were erupting with troubling frequency across the South,
nearly every moment of contact between blacks and whites—no matter
how trivial—was fraught with the possibility of racial confrontation.[30]

At the dawn of freedom—when no one quite knew whether freedom
would mean equality—the vote sustained the District's blacks. The freedpeople were poor, but their power on Election Day meant a good number
would get city jobs. The all-white police force often treated them as con-
traband, criminals, even savages in need of "rudimentary civilization." But
colored votes meant that the police superintendent, A. C. Richards, was an
ally. When some whites asked for separate lines at polling places, Richards
refused.[31]

Equality ruled the day in Washington. The city council banned racial
discrimination in restaurants, theaters, and other places of public accommodation. Directories for Washington and Georgetown stopped marking
black residents with asterisks or the letter *c*. Congressional bills establishing integrated schools came tantalizingly close to becoming law.[32]

Still, the major order of business for Washington's new government was turning the city into a modern capital. Nearly every street had to be graded and paved, with cobblestones, wood blocks, bituminous coal tar—anything that would cover up the putrid and stinking "mudholes and mantraps" that, in the words of one newspaper, "swarm[ed] in all directions as thick as the leaves of Vallombrosa." The task was almost as massive as building a whole new city. Costs far outstripped any amount of taxes the city could raise. Mayor Bowen's government borrowed heavily and, after two years of shrill accusations of corrupt contracting, was voted out of office.[33]

Under Bowen, the roads were at best rough cobble that destroyed cart-wheels, and in wet weather the mud returned in such quantity that, as Bowen's assistant remembered, "fire apparatus was occasionally obliged to travel on the sidewalk, in responding to alarms." The businessmen who had the most at stake in modernizing the city—men who had invested in paving companies and bought up vast swaths of property in anticipation of rising land values—held private meetings in brownstone homes, "juntos" who agreed that a municipal government was simply not up to the task of financing and completing such a massive public works project. After these businessmen hosted steamboat cruises on the Potomac and "other func-tions where the gustatory proclivities of Congressmen were gratified, ac-companied by the alluring influence of genial companionship," a proposal was introduced in the Senate to dissolve the charters of Washington and Georgetown and create a single national territory. While District residents would be able to elect a lower assembly, the president would appoint the governor and the upper legislative house, as well as a board of health and a board of public works with plenary power to turn Washington into a tolerable city.[34]

Although some worried that the proposed territorial bill would strip away black political power, the measure easily passed Congress in February 1871. President Grant's appointments alleviated most such fears—they were all Republicans and three were colored men, including John Mercer Langston on the board of health. The vice president and "moving spirit" of the board of public works, the real estate developer Alexander Robey Shepherd, had been the mastermind of the territorial reorganization. Now he became known as "Boss Shepherd." In elections that followed, two black candidates were sent to the lower house. The territory's plans for massive construction projects promised thousands of jobs for black laborers. Although the police magistrates were replaced by a centralized police court, Wall landed positions as a tax assessor for the territory and sanitary inspector for the board of health.[35]

On May 15, 1871, the territorial assembly gathered in its new chambers at Metzerott Hall, on Pennsylvania Avenue midway between the Capitol and the White House. Once the site of plays, music recitals, and public séances, the hall was now home to a different kind of theater. As justice of the peace, Wall administered the oath of office to the legislators, ushering in a new era of District government. Following the ceremony, the officials stepped outside, where the territory's fire department, militia, and many Republican clubs were pounding their way up Pennsylvania Avenue— now paved with wood planks—to the White House for President Grant's review.[36]

AFTER THAT INTERMINABLE WEEK in June 1871 when Wall lay dying, he did something remarkable: he lived. "Though he is still in a very critical condition and suffers much from his wound," the *New National Era* reported, "hopes are entertained for his recovery." Another week passed, bringing "high hopes of his recovery from effects of the assassin's bullet." In July, James Davenport was released on bail, "Wall's recovery now being certain." At summer's end the shooting ceased to be news. "Wall is now recovered," reported one paper with evident disappointment, "and the case loses the more tragical interest which attached to it while the life of the victim was in jeopardy."[37]

Wall rose from his deathbed to find the street outside his house unrecognizable. In the scorch of late summer, dozens of men were hacking away at Seventh Street with shovel and pick, widening the road threefold and leveling its steep rises to a grade gentle enough for a horse-railway all the way to Boss Shepherd's estate near the Maryland line. Having excavated mud and rock from the roadbed, laborers erased Seventh Street's notorious ravines, gulleys, and mantraps. In the middle of the road, tons of crushed stone were being slowly rolled and pounded into a foot-thick layer of macadam, while crews graveled the rest of the street and sidewalks. From the Boundary north, Seventh Street was becoming, in the project engineer's words, "a first-class road, a leading, important thoroughfare." Teams of horse carts trucked in tons of rock from a nearby quarry that happened to be owned by Joseph T. H. Hall, the area's delegate in the territorial assembly.[38]

The road crews were day laborers hired from the neighborhoods surrounding Wall's house. Most were colored. Instead of organizing into unions, the crews belonged to local Republican Party clubs. Soon after Wall was back on his feet, his name started circulating as a possible challenger to Hall. The incumbent, Wall said, "was a lover of office; rather restless and fidgety about the matter." One of the timekeepers on the Seventh Street project, a Howard University undergraduate named R. D. Ruffin, had spent the previous several years giving stump speeches in his home state of Virginia in favor of black candidates. Although Ruffin worked every day on Seventh Street, the job did not interfere with his passion for politics—"I had night-time for that," he would remember. He soon decided to devote all his energy and "political influence" to Wall's candidacy for the House of Delegates. For Ruffin, Wall's election would mean that the Seventh Street project's supervisors "would treat the colored laborers as the white laborers were treated, and . . . would treat the colored bosses as the white bosses were treated."[39]

At a meeting in early September, Ruffin spoke out against the incumbent and promptly lost his job. "I shall certainly try to take care of my friends," Joseph Hall scolded Ruffin, "and not of those who are going to oppose me." Two others—one white and one black, foremen in charge of gangs of thirty laborers—were similarly fired for being a "Wall man, and not a Hall man."[40]

Talk of a Wall candidacy rattled not only the incumbent but also the board of public works. Wall supported the board's plans—he said that God Himself, "with His knowledge of the state of things in this old District, . . . was in favor of improving it." But the incumbent was the board's business partner in the street-paving effort. When Wall had an audience with Boss Shepherd to insist that Ruffin be rehired, Shepherd said that the timekeeper would be reinstated as soon as he "repented." Ruffin refused.[41]

Individual members of the board confronted Wall to tell him not to run. Wall was unbothered by what he described as a "little set-to." "I don't think any the less of a man who don't think much of me," he said. "If they knew as much of me as I do, I could not blame them for not voting for me." The board bankrolled Hall's campaign; Wall had no money, just "God and the people with us." The District's governor, Henry Cooke, met with Hall and Wall and suggested that one candidate drop out of the race before the election. As Wall recalled the governor's position, "The only difference with me was, who should withdraw." Every morning leading up to the election, Joseph Hall would walk among the laborers on Seventh Street, alternately offering them money for their votes and threatening to discharge them if they considered voting for Wall.[42]

Campaigning at the Old Soldiers' Home in the fall of 1871, Wall could look out over all of Washington. From the hilltops three miles above downtown, the city appeared serene, almost beautiful. Festooned by autumn foliage, Pennsylvania Avenue looked as if it had always been grand. The Washington Monument—stunted at quarter height for nearly two decades—seemed to kneel before the Potomac and the National Cemetery beyond. The Soldiers' Home itself was at once a monastery and leper colony—a soothing retreat and a place where some wounds never healed. The main dormitory looked like a Norman abbey, and the large gabled cottage in its shadow had served multiple presidents as a summer residence. President Lincoln had found particular solace at the Soldiers' Home during the worst of the rebellion, when the District faced constant threat of attack. Here he reputedly drafted the Emancipation Proclamation.[43]

Wall had not come to the Soldiers' Home to escape or disappear. He stood before its residents asking them to reengage with the world outside and vote for him for the District's House of Delegates in the upcoming November election. Wall was darker than any of the old soldiers—they were all white. He claimed to be uncomfortable making political speeches. But he had complete confidence in his ability to represent the men he faced. Rather than discussing the dominant issue in the election—approval of a massive loan for the District's streets and sewers—the candidate spoke plainly, giving them, in his words, "a little Wall-wise." "I talked about their lives and their loyalty to the Government," he later remembered, and said that he "thought they ought to be properly appreciated." Just as the old soldiers were defined by their service, Wall viewed his commission as a singular distinction in his life. They had fought for the same cause. Wall was still fighting it, and now he bore the scars of battle.[44]

ELECTION DAY DAWNED UNDER gray skies, a damp autumn wind seeping under people's skin. At Fort Slocum, north of Howard University, eighty-two men gathered under the banner of their Republican club— seventy-five colored, seven white, all employed on the Seventh Street road. They had resolved the night before to assemble just after dawn and march together to the polls. They walked behind the club president, the time-keeper who had replaced Ruffin. Approaching the voting station, Hall's men made a "grand rush" and tried to give them their candidate's tickets. To a man, the Fort Slocum club refused. As their president described it, "They only asked for Wall tickets." They lined up, eighty-two strong, and cast their ballots one by one. It was the exact margin of Wall's victory.[45]

CHAPTER ELEVEN

SPENCER

Jordan Gap, Johnson County, Kentucky, 1870s

JORDAN SPENCER ARRANGED HIS hand and studied the other players. They were neither cardsharps nor tenderfoots, just a group of men who had known one another for years and enjoyed a regular game of poker out at the Jordan Gap. A game in the hills—cooled by the night breeze, calmed by a serene wash of stars—would have had little of the tension of a saloon or riverboat. Still, no one was out to get skinned.[1]

Sam Estep owned a farm two miles away on Rockhouse Creek. Tom Baldwin, a blacksmith, had a daughter and grandchildren nearby on Barnett's Creek. Two other players, John Preston and Hiram Strong, had come out from town. Preston ran a hotel on Main Street, where Jordan sometimes worked. Strong was Paintsville's doctor. It was a collection of imposing personalities. Spencer was nearly sixty years old—most of his children had children of their own—but worked as if he were decades younger. Preston came from the county's richest family. And Dr. Strong always made sure that people knew he was there; he had his boots specially crafted to squeak loudly at every step.[2]

Spencer had lived at the Jordan Gap close to twenty-five years. He was now known in the hollows west of Paintsville as "Old Jordan" or "Old Jord"; to outside ears, it sounded more like "Jerd." Despite his age, he still spent long days farming and timbering. If anything, the survival of eleven

Spencer children—seven boys and four girls—to adulthood made the farm the most productive it would ever be. Jordan's oldest were in their thirties and had children of their own. His youngest son, Jasper, was just entering his teens. As they grew, the boys tended the cornfields, hauled logs, and split fence rails. The girls weeded the garden, cooked and canned for the winter, made clothes, and handled the youngest boys and girls. Their aunt, Clarsy Centers, Malinda's sister, had moved from Clay County to spend her last years with the Spencers. For Jordan, it made no sense to slow down and divide the farm. He was single-minded about getting the most out of his land and his labor force. "Spencer was a man who never sent his children to school," remembered a neighbor. "He worked them pretty hard."[3]

The poker players got along, though they well remembered the time they were trying to kill one another. When the war broke out, Dr. Strong rode to his home state of Virginia and joined the Confederate cavalry as a surgeon, and Jordan Spencer's oldest son, George, fought with the rebels in the Ragamuffin Regiment. On the other side, while Sam Estep lasted only a month in the Union army before being discharged, John Preston enlisted as an eighteen-year-old and survived nearly three years of grinding battle as a mounted infantry sergeant in the Kentucky and Virginia hills.[4]

After the war Strong spent a couple of years in self-imposed exile out in Wyoming, but he returned to Paintsville unrepentant, casting a Democratic ballot in the first postwar congressional election even though his voting privileges had not yet been restored. There was peace, but people continued to disagree over politics and refused to forget years of killing and robbery and destruction at the hands of soldiers, irregulars, and criminal marauders. County residents filed more than two dozen lawsuits to recover wartime losses, and the courts ordered local defendants' property sold to satisfy judgments. Paintsville Republicans split from the Southern Methodist Church and organized a Northern congregation two blocks away. For more than twenty years Paintsville's two elementary schools were segregated by wartime allegiance—one for Confederates and Democrats, the other for Unionists and Republicans.[5]

Despite the lingering division, people in Johnson County found ways to move forward. What had once been a unanimously Democratic county now voted two-to-one Republican, and at least some of the former rebels changed their allegiance to Lincoln's party. Many of the local combatants were related to one another, and kinship ties fostered reconciliation. As a Union veteran, John Preston might have found it easier to sit down with a former Confederate because two of his older brothers had joined the rebel army. Veterans of both sides started gathering at Constantine Conley's shoe shop in Paintsville; while Conley, a former Union soldier, awled, stitched, and lasted, the men put aside their differences and swapped stories. They could do the same at Jordan Spencer's poker game.[6]

The poker players looked at the cards they had been dealt. They went around the table in a slow circuit, betting or folding, discarding and drawing, raising the bet, and finally calling. In a game where, according to one nineteenth-century cardsman, "it is a great object to mystify your adversaries," the moment when the men revealed their hands was a reminder that nothing was ever as it seemed. The fellow talking chaff might have little more than a high card, while the quiet man held nothing but spades.[7]

To all appearances, everyday life in Johnson County, Kentucky, was no different from what it had been like a generation earlier. But something had shifted. The war had introduced many of Johnson County's veterans to the world outside, and it had also brought outsiders in. Northern speculators and investors began contemplating the ancient hardwood forests and seemingly inexhaustible deposits of coal in the Kentucky mountains. In 1864 a local businessman took a steamboat to Pittsburgh to tell investors in the Pennsylvania Rock Oil Company about Johnson County springs that bubbled with petroleum. With interest rising in the potential uses of oil as medicine and fuel, speculators and wildcatters from the Pennsylvania oil fields started showing up in Paintsville, forming five stock companies in six months. Veterans tramping through the county on their way home from the war were amazed at the sight of oil derricks along Paint Creek. The way mountaineers thought about themselves, their land, and their place in the world was changing.[8]

With each poker hand, the responsibility of shuffling and dealing would rotate from player to player. It was a practice that began on Mississippi steamboats as a way to eliminate the dealer's advantage, to make it harder to mark cards and deal from the bottom of the deck. There was little such danger in the Jordan Gap, but the players followed the ritual. The dealer held a marker—a button or silver dollar or buckhorn knife, known as the "buck"— that denoted his position of authority. As soon as one hand was over, the buck would be passed to the next hand's dealer.[9]

When it was time to pass the buck to Jordan Spencer—when it was his turn to deal—Dr. Strong looked straight at him and said, "Buck, nigger!"[10]

John Preston was jolted. He had heard Tom Baldwin say that Spencer had once been a slave and had bought his freedom, but Preston had never heard anyone speak so bluntly to Spencer's face. Was Strong cracking a joke—say, punning on the word *buck*, a common slur for a black man? Or in a moment where whiskey was being drunk and money lost, did something more serious slip out of the doctor's mouth?[11]

Johnson County had been spared the wrenching transition from slavery to free labor because there were so few blacks to free. But more families had owned slaves in Kentucky than in any other border state. The state had remained in the Union, so it was not subject to the terms of the Emancipation Proclamation. Even after the South surrendered, there were more than 65,000 slaves in Kentucky, and the state legislature voted against ratifying the Thirteenth, Fourteenth, and Fifteenth Amendments, which ultimately freed Kentucky's slaves and guaranteed them equality and voting rights. As people of color organized and declared themselves, as the Kentucky Colored People's Convention did in 1866, "part and parcel of the great American body politic," Southern whites responded with violence but also with pointed assertions that blacks had no claim to equal rights because of an inferiority carried in the blood.[12]

Immediately after the war, Kentucky's legislature barred interracial marriage, limited the free movement of blacks, forbade their testimony against whites, punished blacks more harshly than whites for the same crimes, and segregated the schools by race. In 1867 the Kentucky Supreme Court declared that such measures were necessary to prevent circumstances that would be "deteriorating to the Caucasian blood." All over the South the boundaries between black and white were shifting and hardening. Before the war slavery had established and supported white privilege. As long as law and violent custom preserved the boundary between master and chattel, privileged whites had had little real need to insist on racial purity; allowing ambiguous people to become white only strengthened the prevailing order. In slavery's absence, however, preserving white privilege seemed to require new, less flexible rules about race and constant, aggressive action to enforce them.[13]

Although Johnson County whites had no reason to organize lynch mobs, gangs of self-described "moderators" and "regulators" were beating, murdering, and otherwise terrorizing blacks across rural Kentucky. In nearby Tennessee the legislature took the logic of racial purity one step further, defining *Negro* to include all people "having any blood of the African race in their veins." In Chattanooga, Richmond, and elsewhere, judges and juries were considering a new set of cases on whether the racially ambiguous clans known as Melungeons were black or white, and courts were delineating drop by drop the amount of blood that made a person white or black. Along Rockhouse Creek, census-takers redefined many of the Spencers' neighbors as mulattoes or Indians.[14]

Hiram Strong's words hovered over the poker table like a storm cloud. They challenged Spencer's status, and if they attained a wider currency, they could undermine his marriage and portend intrusive and damaging attention from the state. A hard man like Spencer could have responded with his fists, a broken bottle, or worse. He could have taken a buckhorn knife to the doctor's racial categories—and his throat. But a good poker player is unfazed by a bad hand, or even a string of them; he does not try to change his luck with desperate play. He works patiently and keeps a calm face even when he wins. Spencer let the cloud pass. If he did not take offense, the comment must have been a joke. He shuffled the cards and dealt out a new hand.[15]

LETCHER DAVIS DID NOT ARRIVE in Johnson County so much as stray there. He reeled through the hills, soaked with whiskey, angry and excitable like a flash flood. He had a runt's build, short and wiry, but he scared people. They were struck by his wildness—no easy feat in hills that were full of hot-tempered, hard-drinking men. At his cabin or off wandering, he was coiled for battle.[16]

Back home in Clay County, Letch Davis had spent much of the 1870s running a "blind tiger"—an illegal saloon—and making his pale face familiar in the criminal court. He collected tippling, assault, gambling, and weapons charges as if he were foraging for roots. At the end of the decade he killed a man in a fight and was charged with murder. Although the charges were eventually dismissed, he left Clay before his victim's family could exact revenge.[17]

If Johnson County had emerged from the war in relative peace, other mountain counties continued to bleed. The war had deprived sheriffs and judges of their monopoly on justice, and private killings spiraled among feuding families, business and political rivals, and criminal gangs. Bushwhackers continued to target their perceived enemies. Returning soldiers on each side were ambushed or assassinated or found themselves settling scores as they had on the battlefield. The decline of farming and the rush to clear-cut and mine the hills fueled the violence.[18]

From the 1860s into the next century, the hillsides cracked with gunplay, as everyday frontier violence crested into waves of revenge killings. There were more killings in Kentucky in 1878 than in all of New England. In Clay County, for instance, rival salt-making families and political opponents, the Whites and the Garrards, repeatedly turned to their shotguns and Winchesters, and by the 1890s they would be engaged in pitched battles that drew national attention. Just north of Clay, on the way to Johnson County, was "Bloody Breathitt," where forces led by a former Union irregular named Captain Bill Strong fought a host of rival families, staged their own courts-martial and executions, waged a gun battle in a county courtroom in 1873, and occupied the courthouse in 1874. Twice in five years the governor had to send in troops to establish order, but the feuding continued for decades.[19]

At some point in the 1870s Davis gave Johnson County locals a glimpse of this darker world. The man he had killed in Clay County would not be his last victim. After settling near Lee City, thirty miles west of Johnson County, he participated in a point-blank shoot-out at a picnic in 1905 and in a separate incident turned his twelve-gauge shotgun on a man at such close range that the victim had to have his leg amputated. Davis's son Letcher Jr. was reputed to have cut a man's throat for looking at his wife. People fled their cabins at his approach.[20]

When Davis reached the hollows west of Paintsville, he was a hundred miles from home, but his wild blue eyes landed on a familiar face. He knew exactly who Jordan Spencer was. Although Davis had been born right when Jordan and Malinda Spencer were leaving Clay County, he grew up just over a hill from the Centers and Freeman families. Davis frequently socialized with them, for good or ill—George Freeman's sons were repeatedly called to testify at Davis's criminal trials. Maybe Davis had heard about Jordan and Malinda while growing up, figured out who they were after talking with them or their neighbors, or recognized Clarsy Centers at the Spencers' cabin. It was even possible that he was staying with the Spencers.[21]

Whatever the connection, Davis spent enough time at Rockhouse Creek to pick a fight with Jordan Spencer. When they "got into a difficulty," Davis could have shot Spencer—he had done worse—but it made little sense to kill a man on his home ground. Far from Clay County, without friends to defend him, testify on his behalf, or vote on a jury to acquit him, Davis might have hanged for the crime, from a gallows or a tree. Instead, Davis started telling people along Rockhouse that their neighbor was a "negro."[22]

For years, Spencer's neighbors had maintained a code of silence, accepting Jordan as white so long as no one ever really had to think about it. Spencer gave them no reason to, always asserting a strong place for himself in the community and creating the circular logic that made it unthinkable that a man with whom whites worked, prayed, drank, and gambled could be black. When Letcher Davis started talking out loud—shouting, even— it seemed that by spreading this forbidden knowledge, he would force a moment of reckoning along Rockhouse Creek.

Men like John Horn, whose farm adjoined Spencer's, heard Letcher Davis out. Horn had spent the Civil War in a blue uniform but was hardly radical. While many Republicans favored voting rights for blacks as well as the ability to make contracts and buy and sell property on an equal footing, almost no one, white or black, would admit to advocating what came to be known as "social equality," which included the right to attend integrated schools or marry across the color line. Horn, who had known Spencer from his first days in Johnson County, was not looking to spend time with black people. "I never fooled around them but little," he would say. "I always had something else to do."[23]

Confronted by Davis, Horn could have rethought his relationship to the Spencers and stopped socializing with, working alongside, and relying on his neighbors. Or he could have decided that he had no problem living with people of color. Instead, Horn simply shook his head and dismissed Spencer's accuser as "a wild, drinking kind of a dissipated man." Horn did not know Davis and had no reason to believe that Davis came from Clay County or even that Davis was indeed his name. Other neighbors followed suit in ignoring the talk about Spencer's blood. Jordan's ancestry stayed his own business, and the Spencers—like everyone else along Rockhouse Creek, whether or not their skin was pale—remained white.[24]

It was more than a convenient fiction. For a generation, the Spencers had lived in the same place. The hollows were filling up with Jordan Spencer's sons, daughters, and grandchildren. If they were suddenly relabeled black, their neighborhood would reveal itself as one that did not guard the line between black and white. And if it were admitted that one family had slipped through, many others had surely walked the same path. Few families would be immune to the kind of talk that Letcher Davis was spreading about Old Jordan. Even as outside demands for segregation and racial purity grew louder, it made little sense to redraw the definition of "white" to exclude dark people. Instead, communities buried the hazy, ambiguous, barely documented past and, in essence, allowed almost everyone who had been living as white to stay white. People could remain secure in their status, safe enough even to give reflexive support to the emerging hard-line politics of race.

With his neighbors standing by him, Spencer had no need to retaliate. And by letting the controversy pass, Spencer helped his community embrace the idea that nothing was amiss. Like a rattlesnake at first frost, Davis disappeared from Rockhouse Creek. The neighbors returned to the everyday struggles, mostly silent, that truly defined their lives.

A WEDDING IN THE MOUNTAINS in the 1870s began with a procession from the groom's family home to the bride's. Two by two, under a new day's sun, the groom's party walked or rode through the hills. They were simply dressed. "If there were any buckles, rings, buttons, or ruffles," went one account, "they were relics of old times." The path might be rugged, the journey slow, through thicket and mud, fording creeks, shrouded by forest, or up steep rises to ridgetops with views for miles. It was a ritual of resolve, a reminder of the struggles of marriage and the countless ways the hills had shaped and would continue to shape the bride's and groom's lives.[25]

When the procession reached its destination, the groom stood with the bride, a teenage girl in a homespun dress, and they exchanged simple vows. Sometimes a preacher solemnized the wedding, but often the couple did without and jumped over a broomstick to signify their union, a custom shared by, among others, blacks across the South. The afternoon and evening passed with what one woman remembered as a "heap o' doin's"— feasting and games and dancing the Virginia reel, horse races through the woods for a whiskey bottle, and groups of young men and women tucking the bride and groom into bed. The next morning, after camping in the fields, the wedding party traveled back to the groom's house for the "infare," a dinner where the entire community turned out to celebrate the marriage. They would gather again soon afterward to raise a cabin for the young couple.[26]

Mountain weddings bore traces of Elizabethan country life, as did the ballads people sang, even the words they spoke. In 1878 Jordan Spencer watched one of his boys marry a girl with a seventeenth-century Scottish name. Alafair Yates was all of fifteen when she decided she liked Jordan Spencer Jr. enough to accept his proposal. In many ways the wedding was typical, two teenagers reciting vows outside a log cabin, surrounded by hills and fields and forest in the early days of autumn. But their union bucked tradition in a crucial way. Alafair and Young Jordan married at his family's home, not hers. Her father did not approve of the union. Perhaps he felt she was too young, or that she deserved more than an illiterate farmer who offered a life of back-breaking labor. He never told his daughter his reasons. But neighbors suspected that Yates did not want his daughter marrying a black man.[27]

Relationships that blurred the color line had once been local matters, subject to whispers and rumors and occasional prosecution by local officials but also to tolerance. After the war, however, the phenomenon became part of a national political struggle and, accordingly, more abstract and dangerous. As the "White Man's Party," the Democrats fixated on interracial sex, or *miscegenation*, a word an anti-Lincoln pamphleteer coined in 1864. Resistance to civil rights for newly freed people expressed itself through a vocabulary of sexual deviancy. The "degeneracy" of black women and the "depravity" of black men required laws separating and ordering the races and excused—even compelled—brutal force to maintain white supremacy. Race-related violence was repeatedly described as retribution for sexual transgressions, necessary to protect the purity of white womanhood. In the decade that followed the war, a black man or woman was lynched somewhere in Kentucky just about every two weeks.[28]

Right at this moment—just as traditions of local toleration confronted the mass politics of racial purity—Jordan and Malinda Spencer's children were reaching marrying age. Old Jordan's neighbors had accepted him at the poker table and stood up to Letcher Davis. Once again, however, they had occasion to classify the Spencers and consider whether they should remain on the white side of the line. Living near and working with the Spencers did not necessarily make it acceptable to marry them.

Although Dick Yates did not want his daughter marrying a Spencer, his objections remained a father's qualms and nothing more. Elsewhere in the South white fathers were threatening to kill or imprison the black men their daughters were marrying. But Dick Yates did not enlist the courts to void the marriage or prosecute Young Jordan, nor did anyone else in the county. Once the couple had exchanged vows, breaking up the union would have been just as damaging to Alafair as to Jordan, rendering her unmarriageable and dependent and potentially exposing her to prosecution too. As long as her husband remained white, she would be a respectable woman. Although lynch mobs constantly invoked the purity of white womanhood, it was also preserved by silence and accommodation.[29]

Other people had less trouble becoming kin to the Spencers. Among Rockhouse Creek families, Spencers married members of the Collins and Ratliff families, who were regarded as dark, but also Esteps and Blantons, who were not. Ben Franklin Spencer married a Hopson girl from John's Creek, several miles south of Paintsville; two members of another John's Creek family, the Seabolts, also married Spencers. When Dick Yates would not accompany his daughter to get the marriage certificate, one of the

Seabolts helped Alafair with the paperwork. Given the choice between what they were hearing about racial purity and what they knew about the Spencers after living with them for a generation, most chose everyday experience over abstract ideas.[30]

Young Jordan and Alafair Spencer settled on Rockhouse, next to John Horn's farm. All his life Jordan had worked his father's fields—no schooling, no rest. Marriage freed him, if only to hire out his labor on other men's farms. Two of Young Jordan's sisters, Minerva and Sylvania, lived nearby with their babies and supported themselves as washerwomen. George, Jackson, and Ben were farmers in their own right, with children who would soon be old enough to push a plow.[31]

Although neighbors provided work and support for the Spencers, no one was more important than family. The Spencers might all gather for Sunday dinners. If one had a particular skill, like shoeing horses, he might shoe the horses of everyone in the extended family. At hog-killing time, when the weather got cold but before the creeks froze, the Spencer men might get together to slaughter and clean dozens of pigs. Family members nursed each other through illness and cooked and cleaned and cared for older nieces and nephews when babies were born. They spent more time talking with family than with anyone else. They spread news and gossip and advice first and foremost among themselves. They joked and dickered and debated and fought. And they came together in times of crisis, natural and man-made.[32]

With the children who remained at home, Old Jordan continued to make his crop. Even the ones who had left the Jordan Gap continued, in a way, to help their father. Their labor had created a working farm, income, and collateral—a basis for forming business ties with neighbors and merchants and claiming Jordan's status as a productive, equal, and white citizen. By marrying, they cemented his status. They gave him a white extended family, in-laws and cousins who had a direct stake in the Spencers' racial classification and would insulate and defend their Spencer kin from outside attack. Jordan and Malinda found their place in the vast tangle of local relations. As their children had children, it became increasingly difficult to distinguish the Spencers from everyone around them.

CHAPTER TWELVE

GIBSON

Washington, D.C., 1878

THE HOUSE WAS A fortress, a three-story brick cube with only the arch of the windows and the bare decoration below the roofline hinting at the "ample and somewhat gorgeous" rooms inside. Edwin Stanton, Lincoln's secretary of war, had built the mansion in fashionable Franklin Square, five blocks from the White House. The president had visited often, usually waiting for Stanton in a carriage outside but occasionally venturing into the library, its high bookcases lined with volumes on military strategy and the laws of war.[1]

In the library on a winter evening, Randall Gibson sat and read by lamp and firelight. His forehead and heavy brow, fringed with a wave of hair, caught most of the light. A thick bristle of walrus whiskers separated his patrician nose from a proud chin, giving way to the barest gray hint of muttonchop. His blue eyes—and the dark rings beneath them—appeared enormous. Whenever Gibson entered the library, it was never far from his mind that this was where "Stanton lived + carried on all his devilment during the war and after." The thought always cheered him up. A bare decade after Stanton had crushed the South with total war and Radical Reconstruction, Gibson was living in his house. His wife hosted elegant suppers in Stanton's dining room. Gibson's daughter and two boys ran up and down the hallways where Lincoln's secretary of war had paced. Federal troops no longer occupied the South. Former rebels had retaken the statehouses and legislatures. Democrats—Southerners, some three dozen of them Confederate generals—once again controlled the House of Representatives. Gibson was serving his second term in Congress. In early 1878 he was contemplating another run for reelection that fall. "Good Confederate likenesses" were now hanging on the walls of Stanton's library, mounted with a keen sense of irony by its new occupant. "When I am seated here," Gibson wrote, "I cannot help but dwell upon the change—for the better."[2]

There was a knock on the door, and Gibson's solitude was interrupted. A man walked in, a reporter for *The Washington Post*. The calming effect of a warm room on a cold night was lost on the reporter. He would remember his mood at that moment as "fluttering through the circumambient atmosphere," jittery in anticipation of the interview to come. Gibson welcomed him inside. The man unfolded a copy of the day's *New York Times* and approached. The lead story on the front page described the College of Cardinals assembling in Rome to select a new pope—a matter not without interest to Gibson, who had embraced his wife's faith. But the reporter directed his eye to the story at the top of the far-left column, entitled "The Louisiana Officials." "Look at this, Mr. Gibson," he said. He shook the paper, in his words, "as a matador might shake a red rag in the face of a bull."[3]

SIX YEARS EARLIER, when Grant won a second term as president, Gibson had despaired that "the day for our redemption is far distant . . . I see no road of escape. I see no power to resist. We are undone." Despite his foreboding the rise of Gibson's South had been remarkable, and Gibson had been instrumental in its triumph. He had arrived in Washington in the fall of 1875 ready to battle "the infernal Republicans, the hostile Party," and help the newly elected Democrats to "get together and agree upon a Southern Policy—+ keep it to ourselves." "It will not do for us to be merely counted as so many votes for this or that Northern aspirant," he wrote. "We must be a power—behind the throne if need be."[4]

While Gibson resolved to "hammer away" at "restor[ing] . . . our power + influence in and on the Government," his blows had a gentle touch.

Almost from the beginning, he relied on a lesson from his college days: a Southerner who could talk to Northerners would never want for influential friends. In Gibson's opinion, the "shallow, puritanical pretentious snob[s]" who dominated Washington "labor[ed] under the prejudice . . . that our culture is local, limited + provincial—+ not catholic nor cosmopolitan." In the Yankee view, the "poor + benighted South" was the antithesis of the North, "the world of thought + culture + modern methods of investiga-tion." As a Yale man, a gentleman, and a professional, Gibson would never fail to confound expectations. Where Northerners were frustrated by re-sistance to their efforts to remake the South, Gibson appeared to be the kind of person who understood their concerns and could be trusted to fulfill their vision for a unified nation.[5]

Gibson's politics embraced a set of formal principles that in the abstract had natural appeal to the other side. While Republicans bristled at reports that white Southerners were unrepentant rebels, Gibson freely expressed relief that "the institution of slavery has been extirpated, root and branch, from the soil of my beloved State," and he did not hesitate to campaign for black votes. "I thank God that to-day every man in my State is as free as I am," Gibson declared, "and that the whole people is in the full enjoyment of equal political rights and privileges." Gibson spent much of his first year in Congress focusing on issues that cut across sectional and party lines: commercial treaties with Hawaii and Brazil, funding for the New Orleans Mint, and the establishment of committees to consider national currency policy. The only reconstruction that seemed to matter to Gibson was the reconstruction of Mississippi River levees. According to one prominent Republican, Gibson staked his turf "on the side of law, order, justice, purity, and honor," consciously invoking Republican rhetoric and values to the point that some Northerners imagined that he would switch political al-legiances if only the Grand Old Party compromised on its Southern policy. When Gibson sought a congressional investigation of the New Orleans customhouse—a hotbed of Republican activism in Louisiana—the measure achieved unanimous consent.[6]

In what passed for social life in official Washington, Gibson and his family found themselves in high demand, even among people he might have regarded as enemies. No matter that their next-door neighbor was the brother of William Tecumseh Sherman—the Gibsons soon befriended the family of John Sherman, the longtime Ohio senator and newly appointed secretary of the treasury, who delighted in Gibson's "character as a man, the purity of his life, [and] the charm of his social intercourse." Well read and well traveled, Gibson could speak thoughtfully about "almost every question of science, ethics, history and politics," yet he did so with a restraint that had his companions hanging on every word. For someone who professed to dislike "puritanical" Northerners, Gibson never said "anything that might not be repeated in the family circle, or that would excite the reproaches of religious men and women." Henry Adams's wife, a Boston Brahmin who sneered at what had become of the "tradition of Southern culture, voices, manners, etc. . . . in these post-bellum days," pronounced Randall and Mary Gibson the worthiest of the Southerners in Washington, "better than any I have seen socially." After dining with them at their house, Marian Adams described the congressman as "a quiet, gentlemanly, attractive man." Visiting dignitaries came away from dinners describing Gibson as one of "the best politicians of the best class anywhere."[7]

Gibson's genial first year in Congress ended with the chaotic election of 1876. The presidential race between Republican Rutherford B. Hayes and Democrat Samuel Tilden was unresolved for months, as the parties threatened a new civil war over disputed returns in Louisiana, South Carolina, and Florida. Although election night vote totals suggested that Tilden had won, Republican-controlled election boards in the three states certified Hayes victories, invalidating returns from counties where overwhelming fraud and violence by white paramilitaries had tainted the vote. In Louisiana and South Carolina, the Republican and Democratic candidates for governor both claimed victory and established rival statehouses. When an independent commission established by Congress gave the election to Hayes on an 8–7 party-line vote, House Democrats threatened to delay the final recording of the Electoral College results beyond the March 4 inauguration.[8]

Ever the strategist, Gibson saw the crisis as an opportunity to secure the withdrawal of federal troops and end Reconstruction in Louisiana. He was closely allied with the state's Democratic claimant for governor,

Francis Tillou Nicholls, a fellow lawyer and Confederate brigadier—one of Gibson's first successes in Congress had been a resolution to restore Nicholls's civil rights. In Nicholls's service, Gibson put his social and political connections to work. Every day Gibson met with prominent Republicans—at their homes, at Gibson's office at the Capitol, and at the Wormley House, a hotel favored by the politically powerful and owned by one of Washington's wealthiest blacks.[9]

Gibson approached Grant's secretary of war, Don Cameron, a Princeton man whom Gibson had known since their college days. Gibson pressed the case for recognizing the Democratic claimant for Louisiana governor, recounting the horrors of a decade of Republican rule in Louisiana. According to one observer at the time, after meeting with Gibson, Cameron became "fully impressed with the conviction that the Nicholls government should prevail in Louisiana." Through Cameron and William Tecumseh Sherman, Gibson gained access to the president on January 2, 1877. It was the first time the two had met since Gibson accompanied a prisoner exchange in Kentucky fifteen years earlier. While Gibson had written then of his visceral disgust for the Yankee officers, now he laughed, reminisced, and spoke easily with the president.[10]

Through Gibson, the Louisiana congressional delegation began channeling any information that it wanted the president to hear. When Grant objected that armed mobs had thrown the Louisiana election, Gibson played his trump card: he assured Grant that the White Leagues were perfectly respectable organizations that counted among their members the president's own relatives. It was the argument that Gibson had perfected in a year of social engagement in Washington. By appearing cultured, thoughtful, and modern—as someone whose company Northerners enjoyed—Gibson was convincing people that Southern whites could be trusted to govern again. Gibson embodied an easy solution to what appeared to be an intractable problem. With Gibson at his side, Grant composed "with the greatest ease" a crucial memorandum denying the Republican claimant for the Louisiana statehouse the protection of federal troops. While initially "morose [and] non-committal" about the election, Grant told Gibson, "I mean to stand by you. I mean to stand by my kinfolk in Louisiana."[11]

Gibson also pushed the kinship of North and South as a theme in his public remarks on the floor of the House of Representatives. "The city of New Orleans is no stranger to New England," Gibson intoned at the height of the crisis. "You can hardly mention a name dear to New England that has not its representative in the great southern metropolis, or within our borders, upon the banks of the Father of Waters." He expressed the hope that the descendants of "Adams and Winthrop and Palfrey and Eustis on the soil of Louisiana, may not plead in vain before an American Congress for simple justice. These are the people you would stigmatize as barbarians!" He urged Congress to aid "the people of property, of intelligence, the law-abiding and Christian elements in society."[12]

Gibson cemented his position by extending the literal kinship of North and South to a figurative kinship of Northern and Southern values. He declared that under Democratic rule in Louisiana "the colored man" would not "be deprived of one jot or tittle of his political rights and privileges." For a secret meeting at Wormley's on February 26, 1877, between Louisiana Democrats and agents for Rutherford B. Hayes, Gibson helped craft a memorandum in which the Nicholls government promised "not to attempt to deprive the colored people of any political or civil right, privilege, or immunity enjoyed by any other class of men," guaranteed equal educational opportunities for blacks, and assured the "promotion of kindly relations between white and black citizens of the State, upon a basis of justice and mutual confidence." Moreover, the Democrats spoke of following the law "rigidly and impartially," with prompt punishment for political violence but without "persecut[ing]" Republicans "for past political conduct." Assured by these and other statements of a formal commitment to equality and the rule of law, Hayes promised a new Southern policy, a withdrawal of federal troops, and recognition of the Nicholls government. The House Democrats, for their part, allowed the electoral vote to be counted.[13]

What exactly "equality" or "rule of law" meant was never spelled out. All the Republicans needed was to hear the words. Just as he had as a lawyer, Gibson had looked beyond the particulars to a set of abstract principles on which everyone could agree. On the floor of the House, the powerful Republican congressman James A. Garfield, who would be elected president in four years, approached Gibson and told him, "On our side of the house we looked coldly on the members on your side . . . but as time passed on . . . we have ascertained at last that you and we are fellow countrymen, that you have the same aspirations, the same interests, the same sentiments in a large measure, on the questions that relate to the government that we ourselves cherish." Garfield had fought Gibson at Shiloh and Chickamauga, but on the fate of Reconstruction, he was handing the Southerner his sword.[14]

Days before the inauguration, Gibson was invited to John Sherman's house next door for supper. Rutherford B. Hayes was sitting at the table, and Sherman and Hayes asked Gibson if he would serve in the new Cabinet. Gibson declined, but he continued to meet with Hayes regularly in the months that followed, establishing a personal relationship of "marked consideration." "The President . . . is extremely friendly," Gibson wrote. "I have been out driving with him on his invitation + went with him to New York + he is very confidential, in part because I have declined + not sought favors." Fewer than two years after arriving in Washington, Gibson was the confidant of two presidents, subtly steering Southern policy, savior of what he called "the White Man's Government" in Louisiana, and touted as a future senator.[15]

UNDER THE REPORTER'S EXPECTANT gaze, Gibson picked up the newspaper and began reading. The article consisted of a long letter written to the *Times* by James Madison Wells. Gibson knew Mad Wells, and Mad Wells knew him. Standing five feet tall with a mane of white hair, Wells was a foul-mouthed, pistol-packing legend of Louisiana politics, either the embodiment of principle and courage or the worst kind of corrupt, opportunistic scalawag. The cotton planter from central Louisiana chaired the state's returning board, which certified election results, and had signed off on Gibson's two congressional victories. As governor at war's end and the start of Reconstruction, Wells had invited erstwhile Confederates back into power and worked with Gibson's father, Tobias, on efforts to finance levee construction—only to declare Radical allegiances and advocate for ratifying the Fourteenth Amendment, giving blacks the vote, and stripping the franchise from former rebels. In 1876 Wells and the returning board gained national notoriety—death threats, congressional investigations, and widespread accusations of fraud and bribery—for certifying the presidential and gubernatorial elections for the Republicans.[16]

When the Democrats finally took the Louisiana statehouse after months of standoff, they indicted Wells and the rest of the board on charges of perjury, forgery, and altering elections returns. In early February 1878 the first board member to face trial was convicted. When Republicans in Congress howled that prosecuting the returning board constituted "the greatest outrage that has ever occurred in American political history," Gibson took to the House floor on February 14 and defended the case as a commendable example of the new regime's "rigid enforcement and execution of the laws." With cool contempt for the opposition, Gibson declared that "men accused of offenses of an extraordinary character should . . . be held amenable to justice."[17]

Free on bail while awaiting trial, Wells wrote the *Times* that the prosecution of the returning board was a conspiracy of "inveterate traitors to the Union" who "had undertaken a contract with the Democratic Party to do their dirty work" by attempting "a renewal in insidious guise of the tremendous conflict of 1876, perhaps of 1861." With efficient dispatch, Wells accused the judge, prosecutors, and a key government witness of embezzling public funds, "beastly . . . intoxication," jury rigging, murder, livestock theft, and "denounc[ing] the female teachers of the [New Orleans] public schools as prostitutes."[18]

Reaching the end of the first column, Gibson saw that Wells had reserved his harshest words for him. Wells wrote that Gibson had stuffed ballot boxes to win his seat in 1874 "and would have been indicted . . . , and in all probability sent to the Penitentiary but for my leniency and forbearance." The smear hit Gibson on a point of particular pride—his commitment to abide by the letter of the law, a pillar of his strategy to convince Northerners that white Southerners could govern peacefully and honorably. All the same, stuffing ballot boxes was of a piece with the rest of Wells's letter, the kind of insult that everyone in Louisiana politics had to face at one point or another. What jumped off the page was an accusation of an entirely different order.[19]

"R. L. Gibson has seen fit, on the floor of Congress, to calumniate the Returning Board, and has attempted a justification of their persecution," Wells wrote. "This colored Democratic Representative seems to claim a right to assail the white race because he feels boastingly proud of the commingling of the African with the Caucasian blood in his veins." What was this? For a man who relished a good insult, Wells had never resorted to this one. Instead of referring to Gibson by name, Wells again called him "this colored Representative of Louisiana in the Congress of the nation." "The lineage of this Representative without a nationality," Wells wrote, "can be fully established by many of the old inhabitants of Adams County, Miss., as well as by many of his neighbors in the Parish of Terrebonne."[20]

Gibson glanced up from the paper. The reporter was studying his reaction. So this was why he had come—to see Gibson lose his temper. The newsman would be disappointed. Sitting comfortably, surrounded by his books, the congressman smiled and gave a "look of astonishment and amusement." Asked for comment, Gibson was "serene as a May day." "I think Mr. Wells is crazy," he said, "clearly demented."[21]

The reporter read Wells's words aloud, and again Gibson "serenely and graciously" brushed him off. "My family," he said, "is of an old Virginia stock. My grandfather settled in Port Gibson, and my mother's family is well known in the country. A great many people, of course, know us well."[22]

For a third time the reporter asked Gibson for his opinion of Wells. The congressman's veneer began to crack. "I think he is certainly crazy," Gibson replied. "I cannot, of course, take any notice of the ravings of an imbecile old man, idiotic through senility, and perhaps inheriting constitutional tendencies to insanity. I must request of *The Post* not to notice anything which this undoubted madman has said in reference to me." With those words—*imbecile, idiotic, senility, insanity, madman*—the interview was over. The reporter walked out onto Franklin Park with his item for the next day's paper, leaving Gibson alone in his library.[23]

ALTHOUGH GIBSON WAS AT the height of his influence, he felt as often as not "a good deal broken + shattered." Crippling bouts of gout and arthritis in his feet, knees, and hands were only partly responsible. He felt beset by loss. In 1872 he suffered the "staggering blow" of his father's sudden death. "He had been my life long confidential friend + companion," Gibson wrote. "I seldom passed a day without writing to him when apart." Two years later his young son Randall Lee Gibson Jr., "the picture of health + beauty—just walking + talking," died of a winter flu, a loss from which Gibson found it difficult to "compose myself." At the moment he was advocating for the Nicholls government, his younger sister Louly was dying in childbirth.[24]

On top of his congressional work, Gibson had to tend to a law practice that had grown to overwhelming proportions since his election. The family properties that he shared with his brothers and sisters were heavily mortgaged. His brother and trusted law partner McKinley was "rickety" with consumption. After two years in the Kentucky legislature and another six as the founder and editor of Lexington's first daily newspaper, Hart Gibson was bankrupt—"crushed," "morbid," forever on the brink of "go[ing] to the dogs." Their younger brother Tobe was living extravagantly in New Orleans—on Randall's tab. "I must get him somewhere else or move away myself," he wrote. Their sister Sarah was nearly destitute, about to lose control of her late husband's land, and holed up with her children on an isolated and overgrown Terrebonne plantation. Randall offered Sarah legal help and money and begged her to move with her children back to Kentucky. "They have nothing in L[ouisiana]," he railed, "free negroes, low whites, a wrecked, debased + corrupt + bankrupt disorganized society—my Lord what a life! for your precious children." Sarah refused all overtures, convinced that Randall was scheming to steal her share of the family property. People in Terrebonne blamed him for Sarah's troubles—whenever he returned to the old plantations, they would pass him "coldly + often without speaking." Randall despaired at the thought of "them sacrificed to the level of free negroes and to a *barbarous* condition of society. I have felt that any day I might hear that she and her Daughters have been murdered out there. They might as well be in the depths of Africa."[25]

Worst of all, the struggle over who would control Louisiana never seemed to end. Gibson might have hoped that the Democrats' guarantees of equality for all and their stated policy of not persecuting Republicans would turn the page on Reconstruction. To his distress, neither side would look forward. While the Democrats in Louisiana were prosecuting Wells and the returning board, Republicans in Washington were continually denouncing and investigating violence and corruption in Louisiana.

In public Gibson defended the way things were in his state—at least in the abstract. On the House floor, he answered the allegations about Democratic rule in Louisiana, not by delving into the particulars of any case, but by taking the discussion to a higher level. As purely internal state matters, Gibson argued, they should not be subject to federal scrutiny. Time and again he presented himself—his character, his honor—as a reason for easing scrutiny on Louisiana. "I have sought during my brief political life to contribute all I could to a good understanding between the people of the North and South," he said as a way to end discussion on uncomfortable subjects, "and I have been gratified to observe a better feeling, a kindlier intercourse, a more generous disposition springing up."[26]

The allegations of violence, corruption, and unfairness weighed heavily on Gibson, all the more because he knew they had a basis in truth. While Gibson had appealed to black voters with high-minded speeches on the campaign trail, other Democrats won elections in Louisiana with the rifle, the lash, and sacks of dollars. When Gibson first entered politics, he wrote with astonishment of the "power *of money* . . . I never wanted a million as much in my life." He was touched when supporters "spent their own hard earnings on some votes . . . and desired that nobody should tell me." Gibson won his seat in 1874 against a Republican incumbent just two months after the Crescent City White League had smashed the Republican-controlled state militia in pitched battles on the streets of New Orleans. Fifteen hundred strong with two artillery batteries, the White League was one of many armed groups across the state that "bulldozed" blacks and sympathetic whites into submission, and terrorized blacks were leaving Louisiana by the thousands. Gibson knew the bulldozers well—the Crescent City group consisted of men who had served under him during the war, members of social clubs that he belonged to, and Democratic Party activists who were among his strongest political supporters. The distance between Gibson's image—law, order, and honor—and the reality of Louisiana politics was wearying. "The fact is," Gibson wrote a friend, "between you and me—our L[ouisiana] politics are disgusting—I mean our Democratic politics. A set of jobbing, half educated, reckless men have the lead + the men of substance do nothing."[27]

THE *POST* REPORTED GIBSON'S reaction to Wells on the front page, alongside stories about horse races and prizefights, a double suicide by thwarted lovers in St. Louis, and tensions between Serbia and Russia. The newspaper sided with Gibson, criticizing Wells's letter as having entirely "too much muchness" to be believed. Still, the paper noted that Gibson had "refused to consider" Wells's charges "long enough to deny them" and was convinced that Gibson had opened himself to a libel suit for calling Wells crazy. The same might have been said of Wells for writing that Gibson was black. The law books in Gibson's library would have told him as much. For nearly a century people had gone to Southern courts seeking damages for being called "Negroes," "mulattoes," "colored people," "mixed blood," "yellow," and "not white." These libel and slander cases became occasions for courts to measure the relative status of the races—the disadvantage of being black, the value of being white. Before the Civil War the courts' calculations had begun and ended with slavery and the possibility of being mistaken for a slave. After the war—and particularly after the Fourteenth Amendment to the Constitution promised equality under the law regardless of race or color—it was less clear that being called black had any tangible consequences. Only one case had gone to court since war's end, and the defendant—a carriage driver in New Orleans who had blackballed the plaintiff from the Hackmen's Benevolent Association—had won at trial and on appeal.[28]

In assessing the truth of an accusation, courts had to consider how the law defined the categories of black and white. Most Southern states classified people as legally black if they had one-fourth or one-eighth "Negro blood"—a black grandparent or great-grandparent. Just before and just after the Civil War, Virginia and Tennessee considered enacting laws that changed the definition of *Negro* to include anyone with any African ancestry. In 1857 a bill was introduced in the Louisiana Senate for the "prevention of marriages where one of the parties has a taint of African blood." Although the bill never passed, it reflected the logical extreme of the proslavery position—that slavery was necessary because black inferiority was permanent, set in the blood, and passed along to future generations. The survival of American civilization depended on keeping "the blood of the Caucasian . . . pure and undefiled." This new way of defining race—the "one-drop rule"—was driven less by slavery than by the prospect of freedom. Only in a world where blacks had the potential to compete with whites for power and privilege was it necessary to articulate reasons for keeping blacks in a permanently inferior status.[29]

In Louisiana the existence of a large, traditionally free mixed-race class meant that whites had long competed with people of color for jobs, land, and status. By 1878, as Gibson had insisted, blacks technically had the right to vote and otherwise participate in civic life. By law, blacks and whites could marry each other, and blacks had a right of equal access to hotels, railroad cars, and other public accommodations. On the streets of New Orleans, it was famously difficult to distinguish one race from the other at a glance—many whites were dark, and many blacks were light. Every day people witnessed the color line bending and breaking. The result was that whites believed all the more deeply in their racial supremacy. They organized their entire political life around it. Racial identity was so important that the *Daily Picayune* omitted the allegations as to Gibson's race when it printed an identical letter that Wells had sent to it. Believing in racial difference—enough to kill for it—was what kept whites separate from blacks. For white Louisianans, knowing that blacks could look like them did not discount the importance of blood purity. Rather, they were as likely as anyone in the South to consider a person with traceable African ancestry, no matter how remote, to be black. The porous nature of the color line required eternal vigilance.

At root, libel and slander cases involving accusations of blackness forced courts to decide how zealously the color line should be policed. Awarding large damages acknowledged a sizable gap between white and black status but also deterred people from asking the kinds of questions and making the kinds of statements that kept blacks from passing for white. Conversely, if courts made it difficult for plaintiffs to collect damages, such decisions minimized the disadvantages of blackness, yet encouraged whites to err on the side of accusing people of being black. In Louisiana the courts required that plaintiffs prove not only that the accusation was false and defamatory but also that the accuser acted with malice. This additional showing of malice was hard to make, so most accusers—even ones who spoke falsely— could defeat a lawsuit. Where whites and blacks looked alike, perhaps there was little point in punishing mistakes that were bound to happen. Or perhaps maintaining white racial purity was a task of such paramount importance—and practical difficulty—that it outweighed almost any damage done to those who stood falsely accused.

GIBSON FOUND IT HARD to hold his pen. Rheumatism had turned his hand into an old man's scratch, uncontrolled, vulnerable even on the stationery of the House Committee on Ways and Means. But he would not have a secretary copy the letter. He wrote through his pain. The subject was private.[30]

When asked about Wells's letter, Gibson had responded with cool confidence that his family was from "old Virginia stock." Given their tone and the desperate circumstances under which they were made, Wells's remarks would have met any standard of malice, if they had been false. But Gibson did not sue Wells for libel. The truth was, Gibson knew very little about his father's family.

In the weeks after the *Times* article ran, instead of demanding satisfaction of Wells—legal or otherwise—Gibson and his brother McKinley began corresponding with two men in Mississippi, one in Natchez and one forty miles upriver in Port Gibson. Both were in their seventies. The Reverend John Griffing Jones had already published his *Concise History of the Introduction of Protestantism into Mississippi and the Southwest* and had just finished the *Complete History*. John Francis Hamtramck Claiborne had been a planter, journalist, and congressman. After years of collecting papers, he was writing a massive history of Mississippi and its best families.

Both men had known Gibson's father's parents, better than Gibson had. "I never saw my Grandfather for whom I was named nor my Grandmother," he wrote Claiborne, explaining that he had been born in Ken-

tucky and raised among "the Harts, Shelbys, Prestons, Breckinridges."
McKinley asked Jones for help constructing a family tree. While Claiborne
did not know anything about the Gibson family origins, he fondly described his days living in the "Gibson neighborhood" just below Vicksburg,
where Gibson's father and uncle—"handsome, dressy, of refined manners
and exceedingly popular"—had been his particular friends. The Gibsons,
Claiborne assured his correspondent, "were numerous—intelligent, generally esteemed, wealthy—and most of them members of the church." Jones
too spoke of his fondness for the Gibsons. "I hope to meet many of the
Gibsons in that bright world where the living never die and friendship
never parts," he wrote. He offered more specifics about the family history:
names and birth and death dates, their settlement on the Great Pee Dee
River in South Carolina, and a theory about what had come before. From
the Gibsons' "elevated intellectuality, morality, religion and enterprise,"
Jones supposed that they descended from "Portuguese Huguenots" who
had settled in South Carolina—a gentle suggestion that along with elite
status, the family also had a tradition of dark skin. "I do not remember ever
to have heard but one of the connexion refer to this as a tradition of the
family," Jones wrote. "I wish we now had the means of demonstrating this
theory."[31]

CLAIBORNE AND JONES DID NOT COMPLETELY resolve the question
of family origins, but the Gibsons were satisfied. If they could not account
for every drop of blood in their veins, they could establish that the family
had lived for generations with, in Jones's words, "an elevated position in
society, on account of their intelligence, morality, refinement and high
toned and honorable bearing in all relations of life." Such status could not
mean anything but whiteness.[32]

While newspapers around the country had run wire stories about Wells's
letter, few treated the accusation as having any merit. Rather than discussing the accusation, papers in Vicksburg and New Orleans recounted Gibson's lofty lineage. When a Mississippi congressman incidentally mentioned
Gibson on the House floor a week after the *Times* had printed Wells's letter, he added a statement about his colleague's "illustrious ancestors" on

both sides of the family. As much as racial purity mattered to white Southerners, they had to circle the wagons around Randall Gibson. If someone of his position could not be secure in his race, then no one was safe.[33]

If the issue ever had life, it receded when the Louisiana Supreme Court ruled in March 1878 that all charges against the returning board members had to be dropped. Wells quietly retracted the charges in his letter soon afterward. Nevertheless the Gibsons could not forget the allegation. When family members published the funeral sermons that had been delivered in the 1830s over their paternal grandparents, they appended the letters from Claiborne and Jones that described the Mississippi Gibsons' sterling reputation. Hart Gibson and Sarah Gibson Humphreys took up genealogy as a hobby, eventually tracing the family line back to a prosperous landowner in colonial South Carolina who played an illustrious role in the Regulator Movement of 1768—a man named Gideon Gibson. Without specifically addressing the charges against Randall, the family was answering them.[34]

Randall Gibson and his family never lost their social position. He was heading toward an easy reelection in the fall. In Washington the Gibsons enjoyed the "pleasant company" of former Confederate generals Joseph Johnston, John Smith Preston, Jubal Early, and Custis Lee. More than ever Gibson found himself reminiscing about the great battles in which he had fought, striving for what he called the *"truth exactly"* about Shiloh, Murfreesboro, Chickamauga, Atlanta, Nashville, and Spanish Fort. Privately, he mourned the loss of close friends from a vicious yellow fever outbreak in New Orleans, including his first law partner and a young man who had risen from office janitor to an associate in his practice. Despite the universal respect and esteem accorded to him every day, Gibson started dreaming of a different life: more time with his children and perhaps a return to full-time law practice, in partnership with McKinley and Hart—in Kentucky. "If you + Hart will go to work at the Law + find a place that would suit me, I will sell my House in N.O. + join you," Randall wrote his brother. "I long to get out of the South—away from a Country of Negroes, outlaws + yellow fever. This is confidential but I mean every word of it."[35]

CHAPTER THIRTEEN

WALL

Washington, D.C., January 21, 1880

O.S.B. WALL'S FOOTSTEPS ECHOED in the hallways of the Capitol. The slap of leather on marble magnified his presence, announcing his arrival. But the echoes diminished him too, heralding his insignificance in a building of grand proportions. If being summoned to testify before Congress was a tribute to his prominence as a politician and a Race Man, the hearing would also provide yet another public occasion to be badgered, vilified, and humiliated.

The hearing was not in one of the Senate's great committee chambers—gilded, frescoed, with a sweeping view of the Mall. Tucked away in the basement, Wall's hearing looked as if it were taking place in the card room of an exclusive club. Bookcases lined the walls. Along the edges sat an assortment of committee clerks and reporters for the newspapers and wire services; some of the clerks were writing articles themselves to supplement their salaries. A large oak table in the middle took up most of the room. Wall knew where to sit. He had testified many times over the past eight years. He walked to one end of the table and faced his inquisitors.[1]

"State your name, age, and residence," said the bearishly whiskered man on the other end of the table. It was Daniel Voorhees, the Indiana Copperhead chairing the newly formed Select Committee to Investigate the Causes of the Removal of the Negroes from the Southern States to the Northern States—a mass migration of Southern blacks in 1879 that was known as the Negro Exodus. Flanking him were four other senators. The committee—three Democrats, two Republicans—reflected the composition and preoccupations of the new congressional majority. Over the past year several thousand blacks from North Carolina had moved to Indiana. Senator Voorhees was convinced that the influx was a Republican plot to tip his closely divided state in the 1880 presidential election. His fellow committee member, North Carolina's senator and former governor Zebulon Vance, viewed the mass migration as a colossal threat to his state's supply of cheap labor. Senator Voorhees vowed to "find out who these infernal damned political scoundrels are, who are trying to flood our State with a lot of worthless negroes." O.S.B. Wall, president of the National Emigrant Aid Society, was infernal damned political scoundrel number one.[2]

LESS THAN A DECADE before, Wall had been a respected politician, elected to two terms in Washington's legislative assembly by a majority white district. After three years of territorial government, Washington's avenues were layered with bituminous coal tar, and Boss Shepherd and his ring of "street paving jobbers" were millions of dollars richer. The whole country was engaged in frenzied speculation on railroads and real estate, betting that extending modern infrastructure to the wild corners of the West would make everyone rich. Wall too was aggressively upgrading. At the end of 1871 he bought a large lot steps away from Howard University and the Freedmen's Hospital and built a two-story wood-frame house. Next door John Mercer Langston was constructing his Swiss-inspired Hillside Cottage, which for the next five decades would be a social center for the District's aristocrats of color. Wall's house was on the same scale as Langston's, which cost the princely sum of $6,300 to build.[3]

With his savings swallowed up by the house, Wall had to support his family on a salary of less than one hundred dollars a month. His wife, Amanda, tried without success to get a charitable association to pay her for the classes she was conducting with freedpeople. In early 1872 she resolved to take music and French classes at Howard University so that she could qualify for a teaching credential. With "no possible way of defraying expense," she appealed directly to Oliver Otis Howard to use his influence to get her hired as the seamstress at the Freedmen's Hospital, replacing the "Jewess of wealthy connections + Southern sympathizer" who currently had the job. But at the end of 1872 Amanda was pregnant. Laura Gertrude Wall was born the next year, and her father now had a family of seven to feed.[4]

When the baby was six months old, the nation's economy, floating on bad loans, foundered. The massive Panic of 1873—or Great Depression, as it was then known—claimed as its victims entire industries and millions of workers. Heavily invested in risky land and railroad schemes, the Freedmen's Bank collapsed in the middle of 1874. Tens of thousands of blacks lost tens of millions of dollars in savings. Wall had made his first deposit in the bank when he moved to Washington, and over the years his wife and children had opened their own accounts. Howard University almost failed.[5]

Across the country voters punished the Republicans, who had held power since the war. The party's 110-seat majority in the House of Representatives became a 60-seat deficit in the 1874 election. Although the lame-duck Republican Congress pushed through the Civil Rights Act of 1875, which guaranteed the "full and equal enjoyment" of "inns, public conveyances on land or water, theaters, and other places of public amusement" as well as the rights of blacks to serve on juries, the new Democratic majority foretold dark days ahead for the nation's blacks. Northern sympathy for civil rights curdled into apathy or outright racism, and Southern whites were openly engaging in coordinated, violent campaigns to suppress black votes and retake power. Within two years there were no federal troops to defend against white attacks, and the Supreme Court had ruled that the federal government could not prosecute individuals who massacred fifty blacks in an election dispute.[6]

The District faced the Panic of 1873 drowning in debt from Boss Shepherd's binge on street paving and other infrastructure projects. Residents and congressmen committed to "good government" joined forces with Democrats to overhaul the District's political structure. The rampant corruption had been driven by some of Washington's richest and most powerful men, men who were at best lukewarm about civil rights. But the problems of territorial government were conflated with the alleged inability of blacks to participate in a democracy. Although blacks had shown independence in their political preferences, providing crucial votes to oust the Radical Republican mayor Sayles Bowen in 1869, whites assumed without discussion that blacks constituted an undifferentiated voting bloc that could be bought off and manipulated. In June 1874 Congress dissolved the territorial legislature and created a three-man commission appointed by the president to run the District. Residents would not cast ballots in local elections for another century. The first jurisdiction during Reconstruction to grant full voting rights for black men became the first jurisdiction to take those rights away.[7]

The tragedy befalling Negro suffrage was played as farce. Newspapers breathlessly reported that upon the dissolution of the legislature, members of the House of Delegates looted the assembly building. Never mind that there were only a couple of blacks in the legislature. The District's experiment with equal voting rights was dismissed as an inevitable failure because blacks were unfit to govern. The dailies developed a derisive shorthand for this failure after one delegate was reportedly caught on his way out of the assembly building with a cleaning implement stuffed in his sock. O.S.B. Wall was no longer a pioneer, leader, or public servant. All black politicians, according to the press and much of its readership, were mere "Feather Dusters."[8]

As the District turned away from civil rights, day-to-day life became markedly more hostile for everyone from freedpeople to colored aristocrats. Blacks and whites stopped socializing. Restaurants routinely refused blacks service despite the local law that guaranteed equal access to public accommodations.[9]

As a justice of the peace and former delegate, Wall remained prominent in the colored community. He agitated for restoring voting rights to the District and led efforts to urge the president to appoint the former mayor Sayles Bowen as one of the new commissioners. When another citizens' group voted to propose a different man to be commissioner, Wall was respected enough to be brought in to inspect and count the ballots. He petitioned Congress for federal land "for the purpose of endowing a home for the indigent poor of the District of Columbia" and helped arrange events celebrating the unveiling of a "Freedmen's monument" in Lincoln Park on Capitol Hill.[10]

Outside his community, however, Wall's stature was fading. Newspapers started ridiculing him. In 1873 he was castigated for a conflict of interest when as justice of the peace he issued an arrest warrant for an accused lumber thief, only to defend the man in his hearing at the police court. The next year the *National Republican* printed a letter full of misspellings that Wall supposedly wrote to the District of Columbia Supreme Court, asking for a copy of his law license because he "lost the fust one." Wall sued the paper's editor for $10,000 for suggesting that he was "an illiterate ignorant and stupid man and a shallow pretender in his profession." A few years later Wall was blasted for issuing an arrest warrant for a three-year-old child. In a letter to the editor of one paper, Wall explained that "justices who issue warrants for the arrest of parties . . . are obliged to depend entirely upon the *exparte* statement of the complainant as to the facts," but for many, the incident confirmed his reputation as a bumbler. "Wall knows as much about *law* as he does about *conic sections*," wrote one man to *The Washington Post*. The *Daily Critic* called him "Oh! S. B. Wall."[11]

Wall's reputation suffered its most serious blow during the 1878 congressional hearings into the conditions and administration of the Freedmen's Hospital. Witness after witness accused Wall of sparking the investigation with baseless charges of corruption and patient mistreatment, all because the hospital's chief, Gideon S. Palmer, refused to buy food from a grocery store that Wall had started. For two years, Dr. Palmer said, he had been "constantly beset" by Wall, "directly and indirectly, to induce me to purchase supplies from him, and to purchase supplies from persons recommended by him." The owner of a clothing concern said that in exchange for the discharge of a forty-dollar debt, Wall promised to use his influence to land him a contract to supply the Freedmen's Hospital with coats, blouses, stockings, and cotton ticking. Wall, another witness testified, often said that he was "entitled to patronage" because he had worked to get the old hospital administrator fired and Dr. Palmer hired.[12]

The testimony revealed a man in financial trouble, alternately begging and bullying for scraps of hospital business. The hearings also showed someone who had learned some fundamental lessons about politics during the Boss Shepherd years. For Wall, power, patronage, and material gain were indistinguishable. He had the confidence to organize alliances and agitate for change, however dubious the cause. He was unafraid to throw his weight around, even with whites. "You will see trouble, I think," he icily threatened Dr. Palmer. "We are going to look into the crookedness of the Freedmen's Hospital, and when we get through I will shake hands with you."[13]

The details only got more damaging for Wall. According to Dr. Palmer, Wall would implore him to "give the patronage to a colored man" and "would often use language like this, 'You won't give a poor fellow a chance to live; it was intended in these appropriations to give us poor fellows a chance to make something.'" Wall's own brother Albert, a dairy farmer who supplied the hospital with fresh milk—and perhaps was struggling to keep his contract—testified that Wall said that if "he should accomplish his purpose, which he was positive of doing, if he would put a man in that hospital whom he could control . . . I would have more patronage from the institution; and a great many things I cannot just think of at present." Wall's old friend Charles Purvis, a doctor at the hospital, called Wall a "rascal" and a "scoundrel." The hospital's meat supplier testified that Wall promised extra cents per pound in exchange for support in his quest to oust Dr. Palmer. "I told him I was not going to place myself in the hands of any colored man as my owner," said the meat dealer. "I never owned a colored man in my life, and I would not own one, or suffer one to own me."[14]

Buried within the bluster and bad behavior was a deep anger over what life in the District had become for an ambitious black man. Wall reportedly called Dr. Palmer a "Yankee scoundrel" and vowed that the "Yankee scoundrels shall not have the patronage down here to do as they please with." The city's colored institutions were run by whites. Howard University in 1875 had rejected John Mercer Langston as its first black president, even though he had ably served as acting president.[15]

Dr. Palmer's predecessor at the hospital—Robert Reyburn, the surgeon who had treated Wall's gunshot wound—was, according to Wall, a member of an all-white medical society and was "indispos[ed] to grant certain privileges . . . to the colored students" studying medicine at Howard. Wall successfully got Reyburn fired but was frustrated in his efforts to get Charles Purvis hired as the new head. "I had my reasons" for "trying and exhausting on Purvis to get him appointed," Wall said, "and they were simply that he was a colored man." Amanda Wall and Carrie Langston led a petition drive, also unsuccessful, to get another colored doctor, Alexander T. Augusta, chosen to lead the hospital. Only a few years before, Wall had been one of the "ruling spirits of the Bowen and Public Works *regime.*" Now that his moment of power was over, he and his race were left with very little. Desperate and disillusioned, Wall risked his reputation over groceries—and lost.[16]

Three months after the Freedmen's Hospital fiasco, President Hayes submitted Wall's name to the Senate for reappointment to another term as justice of the peace. The nomination did not go unnoticed. "Everyone knows he has been charged with being notoriously corrupt," one man wrote *The Washington Post.* "Besides his corruptness, the public is well aware of the fact that many of his warrants have been thrown out at the Police Court on the ground of informality." Even though others described Wall as having "unimpeached integrity" and a solid professional record, the Senate rejected his appointment in June 1878, along with the one other colored nominee for justice of the peace. After almost a decade of public life, Wall was left scratching out a living as what he called a "one-horse lawyer," representing petty criminals in the police court. In his spare time he started occupying himself with a new political cause. It was about freedom, equality, and, above all, escape.[17]

AT THE DEPTH OF his disgrace in the spring of 1878, Wall had become president of a group called the Western Emigration Society. Its goals mirrored his work eleven years earlier in the local field office of the Freedmen's Bureau: to find the District's indigent blacks land and jobs elsewhere. One of Wall's first acts on behalf of the Emigration Society was to petition the Senate in May 1878 for $75,000 "to enable the helpless poor of our race in this section to locate as farmers on lands of the United States dedicated to homestead purposes." He asked Oliver Otis Howard, now commanding an army in the West, to send him "some reliable information respecting the advantages offered to settlers in Wash'n Territory . . . What we want to know is with reference to the climate, productiveness of the soil, present condition and future prospects of the Territory &c., &c." Wall's focus on migration was a focus on escape—escape from what his friend and fellow emigrationist Richard T. Greener would call the "fetid and vitiated political and social atmosphere of Washington which we have breathed so long." The District no longer promised blacks a rising community, a pathway to equality. Blacks had lost the vote. Congress was retreating from its commitment to civil rights. Whites in Washington were expressing their racial contempt openly. Just about the only "manly and dignified step" that blacks could take, Wall supposed, was to exercise their right to move away.[18]

If the Emigration Society initially had modest goals, it would soon be swept up in a much larger tide. By 1878 whites had forcibly pushed blacks out of government in every Southern state, resorting to military-style campaigns responsible for thousands of murders. Terrorized blacks were stuck in sharecropping contracts and trapped in spiraling debt. Their children had little hope of getting an education. Blacks across the South had long been gathering quietly to discuss leaving for the western states or Liberia. Outraged at Southern atrocities, Northern Republicans started speaking publicly about "emigration." In January 1879 Senator William Windom of Minnesota proposed convening a committee to explore the possibility of "a partial migration of colored persons from those States and congressional districts where they are not allowed to freely and peacefully exercise and enjoy their constitutional rights as American citizens."[19]

Two months later, after the cotton crop failed in Louisiana and Mississippi, river landings were thronged with hundreds of blacks boarding boats for points north. Groups from other states—Arkansas, Tennessee, and Texas among them—were also reported to be leaving. Almost immediately the mass migration had a name: the Exodus. Within weeks *The Atlanta Constitution* was reporting, "If the negro exodus continues, St. Louis won't know whether she is in Missouri or Africa." Most of the "exodusters"— numbering some twenty thousand—were heading onward to Kansas, where they had heard by word of mouth and from railroad circulars that jobs and freedom awaited.[20]

Wall recognized that the "modern exodus . . . of the colored people," "linking their destiny for weal or woe with that of the young and thrifty States of the great Northwest," was "really the most practical or available solution of one of the most vexed political problems which has thus far menaced the Republic." In April 1879 the Western Emigration Society became the National Emigrant Aid Society, newly dedicated to the "immediate assistance to persons already immigrating . . . from the South to the West." Wall assembled a group of notable District residents to serve on its board, including former mayor Sayles Bowen, First Congregational Church pastor Jeremiah Rankin, and *Daily Republican* editor A. M. Clapp. The society also gave him the opportunity to have regular contact with top Republican Party officials, black leaders including Frederick Douglass and Senator Blanche Bruce, and even his erstwhile enemy Charles Purvis. In May, Wall organized his first mass meeting at the grand downtown auditorium Lincoln Hall, where Senator Windom and Richard T. Greener, among others, appealed to a "good audience" to contribute money to pay for train and boat tickets for exodusters.[21]

The Exodus created an excitement that the District's blacks had not felt in years, and it restored their commitment to one of the original Republican articles of faith—what had guided Wall as a Freedmen's Bureau agent—that free labor in a free market could cure the nation of its most serious political, economic, and moral failing. In early October, Wall arranged another meeting, this time featuring John Mercer Langston. "Neither the old slaveholding spirit, nor the old slaveholding purpose is dead in the South," Langston told a packed auditorium. "That plantocracy, with its fearful power and influences, has not passed away; . . . the colored American under it is in a condition of practical enslavement, trodden down and outraged by those who exercise control over him." Langston was speaking like the abolitionist orator he had been decades ago, and his words took the crowd—colored and white—back to a time when it was easy to distinguish right from wrong, when the call to action was clear. "It is . . . possible and practicable to so reduce the colored laborers of the South by emigration . . . as to compel the land-holders—the planters—to make and to observe reasonable contracts with those who remain," Langston said, "to compel all white classes there to act in good faith; . . . obeying the law and respecting the rights of their neighbors."[22]

Whatever interest among the District's blacks the Exodus had sparked in the abstract, the movement entered a new phase on a November afternoon when more than fifty men, women, and children from eastern North Carolina appeared in Washington, asking the Emigrant Aid Society for train fare to Indiana. For six months they had been meeting in churches to discuss leaving for the West. In September two leaders of their movement stopped in Washington on a trip to scout out possible locations for resettling. At the suggestion of a member of the Emigrant Aid Society, they went to Indiana. The two men returned to Carolina with a circular written by a black minister extolling how "in Indiana all stand equal before the law—the black man being protected in his contracts, property, and person the same as the white." "Thousands of good farm hands and house servants can readily find employment at remunerative wages," went the circular, "and when you have earned your money the law will compel payment, should it be refused, which is not likely to be the case." It was all anyone needed to hear.[23]

Wall met with the refugees, talked with them about conditions in North Carolina, and negotiated a group rate with the Baltimore & Ohio Railroad—nine dollars a head, with a one-dollar "drawback" going to the National Emigrant Aid Society. The society contributed $270 to send them to Indianapolis. Two weeks later 164 more arrived in Washington. Wall created committees to organize another mass meeting, a fund-raising lecture, and a benefit concert by local church choirs and to solicit donations from the District commissioners, churches, federal workers, and more. The goal was to raise $1,000. Soon after, another three hundred people arrived.[24]

As the Exodus got more and more attention, Wall started receiving letters from people in Pennsylvania, New York, and Ohio expressing their willingness to employ "Exodusts Emigrating to Our Western States," as well as testimonials from emigrants describing Indiana as a place with "a greate meny friendes" where blacks could "meate with suckses." At the same time the newfound prominence of Wall and his cause drew attacks from blacks and whites. Some opposition in the colored community tracked the views of Frederick Douglass, who routed large contributions to the society but warned that the Exodus was "an abandonment of the great and paramount principle of protection to person and property in every State of the Union." Others, particularly blacks who remained leaders in the South, railed against the disappearance of communities and constituencies that still had some strength. A newspaper editor in North Carolina gave a speech advocating that "our righteous indignation and censure should be unsparingly poured" on Wall and Richard Greener, whom he identified as "the original promoters of the exodus movement." "We say to Professors Greener, . . . Wall, and to all others engaged in the nefarious work of deluding the negro by misrepresentation and falsehood—stop; hands off; let us alone," the editor said. "You do not represent us, you have no constituency, you have nothing but impudence, cheek, and cunning, and an inordinate greed for filthy lucre." For a third group, the opposition was more personal. At the end of December 1879 a small number of prominent local blacks gathered to denounce the Exodus. One attendee, reported The Washington Post, "made allusions which were assumed to be attacks on Mr. O.S.B. Wall," describing him as someone who "believed neither in God nor Heaven" and who had "arranged with the railroad companies for a drawback of fifty per cent. on the fares, which went into their own pockets."[25]

Among white Democrats north and south, the Exodus was a sham, a naked plot by Republicans to "ship negroes enough to doubtful States to change their political complexion." Beyond the political machinations, the causes of the emigration, according to Democrats, were simple: unscrupulous railroad agents eager to drum up business and other outsiders who profited by sowing discontent. Wall was not a hero—he was the "colored manipulator of the Exodus movement." As Democrats saw it, life in the North was inevitably terrible for the emigrants, and conditions in the South were perfectly fair.[26]

AT THE START OF the hearing on the Negro Exodus, Senator Voorhees asked Wall to list everyone he knew who was helping thousands of Negroes leave the South for points north and west—their names, the names of their organizations, how the groups operated, whether and how regularly they communicated with one another. Wall parried even the simplest questions with artful indirection. Asked if the Emigrant Aid Society—the group he had founded—had any branches, Wall answered, "None that I know of." Asked if there were "other similar societies . . . in the United States," Wall said he had learned of some "by the papers and by hearsay," but he never actually named a single one. Was the Emigrant Aid Society's correspondence secretary "white or colored"? Wall answered that the young man holding the position was a "very handsome mulatto." Who kept the Emigrant Aid Society's records? "We have been going on very much as the English Government does," Wall said, "without any written constitution."[27]

Testifying at the Freedmen's Hospital hearings two years earlier, Wall had been prickly, defeated—pathetic, but for the ugly accusations against him. Now he was a different witness. Facing a hostile committee ready to charge him with luring blacks to lives of misery in order to rig the 1880 presidential elections, Wall was nimble and defiant. His confidence reflected his commitment to the Negro Exodus. Once again he had a cause worth fighting for.

Senator Voorhees, for one, was convinced that the Exodusters had no rational reason to leave their homes in the South. "Do you not know," he asked Wall, "that North Carolina has been more friendly toward the colored race; has been more kind in its treatment of them; more liberal in its legislation in their behalf; and has actually done more for their benefit than any other State, North or South?"[28]

Wall could barely contain himself. "Now, Mr. Senator, that is a very nice little eulogy on North Carolina," he said. Gesturing toward the North Carolina senator at Voorhees's side, he continued, "Governor Vance, there, himself could not have done it up any better." Wall's passive protest—his refusal to give clear answers to Voorhees's questions—was over. The witness proceeded to take over the hearing. First, Wall preempted Voorhees's point by appearing to concede it. "Seriously, Mr. Senator, I will agree with you that North Carolina has been one of the mildest and most considerate slave States in the Union," he said. "Since emancipation she has treated her colored population as fairly as could be expected of a master class toward their ex-slaves."[29]

Then Wall slammed the door: North Carolina, he insisted, was nevertheless a "grand good State to emigrate from." "If I were a white man and were able to do so; that is, if I had the wealth so that I could, and the privilege of doing so," he said, "I would go down to North Carolina and would educate and instruct those negroes, not with reference to politics or religion or social systems, but I would say to them if you want to educate your children to be men, to imitate the white race, to own property, to become successful in life in any respect, you must leave this poor, wretched, God-forsaken country, where the soil does not seem able to sprout black-eyed peas, and go out into the broad, rich, fertile West, where they can buy farms on those alluvial prairies at a less price per acre than the rent that they pay every year down there."[30]

When Voorhees challenged Wall's "sweeping assertions" about North Carolina's poor soil by asking if he had ever "examine[d] the census returns of North Carolina as regards its productiveness," Wall cheerfully responded, "O, yes, sir; I certainly have; I love the State."[31]

Exasperated, Voorhees asked Wall to "point out some other evils that you think the people will be relieved of by going to Indiana." Wall took the opportunity to expound upon the poor state of "the education and schooling of the children" in North Carolina, where students in rural districts received little more than three months of instruction out of the year. "From the fact that school privileges there are not so good as they are in the north generally," he said, "I would urge them to leave there and seek some place where their children can find better opportunities for education."[32]

Rather than contesting Wall's facts, Voorhees tried to narrow the inquiry. An Emigrant Aid Society circular had declared that the "disposition to escape beyond the reach of oppression has been of course greatest in those sections of the South where in their opponents have displayed the least regard for their rights to 'life, liberty, and the pursuit of happiness.'" Referring to the circular, the senator asked, "Does this emigration come from parts of [North Carolina] where the white people treat the colored people more unjustly than in other parts of the State?"[33]

"Well, now, I think they treat them quite unjustly there," Wall answered simply, without comparing the treatment of blacks in different sections of North Carolina.

"Quite unjustly in what way?" Voorhees interrupted. Instead of forcing Wall to address the narrow issue presented—what a skillful cross-examiner might have insisted upon—Voorhees gave his witness an opening.[34]

"I think they treat them unjustly in the way they take advantage of them in paying them for their labor," Wall declared.

"How do you know they take advantage of them?" the senator asked.

Where Wall had ducked these kinds of questions earlier in the hearing, now he spoke plainly. "I know it, because I have it directly from the mouths of many intelligent, honest-appearing men who have come from there," he said. "Quite a number of them have told me that . . . they can get but about thirty cents a day for their labor . . . After they have made four or five bags of cotton, and so much corn, or whatever else they may be raising, at the end of the year . . . the man from whom they rent, who has the measuring and weighing of the crop, and the handling and calculating of these orders, makes it out, somehow, so that they not only have nothing, but are in debt, with a mortgage on them, as one might say, for the future."[35]

Now it was Voorhees's turn for sarcasm, as he tried to cut Wall and his claims about Southern injustice down to size. "Have you sufficient knowledge of the world," the senator asked, "to know whether the same thing is or is not true of large numbers of persons in other places, everywhere, white as well as black; or does everybody get rich outside of North Carolina?"

"O, no, sir, not everybody," Wall said, "but in most places, anybody that is hardworking and economical can manage to save up something."[36]

Rather than letting the issue go, Voorhees sensed weakness in Wall's seemingly naïve answer. Hoping to force Wall to admit that blacks in North Carolina did not understand how the economy worked and were expecting special treatment, the senator repeated his question: "Is it not true of the laboring class in all portions of the country, to a large extent, that at the end of the year they are still behind; is not that a very common complaint everywhere?"

If Voorhees thought that Wall would fold, he was wrong. With his deceptively simple answer, Wall had lured the senator into inviting him to speak at length. Now Wall would spring the trap. "Mr. Senator, I will frankly give you my reasons for concluding that there is something wrong about this matter," he said. "I understand a little about human nature. The master class, who have for two or three hundred years held these colored people in abject slavery, have not so soon lost all their feeling of superiority and ownership and their determination to get and to keep the upper hand of them.

"Human nature," he continued, "does not change so suddenly but that, if this class to a man remain right there, in the same localities, and in the same relation as servants, as abject hewers of wood and drawers of water, the upper class, with their dislike of labor and their contempt of laborers, are not likely to be so pure, so immaculate as to treat these people fairly and as their fellow-men."[37]

In words that invoked the book of Joshua and echoed abolitionist speeches by, among others, Frederick Douglass, Wendell Phillips, and John Mercer Langston, Wall depicted the Negro Exodus as nothing less than a patriotic response to an unfair, impure, un-American "master class." While Democrats like Voorhees took on faith that blacks were treated fairly in the South, Wall described the everyday reality faced by his people. "When I hear these statements of unfair and unjust and oppressive treatment from dozens and hundreds of people, bearing upon their countenances the seal of wretchedness and the impress of despair, I hold myself justified in believing it to be true," he said. "If it be a fact that the whole population of the South cannot do any better by the colored people than they do—if, on account of the poverty of the soil, they cannot do any better—that does not make it any the less their right to leave such a country, nor any less their duty to move to some better one, which will afford them greater advantages in life for themselves and their children."[38]

Senator Voorhees had no response to Wall. He changed the subject.

THE NEXT DAY, WALL was called back to the committee so that other senators on the panel could question him. Defending his home state, Senator Vance suggested that Wall was wrong about conditions in North Carolina because he did not consult official government reports or "intelligent white men of the State." The two Republican senators in the minority offered Wall more of an opportunity to attribute the Exodus to "the abuses the colored people have received." "I think where they are even treated best their treatment is such as to demoralize them and frighten them," he said.[39]

After fifty-three days of testimony from dozens of witnesses, the committee's Democrats reported to the Senate that their initial suspicions had been confirmed: that the motive for "promoting this exodus of the colored people was purely political," to traffic blacks to "close States in the North, and thus turn the scale in favor of the Republican party." They found that no racial inequality, mistreatment, or vote suppression existed in the South. "The condition of the colored people of the South is not only as good as could have been reasonably expected," they reported, "but is better than if large communities were transferred to a colder and more inhospitable climate, thrust into competition with a different system of labor, among strangers who are not accustomed to them, their ways, habits of thought and action, their idiosyncrasies, and their feelings."[40]

In reaching their conclusion, the Democrats attacked Wall's testimony by suggesting that he had received kickbacks from the Baltimore & Ohio Railroad—one dollar for every passenger sent to Indiana. Wall insisted that the "drawbacks" went to buy more tickets, and even witnesses who objected to the Exodus as politically motivated testified that no one profited from the Emigrant Aid Society, which aimed solely "to help men fleeing from oppression." The sharpest attack on Wall came from W. Calvin Chase, a journalist two years away from starting his influential Negro newspaper *The Washington Bee*. Chase told the committee that Wall's "only object was to speculate on the ignorant people of the South." "I have known him for five or six years," Chase said, "and I know he never enters into anything except he makes something out of it." Without mentioning the Freedmen's Hospital investigation by name, Chase suggested that Wall had a reputation for being "very dishonest" and that "the people in the District have no confidence in him."[41]

DESPITE CHASE'S PRONOUNCEMENTS, Wall emerged from the hearings a pillar of Washington's colored community. "Capt. O.S.B. Wall deserves great credit for his untiring energy and interest in behalf of the fleeing emigrants from the Southern States," opined the *Argus*, whose editor opposed the Exodus. "We have a high opinion of Captain Wall . . . He is a public benefactor." The following winter, the District commissioners appointed Wall to work with the police in his precinct to coordinate relief for the local poor. By early 1882 Wall was chairing the committee to plan the twentieth anniversary of emancipation in the District. On Emancipation Day that April he would ride in a parade down Louisiana Avenue through a "ringing mass" of thousands of black residents and introduce the day's orator, his fellow Exodus activist Richard T. Greener. In 1884, just four years after publicly denouncing Wall, W. Calvin Chase printed in the *Bee* that it would be "a very handsome thing" if the president would appoint Wall "to some important position." "Capt. Wall is a member of the District Bar and a man who is respected by the entire population both white and colored," Chase wrote. "He is unlike many of our great Negro leaders who is for self all the time, but, he believes in aiding those who aid him and assisting those who have got sense enough to assist themselves." Once again Wall was confident in his place in the colored community and his claim to racial equality. When his youngest daughter, Laura Gertrude, reached the first grade, he quietly got approval from one of the school board's colored members for her to attend a white primary school near the family house on Howard Hill.[42]

Although Wall maintained that the Emigrant Aid Society had nothing to do with politics, his ties to the Republican Party grew stronger than ever. Almost immediately following the Exodus hearings, Wall was appointed a special agent in the Treasury Department. He was also able to land government positions for his sons, both in their early twenties; Edward was a post office clerk and Stephen an apprentice in the Government Printing Office, learning a skilled trade that promised status and stability. In the fall of 1880 James Garfield—the Union general who as an Ohio congressman introduced a bill to provide $75,000 to aid the Kansas Exodusters—was elected president, and Wall found himself at his peak of influence. When his old political ally Sayles Bowen again sought an appointment as District commissioner, Wall went to the White House to seek a personal audience with the president.[43]

As Exodus fever subsided after 1880, the District seemed to hold renewed promise for its colored community. The Exodus had created a sense of progress, the feeling of a certain measure of control over their lives. For the first time since losing the right to vote in 1874, they had shown themselves capable of organizing for social change and restoring something approaching abolitionist fervor among Republicans nationally. Whether blacks would be able to translate the energy of the Exodus into a better life in Washington was a hazier proposition. Fundamentally, the strength of the Exodus among the District's blacks was that it revived the hope and promise of Emancipation, while allowing a collective outpouring of rage and grief over the death of Reconstruction. But if the Exodus was about movement—political organization and physical migration—the District's blacks still found themselves standing in the same place. Only at the end of a remote chain of events, only in the most abstract reaches of free labor theory, would the Exodus ever lead the South back from the abyss of, in Wall's words, "this intimidating, and white-liners, and night-riders, and ku-klux."[44]

Toward the end of Wall's Senate testimony, New Hampshire's Republican senator Henry Blair asked him to explain his "philosophy of the exodus." For Wall, it embodied the tragedy of the past and the uncertainty of the future. "This would be my theory," he said. "Just after the war our people were in good condition. From the wreck of matter and the crush of worlds that passed over us our people emerged into a condition where there seemed to be a little sunlight, and into what was for a while a better state of things." It did not last. "We got along for several years very well," he continued, "until . . . the men who had been in the rebellion came into power in those States, . . . and then the things relapsed into pretty much their old condition." Try as they might to imagine a new life in a new place, blacks were still suffering the loss of that moment in the light. "We have got into a state of things so dark and oppressive that there must be some ventilation," Wall said. "There must be something to make us free again."[45]

CHAPTER FOURTEEN

GIBSON

Washington, D.C., New Orleans, and
Hot Springs, Arkansas, 1888–92

THE ROOM WAS NEARLY silent. In the squeezing heat, it was as if all possibility of sound had evaporated. Sunlight trickled through small windows high overhead but never seemed to penetrate the thick cloud of steam that billowed from floor to ceiling. Along the sweating marble walls, attendants stood invisible, their white uniforms perpetually on the verge of losing their starch and buckling over black skin.[1]

Randall Gibson closed his eyes, and for a moment it seemed that he had fallen asleep. But a low word, a gentle shake, from his attendants could not wake him. They pulled his body from the water and out into the waiting area. Skeletal, slack except for arthritically gnarled fingers and toes, Gibson looked decades older than his sixty years. Unconscious, he was wrapped in a thick white robe and wheeled back to his room, past a line of robed gentlemen in caned rocking chairs, all waiting for their turn in the baths.[2]

Gibson had not planned to spend November 1892 in Arkansas, but his doctors had told him that his heart and kidneys were failing. After summering in Westchester and stopping briefly back in Washington, he had gone to New Orleans to campaign for Grover Cleveland's bid to unseat Benjamin Harrison and win a second term as president. But Gibson could barely leave his room at the St. Charles Hotel. Although he had for years described how the journey home would leave him "flat of my back," his city friends were aghast at the man they saw—gray hair, gray skin, in panting agony with every slow step. Before Gibson could vote in the election—before he could toast the Democrats' reconquest of the White House—his doctors ordered him to leave New Orleans immediately before the damp of early winter killed him. He wrote out a codicil to his will and canceled an order of horses and cattle for his property in Terrebonne Parish. He met with his law partner Gilbert Hall in the lobby of the St. Charles, told him about the diagnosis, and said that he dreamed of the day he could retire to his sugar plantation, his "old family mansion, full of rich and comfortable furniture, with a library which he had been gathering for years." Then he boarded a train to points north and west—to Jackson, Memphis, Little Rock, and finally Hot Springs.[3]

Gibson did not know if he would ever see Louisiana again or, for that matter, if Louisiana would even notice that he was gone. During eight years in the House of Representatives and another ten in the Senate, Gibson had channeled millions of dollars to his state: creating federal offices and agencies in New Orleans, committing the government once and for all to building and maintaining Mississippi River levees, fighting to preserve the tariffs that shielded the sugar plantations from competition in Hawaii and the rest of the world. In Terrebonne Parish, the town that was closest to his father's plantations—Tigerville—had changed its name to Gibson in his honor. But the Louisiana that he had seen on several visits in 1892 barely appreciated what he had accomplished for it, let alone what he aspired for its future.[4]

Perhaps the culture of politics in Louisiana—what Gibson called the "pepper + salt atmosphere," the petty jealousies, the "flatterers + schemers + political wreckers," the cash exchanging hands—made it impossible for any elected official to feel loved. Gibson's votes in Congress, the positions he took in local politics, and the patronage appointments he secured seemed to create loyalty and loathing in equal measure. For everyone who benefited from his work, others—from scattered individuals to entire factions of the Democratic Party—felt shut out. Gibson earned their undying enmity, the declaration of a "relentless war" in which he was routinely accused of corruption. People he had worked with in 1877 to end Reconstruction now minimized his contribution. "I have received any number of letters," Gibson wrote, "some threatening my life + others warning me of assassination."[5]

When Gibson's positions did not inspire hatred, they were simply alien to what life in Louisiana had become. As Louisiana's Democrats consolidated their rule after Reconstruction, the structure of state government was molded around three goals: keeping power, enriching the powerful, and maintaining white supremacy. Reconstruction-era policies that benefited whites and blacks alike, such as public education, were scrapped. More white Louisianans were illiterate in 1892 than when Gibson first took office. When Gibson voted in the Senate for federal education funds to be equally divided between blacks and whites, for a modern civil service to replace patronage, and for direct election of senators, it was hard to know what constituency in Louisiana he represented. He was spending more time in Washington, in Westchester, on the New England shore, and in European spas than in New Orleans. In the spring of 1892, as Gibson stood for reelection to another term in the Senate, he faced a strong slate of challengers. The legislature deadlocked and decided to postpone the vote. Gibson was denounced as the senator from New York.[6]

In Washington Gibson was among friends, but there too he was alone, left to hobble around an empty home. His wife, Mary, only forty-one, died in 1887. She had been sick for two years, but the end was sudden. Their three boys were gone, sent away to boarding school and college. The youngest, Preston, now spent days worrying about his father's health, wishing in vain for a letter from him. "I sincerely hope that you will allow me to come home Easter," the twelve-year-old wrote in 1892. "Please write and tell me so if I have good marks and am a good boy I can go and I will be a good boy if I have to get up at 6 o'clock in the morning to study."[7]

Gibson was surrounded by admirers in Washington, but the politics of North and South remained an embarrassment to him. In 1888, more than a decade after the compromise that had ended Reconstruction, Gibson was elected to a second term in the Senate. The Republican majority held up his credentials and threatened a meticulous investigation into election-related violence and fraud in Louisiana. For nearly a year Gibson sat through speeches detailing his state's failings: ballot-box stuffing, homes of blacks and sympathetic whites riddled with bullets or burned to the ground, and the weekly "political murders of negroes," by noose and shot-gun blast and throats cut ear to ear.[8]

Worst of all were the allegations of "terrorism attempted in Terre Bonne Parish," which included multiple references to violence instigated by Randall's younger brother Tobe, now an attorney living on a family plantation. Tobe reportedly had said that he was leading mobs of night riders to help his brother win reelection to the Senate. After years of float-ing above the nastiness and corruption, Gibson was mired in the moral swamp of Louisiana politics. The Republicans were forcing upon him a hard realization: that he directly benefited from Louisiana's political ter-rorists and was no different from them.[9]

As he had in years past, Gibson assured his fellow senators that white Southerners shared the same values as Northerners. "The great body of the population reposes solidly upon those sentiments of religion and char-ity," he declared, "of good-will and patriotic endeavor, that constitute the basis upon which the structure of every enlightened government must rest." The South, according to Gibson, was "rallying around the great central ideas of constitutional government, building railroads, starting fur-naces, building up great institutions of learning . . . reducing governmental expenses, inviting foreign immigration and immigration from our country-men in the North." He said that blacks and whites "live in relations of kindness and amity so far as I know everywhere in the State of Louisiana" and that Louisiana's Democrats aimed only to "obliterate the color line in politics and consolidate the people on the basis of equal rights and common interests." Finally, Gibson reminded the Senate that blacks were "a race marked as distinct from the white race, and which has not yet the capacity because perhaps it has not had the opportunity to fit itself for the respon-sibilities of self-government." Most white Northerners agreed, and Gibson sounded eminently reasonable in urging patience as "the experiment of universal suffrage in the South" would yield equality in time.[10]

Such words had been seductive in 1877, but throughout 1888 and into 1889 Senate Republicans kept up the drumbeat of accusations of atrocities and irregularities. Gibson shifted his response, attacking the Republicans' evidence as unreliable. The allegations concerning his brother, he said, were made by "a single man in the parish, of whom I never heard, and I doubt if the man ever lived there." New Hampshire senator William Chandler promptly produced a letter from a Terrebonne Parish newspaper editor suggesting that Gibson knew the man well and accused the senator of "untruth, in whole and in every part."[11]

Again, Gibson changed tactics. "I did not know, until informed by the Senator from New Hampshire, that I had an enemy in my old parish or that there was any person in it who would characterize any statement I might make as untrue," he said. "Nor did I believe there was a Senator in this body who would so far forget decorum and good manners, which always mark the relations of gentlemen and which we have the right to expect from American Senators, as to read a letter, with the view to wound the sensibilities of an associate, from one of his political correspondents."[12]

Gibson turned the issue of racial violence and fair elections into broad questions of senatorial etiquette and, ultimately, federalism: how much courtesy and deference senators owed to one another and whether the Senate should regulate its own membership by investigating a state's internal affairs. A dozen years after the 1877 compromise, Gibson, with a lawyer's skill, could still turn unacceptable facts into palatable abstract principles. At the same time he personalized the matter. Senator Chandler's accusations had hurt his feelings. Gibson himself hardly ever went to Terrebonne Parish, and to his mind, the blacks there had trampled on his rights. He described the plantation that he still owned. "For many years past, with the exception of the main house and yard, the entire property has been in the possession and use of the former negro slaves . . . without paying a sou of rent or of the taxes," Gibson told his colleagues. "So much for my contribution to the reign of terror in Terre Bonne Parish; so much for my oppression and denial of rights and privileges to my former negro slaves." Without ever responding directly to the charges of political terror, Gibson had found the vulnerabilities in the Republican position and declared himself a victim, not a victimizer. For Republicans and Democrats alike, the relationships that senators had with one another, the personal dynamics that kept their small community running, mattered more than the workings of democracy in Louisiana.[13]

Gibson was quickly seated in the new Senate, but the effort had exhausted him. He had spent fifteen years selling the idea that the New South's leaders and their values were indistinguishable from those of the North, that together they formed a single national elite. He had put himself forward as a leader whom Northerners could trust and accept as one of their own. Now he knew that he would always be different, always suspect, always tainted. Gibson wore the South—its sickening past, its vicious present—like an indelible mark on his skin.

IN THE WOODS RINGING Hot Springs, the chill air of late fall was heavily perfumed. The smell mingled different notes: tree bark and mud, pine needles green on the branch and decaying on the forest floor, resin oozing down limbs and dripping off branches. It was thick, inescapable, almost tarry as a person inhaled, but somehow it lightened the air, creating an illusion of purity, like the smell of salt and seaweed by the shore.[14]

Randall Gibson sat in an open carriage bumping and flickering through the shadows. Sitting next to him was a man in a well-cut suit, stark bald with a full white beard, tall and wiry, eyes undimmed. William Preston Johnston had accompanied Gibson from New Orleans. Over several days they had been taking walks around the resort and rides through the hills together.[15]

On their way back to the luxurious Park Hotel, which styled itself as Hot Springs's "palace of purification," Gibson and Johnston passed through town. Even in the short days leading to winter, Hot Springs had, according to the writer Stephen Crane, "the same quality as the gaiety of the Atlantic Coast resorts in the dead of summer." The resort could have been anywhere. The tidy paved streets, Crane wrote, "mingled an accent from the South, a hat and pair of boots from the West, a hurry and important engagement from the North, and a fine gown from the East."[16]

In many ways it was the South Gibson had worked to create. It was uncurious, "purely cosmopolitan," with its local accent—its local prejudices—erased. As with the Mississippi River levees, the government had helped open Hot Springs for business, diverting mountain streams underground and piping water from the springs into the resort. It was a manufactured town with, Crane wrote, "a wide sympathy, not tender, but tolerant." It was a place where a visitor "may assure himself that there are men of his kind present."[17]

Sitting in his carriage, Gibson needed no such assurance. Few people understood him as well as Will Johnston. They had known each other the entirety of their remarkably similar lives. Johnston was Gibson's age almost exactly. Cousins on their mothers' side, they had been raised among the Kentucky aristocracy, with their fathers frequently absent, down the Mississippi River on business in Louisiana and East Texas. Gibson and Johnston had gone to Yale together, read law at the same time, and become officers in the rebel army. After the war they both had sought solid ground by practicing law. When Gibson established himself in New Orleans, he had asked Johnston to leave Louisville and become his partner. Instead Johnston became a college professor and wrote a mammoth biography of his father, the Confederate general Albert Sidney Johnston. As Gibson worked in Congress to restore former rebels to power, Johnston was shaping how Southerners and Northerners alike would remember the rebellion.[18]

In 1883 Gibson finally succeeded in bringing his cousin to New Orleans. Two years earlier Paul Tulane had summoned Gibson to the vast estate where he lived alone in Princeton, New Jersey. The eighty-year-old bachelor offered him control of property worth hundreds of thousands of dollars to support education in New Orleans, where Tulane had made millions as a young man in the cotton trade. Gibson's father-in-law had been his best friend. Gibson organized a board to run the Tulane Education Fund, which decided to create a university with Will Johnston as its president.[19]

From Washington and Westchester, spas in Virginia and European resorts, through arthritis and gout and his wife's death, Gibson spent years in constant correspondence with Will Johnston, Paul Tulane, and Tulane's personal attorney James McConnell. Creating the university required all Gibson's skills as a lawyer and politician. In 1883 the Louisiana Supreme Court ruled that income from the Tulane Education Fund's properties was not tax exempt, potentially exposing the fund to pressure from whatever political faction had the power to set the rates. Working around the decision, Gibson pushed the legislature to give the Tulane Education Fund full control over the University of Louisiana's New Orleans campus. Although the board would run the university as a private institution—it would now be the Tulane University of Louisiana—arguably this new hybrid was public and therefore tax exempt. Gibson's enemies fought him on tax status and circulated rumors about mismanagement of the bequest, rumors that frequently reached Tulane himself. Still, in 1886 the Louisiana Supreme Court decided that the university and the fund would be tax exempt. It did not matter how the institution actually functioned; a bare classification, Gibson's legal fiction, saved the school from the poison touch of state politics.[20]

Beyond his work as the board's chair, Gibson worked closely with Johnston to shape what kind of university Tulane would become. They were creating an institution in their own image. It would be devoted to practical subjects and science, as Paul Tulane had insisted, but also literature, history, and philosophy. Its teachers would be unmarried recent graduates of Yale, Harvard, Oxford, and Cambridge, grounded in the best traditional knowledge and the latest advances, devoted without distraction to educating their charges. Tulane's graduates would be well-rounded people, not "mere cog[s] in the great wheel of society," as Johnston once said, but adults equipped to make independent critical judgments about themselves and their worlds.[21]

As Paul Tulane continued to give gifts and promised more at his death, his bequest was becoming Gibson's legacy too. The new university—cosmopolitan, idea-driven—would create a new South, led by a rising generation of people trained to think like Gibson and Johnston. In a nod to modernity—and the possibility of attracting additional large donations—Gibson urged Tulane, above strenuous objections from others, to revise his bequest to serve not just the "young men in the City of New Orleans" but "young persons," opening up the possibility of educating women. Gibson also suggested that Tulane insert one more word between "young" and "persons"—"white"—in order to "confine [the bequest] to white persons." After much "consultation and consideration," Gibson wrote, "he did so finally." It was just one word, but it meant so much. For Gibson, limiting the gift to whites was arguably the key to making the bequest effective, removing it from the scorched-earth politics of white supremacy. At the same time the limitation insulated him from another round of attacks from his political enemies.[22]

On the cusp of realizing their vision, Gibson and Johnston had to watch it founder. The crippling of their dream was remarkably quick, in a succession of events worthy of a Charles Dickens novel. When Tulane died in March 1887, his lawyer McConnell searched the Princeton mansion for the will that he had drafted for the old man, a will giving a large final endowment to the university. He found nothing. McConnell searched every safe-deposit box where Tulane could have kept it—nothing. No will was ever found. Tulane's millions were divided among his nieces and nephews. In the Princeton Cemetery, the heirs erected an elaborate monument crowned with a sculpture of their uncle. But the university that carried his name—the university that was supposed to be Gibson's monument—would always be strapped for money. It would never stand at full height.[23]

THE SOFT SHOCK OF damp cloth, cool air on wet skin, interrupted Gibson's exhausted drift from day to night to day. It gave the man a moment of relief, but the slow tide of pain always rose again. Gibson opened his eyes. The room would never be familiar. He was still at the Park Hotel, just two weeks after fleeing New Orleans for his life. But he recognized the woman leaning over him. His older sister Sarah was taking care of him.

For several days the strolls and carriage rides with Will Johnston had had a tonic effect on the ailing senator. But after collapsing in the baths—from dehydration, perhaps, or heatstroke, or even a heart attack—Gibson could not leave his bed. He could barely tolerate spoonfuls of warm milk. Warned by wire that her brother was failing, Sarah Gibson Humphreys had come down from Kentucky to nurse him back to health.[24]

Randall's sister had been a widow for almost thirty years. As her brother prospered and advanced in American politics, she suffered through decades of financial and personal hardship—mortgaging and leasing out her land, scrimping and economizing, scheming to grow tobacco and sell timber rights, doing anything to keep her family afloat, to hold on to her Louisiana and Kentucky estates, and ensure that her children would remain the equals of her brothers' children. The challenges were severe in the decades after the war, as the country reeled from financial panic to financial panic. Often she found that she could not conduct routine business or secure loans because she was a woman. Although she had the legal capacity to enter into contracts—most states by the 1870s allowed even married women to conduct business and own property independent of their husbands—the law did not affect day-to-day business customs, which continued to treat women as "being infants in reality as well as in law."[25]

For a time Randall and Sarah had jointly owned their father's plantation, Live Oak, an experience that convinced her that Randall was out to take her shares and reduce her to one of his dependents, like a child, or a slave. After years of mistrust Randall and Sarah settled their financial differences in 1883, when Randall traded another plantation and much-needed cash for his sister's share of Live Oak. Sarah and her family became regular visitors in Washington. Her children married well, and she began to feel a measure of security.[26]

Still, Sarah found herself arguing repeatedly with her brother about the rights of women in an advanced society. Although their discussions may have swayed Randall to include women in the Tulane bequest, the senator insisted that the status of women was fixed by nature. "I *talked* and *talked* down his foolish ideas of women being infants in reality as well as in law," Sarah wrote. "He couldn't understand how a woman, a 'female thing,' a 'chattel' in the common law could feel the same human necessities, to eat, to sleep, to be clothed and sheltered and get ahead in the world, that he did. He couldn't realize that a woman felt human aspirations and were open to human convictions and that they didn't all propose to give their lives up to replenishing the earth just to please men." While Randall told her that "the mistake of my life had been that I had always been trying to *do* something, when . . . I should have sat down and been simply a lady," Sarah resolved that "we can't give up if we are *ladies*."[27]

In 1888 Sarah helped found the Kentucky Equal Rights Association and began campaigning and writing articles in favor of women's suffrage and legislation to raise the age of consent from twelve to eighteen. In her view, merely amending the law would not give women freedom. Only if women fought for their rights, Sarah thought, would equality follow. By struggling and striving—by embodying freedom and equality—women would prevail.

Sarah packed a pistol. In the view of one Kentucky newspaper, she was becoming a skilled orator, good enough to "beat half the members of Congress at stump speaking."[28]

At Hot Springs, though, Sarah kept her voice soft as she tended to her brother. Outside his room she sent increasingly hopeless accounts of Randall's health to family and friends—he was "vomiting blood, his body broken out with a terrible rash, his throat and tongue swollen—in short he seems to be on fire," she wrote. But by his side she was gentle, encouraging. Randall was visibly comforted by her presence. Soon two of Randall's sons joined her. Richie arrived on his own; he was prepping for Yale at Fordham College in New York, near the family home at High Bridge. Young Preston, born while his parents were still mourning the loss of their daughter Louisiana in 1880, was pulled out of boarding school and accompanied to Hot Springs by his mother's sister, Leita Kent. He had been seven when his mother died. He would reach adulthood with a large family fortune but without a parent's love.[29]

Sarah, Richie, Preston—they would carry Randall's memory and the Gibson name, as would his two surviving brothers. Like Sarah, Tobe shuttled between Louisiana and Kentucky; he had built a successful law practice and helped organize gatherings of Confederate veterans. Hart, who had dodged bankruptcy in the 1870s without ever having to go to work, was conspicuously ensconced in a turreted Gothic castle just on the edge of Lexington, a fixture of the society pages, an active Yale alumnus, and a state university trustee. It was well known in Kentucky that "had it been necessary for [Hart] to exert his talents for a livelihood there is no distinction to which he might not have aspired." As it was, he was one of Kentucky's "most noted breeders of thoroughbreds."[30]

Looking at his two boys, Randall Gibson could not have helped but think of the one who was not at his bedside. Montgomery, his oldest son, was in Lexington, drinking himself stupid. Upon sobering up, he would contemplate how to cash out his share of his father's home in New Orleans and sugar plantation in Terrebonne Parish. Although his mother had expressed in her will the hope that "my sons will ever respect and obey their father," Montgomery was "not a very steady boy," one newspaper reported, "and, to use a street phrase, keeps his father guessing all the time as to what scrape he will turn up in next." A year after his mother died, he entered Yale. A generation earlier Randall and Hart Gibson had fascinated their classmates by clothing a striving, middle-class sensibility in the manners of Southern planters. But at Yale Montgomery became a wastrel, or worse. While Randall and Hart had spent much of their college years meticulously accounting for every penny spent, as a freshman Montgomery disappeared with a large check that his father had sent to cover his expenses, turning up several days later in Chicago, the money gambled away. Newspapers gleefully reported sightings of "young Mont," describing a young man without an overcoat talking to strangers at a rapid clip about his trust fund and the trouble he was causing his father, "evidently not intoxicated, but very plainly . . . excited and flighty."[31]

Montgomery's distance, figurative and literal, his idling ways, his incapacity—they made Randall weep on his deathbed. They were a sign of failure, the end of his line. Yet they also revealed a deeper success. Montgomery did not have to approach his father's achievements. He was a person of consequence because he was a Gibson. The newspapers would cover his comings and goings, his highs and lows, however petty. It had taken fewer than thirty years for Randall Gibson to build a successful law practice, marry into great wealth, and vault to the highest level of American politics. Now his children were aristocrats.[32]

Lying in bed, attended to by Sarah, Richie, Preston, and a retinue of doctors, Randall Gibson spent many of his waking hours reviewing his will. He would be buried in Kentucky, not in Louisiana. The boys would get watches and seals like the ones he had worn every day, and Will Johnston would also get a gold seal, a fitting tribute from a man who had written him hundreds of letters over thirty years. Gibson provided $500 annuities for his three siblings and then added an extra $2,000 gift for Sarah. His sister-in-law Leita Kent would get jewelry, books, diaries, and other personal effects, to keep in the family or dispose of as she saw fit.[33]

Although his three sons were already rich from their mother's family fortune, Gibson resolved to split nearly the entirety of his estate among them. If Tulane University was expecting something more than the $2,500 Gibson had set aside for the study of Southern history, it would once again be disappointed by a will. The boys would get Randall's homes in Washington and New Orleans as well as Oak Forest Plantation in Terrebonne Parish on the banks of Bayou Black, bordering a colored church on forty acres that he had given a favorite servant. Shortly before he left New Orleans for Hot Springs, Gibson had amended the will to instruct his executors and trustees not to sell the real estate before Preston had reached his majority. The properties were pieces of himself, who he was and what he valued, elegant townhomes and sugar fields and cypress forests. The experience of owning them would bring his boys to maturity as surely as if Gibson himself were at their side, teaching them "the value of property and . . . how to economize and take care of it."[34]

Besides the implicit shaping effect of owning property, Gibson's will provided very little guidance to his sons beyond urging them to follow the Ten Commandments and the Sermon on the Mount. He did not name a guardian for Preston. Instead he appointed four men as his executors and the trustees overseeing the bequest to his sons: Washington banker Charles Glover, New York lawyer and High Bridge neighbor Fielding Marshall, his New Orleans law partner Gilbert Hall, and longtime political ally, Tulane trustee, and Louisiana's junior senator Edward Douglass White. Gibson urged his boys to "defer to and confide in" them. It was a move that equated his sons' aristocratic stature with an ability to live independently. It may have acknowledged that the boys were far richer than his brothers and sister. Perhaps they needed distance from the rest of his family.[35]

November darkened into December. Newspapers across the country printed daily updates on his condition, describing him as hovering between life and death. His doctors gave up any hope for his recovery and could only comment on the "amount of vitality he possesses, which has kept him up this long." Will Johnston and Gilbert Hall came up from New Orleans to say good-bye. A Catholic priest gave Gibson last rites. On December 15, in the low afternoon sun, Richie, Preston, Leita Kent, and Sarah sat by Randall's side. He spoke with them quietly, then closed his eyes. For a silent minute they thought he was sleeping. Then they began to cry.[36]

CHAPTER FIFTEEN

WALL

Washington, D.C., 1890–91

O.S.B. WALL SPENT HIS nights among the District's best people, at classical recitals and summer cruises down the Potomac, weddings with hundreds of guests, progressive euchre games that broke near midnight for sumptuous suppers, formal gatherings to honor distinguished visitors, and meetings of any number of political and charitable clubs. Wall shared pleasantries and confidences with Harvard graduates, doctors, educators, and former members of Congress. Over waltzes and oratorios, the trill of laughter, and the syncopated report of silver on china, it was possible to forget that these men had been blackballed from the Harvard Club and District Medical Society, forced to work in segregated school systems, drummed out of Congress, and hounded from their homes by murderous mobs.[1]

In Wall's nighttime world, he was a distinguished gentleman with a "most paying law practice," "one of the most industrious and intelligent lawyers of the district." To his friends, he was Captain Wall, a leader of the race. His status was cemented by his close relationship with John Mercer Langston, who had served until 1885 as the government's minister to Haiti, became the first president of the Virginia Normal and Collegiate Institute for colored men and women, and then in 1888 was elected to represent Virginia in Congress. Wall's status was undiminished by the fact that white

Democrats had stolen the election, or that Langston had been contesting the results going on eighteen months.[2]

At public orations by Douglass and Langston before "large and brilliant audience[s]," Wall sat confidently on the dais alongside other Race Men like Blanche Bruce, Charles Purvis, Richard Greener, and the young Harvard graduate Robert Terrell. In 1885, when the crusading black newspaper editor T. Thomas Fortune sought an opinion on how colored Washington was weathering the Democrats' ascent to the White House, he asked Wall. After many blacks denounced Frederick Douglass's 1884 marriage to Helen Pitts, a white woman, Wall emerged as one of Douglass's most articulate defenders. "I think it is carrying out practically the theory and principles advocated by Mr. Douglass for the past thirty years with reference to the equality of the race," Wall said. "Mr. Douglass is a distinguished man, and he is now in the full strength of his intellectual vigor, and therefore it should be regarded as a deliberate and mature choice. Marriage is a question to be determined alone by the high contracting parties, and I can see no reason why Mr. Douglass and Miss Pitts should be made an exception. I see no reason why the public should be exercised over this matter more than any other marriage."[3]

Wall had long mingled comfortably with whites. Even as most were shutting blacks out of their lives, some remained sympathetic to the cause of equality and still showed their support openly and proudly. Wall might see a white ex-senator or a retired Supreme Court justice at an event. He might even imagine that the promise—the openness—of the days after the war had not withered on the vine.[4]

At their "charming house" on Howard Hill, O.S.B. and Amanda Wall held "most elaborate" evening parties for eminences such as Douglass and his wife, former Mississippi congressman John R. Lynch, and former South Carolina congressman Joseph H. Rainey. Firm believers in equality for all, priding themselves on views that were "radical and correct," the Walls even hosted Susan B. Anthony at the house for a night of music and "bright and animated conversation." By candle and firelight, Captain Wall delighted guests with stories of his "hairbreath escapes when he was conveying slaves to freedom by the Underground Railroad thirty-five years ago." "But it moves one to tears," wrote one visitor, "to hear him tell how that, upon one occasion when he with others rescued a boy at Wellington, Ohio, . . . he, Mr Charles Langston, brother of our Minister to Hayti, and his other comrades were cast into the Cleveland jail."[5]

When a young lawyer named Reuben S. Smith dined with the Walls, he thought that "a more ideal and happy family could hardly be found." With his "amiable" wife, "stalwart sons," and "beautiful and accomplished" daughters—the youngest, Laura Gertrude, was prepping at Oberlin—Wall was the picture of a "devoted father." The impression was shared by Henry Wall, a white first cousin on O.S.B.'s father's side who had come to Washington to work for the Democratic senator from Tennessee Isham Harris, a former Confederate officer and aggressive opponent of Negro equality. For nearly a century the story "about that time Uncle Henry Wall ate with those colored Walls in Washington" would be repeated among the white side of the family down south. Henry had found his cousins "culti-vated and charming and when they asked him to stay for dinner, he ac-cepted and enjoyed the entire evening," wrote one descendant in 1969. "As this part of the story was told and retold[,] the only person who received any censure here was Uncle Henry for his straightforward acknowledge-ment that he enjoyed himself. For that, they never forgave him."[6]

THE RESPECT AND DISTINCTION, the intellectual exchanges and ele-vated pursuits of Wall's night hours, faded in the sunlight. After evening revelries Wall awoke to a less rarified existence. He had borrowed heavily on his charming house and had no certain way to pay his ballooning debt. He spent his days at the police court among the District's petty thugs and thieves, the abjectly poor and morally lost, hustling and scraping for clients who could barely afford to pay his five-dollar fees.[7]

At the police court, he argued before Judge William B. Snell, a Maine Yankee whose appointment to the bench in 1871 had terminated Wall's position as a police magistrate. Although Wall once described Snell as being evenhanded in his treatment of colored lawyers, the judge did not hesitate to put Wall in his place. While defending an accused harness thief, Wall tried to impeach the credibility of witnesses by asking them if they had ever served time in the penitentiary. Judge Snell declared in open court that Wall's cross-examination was "a disgrace to the profession." "If a man would ask me that question," Snell said, "I would knock him down." When Wall tried to introduce hearsay in a larceny trial, the judge responded with what seemed like a personal insult to someone who had regularly testified on Capitol Hill. "No sir. No hearsay evidence here," Snell said. "I am not a Congressional committee, and I despise the methods of those committees and the kind of witnesses that testify before them."[8]

Judge Snell's lack of regard for Wall carried over to the prosecutors. When Wall defended a man who had been accused of carrying concealed weapons, the district attorney told Wall's client that he should get his money back and named the client to the court as someone who had a "dishonest lawyer." Wall stood before the judge. "The client was a client of mine," Wall said. "My children and my friends, their wishes and sentiments are at stake. I am nearly sixty years old, have held eleven commissions and have never dishonored one of them. I never had a charge against me except once in Cleveland for rescuing a slave."[9]

The white press took every opportunity to portray Wall as a buffoon or worse, better dressed perhaps than the "piratic-looking young negroes" he defended on charges ranging from vagrancy to stealing a sixteen-cent harmonica, but no more worthy of respect, let alone equality. The papers regularly reported Wall's doings in court as comic relief. When Wall pleaded for mercy for an admitted thief on the grounds that "my client is an imbecile," the defendant interrupted to ask "in a business-like manner how long he would get on [a guilty] plea." "I guess he is a pretty bright imbecile," joked the judge. In October 1885 the dailies titillated readers with news that O.S.B. Wall had been caught by Amanda in flagrante with the wife of a "white policeman" whom Wall had previously recommended for appointment to the force. The Walls and the policeman and his wife vehemently denied the story, and two months later an investigative report to the District commissioners by a police major stated that "nothing occurred to warrant the scene described in the newspapers at the time." Wall blamed unnamed "enemies" for circulating the story.[10]

Perhaps most galling of all, Wall suffered the disrespect of younger black lawyers. Over the course of the 1880s, whites in Washington isolated their colored neighbors. The tens of thousands of blacks living in alleys behind tidy white residential blocks were erased from the civic conscious-ness except as criminals and carriers of communicable disease. Blacks with money were increasingly consigned to segregated enclaves on the District's fringes. The local government, no longer elected, shut blacks out of the city jobs that had sustained the community through the 1860s and 1870s. The election of Grover Cleveland in 1884—the first Democratic president since the Civil War—caused widespread fear that the federal government would stop hiring blacks too. The District had more black lawyers than anywhere else in the country, but there were not enough paying clients to support them. The colored aristocracy often hired white lawyers, a logical extension of their elitism and color snobbery, or perhaps a sign of surrender to the pervasive unfairness blacks faced in and out of the courtroom. Wall himself retained a white lawyer—his old friend, the abolitionist, Radical Republican, and former police chief A. C. Richards—to handle his estate. Black lawyers were left fighting for the scraps in police court. When de-fendants were led from the basement holding cells into the courtroom, they were set upon by hungry lawyers "as a rat by a congregation of cats."[11]

Some lawyers tried to poach Wall's clients. Others insulted the old man to his face. Occasionally Wall was able to remain good-humored. When a judge urged Wall and another lawyer to settle their differences outside, Wall responded, "It'll be pistols and coffee for two." But the daily struggle was grinding him down.[12]

The erosion of race pride and solidarity that Wall witnessed in the gritty chambers of the police court was a symptom of a larger sense of hopelessness that pervaded black America. In an 1885 speech that Wall attended, Frederick Douglass observed that the "sullen discontent and deadly hate" of white Southerners after the war had become a governing principle. From the moment federal troops abandoned the South in 1877, Democrats had had carte blanche to "encourage violence and crime, ele-vate to office the men whose hands are reddest with innocent blood; force the Negroes out of Southern politics by the shotgun and the bulldozer's whip; cheat them out of the elective franchise; suppress the Republican vote; kill off their white Republican leaders and keep the South solid." Countless thousands of Negroes in the South lived in conditions approxi-mating slavery, shackled by sharecropping contracts, arrested on trumped-up charges, and sold as convict labor. Every few days a Negro was lynched: burned, shot, castrated, hacked to pieces.[13]

Whites in the District and points north had scant consciousness of the terror and bloodletting, let alone sympathy for civil rights. Most Americans thought blacks were stupid, lewd, immoral, predisposed to crime, unfit for full citizenship—deserving of everything they suffered. Unless they were kept entirely separate from whites, unless whites took every effort to preserve absolute purity of their blood, Western civilization would fall. Given the horrors of Southern life—and the passive approval of the rest of the country—Douglass wondered aloud if blacks would be driven to revolution, "imitat[ing] the example of other oppressed classes and invok[ing] some terrible explosive power as a means of bringing [their] oppressors to their senses, and making them respect the claims of justice."[14]

Instead the violence turned inward, and no one—not even those in Wall's elite social circle—was spared. The collapse of civil rights cast adrift young colored aristocrats like Wall's children, educated in the 1870s among whites and raised to expect equality. Just after sunset on March 4, 1884, John Mercer Langston's twenty-year-old son, Frank, found himself caught up in a crowd watching two men—black and white—brawl just a few blocks from home. On his way to a lecture at the high-toned Bethel Literary and Historical Association, dressed in a steel-colored suit, light overcoat, and derby hat, Frank was the picture of a colored aristocrat. But in the heat of the moment, he pulled out a pistol and fired two shots, killing one bystander instantly and wounding another in the neck.[15]

John Mercer Langston was away on government business in Haiti and Caroline was "prostrated with grief" at news of the killing, so O.S.B. Wall took responsibility for his sister's family. Rather than trusting the legal system to treat Frank fairly, Wall gave his nephew a horse and buggy and a hundred dollars, enabling him to escape to cousins in Memphis. When an "anguished" Langston arrived home from Haiti in May, Frank returned to town and surrendered. Wall helped put together a team of distinguished white lawyers who eventually won an acquittal. Just three years later, however, Frank killed a man who called him a "damned liar," this time in Petersburg, Virginia. Again Wall assisted in finding "excellent" lawyers to represent his nephew and attended the trial. But with a less forgiving jury, Frank wound up serving nearly five years in the penitentiary.[16]

The unmooring of the younger generation plagued Wall with anxiety. His son Stephen, after six years in a supposedly secure position at the Government Printing Office, was fired by Democrats appointed by Grover Cleveland. Stephen opened a cigar shop in the Shaw neighborhood, not far from home. The shop doubled as a pool hall, and by the end of 1887 there was a room in the back with a counter and shelves stocked with demijohns of gin and rye, shot glasses, and cases of beer. In January 1888 police raided the establishment, and Stephen was arrested for operating a "tippling-house, bar-room, [or] sample room" without a license. O.S.B. Wall had to go back before Judge Snell in police court not to defend some illiterate, starving, tubercular wretch but to see his "stalwart" son—the boy he had named for his father—stand in shame. Wall had to hear witnesses testify, as one did, that "I bought a cigar and called for a drink—got a drink of gin, paid for it, and *drank it*," and he had to bear the humiliation of watching Judge Snell pronounce Stephen guilty and hand down a sentence of $105 or sixty days in the workhouse.[17]

Wall posted an appeal bond for his son, hired a white lawyer, and took the case to the criminal court for a jury trial. Stephen Wall and his employees testified that they had never sold beer and whiskey but rather had been serving it at private gatherings of Republicans gearing up for the 1888 presidential campaign. The liquor was meant to "advance his political interests," Stephen said, and an employee clarified that he had advised Stephen that "if he would have some drinks on hand he could get the men to vote any way he wanted them to." After Stephen's lawyer alleged that the police drank most of Stephen Wall's liquor during the raid, "leaving nothing except a pile of empty bottles," the jury returned a verdict of not guilty. Near the end of 1888 Stephen applied for a barroom license and was rejected. Soon afterward he sold his shop. When it was raided again in 1890, it was called the Columbia Social and Literary Club. Police found "half a hundred negro men in the shabby, low ceilinged rooms, many of them gathered around a rude table on which a spirited game of crap was in progress."[18]

O.S.B. Wall's other children were contemplating different lines to cross. His oldest son, Edward, left his job at the post office and moved all the way to Montreal. Like his brother, he became a saloon keeper. Unlike anyone else in the family to date, he married a French woman and presented himself to the world as a white man. Wall's daughter Bel, who had been working as a substitute teacher in the District's public schools, was dreaming of a life in the New York theater—and a new role offstage. She studied acting at the Martyn College of Elocution and Oratory. The school shared space with the Martyn Commercial College, which advertised "Colored students not admitted."[19]

The harder whites made it for blacks to earn a living, educate their children, and just make it through a single day without threat or insult, the greater the incentives grew for light-skinned blacks to leave their communities and establish themselves as white. If anything, the drumbeat for racial purity, the insistence that any African ancestry—a single drop of blood—tainted a person's very existence, accelerated the migration to new identities and lives. The difference between white and black seemed obvious, an iron-clad rule, a biological fact. But the Walls knew that blacks could be as good as whites and as bad, as smart and as stupid. Blacks had just as much claim to schooling and jobs and love and family, to common courtesies each day. The Walls knew that blacks could be every bit the equal of whites—and that their skins could be equally light. As the United States veered from slavery to Jim Crow, O.S.B. Wall's children did not stand up and fight. They faded away.

HIS FINANCES TIGHTENING, HIS people crushed, his family dissolving, Wall started losing his grip on his decorum and dignity. After an "aged white lawyer" called Wall "a— fool" during a break in court proceedings, Wall slapped him in the face, stunning onlookers. When a lawyer tried to claim one of Wall's clients as his own, Wall screamed in the middle of the police court that the lawyer should be sent to jail for "shystering." Wall drew looks of "interest and dismay," while an officer whispered to the old man to "Shut up!" On a third occasion at the courthouse, Emanuel M.

Hewlett, who represented Frederick Douglass and his family, referred to Wall as a "50 cent lawyer." In response, Wall promptly "sent out his right hand with terrific force, and the blow caught Hewlett on the jaw, forcing him against the door and sending his silk hat and cane in different directions across the witness room." Hewlett punched Wall in the face, and Wall reportedly bit Hewlett's finger. The daily papers crowed that "Hewlett claimed the fight on a foul."[20]

Wall's money problems were intruding into his family relationships. When his sister Sarah died in 1886, leaving valuable land and personal effects in Ohio and the District, John Mercer Langston was appointed executor of the will. Wall wrote "my dear professor" a series of increasingly insistent letters, practically begging for fees as well as for a larger, presumably more remunerative role in handling the estate. Wall described himself as "restless" and "anxious" to have his sister's property inventoried and divided as quickly as possible. He demanded prompt payment for every bit of aid that he had given Mercer. "I have received not one cent of my bill . . . after I spent a day with you to assist to get in your possession all the money of the estate in this District," Wall wrote. After Wall left town to handle his sister's funeral arrangements, he sought reimbursement for the "*honest* and *necessary*" expense of keeping his horse at a boarding stable "for two or three days when I had no one in the world to take care of [it] while I was absent from home." "I am not able to lay out of the use of my money and would not if I could help myself," he admitted to Langston.[21]

At work, Wall suffered occasional episodes of speechlessness. He would stand up to argue a case but find himself "unable to articulate a word," seized with the feeling that his tongue was swelling. Each time Wall had an attack, he would need several days of rest. Then he would put on his suit and head back to the police court.[22]

ON APRIL 12, 1890, Wall readied himself for work—suit, tie, watch, papers. He appeared to one daughter to be "unusually bright and . . . in good spirits." It was a Saturday morning, warm, breezy, and fair, the loveliest kind of day in the District's short spring. The police court was eighteen blocks south, and the ride into town would be beautiful. From Howard Hill the entire city unfolded before Wall. The foul swirling dust, deep muck, open sewers, and roaming livestock that he had first encountered after the war had given way to stately avenues and graceful parks, charming townhomes on tree-lined streets, mansions and monuments. Wall saw a Washington that was prettier than ever, and uglier at the same time. Two blocks down the hill, LeDroit Park was elegant, understated, and in bloom. Developed at the same time that Wall was building his house, the subdivision of picturesque Victorian homes and lush rose gardens had long been fenced and patrolled by guards, signaling that it would have nothing to do with the surrounding neighborhood and its black residents. Although Howard students tore a gap in the fence in 1888, LeDroit remained all white, its wrought iron reinforced with barbed wire.[23]

The Saturday police court was cleaning up Friday night's mess. On his arrival Wall took his place in the familiar choreography of defendants, police, bailiffs, lawyers, and onlookers. The courthouse had once been a Unitarian church, but few prayers were answered there now. In his well-cut suit and languid bow tie, his hair and mustache touched with gray and neatly trimmed, Wall occupied a different world from the ragged client beside him. Behind Wall were more of the same, shadows of men whispering with lawyers eager for their business or silently waiting their turn for justice, all accused of petty crimes—theft, profanity, assault, carrying a concealed blade. Police officers and bailiffs paced the vaulted chamber and the corridors outside, ready to testify, on guard for disturbances. Women and children sat on hard benches, craning for glimpses of loved ones.[24]

Surrounded by old acquaintances, friends, and enemies, Wall joined the procession of pleas and fines, crime and punishment. It seemed endless— his clients looking up to him, the judge looking down, Wall floating in the middle like dust trapped in sunlight, buffeted by contending currents, wealth and poverty, right and wrong, liberty and bondage, black and white. But then it stopped. He stood and faced the judge and opened his mouth to argue his client's case. His lips began to move, but there was only silence. He stopped and tried again. The silence stretched. He looked at the judge, bewildered. He could not say a word.[25]

Wall faltered and fell. His onetime slanderer Emanuel Hewlett gathered him in his arms and with another lawyer carried Wall out of the courtroom. On the street they hailed a carriage and raced back to Howard Hill. Charles Purvis was sent for from the Freedmen's Hospital. The doctor found a man paralyzed by a massive stroke.[26]

Though Wall could not talk, Purvis was encouraged by the fact that his patient could understand his questions and seemed to comprehend what was happening around him. Wall recognized his wife and children and the many friends who were making "anxious inquiries as to his condition." Purvis told the press that Wall was a "very sick man" but held out hope that "with close watching and treatment he would pull through."[27]

Immobile and anguished, Wall suffered through two months of pain and prayer. Howard University's president Jeremiah Rankin visited regularly. After blacks had been allowed to join the First Congregational Church more than two decades earlier, Rankin had become the minister and baptized Wall. Now he cheered O.S.B. and Amanda Wall "many times by his calls to sympathy in our affliction." As spring ripened into summer, Wall rose from his bed. Writing to General Oliver Otis Howard of her husband's "wonderful" recovery that August, Amanda exulted that "God has again placed him on his feet + with use of a cane only he has been going, the past week, about the neighborhood."[28]

As he gained strength, Wall's first thought was that he had to start working again. "When brought home from court," Amanda wrote, "he had six dollars, all we possessed. Our home mortgaged for $1600." Going back to the police court was out of the question "because of lameness + inability to use his pen." Amanda took charge of finding something for him to do. She knew that William Windom, a former senator from Minnesota who had supported Wall during the Negro Exodus hearings, was now treasury secretary in the new Republican presidential administration. She asked General Howard to contact Windom on Wall's behalf to see if there was an opening for a "night or day's watchmen's position; day watchmen's preferred." Upon receiving Amanda's letter, Howard immediately wrote the treasury secretary to see if Wall could get some "light work." "Anything you can do for Wall," Howard wrote, "will be greatly beneficial to a worthy man + his family and appreciated by me + his numerous friends."[29]

Wall never got to use Howard's recommendation. He wilted in the late-summer heat. When the weather broke, he rallied again, but Amanda described a family left waiting "from day to day hoping for the fulfillment of our desires." O.S.B. and Amanda now refocused their energy on getting Stephen reinstated at the Government Printing Office and securing their son's position as a respectable member of the middle class. Even though blacks had lost considerable clout in the fifteen years since the end of Reconstruction, the Walls had retained their ties to prominent whites—connections from Ohio, the war, and from Wall's days as a Republican official and activist. At the time of Wall's stroke, the family had just started lining up influential men to contact the public printer on Stephen's behalf. While an initial letter from an Ohio congressman tepidly described hiring Stephen as a "personal favor," the entreaties took on a new urgency by the beginning of 1891. Alvred Bayard Nettleton, assistant secretary of the treasury, pleaded that rehiring Stephen would "make the difference between the comfort and the absolute distress of Captain O.S.B. Wall, who was a faithful Union soldier and officer during the war and now lies paralyzed and helpless." "I do not often consent to write letters of this nature," Nettleton said, "but the case of Captain Wall appeals to me so strongly and pathetically that I cannot refrain from asking your special consideration for it."[30]

As winter turned to spring, Wall grew increasingly feeble. Practicing law, organizing his community, stumping for votes, and fighting for liberty before, during, and after the war—a journey of sixty-five years receded into the dim corners of his sickroom. From his bed he learned of Bel's stage performances and Laura Gertrude's studies at the Oberlin Conservatory. In March he quietly rejoiced in the news that Stephen had been summoned back to work at the Printing Office. A month later, "peaceful and without a struggle," O.S.B. Wall died.[31]

CHAPTER SIXTEEN

SPENCER

*Jordan Gap, Johnson County,
Kentucky, ca. 1900*

F OG SEEPED THROUGH THE hollows like a slowly spreading stain. First the ridges faded and disappeared, then the
budding treetops up and down the slopes, followed by the hillsides themselves. The pale shroud poured through split-rail fences, smothered the
fields, swallowed coops and cabins. Places where people had spent their
entire lives became new and unfamiliar. No mountains above or hard ground
below. Everyone was alone. People startled, lost their footing, bumped into
things that were not there. It was widely believed that the fog was a play-
ground for ghosts and haints. After a shivering moment, the calls of birds
and people, the sandy grind of hoof on trail, or the bubbling rush of a
spring creek grew crisp in the white darkness—sounds that kept a man
from thinking he was dreaming, or dead.[1]

With each passing year, the mists were haunted by new and unfamiliar
noises: a shriek, whistle, or whine, a percussive blast. The fog could lift
quickly, but other clouds—red, brown, and black—remained. From high
in the hills, one might see dust rising from dynamite and falling timber, or
a steady column of smoke along the Big Sandy River. For more than twenty
years, the Chesapeake & Ohio Railroad had been extending its line eighteen miles from Lawrence County into Johnson. Paintsville was almost in
sight.[2]

The train would be a rumbling envoy for the new century. Almost since the Civil War, businessmen in town and in faraway cities had dreamed of, dealt for, and plotted its course through Johnson County. The Chesapeake & Ohio was joined by the Louisville & Nashville and Norfolk & Western railroads in extending deeper and deeper into the mountains from north, south, east, and west. On a map, the lines were wrapping around the eastern Kentucky hills like a lariat slowly pulling tight.[3]

The train would connect Johnson County to the rest of the country—to the world, even—better than any Big Sandy steamboat. It would bring new markets and new jobs to the area, and it would kill old ones. It changed the way people thought about and fashioned their lives. They would keep time differently—railroads and the industries that typically followed insisted on standardized clocks. Homespun linen and wool would give way to store-bought clothes. Within a generation a county historian would be describing local wedding customs as "comparable to those in 'The Little Church Around the Corner' at East 29th Street, New York City." The train would take people from the hills to big cities, and new people would come in.[4]

In addition to standardizing time, railroads ordered space in novel ways, introducing new encounters with outside authority. A train might roll through the Big Sandy Valley, but each railcar enclosed a different world, with rules set by faraway corporate officers and state regulators and enforced by conductors. These rules dictated how people could act: whether they could talk loudly or play cards, smoke or chew tobacco. They also dictated where people could sit—in first class or in the ladies' car, the smoker, or the colored car.[5]

For nearly thirty years after the war, blacks in central and western Kentucky demanded equal access to trains and streetcars, protesting and repeatedly suing over racial segregation. By the time the railroad was within sight of Paintsville, however, the state had resolved the issue in favor of absolute separation. In 1892 the legislature required all railroads, on pain of heavy fines, to provide separate coaches or compartments for black and white passengers, marked by "appropriate words in plain letters indicating the race for which [they are] set apart." Four years later the United States Supreme Court held that such statutes were constitutional, and the Southern landscape was transformed with signs labeling everything white or colored.[6]

Johnson County did not experience the critique of white supremacy and display of black political energy that developed during the years of Reconstruction, nor was it gripped by the white majority's harsh backlash, its rage for separation and purity, that swept far beyond Kentucky. The county responded to Jim Crow by declaring everyone white. But each day the railroad brought a new occasion for train conductors, unfamiliar with the local accommodation, to disagree. Some state courts helped preserve local customs by allowing whites to sue railroads for being assigned to the wrong car; in essence, these suits forced conductors to give ambiguous passengers the benefit of the doubt. Kentucky courts, however, shielded railroads from defamation suits. "What race a person belongs to cannot always be determined infallibly from appearances," the state supreme court held in 1906, "and mistakes must inevitably be made." The importance of maintaining racial purity outweighed any individual right to be recognized as white.[7]

Despite the changing times, Jordan Spencer traveled every spring to a place beyond the C&O's grasp. He was as old as men got, but he could still handle a horse. Well into his eighties, he rode a fine stallion into the hills toward Virginia. No train conductors asked him where he was going or made a judgment about who he was. His children presumed he was returning to somewhere he had known as a young man. Given the impossibly rugged terrain, their father could have managed the journey and returned home only on horseback.[8]

In Virginia, Spencer rode from farm to farm, offering his stallion's services as a stud and collecting fees for the previous year's successes. Breeding horses required no modern technology, but new imperatives increasingly held sway. "At one time in Virginia horse-breeding, blood and record was everything," reported Virginia's agriculture commissioner in the 1890s. "Now a more utilitarian time has come, and the horse that will produce the greatest profit . . . whether for the turf, the road, the farm, or the team, will be sought for in the section to which the breed is suited."[9]

Whatever the bloodlines of Spencer's stallion, it thrived in the mountains. Jordan made enough money to leave a good deal of it behind at stills and speakeasies known as "blind tigers" on the ride home. After a certain point on the road, the horse knew the way back to Rockhouse. It carried him along the creek bed and up the path to Spencer's cabin, where it stood calmly, waiting for someone to pull the old man down and put him to bed.[10]

All of Jordan and Malinda's children were dead or grown. Malinda, now in her seventies, had survived fifteen childbirths. Eight sons and daughters—mostly sons—were still alive. Their youngest girl, Lydia, had married in 1895. Their youngest boy, Jasper, was thirty-two and had been married twice, with two sons and a daughter. Jordan Jr. was the father of nine. For a time the old couple probably lived alone in their cabin, in silence they had never known as children or adults. Even though Old Jordan took pride in doing hard fieldwork until the end of his life, he and Malinda could survive with just a cow, some hogs, and what they grew in gardens by their home. They started selling off small pieces of land to neighbors. Jordan and Malinda lent them money to complete the purchases, just as their neighbors' parents and grandparents had helped the Spencers finance their own acquisitions half a century earlier.[11]

But Jordan and Malinda's cabin did not stay silent more than a few years. Shortly before 1900 their son Tobe moved back in after his wife died, with two teenage boys and two younger girls. The five of them gave Jordan and Malinda a workforce. The farm had new life, and the cabin was crowded again.[12]

When Old Jordan went visiting along Rockhouse Creek and elsewhere in the hills, people saw a dignified man. He sat tall on his horse, walked strongly, and still paid meticulous attention to his appearance. A handful had known him from the time the Spencers moved to the hollow. Most could not remember a time without him; none was his elder. He reminded them of their parents, long-dead brothers and sisters, lost days.[13]

No one seemed to think about Old Jordan's race—that had been something for the bygone generation to puzzle out. His children and their children were white, without question. Many of them were kin by marriage. When the 1900 census-taker looked at Jordan, he initially marked a *B* by his name. But then he had second thoughts—perhaps after gauging community opinion—and wrote a *W* over it, retracing the letter again and again until it was bolder than any other classification on the page. The old man had become emphatically white.[14]

Although Spencer was well composed in public, his grandchildren remembered someone different at home—a man who had spent decades working children hard in the fields, remained able to do heavy lifting, and, when he got drunk, stayed strong enough to administer beatings. Like their parents, the grandchildren living with Jordan worked instead of going to school. They never forgot the man, and as they grew older, they repeated stories about him that their children, in turn, never forgot. In one telling, Spencer was so full of rage, so uncontrollable one night that a grandson reached into a coal bucket, grabbed a rock, and beat Jordan until he collapsed to the cabin floor, bloodied and unconscious but still terrifying in a coal fire's glow. He would be a new man for the neighbors the next day.[15]

EVERY EVENING AN ARMY of Kentucky men sat in washtubs and tried to scrub themselves white. They scoured their cheeks and eyelids and ears and hands, under their fingernails. Their skin was dull black, head to toe. The black had worked through their sleeves and pants and long johns, burrowed into their arms and legs like the little red chigger bugs that infested the hills—perhaps the reason some called it "bug dust."[16]

In the last minutes of light, the men washed themselves with lye soap until they tasted it and felt it burning their eyes. The tub water grew dull and dark and sulfurous as it cooled. Some of the black never came out. When coal dust got into a cut, it dyed the skin like a tattoo. Even after their nightly baths, the men could still smell coal, and they still spat black.[17]

The railroad had come to Paintsville for one reason: to tap eastern Kentucky's millions of tons of bituminous and cannel coal. People in Johnson County had been mining bits of it for as long as Jordan Spencer had lived there, but mainly for their own use, picking away at their hillsides when they had some spare time. Without an easy way to ship to the large factories, blast furnaces, and gasworks that needed it, there was no use in doing anything more. Rising industries in the North could rely on coal from Pennsylvania, Ohio, Indiana, and Illinois; as late as 1900, western Kentucky's mines still produced more than the Appalachian counties. Once the railroad snaked up the Big Sandy Valley, however, the massive fields between Paintsville and Elkhorn Creek near the Virginia line would yield cheap, high-grade coal by the mountainful.[18]

It was common knowledge that eastern Kentucky was rich with coal. It jutted out of the ground in large rock formations, plainly visible to people passing by. For decades everyone from a local Johnson County teacher to financiers in Boston, Chicago, and Pittsburgh had been busy buying up hundreds of thousands of acres of mineral rights. They took rooms at the Alger House in Paintsville and carried suitcases full of cash. They rode through the hills with saddlebags heavy with gold pieces. Mining companies were financing the railroad construction. When the line first crossed into Johnson County in 1888, coal operations immediately opened along the way. Within months Johnson County coal was burning in New York City, Toronto, Chicago, the Dakotas, and elsewhere. As Jordan Spencer was selling off small parts of his farm, his deeds stopped referring exclusively to stone markers and tall trees in delineating property boundaries. In 1895, nine years before the railroad reached Paintsville, Spencer sold a parcel that began at "a rock and locust near a Coal Bank."[19]

It was less clear how life would change once the mines along the Big Sandy Valley began producing tens of thousands of tons of coal every day. For a farmer like Jordan Spencer, coal companies paid good money for crops to feed the workforce and for timber to strengthen support walls inside the mines and to build housing outside. Although Clay County's saltworks and Johnson County's small-scale coal and timber operations must have given Spencer some understanding of industrial life, the old man could not have foreseen how different his children's and grandchildren's lives would be from his own.[20]

Jordan Spencer had spent his eighty-plus years surrounded by forest. His daughter Lydia sold her mineral rights and used the proceeds to buy a home for her family in town. Many more Spencers wound up in the mines. Men who had spent their childhoods in the hills took jobs chiseling and blasting their way through them. Many miners almost never saw the sun. In winter their days started before sunup and ended after dark. They entered the mine through a wide mouth gashed into a hillside. The main tunnel branched off about every eighty feet into smaller tunnels, known as "rooms." Miners claimed their own rooms and returned to them every working day. They used their own time to buttress the walls and ceiling with timbers. At the end of a room was the rock face, and each day the room grew a little longer.[21]

In the dim, stinking light of lard lamps, the miners picked and drilled under masses of coal while lying on their sides. Packing and lighting gunpowder charges and diving for cover, they spent hours shoveling rock into carts. Slouching under beam and ceiling, feet soaked from the slush and puddle that slicked the mine floors, throats burning from powder smoke and dust, they pushed cart after cart to the main tunnel, where mules pulled them out of the hills.[22]

In the early years miners were paid by the weight of what they had carted out, usually two or three dollars a day, sometimes given as scrip redeemable only at the company store. In certain ways the mining life was not unlike farming in a mountain hollow. Plowing, clearing trees and brush, splitting wood and building fences, and harvesting could be grueling, repetitive, and lonely tasks. Miners who were paid by the ton could work at their own pace, with little supervision. The timbers that framed the tunnel walls and ceilings were notched like logs for cabins. Perhaps the most visceral reminder of life outside was the steep pitch of the mine floors. In the 1870s one miner described his daily routine as "very much like asking a man to stand on the roof of a house while working." It was a sensation familiar to anyone who had ever picked corn in the Jordan Gap.[23]

Outside were hollows crisscrossed with tracks and crammed with mine tipples, workmen's cottages, and the company store. Creeks ran foul and were littered with garbage. And everywhere, in the miners' homes and on their stoops, in their hair and teeth and eyes, was the coal dust, "like sand on the desert. It was in their food," wrote a folklorist who would travel throughout coal country. "Their clothes grated with it . . . The white satin ribbons for their children's christenings were soiled by company-store clerks who measured with grimy hands." In the middle of the mountains, they might as well have been in Chicago, Pittsburgh, or Detroit.[24]

Jordan Spencer had established himself in his community and created relationships and alliances in part by borrowing money from neighbors and local businessmen and paying them back over time. Miners, by contrast, stayed in hock to the mining companies, for their housing, food, clothes, and supplies. It was as if the railroad and mines were creating a new world in the hills, a new beginning, and a new history. In Kentucky, towns were established bearing the names of executives from faraway corporations: Miller's Creek, about five miles from the Jordan Gap, would become Van Lear, Kentucky. In Virginia, Roanoke was not the failed colony that Sir Walter Raleigh had tried to establish in the late sixteenth century; after 1882 it was the Norfolk & Western's gateway to the mining areas of the south-western Virginia mountains, a town formerly known as Big Lick. Pocahon-tas was no longer the princess who saved John Smith's life. Now it was the giant coalfield spanning the border between Virginia and West Virginia.[25]

With policies set hundreds of miles away, the coal companies controlled the kinds of relationships that miners and their families could form among themselves. In large part this control stemmed from their ability to select who worked in the mines. They balanced locals with outsiders to create communities where it was difficult to develop norms and values and rules that conflicted with maximum productivity—communities where no one had roots.[26]

Many of the mine workers came from far away: Virginia and Alabama, but also Italy and Hungary and Poland. For the first time ever, appreciable numbers of blacks would live in Johnson County. Until then many local residents would have said they had never seen a black person before. Within fifteen years the federal government would be investigating whether the coal companies were moving blacks in from the Deep South in order to tip coal-mining states Republican in the 1916 presidential election. Above-ground, the area began to resemble the rest of the South, with freshly painted "whites only" signs and housing and schools and religious services segregated by race. But in the darkness and dust, the rules were relaxed. The imperative to extract as much coal as possible trumped the discipline demanded by Jim Crow. Although blacks were excluded from management jobs, down in the mines they labored side by side with white miners. They called whites by their first names, and at the end of the day they earned the same wages.[27]

Filled with outsiders and confronted with the task of separating blacks and whites, coal-mining communities were far from Rockhouse Creek, if only a few ridgelines away. Even in this unsettled world, however, the Spencers remained white. The camps were places where memories were lost— no one would take the time to explain who Jordan Spencer was, or find someone who would listen. It was hard to tell what Jordan's descendants looked like inside the mines or in the dusty twilight outside. Their status was fixed as locals, and as far as anyone was concerned, the locals were all white.

THE HORIZONS WERE NARROW in the creek valleys and bottomland that wound through the hills. Every moment brought a new turn, a new outcropping, a rise or fall, an obstacle to overcome. It was a landscape that put people in blinders, demanding complete attention to the present moment. There was little future to contemplate when one had no way of seeing what waited ahead. Nor was there anything to look back to. An old man and woman standing by a path would not be visible long. Within steps they would blend into the wilderness, obscured first by trees, then by rock.

Jordan Spencer Jr. and his wife, Alafair, had lived nearly twenty years along Rockhouse Creek. They raised their oldest children nearly to adulthood there. The neighbors knew and would remember them fondly. Now Young Jordan's family was moving slowly through the hills. Their horses and mules staggered with everything they owned, food for the journey, and eight children. Their five boys all shared names with Jordan's brothers; their three girls were Virgie, Mary, and Liengracia. With George age sixteen and Mary a few years younger, the oldest could wrangle the babies. Alafair was probably pregnant with their ninth, a boy they would name Paris.[28]

South and east up the Levisa Fork, the hills peaked higher, and the hollows cut steep. It would be years before the railroad would extend that far. Around 1900 the paths were at best treacherous, often too narrow for wagons. The difficulties of riding through the area became the stuff of legend for the would-be coal barons trying to convince local farmers to sell them mining rights in the area. In any season but summer, the creeks would have been too high and fast for a family to cross them. At most the family might manage to move a mile every hour. It was impossible to travel in the dark. South of Paintsville the Spencers might have stayed with Jordan's brother Jasper and his family. But their journey was just beginning, and they probably slept outside most of the way.[29]

Unlike Old Jordan and Malinda, Jordan Jr. and his family did not strike out for a new life because anyone disapproved of them. Still, they prepared to travel far away. It was unlikely they would ever see their parents, brothers, sisters, and cousins again. Perhaps Rockhouse Creek was getting too crowded for the family to feed themselves. Across Appalachia, what had once been sparse settlements in remote creek valleys were becoming dense neighborhoods, as dozens of children of the original settlers were having dozens of children themselves. There was less available land, and it was higher up in the hills. It was harder to grow food or hunt for it in the woods. If Jordan Jr. had expected to inherit land from his parents, their remarkable longevity was forcing him to wait decades for a better life. With so many siblings nearby, he would not inherit much.[30]

Instead of going downriver to Louisa or Catlettsburg, Cincinnati or Louisville, the family went farther into the hills, through Floyd County and Pike, into Virginia. As they rode up the Levisa Fork, rafts of hardwoods floated down. While it was impossible to extract coal by the ton without the railroad, large timber companies were clearing the hills and moving logs out by the creeks and rivers. In the years before the cutting started, locals and outsiders anticipating the timber and coal boom and rising land values had rushed to buy property. The fields and hunting grounds of many small farmers in the hills shrank or disappeared. Jordan Spencer Jr. may have been similarly constricted by new realities.[31]

At Pikeville the steamboat line ended. In the late 1880s Pike County and nearby Logan County, West Virginia, had fascinated the nation, as the Hatfields and McCoys waged a legendary feud. With a public hanging of one murderer, Pikeville officials had declared to the world that the area was ready for coal and timber investment, that law had conquered the mountains. In reality, the coming of railroads and timber and coal was making the hills increasingly violent, as uprooted locals adjusted to new lives and jobs, fewer opportunities, and competition from newcomers. The violence, in turn, allowed outsiders to develop the area without regard to the effect on local lives; if the mountaineers were savages, whatever industry did to them would only be an improvement.[32]

The Spencers kept moving, and the land became almost impossibly rugged. They rode to the end of Kentucky, to the point where, in one writer's words, the mountains themselves "crumble[d]." The Breaks of the Sandy were a stretch of rapids cutting through canyons a quarter-mile deep. With two sandstone towers rising sixteen hundred feet at the entrance of the Breaks, the area seemed defiantly wild. But just downriver was the place that investors already knew would become the Elkhorn coalfield, with some of the largest and purest deposits in the mountains. In only a few years the Breaks, a "shrine of things primeval," would confront the "furnace, ore-mine, coke-cloud, and other ugly signs of civilization."[33]

The Spencers passed north and east of the Breaks and continued higher into the hills, following the Levisa Fork into Buchanan County, Virginia. After seventy-five miles of steep struggle, the state line was the easiest of boundaries to cross. Although Old Jordan regularly traveled to Virginia, no one knew him here. Young Jordan and Alafair had enough children to establish a successful, productive farm, but they would have to start over to become part of a new community. About four miles in, they branched off the river and walked up a narrow valley with an auspicious name: Home Creek.

CHAPTER SEVENTEEN

WALL

Washington, D.C., 1909

I N THE MOMENTS BEFORE sunrise, as signs of life filtered through the blackness outside—roosters crowing, strays howling, farmhands calling as they loaded horse carts for market—Stephen Wall could have imagined that he was far away. The feeling that he was living a different life from what he had known before persisted in the light of day. Walking to the streetcar down a rutted dirt road, he passed small farms, dense woods, cottages, and houses under construction much like the one he had built over the past year for his family. The landscape was more like the Oberlin of his early childhood than Washington, D.C. It was a quiet walk. The air was fresh.[1]

Some of the sights along the way were familiar: men dressed like Wall in three-piece suits, carrying briefcases or lunch pails, checking their pocket watches. These were men entrusted with keeping the government running, having sworn an oath, as Wall had, to "support and defend the Constitution of the United States against all enemies, foreign and domestic." But Wall might also pass monks in cassocks and nuns in full habit, people walking in a different world, speaking languages he didn't understand. Brookland was not the city, nor was it the country. Ringed with cloisters, seminaries, and Catholic universities, the neighborhood was sometimes called Little Rome. It was a new place. No one had lived there long or quite knew whether it would be rich or middling, respected or just respectable.[2]

The streetcar to work rattled Wall back to Washington. Three miles south and west, and he could see the Capitol dome, its clean line wavering in the heavy air. The area around the Government Printing Office was barely recognizable to him. Over the past few years, the notorious shantytowns called Swampoodle had been cleared to make way for Union Station. The foul waters of Tiber Creek ran underground now. Goats no longer foraged in mounds of garbage. The poverty, suffering, and rot had been bricked over.[3]

Even from the outside, the Printing Office's enormous new building—twelve million bricks, six thousand tons of steel, miles of cable and wire—buzzed with industry. Day and night, the presses never stopped running. The walls contained gas, water, electricity, steam, and compressed air—enough to illuminate ten thousand Edison bulbs, operate fifteen elevators, melt pigs of lead by the ton, and provide cold drinking water from seventy-five fountains spread over more than ten acres of floor space. The building was a monument to the Republic's limitless productive capacity. It was a machine.[4]

Thousands of workers filed in for the morning shift. Inside, hundreds of presses were printing more documents, faster, than anywhere else in the world. As an apprentice in 1880, Wall learned the art of typesetting as it had been practiced for four centuries. He spent his days on his feet assembling lines of type on his composing stick, letter by letter. The conversion to automated typesetting that began in 1904 changed Wall's work life. Now he sat during his eight-hour shift inputting thousands of "ems" of text—for patents, Treasury reports, the *Congressional Record*—into an enormous keyboard, creating perforated paper rolls that would enable the newly invented Monotype machine to cast an entire page out of molten lead.[5]

In the Monotype composing room, row after row of keyboards mechanically clacked over a baseline hiss of compressed air through the pipes overhead. Whistles periodically blasted, loud and shrill enough to be heard over the largest presses. Submerged in this deafening sea, Wall had no way of knowing whether he had composed his pages correctly until they were cast. The compositors' skill was total concentration, an ability to shut out the entire world, everything except for the next letter to be keyed in.

Wall's supervisors monitored his speed and accuracy, and the tidiness of his work space.[6]

Though Wall was one of hundreds of men and women performing the same tasks in a giant room, he knew he did not blend in completely. In the three decades since he started at the Government Printing Office, he had been fired twice, both times for five-year stretches, by newly elected Democrats. Seeking his second reinstatement in 1899, Wall would remember the "reductions in force" as mass purges of skilled black printers—"prejudice, pure and simple because I am a colored man." By 1909 the number of black compositors could be counted on one hand. Wall had reason to feel secure in his job. He had a high civil service score, and there had been successive Republican administrations during his ten years back at work. He had survived the much-feared transition from hand type to machines. And his bosses warned that racism had no place at the Government Printing Office. "I wish to declare with all emphasis," the public printer would say in 1911, "that any employee of this department who tries to precipitate the devilish stricture of race prejudice will be immediately dismissed and will not again be employed!"[7]

But at century's turn the "devilish stricture of race prejudice" was inescapable. In every state of the former Confederacy, blacks had been violently kept away from the polls and then stripped of the vote. After George White of North Carolina finished his term in 1901, Negroes in Congress—a bastion of protection for black federal workers—were merely a memory of Reconstruction. "Whites only" signs confidently announced a new segregated order, repeatedly validated by the Supreme Court. Best-selling novels and scientific studies alike described blacks as innately stupid, lascivious, violent, and diseased. With sickening regularity, often approvingly, newspapers reported lynchings.[8]

Washington, in the words of Wall's onetime neighbor Anna Julia Cooper, was overrun with "hysterical negrophobics" and "Angry Saxons." Blacks were shut out of most jobs—even advertisements for maids and butlers were increasingly requesting whites—and were routinely excluded from hotels, theaters, and restaurants. "I may walk from the Capitol to the White House," wrote one woman in 1907, "ravenously hungry and abundantly supplied with money . . . , without finding a single restaurant in which I would be permitted to take a morsel of food." In the winter of 1908, Alabama congressman Thomas Heflin, whose district included Tuskegee, proposed segregating public transportation in Washington. A month later, on his way to deliver a temperance lecture at a Methodist church, Heflin shot a black man in the neck on the Pennsylvania Avenue streetcar.[9]

At the Government Printing Office, white printers, bookbinders, and other tradesmen denied black workers union membership and regularly complained about their competence. As one of the last Negro compositors, Wall wanted to call as little attention to himself as possible. Nevertheless he tried to muster the courage to ask for a promotion. Since his reinstatement in 1899, Wall had made the same salary: four dollars a day. In the meantime he had married and had three children. Now in his fifties, he knew he was running out of years to support his family. After his daughter Isabel was born, he succeeded in getting a three-cent raise as an imposer, adding footnotes and putting pages into final form for the presses. He lasted a few months before being demoted to his old job.[10]

Around the time Roscoe was born in 1906, Wall twice applied for jobs supervising other compositors. He phrased the requests almost as apologies. "Mr. Stillings," he wrote the public printer, "do not think that I mean to take advantage of the kind treatment accorded me by you." Wall arranged to meet with Stillings to talk about his long-term prospects. "You made me feel that if an opportunity presented itself, and the person worthy, you would give them a favorable consideration," he wrote afterward. "I can assure you that no one will be more diligent, faithful, or strive harder to give perfect service, nor would anyone appreciate more highly the confidence placed in me by you." The public printer promised to give Wall's situation his "most careful consideration." The promotion never came.[11]

STEPHEN WALL'S ESCAPE FROM blackness began after the death of his mother, Amanda Wall, in 1902. On a bitter mid-November day, Stephen stood beside her open grave in an isolated corner of Arlington National Cemetery, the sunlight broken by the bare branches of surrounding trees.

His brother and three sisters hovered nearby. In front of him a granite obelisk announced his father's name in large capital letters. His mother's name would be etched inconspicuously on the side. Surrounding them were markers for men the Wall children had known growing up, officers in the war and fixtures of elite colored Washington, their carved and gabled stones clustered like a block of Victorian houses.[12]

When O.S.B. Wall died in 1891, a mass meeting had gathered to express their "profound sorrow" and pay tribute to the man's service to his people. The leaders of the race packed his funeral—former U.S. senator Blanche Bruce and congressman John R. Lynch, doctors and lawyers, professors and reverends and bishops. *The Washington Post* described the service as "very impressive." It had been conducted by the distinguished pastor of the First Congregational Church, the elite institution that Wall had integrated shortly after the Civil War.[13]

By contrast, Amanda Wall's funeral in 1902 was a "short and simple" affair. Aside from a few close friends, the Wall children grieved alone. A white undertaker had prepared her body. Looking at Edward, Isabel, Sallie, and Gertrude, Stephen had reason to wonder if they would ever stand together again. Edward was married to a French woman in Montreal and working as a sleeping car conductor on the Canadian Pacific Railway, a position that would be off limits to blacks for another half century. At the time of their mother's death, Isabel was already Mrs. Gotthold Otto Elterich of Manhattan and Freeport, Long Island, the wife of a railroad capitalist. Sallie had become Helen Easton on New York's Upper West Side. They were new people now, scattered, anonymous. The youngest, Gertrude, had lived at home during their mother's final illness, but she would soon move to a decidedly paler section of northwest Washington and start going by her given first name, Laura. Despite their family's proud history, all of Stephen Wall's siblings found it necessary to disappear and had no problems doing so.[14]

While the Walls' neighbor Howard University professor Kelly Miller pondered "the self-degradation and humiliation of soul necessary to cross the great 'social divide,'" becoming white loomed as a temptingly simple option for Stephen Wall. His siblings were hardly the only people he knew who had crossed the line. At roughly the same time that Stephen's older brother moved to Canada, his cousin Ralph Langston, who grew up next door and apprenticed with Stephen at the Government Printing Office, was arrested in New York for seducing a young woman who claimed not to know that Langston was colored. The daughter of O.S.B. Wall's old friend Richard Greener was now J. P. Morgan's personal librarian—of exotic Portuguese origin—Belle da Costa Greene. Around 1902 another scion of the District's colored elite, Theophilus John Minton Syphax, was establishing himself as a white lawyer in New York by the name of T. John McKee.[15]

Stories of the blurred boundaries of color were cultural commonplaces in turn-of-the-century American life, fodder for popular novels, Broadway plays, and front-page news. Black Washingtonians sat through Sunday sermons on the perils of passing for white, then whispered about the people they knew who had gone to the other side. *The Washington Bee*, the venerable weekly edited by O.S.B.'s and Stephen Wall's old acquaintance Calvin Chase, described the colored elite as gripped by a "white fever craze." Even as the paper opined that the fever "ought to be cured," it advertised whitening cosmetics like Complexion Wonder Creme, which promised to "improve any colored countenance like magic." People of Stephen Wall's class and complexion might have said the real struggle was to stay colored rather than cross over. They spent their days arguing with train conductors who insisted that they be seated in the white car, and parrying the hostile reactions from police and passersby when walking with darker friends, colleagues, and spouses. Being white could be as simple as keeping one's mouth shut.[16]

But Stephen did not cross the line, at least not in 1902. While most of his family disappeared, he held on to his old life. During his years laid off from the Government Printing Office in the 1880s and 1890s, he ran a pool hall, then a cigar shop, and finally a bicycle store, all in black neighborhoods and all serving black people. He remained in the neighborhood where he grew up, in the shadow of Howard University and the Freedmen's Hospital, near his mother and old friends. Just up the street were Hillside Cottage and his uncle John Mercer Langston and his aunt Carrie, who provided an immediate connection to family, community, and history. In the years before his death in 1897, Langston would hold court on the porch, regaling neighbors with stories about his garden, the graceful trees that lined Fourth Street (the sycamore, spruce, white birch, and sweetgum were personal gifts from Charles Sumner), and most of all, "important facts and stirring episodes in the history of the Negro race, of which he never tired of telling." "He was," according to Kelly Miller, "a talking encyclopedia upon the events of the Civil War and the tragic era of reconstruction."[17]

When Stephen sought his second reinstatement to the Government Printing Office in 1899, he stated his race outright in letters to the public printer. Moreover, he stressed that the earlier firings had been motivated by prejudice and politics, not by job performance. He returned to work in 1899 as a black man. He described himself as "Colored" in a questionnaire distributed at work and detailed his father's service in the United States Colored Troops.[18]

Although Wall was outspoken about his race at work, his ties to his community grew ever more tenuous. In 1900 he married a white woman. Contemporary writers imagined that passing for white often began as a lark, only to become irreversible because of love and marriage across the color line. But Lillie Slee knew that Stephen was colored. Raised by a Canadian mother in Massachusetts port towns, she simply may have ordered her world differently from the average Washingtonian. She prayed at the First Congregational Church, where she may have met Stephen. Or perhaps the immediate necessities of life caused her to regard racial integrity as less imperative than others did at the time. She had been married before. Stephen was already in his forties. Their relationship could have been the last chance for either of them to start a family. Stephen and Lillie understood that they were living beyond a boundary—they eloped and married alone in Philadelphia. Lillie knew Stephen's mother, but the couple did not live with her.[19]

Marrying Lillie eroded Stephen's connection to the black community, as he decided he could no longer be a "good fellow" and stopped socializing with old friends. As a devoted husband—and, by the end of 1901, father—he hardly left the house anymore except to go to work. He continued to view himself as part of the Wall family and continued to identify as black. He named his first child for his sister, Isabel Irene. His son would be Roscoe Orin, after Orindatus Simon Bolivar Wall.[20]

Soon after his mother died, Stephen moved his family back into the rambling frame house his father had built—a move in the opposite direction from the one chosen by his siblings. Sparsely furnished, with tattered mats on the floor, the house was past its proudest days. Amanda Wall had spent the decade she outlived her husband close to poverty. At the same time she regularly made loans to friends, and she always had something for the steady stream of poor blacks whom she continued to receive. Being part of the colored elite was never simply a question of money.[21]

The house had kept Amanda afloat—she borrowed on it repeatedly. When creditors came knocking, Amanda deeded the house to Isabel and two apartment buildings to Helen and Edward. The maneuvers—disguised as sales—served a dual purpose. She was able to shield the house from foreclosure after a creditor sued her in 1896. And more important, the land transfers tethered her children to her even as they made their way in the white world. As long as they held the family property, they remained part of the family.[22]

If the web of property initially tied the Walls together, it would soon push them apart. Separated by physical distance, financial need, and identity, the five children were incapable of untangling their mother's estate on their own. They turned to the equity courts of the District of Columbia, which promised an efficient but painful way to resolve the mess. Their father, O.S.B. Wall, had spent many hours arguing equity cases as an attorney in private practice. His children hired white lawyers for the job. Only two weeks after Amanda died, Gertrude sued her siblings for a share of what their mother had signed over to them. In the meantime Stephen, Helen, and Isabel fought over who would be their mother's executor. But with three children out of town and a fourth—Gertrude—living under an assumed name, nothing was resolved. Subpoenas went unserved. Gertrude dropped her case almost immediately after filing it, only to bring—and again drop—an identical suit three months later.[23]

It took until the end of 1907 for everyone except Gertrude to reach an agreement. Edward sued his siblings to force them to sell the house, claiming they owed him money. The plaintiff and defendants were colluding, using the suit to engineer a particular result: a forced sale to which Gertrude could not object. Edward's lawyer had represented Stephen in earlier cases involving their mother's estate. Stephen, Helen, and Isabel conceded the case. But Gertrude was nowhere to be found. In early 1908 a judge ordered the sale. The District of Columbia bought the house and promptly knocked it down. In its place the city built a colored school.[24]

IN JULY 1908 STEPHEN used his share of the sale money to start building his house in Brookland. That same month he received an official reprimand for making three mistakes on a single galley—an "exceptionally bad proof." Shortly afterward he and a few dozen others were removed from the Monotype composing machine and demoted to checking proofs for errors, which required standing all day by roaring presses and molten lead casting machines. His foreman told him it was part of a large-scale reorganization of his division. But most of the others were soon "sent back to the machine," Stephen would complain. Less qualified people were operating the Monotype keyboards. Stephen was reminded of this fact every day because it was his job to correct their "horrible composition, which takes three times as long to get in proper shape." "An injustice has been done me," he seethed.[25]

At the end of each day Wall collected his four dollars in pay, walked out the arched doorway of the Government Printing Office, boarded the streetcar, and retreated to his new house. It was fancier than his father's had been: a three-story colonial with a tile bath and a hot-water heater in the basement, "one of the best homes" in the neighborhood. Its grandeur was muted by its pebbled stucco siding, which helped the house blend a bit into its surroundings. It was a fortress and a blind.[26]

After years of working to stay colored, years of experiencing what W.E.B. DuBois had called "this sense of always looking at one's self through the eyes of others, of measuring one's soul by the tape of a world that looks on in amused contempt and pity," Stephen had finally decided to shed the burden of race. His family was taking to their new community. Neighbors regarded his wife, Lillie, as a "woman of culture." In April 1909 his seven-year-old daughter Isabel was invited to attend Sunday school at Brookland Baptist Church. That fall she would enter the first grade at the graceful brick elementary school two blocks away. The people and places of his past fell away. Stephen Wall saw more and more that being somebody depended on being nobody.[27]

AFTER ISABEL HAD BEEN going to Sunday school for a month, there was a knock on the Walls' door. It was a neighbor, David Oertly. In many ways Oertly was like Stephen Wall. He also commuted into town and worked for the government in a skilled position—he was a draftsman at the Navy Department. In his spare time he played second base on the Brookland Brotherhood's baseball team and grew irises and dahlias. His yellow roses were prizewinners. His oldest son was the same age as Isabel and went to Sunday school with her.[28]

Oertly was calling on church business. Lillie Wall was home with the three children. In the time Isabel had been attending Brookland Baptist, he said, a number of parents had withdrawn their children from the Sunday school. If Lillie showed any confusion about his point, Oertly told her that the "congregation had determined that Mr. Wall was a negro." He left the Walls with a blunt request: "either identify themselves as white or discontinue their attendance upon the Church and school." Oertly may have been apologetic, but he was firm: "although they regretted having to ask the parents to withdraw their children," a newspaper later explained, "it was necessary."[29]

If Isabel was too young to know what was happening, her parents understood. Brookland did not feel like Washington, but it was still a swamp. As a new neighborhood being built from the ground up, it could be even more segregated than the rest of the city. For years leading up to the time the Walls moved there, the neighborhood citizens' association had doggedly protested plans to build a colored school nearby—Negroes simply were not moving there, they argued, and besides, the school would lower their property values. When Congressman Heflin proposed segregating streetcars in the District, the association sent a letter of support. Neighbors such as David Oertly may have looked and acted like the Walls, but their worlds were profoundly different. Oertly's wife was a proud member of the United Daughters of the Confederacy; his father-in-law had been a private in the Virginia cavalry and attended every Confederate reunion he could for decades after the war. Being white did not mean freedom from race. If blackness for Stephen Wall forced a continual consciousness of who he was, being white required a constant display of who one was not.[30]

The Walls faced a dilemma. They were no longer anonymous. Neighbors knew *who* they were, and now they were voicing suspicions about *what* they were. They could leave Brookland and return to Stephen's old neighborhood and old identity. Or they could follow his brother and sisters' example: move somewhere else, and thoroughly cover their tracks.

Instead, Stephen and Lillie sought a third option. Without any protest they stopped sending Isabel to Sunday school and waited out the summer. On a warm, cloudy September morning, mother and daughter made the short walk to the Brookland School, entered the brick archway, and found the principal's office. With fair skin, blue eyes, and hair in long blond curls, Isabel was nothing but a "pretty little miss about to make her bow to the world by entering first grade." After making "the usual inquiries," the principal admitted the girl. Her mother spelled her name for the paperwork: Isabel "W-h-a-l."[31]

Ten days later Isabel was sent home from school with a note from the principal. "My dear Mrs. Whal," wrote Mary Little, "in consequence of information subsequently obtained, I will have to withdraw the ticket of admission to Brookland School issued . . . to your daughter Isabel Irene." It was signed "Respectfully." Following up on what the principal meant by "information subsequently obtained," Lillie learned that in response to complaints from parents and possibly the Brookland Citizens' Association, the principal had determined that Isabel was a "colored child" who was legally forbidden to attend the District's white schools. Her teachers were stunned. "None of them even suspected that she had colored blood," one said, "and it is difficult to make them believe it now."[32]

Stephen Wall echoed their disbelief. "My child is as white as any in the Brookland School," he said. "If it had not been for some talkative busybody who set the story going, no one would ever have dreamed of raising the question." He had tried to become white by keeping his mouth shut, only to find himself and his family targeted for their race more than ever before. He faced the bitter prospect of explaining the situation to Isabel. The girl did not know she had been kicked out of school. At the moment, she was sick in bed. Perhaps by the time she got better, the issue could be resolved. Unlike the situation with the Baptist church, Stephen would not go quietly. He resolved to appeal the expulsion.[33]

It was uncertain what such a challenge would accomplish. The Walls' secret was out, and the harder Stephen fought, the more people would know. Even if Stephen and Lillie succeeded in getting Isabel reinstated to the first grade, a ruling by school officials in her favor was unlikely to change the community consensus that the Walls were not white. Isabel would have to face classmates and parents who did not want her at school. The Walls would have to live among people who did not want them as neighbors.[34]

Stephen Wall's refusal to give in was not merely an expression of rage or pride. He could not let go because he was convinced that the principal had violated the law. As he understood it, the District's Civil War–era statutes established separate schools for blacks without prohibiting them from attending white schools. Even if the law did mandate segregation, he could not imagine that one elementary principal had the authority to classify his children as colored. While Lillie wrote a letter to schools superintendent A. T. Stuart asking him to reconsider the principal's decision, Stephen contacted the press. On Sunday, October 10, next to pieces on President Taft getting sunburned at Yosemite and Ty Cobb stealing home against the Pittsburgh Pirates, *The Washington Herald* ran a front-page story under the headline "May Bar Young Girl from School: Controversy as to Whether She Is a Negro." Three more boldface subheads followed, announcing, among other things, that the "Claim of Negro Extraction Affects Stephen Wall, Employe[e] of G.P.O."[35]

Having embraced the anonymous life, Stephen Wall cast it aside in his bid to get Isabel admitted to a white school. In addition to mentioning where he worked, the story pinpointed the intersection in Brookland where the family lived. In his comments to the reporter, Wall all but placed a spotlight of racial scrutiny on his head. "They say she shall not go to this school because they think her father has negro blood," he said. But he refused to "confirm or deny the report on his extraction."[36]

Wall "hinted significantly about damage suits if his rights were not given him," the *Herald* reported. But what did he mean by "his rights"? Wall was not arguing that he was white or, for that matter, that his daughter was white. Nor was he arguing that segregation was wrong. Rather, he was asserting a right not to admit his race and not to be classified as black without evidence provided by the government. "The burden of proof is on them," he declared. "If they believe I have negro blood, very good. Let them prove it. For my part, I only know the law compels me to send my child to a public school, and that I have obeyed the law."[37]

The point Wall was making was fundamentally about process. In the absence of an official reason backed by evidence, the school had no authority to expel Isabel. "I am certainly going to send my child back to school as soon as she is well," Wall said. "As I understand it, the case is not yet settled. I do not know why my little girl has been barred from school. She has not attended this week because she is sick." It was a technical argument about Isabel's entitlement to attend the school two blocks from home—an argument, perhaps, that only a lawyer could love. Even as Stephen turned his back on the colored world, he remained O.S.B. Wall's son.[38]

THAT WEDNESDAY THE SCHOOLS superintendent wrote Stephen that he had "the honor to inform you that I sustain the action of the principal." *The Washington Post* and *Washington Times* picked up the story. The next day Stephen Wall was laid off from work.[39]

Reaction to the controversy rippled through colored Washington. People in Wall's former social circle were indignant on his behalf. Wall may have been trying to escape the race, but he was still suffering like a black man. "I am in sympathy with Wall," wrote Charles Purvis, the physician who had treated O.S.B. Wall in his final illness. "It is damnable to have such a question raised. What a country!! Where is our boasted religion? Liars every one of them."[40]

If Wall's plight appealed to members of the black elite, so did his technical view of his legal rights. Alongside their outrage at America's "race hatred," members of the black elite firmly believed that "the law is with Wall." Purvis's letters were both cris de coeur and legal briefs, citing slave laws mandating that "a child shall follow the condition of the mother," an 1856 Ohio court decision establishing a one-half rule as "what constitutes a white man," and an 1868 case in the District holding that the mixed-race child of a prominent abolitionist was white. "If 25 percent can make a fellow black," Purvis declared, "75 should surely make him white."[41]

Although newspapers did not report Wall's firing, the story circulated by word of mouth. Purvis, in retirement in Brookline, Massachusetts, received clippings and letters about the case from Whitefield McKinlay, a Washington real estate broker with ties to Booker T. Washington and the Roosevelt and Taft administrations. "Wall is passing 'thru' a serious experience; he is being punished for asserting his rights," Purvis wrote. "Taft should order his reinstatement. Of course the Public Printer will deny that he was influenced by public opinion, but the action speaks for itself. I hope Wall will fight it out. I hope he will call upon the President."[42]

It was not out of the question for Stephen Wall or someone acting for him to meet with President Taft. Wall knew members of the "black cabinet," the handful of federal appointees who had the president's ear on matters relating to the race. Years before, his father had called on President Garfield. But mobilizing his elite support would require him to acknowledge that he was black. As an anonymous white man, Wall had decidedly lower connections. Whether or not someone intervened, he was reinstated at the Government Printing Office for a third time two months later.[43]

On October 29 the Walls wrote the board of education appealing the superintendent's decision and requesting a hearing. They received no reply. By mid-December Stephen retained John Ridout, the lawyer who had represented him in the lawsuits untangling his mother's estate. Ridout threatened to seek mandamus to force an "official action of the Board expressed and recorded at a Board meeting." A month later, on January 28, 1910, the board formally affirmed Isabel's expulsion by an 8–1 vote. Two in the majority were black; the sole dissenting vote was from Mary Church Terrell, a civil rights leader and fixture of the colored elite who was long acquainted with the Walls. Her reasoning echoed Purvis's balance of protest and legal principle. She sought to spare Isabel "many of the hardships, humiliations and injustices of which she would be the helpless victim if she were forced to cast her lot among colored children." And she argued that "during slavery it was customary in some southern states for the child to follow the condition of the mother, and, since the mother was white, the child should be allowed to attend the white schools."[44]

Although Wall was committed to the notion that the board of education affirmatively had to prove his race, that position was bound to intensify the scrutiny on him and his family and, ultimately, affirm his black ancestry. His father, after all, had been prominent in broad legal and political circles in the District of Columbia. On March 17 Stephen Wall filed suit in the District's trial court to force the "immediate re-admittance" of Isabel to the Brookland School. His petition conceded that Isabel's "great grandparents were a white man and a very light mulatto woman; her grandparents were a son of said great grandparents and a white woman, and the parents of petitioner are a son of the said grandparents and a white woman." The board of education responded that this admission was enough to justify the expulsion, and its lawyer started investigating Wall's background.[45]

Two months later the presiding justice, Daniel Thew Wright, heard from ten witnesses. Three policemen testified that the "reputation of the Wall family was that it was colored"—that they had lived in a colored neighborhood, that O.S.B. Wall was "regarded as a colored man," that "the mother was yellow in appearance," and that Stephen had conducted "a colored pool-room" in a "colored neighborhood." The undertaker who prepared Amanda Wall's body for burial "supposed the deceased to be colored" because "when he handles a colored body, it has an odor which to him is very offensive, and he perceived that odor on this body."[46]

Stephen Wall admitted that his father "was known as a colored man" but asserted that his mother "was, and was recognized as, a white woman." Lillie testified that she had known her mother-in-law, "who was a white woman." Asked about her first marriage, Lillie said that she "had been married to a Japanese." From there Justice Wright, who was four years away from impeachment hearings on an array of personal and professional misdeeds, took over the questioning. The judge elicited that Lillie had married Stephen on the spur of the moment, as they "were on a trip to

Atlantic City." The judge then asked about her own racial background, implying that her conduct was somehow less than white. When Lillie said that she had "no African blood in her ancestry," Justice Wright followed up with a question about a "mark of color just below her jaw." Lillie explained it was "a birth mark or from the liver." The testimony was uncomfortable, invasive, and humiliating. It was also the last time that O.S.B. and Amanda Wall would be publicly remembered.[47]

At Justice Wright's urging, the board of education convened its own hearing the next week and read the court transcript into the record. A delegation of the Brookland Citizens' Association showed up "with an avowed determination to contend 'to the last ditch' for the little girl's exclusion from the public schools for white children," but John Ridout convinced the board not to allow them "to come here making speeches." The only person put in the witness chair would be Isabel Wall.[48]

Ridout called her to the stand and announced, "I will rest my case upon the personal appearance of the child." By all accounts, Isabel was a vision of Victorian girlhood, "decidedly pretty" and charmingly unaffected by everything happening around her. According to *The New York Times*, she "laughed and talked with her mother . . . and showed no fear of Capt. Oyster," the school board president. "Isabel," reported the *Times*, "is a great deal more concerned over the way her dolly's complexion is wearing off than the manner in which her own cheeks are scrutinized by every one she meets."[49]

Although the District's laws established separate "white" and "colored" schools, there was no definition of "colored" on the books. Relying on Isabel's skin, eyes, and hair, Ridout argued that "'colored child' means a child so colored as to be recognized as such." After briefly noting that in the past the board of education had allowed light-skinned children to attend white schools, Ridout returned to Isabel's appearance. "No human being could look at that beautiful little child and not admit instinctively that so far as personal appearances is concerned she is a white child," the lawyer said. "God almighty has designed this child and the fact that the school law should be construed so she will be declared a colored child will never make her so . . . I am sure you will pardon me for the personal feeling I have in the matter because I confess that this little child appeals to me."[50]

Ridout's pitch for the "instinctive" belief that Isabel was white may have struck him as a plea for common sense, but it was a tone-deaf argument at a time when whites reflexively believed that any African ancestry made a person black. The one-drop rule had motivated the citizens of Brookland to demand Isabel Wall's expulsion in the first place, and the school board relied on something like it in arguing that Isabel's "very light mulatto" great-grandmother settled the question of the girl's race. "The people generally hold, of course, that one drop of negro blood makes a negro," reported the *Post* in 1907, "and their steadfastness of purpose and the strict social lines that are drawn are considered the only real safeguards of the white race in the South." It was such a commonplace belief that Booker T. Washington could invoke the rule casually and without comment: "It takes 100 percent of white blood to make a white man, but only one drop of negro blood to make a negro." A popular play at the time concerned a Southern governor who learns that he has an imperceptible trace of black ancestry—it was called "The Nigger."[51]

While the white public constantly stressed the importance of racial purity, the statutes in effect across the South were considerably less strict. Most states, including Maryland, drew the color line with a one-eighth rule—one black great-grandparent made a person legally black. Virginia had a one-fourth rule. Only Oklahoma defined *colored* as "all persons of African descent." Ridout could have hewed close to the formalism of laws defining race and argued that the common legal definition of *colored* at the time the District of Columbia enacted its schools law was a one-eighth rule. Lawyers litigating similar cases in Louisiana, North Carolina, Virginia, and elsewhere were winning on the basis of strict, technical readings of blood quantum requirements. Such arguments succeeded not because they enabled people of color to become white but because strict readings of the statutes prevented people who had long lived as whites from being reclassified as black. In the absence of a statutory definition in the District of Columbia, the strongest argument in Isabel Wall's favor had little to do with "instinct."[52]

With little besides Isabel's appearance to go on, the board voted 8–1 that the girl, "for the purposes of school classification, is a colored child." The two black board members in the majority issued a separate statement suggesting that they disapproved of Stephen Wall's move toward white-ness, a view repeated soon afterward in the black press. "We cannot stultify ourselves to the point of admitting that our own children are stamped as inferior because of attendance on the schools provided by the Board of Education for colored children," they said, "nor are we disposed to grant that there are any superior privileges attaching to attendance on a white as compared with a colored school." "I am very sorry to have to disagree," said Mary Church Terrell, the lone dissent, "but my conscience will not permit me to adopt the attitude of the Board." "I have seen Isabel Wall," she said. "I know Isabel Wall's grandmother, and I have seen Isabel Wall's mother and, as I understand that the rule is that all children follow the condition of the mother, I am of the opinion that Isabel Wall is a white child."[53]

Ten days later Justice Wright issued his opinion. Like the school board, he was unimpressed with the argument based on Isabel's appearance. Al-though she had "no physical characteristic which afforded ocular evidence suggestive of aught but the Caucasian," the judge observed that "her father presents to the eye racial characteristics which identify him of Negro blood" and that her mother was "formerly wife to a Mongolian." In the absence of a statutory definition, Justice Wright defined *colored* in the "common parlance of the people." As he saw it, "persons of whatever com-plexion, who bear negro blood in whatever degree and who abide in the racial status of the Negro, are 'colored' in the common estimation of the people." Wright's definition stopped short of a one-drop rule—people who had established themselves as white could argue that they did not "abide in the racial status of the Negro." But ultimately, the definition shut out Stephen Wall, whom Justice Wright specifically identified as someone whose status had "been always that of the negro."[54]

Wall appealed to the District of Columbia's high court. His brief cata-loged Southern statutes that defined who was black and who was white yet conceded that "the term 'colored' when not defined by statute is to be given its common significance." After positing a weak argument that the common definition of *colored* hinged on appearance, the brief argued—contrary to a century of case law—that Isabel's racial status had nothing to do with her father's "negro associations." While successful lawyers in other cases had argued that hypertechnical racial definitions were necessary to prevent whites from being reclassified as black, Wall's counsel never imagined the possibility that many whites could have African ancestry.[55]

Six months later the District of Columbia Court of Appeals affirmed Justice Wright, quoting his opinion at length. The court regarded physical appearance as a "delusive test of race" and after consulting the dictionary definition of *colored* concluded that it meant "persons wholly or in part of negro blood, or having any appreciable admixture thereof." It was as close as a court had gotten to adopting the one-drop rule. The year 1910 ended with the Wall family identified and exposed in legal precedent and in newspaper articles that ran coast-to-coast.[56]

SOON AFTER THE COURT'S decision, Stephen Wall sold the house in Brookland. For the next ten years the family moved repeatedly from neighborhood to neighborhood and from white to black to white again. The courts could not keep them from becoming white, but affected only how they did so. From 1916 to 1920 the Walls rented a home just a couple of blocks down Fourth Street from where Stephen had grown up. Their landlady was Mary Church Terrell, the one school board member who had voted in Isabel's favor. But by 1920 the Walls had moved again, settling in Georgetown. They changed their first and last names. Now they were the Gates family: Steven, Elizabeth, Lillian, Ethel, and Russell. In many ways their new community was like Brookland. The neighbors were lower-level federal employees, all white. The major landmark was another Catholic university. Here Isabel, Ethel, and Roscoe had no problem attending the white schools down the street. Stephen was back on the Monotype machines at the Government Printing Office. By this point he preferred working the night shift.[57]

CHAPTER EIGHTEEN

SPENCER

Home Creek, Buchanan County, Virginia, 1912

B UCHANAN COUNTY, VIRGINIA, WAS an island far from the sea, one of the most isolated parts of Appalachia. It had barely any level ground, just mountains on mountains pushing into Kentucky and West Virginia, each ridge like an ocean to cross. The hills were so steep that they had names like Big A. Most of the county was ancient towering forest—chestnuts on the ridgelines, white oak down the slopes, and yellow poplar and black walnut in the coves and bottoms, at the heads of ravines, and along narrow twisting creeks. During winter only four or five hours of light reached the deep hollows between the hills; the sun rose over one mountain and set behind another.[1]

Buchanan's county seat, Grundy, was barely a town, just a collection of buildings perched between the mountains and the Levisa Fork of the Big Sandy River. When Grundy wasn't flooding, it was burning, and when it burned, it burned to the ground. There was no fire department, nor was there running water. Telegraph lines had not found a way into the county. Election results reached the state capital days after every other county in Virginia had reported them. A few long-distance telephone lines had been strung, but mostly by moonshiners seeking advance warning of raids by state revenue agents. When convicts escaped from the penitentiary, they made for the area as if it were Mexico.[2]

Nine miles northwest of Grundy, four miles shy of the Kentucky line,

Home Creek curled off the Levisa Fork. The creek twisted several miles east through the hills, branching off into ever-smaller hollows. Journalists, ethnologists, and geographers who wandered the area and regularly recounted their travels for Northern readers described places like Home Creek as ones that "the current of time has swept by and left . . . in an eddy," inhabited by people "rich in the local colour of an age long past." The locals spoke seventeenth-century English, spun the cloth on their backs, shoed their own horses, and hunted small game "with the old English short bow" and "arrows hefted in the ancient manner." They led lives almost entirely confined to the few miles surrounding their windowless cabins.[3]

Most of the people living along Home Creek descended from the men and women who had originally moved into the area from more civilized parts of Kentucky. Some 150 years later they were still pioneers, scratching gardens and cornfields out of hillsides that washed down to bare rock after a season or two. They tethered shacks to large trees to anchor them for the inevitable floods. Aside from church, they could gather at a mill for grinding corn and a small country store where they could pay for bolts of calico and children's shoes with chickens and eggs. Home Creek's mill and store were owned by the same short, stout, and foulmouthed man. If anyone had a secure place in this jagged hollow, it was George Looney. He was about thirty-five years old, with eyes the same color as his gray hair, the father of two sons and five daughters. Where most people owned a few dozen acres, he claimed several hundred. His ancestors were among the county's very first settlers. Less than a mile to the south, over one ridge of hills, was Looney's Creek.[4]

Although outlanders assumed Buchanan County was a place that time forgot, George Looney knew better. Every day his world was changing. Although most of the county was wooded, very little forest was untouched by 1910. Over the previous decades most of the yellow poplar and other ancient hardwoods had been chopped down, "ball hooted" down the hillsides, and floated out the creeks. The nearest train station was forty miles away, but a large outside logging concern had already extended narrow-gauge rail from the Norfolk & Western line in West Virginia to Hurley, just northeast of Home Creek. At Hurley the W. M. Ritter Company had built an enormous lumber mill that employed six hundred men. It was surrounded by a boomtown and, beyond that, thousands of acres of bare hills studded with tree stumps. In addition to employing mill hands and lumberjacks, the company had crews hard at work expanding the rail line, one hollow at a time, to new tracts of virgin timber. It was close enough that Looney could probably hear the Shay locomotive's shrill whistle.[5]

While coal mining was still twenty years away, the counties surrounding Buchanan were being hammered and chiseled and dynamited to dust. It was common knowledge that Buchanan would be next—that the hills were hiding twelve billion tons of "high-grade, coking, bituminous coal in beds of minable thickness"—it was only a matter of time. When that time came, George Looney, Home Creek's resident businessman, would be ready to sell his mineral rights. While the train carried logs out of the county, the return trip brought crates of liquor and bags of mail from the outside. Ninety percent of the mail was addressed to the Ritter mill. Logging had attracted new people to Buchanan County, a slow but constant stream. While most were strong men headed to Hurley, at least one family moved into Home Creek.[6]

In 1898 Jordan Spencer Jr. arrived from Kentucky with his wife, Alafair, and their nine children, the youngest an infant and the oldest seventeen. Within two or three years they might as well have lived in Home Creek forever. They bought land and started farming it. Jordan's eldest son, George, soon married Arminda Justice, the daughter of an established local family—at twenty, almost beyond marriageable age. George and Arminda moved to land nearby that she owned, and within a decade they had five children. Just like that, the Spencers found themselves kin to almost everyone around them.[7]

For the better part of a decade, Jordan Spencer and his sons and daughters worked for George Looney, whether it was harvesting corn or clearing trees. The Spencers and the Looneys got along well. They often ate together and stayed over at each other's houses. In 1909, when George and Arminda Spencer's oldest son, Melvin, turned six, they sent him to the same school that George Looney's children were attending. The teacher was Looney's third cousin and related by marriage to the Spencers.[8]

If the Spencers found easy acceptance along Home Creek, it abruptly ended in late October 1910. As the hillsides slicked with fallen leaves, George Looney's older brother was shot dead. Henderson Looney had been boarding with George. He was divorced, in his forties, laboring for his keep. His killer was Andrew Jackson Spencer, the third of Jordan Spencer Jr.'s nine sons. Jack was nineteen, just married, farming a small plot of rented hillside in the hollow. No one knows why he shot Henderson Looney, who had been a neighbor since Jack was a little boy and had a daughter near his age. Spencer was charged by the sheriff and put on trial, but he was never convicted. The acquittal allowed him to resume something resembling a normal life on Home Creek in early 1911. He soon had enough money to buy land and years later was enough of a law-abiding citizen to help the sheriff raid and shut down local moonshine stills. But George Looney would not forget what had happened.[9]

After Henderson Looney's killer went free, it seemed preordained that George Looney would exact justice on his own. The occasional items about Buchanan County in big-city newspapers described a place without law—or more accurately, a place with its own code that existed alongside the law. While Hatfields and McCoys had periodically slaughtered each other in nearby Pike County, Kentucky, and Logan County, West Virginia, more than once the killers had fled to Buchanan, which was too rugged for the sheriff's posse. Buchanan County families did not have feuds. They had wars.[10]

"These mountaineers are men who hold life as light as a laugh," pronounced one of the first anthropologists to study the Appalachians at the turn of the century, and in Buchanan people lost their lives for reasons big and small. Sometimes they died for money. In 1909 six members— three generations—of one family were shot, hacked, and burned to death for several hundred dollars' cash and a thousand more in gold and silver coin buried on their land. People died "in the madness of moonshine intoxication"—in fights over ten cents to buy whiskey, and fights after all of it was drunk. And people died for no reason at all, cut down at their ramshackle home places and on their way to church parties, along lonely mountain passes, and in the muddy streets of Grundy. No one was too law-abiding to partake of a little killing. When a local judge's son encountered a deputy U.S. marshal's son in 1901, they blasted each other with revolvers point-blank "as rapidly as they could draw the triggers."[11]

George Looney's war on the Spencers began immediately after Jack Spencer went free. In newspaper stories, silent films, and anthropological studies, Southern mountaineers invariably reached for their rifles, but Looney did not fight with bullets. Words were his weapon. Everywhere he went, Looney would talk about the Spencers. "Nothing but God damned negroes," he called them, "and I can prove they are God damned negroes." At his mill and at the store, at home and when visiting, he spread the rumor to anyone who would listen. In the summer of 1911 his words drifted down the creeks and forks and branches wrinkling through Buchanan County.[12]

It was a strange accusation, considering that there were no blacks to hate in Buchanan County. It was almost entirely white, possibly the whitest place in the South. Out of twelve thousand county residents, the census counted four blacks in 1910, down from five a decade earlier. The rest of the South had spent the last twenty or thirty years building a social wall between blacks and whites. In Virginia and elsewhere, new statutes required the separation, and it would be stricter than ever before. Since the eighteenth century, Virginia had defined a black person as anyone with more than one-quarter "negro blood." In 1910 the legislature tightened the definition to a one-sixteenth rule. Other states took the idea of racial purity to the limit, defining anyone with any African ancestry as black. While established by law, the new order assumed a concrete form every day on streetcars, in restaurants and hotels and shops, at job sites, and in random, momentary face-to-face encounters. Segregation was also being enacted and enforced with slaps, slurs, punches, and kicks, by rope and bullet and pine torch.[13]

Segregation and lynching and the idea that blacks were genetically inferior—a contagion that had to be quarantined—seemed to make the most sense where blacks and whites lived in great enough proximity that whites could imagine a world where blacks had an equal claim to power and privilege and justice for old wrongs. Most people in Buchanan County had never even seen a black person, and segregationists looked longingly to the hills as an Eden of white racial purity. Although outsiders were

constantly describing the backwardness of the mountains, the drunken-
ness and violence and primitive Christianity and child brides, the "bare
feet, ragged clothes, and crass ignorance," the highlanders also symbolized
something else: what one anthropologist called "the inextinguishable excellence of the Anglo-Saxon race." Where everyone was white—where
black people posed no threat to the social and political order—the question
of whether or not the Spencers were "God damned negroes" seemed to
have little consequence.[14]

However, the fact that Looney could think of his whisper campaign
as vengeance for his dead brother suggested that Buchanan County was
less isolated than most outsiders could imagine. Although hardly any blacks
lived in the mountains—although the South's highland counties had
fewer slaves before the war, were less likely to support secession, and were
more likely to ally themselves with Northern Republicans after the war—
upcountry whites had long resented the counting of blacks for appor-
tioning seats in the state legislature, which tilted political power to the
plantation regions. "This hill folk were . . . opposed to slavery," wrote Harvard geologist and Kentucky native Nathaniel Shaler, "and even more to
negroes." Fifty years after the war, industry and capital and the outside
world were steadily creeping closer to the mountains, bringing with them
the politics of segregation and a rigid vocabulary of difference.[15]

Just as their lives were changing, the people of the mountains associated
blacks with an uncertain future. Although southwestern Virginia had a
minuscule black population, more blacks were lynched there between 1880
and 1930 than in any other part of the state. Although isolated from the
surrounding counties, Buchanan was not untouched by the killing. When
two Buchanan County merchants were robbed and murdered in 1893 by
a train depot in nearby Tazewell County, more than one hundred Buchanan men rode to the scene of the crime and lynched five blacks. As the
mob rode home, they proudly proclaimed Buchanan "altogether a white
county."[16]

Looney did not want to kill the Spencers, but his accusation threatened
to turn the Spencers back into outsiders. Looney also understood that
community standing and security were not the only things that hinged on
the issue of race. He had something bigger in mind, something that would

require traveling beyond Home Creek. He enlisted the aid of a younger cousin in Grundy—an attorney at law named Glenn Ratliff—as well as a trustee of the Rock Lick School District. Together, at Looney's expense, they traveled eighty miles to the northwest, until they appeared one summer day at a Paintsville hotel. After asking the proprietor a few questions, they found themselves riding through the Jordan Gap, looking for people who knew the Spencers.[17]

Before the school on Home Creek opened for the fall term, Looney approached his third cousin the teacher and told him to tell the Spencers that he had called them "damned niggers." Because there were Spencers enrolled there, Looney declared, he would have to take his children out of school. "They shan't go with negroes," he said.[18]

While each Appalachian hollow appeared to be entirely self-contained, Looney understood that the people in Home Creek lived in direct daily contact with outside authority. For about forty years there had been public schools in Buchanan County. More than the railroad or the revenue inspectors who periodically raided local moonshiners, these schools connected the mountains with the world beyond. George Spencer signed his name with an X. His wife, Arminda, could not read or write either. But they were sending their oldest son to school. He would learn to read and write. This opportunity—this relationship with the state—was one of the few things the Spencers had. Looney intended to take it away. When Looney returned from Kentucky, he asked the Rock Lick school trustees to convene without telling Spencer. Looney produced sworn affidavits from the men he had interviewed in Kentucky and convinced the board to expel Melvin Spencer from the third grade.[19]

If George Looney had a modern outlook on the world, his neighbor George Spencer resembled a stock character in a silent melodrama about feuding mountain families. Spencer was thirty. He spent his days farming the hillsides and came home to a pregnant wife and a cabin full of children. He had a taste for whiskey and was not above going on "a drunk." George Looney had essentially ambushed him with his affidavits and the school board decision. For most whites anywhere in the country in 1910, "God damned negroes" were fighting words. In the mountains one might have expected an illiterate farmer to kill over them.[20]

But once again the Spencer-Looney feud did not follow the standard script. Instead of loading his rifle, George Spencer mounted his horse and rode out of the hollow. He went to Grundy and discussed his situation with a man named William Daugherty. Daugherty was Spencer's age, and like Spencer, he had recently moved to Buchanan County from Kentucky. In his younger days Daugherty had taught school. But in Virginia the law was his business.[21]

Daugherty would eventually gain a reputation for his "legal prowess," and in a few years he would help coordinate the World War I draft in Buchanan County. But when Spencer met with him, he had just escaped discipline from the Virginia Bar for practicing law without a license. Although Daugherty was barely established, he had formed a partnership with one of the most experienced and well-known lawyers in the region. Roland E. Chase had practiced for more than twenty years, and unlike most attorneys in the area, he had actually attended a law school. Long active in Republican politics, Chase was serving his second term as state senator for Buchanan and three other mountain counties. He lived forty miles away in Dickenson County, in a massive brick mansion that he had built next to the courthouse. He routinely traveled throughout Virginia in his capacity as grand master of the state's Odd Fellows.[22]

Spencer retained Daugherty and Chase. He was not going to kill George Looney. He would sue the man for slander.

Perhaps Spencer was following Looney's lead. Looney, after all, had hired a lawyer, taken evidence, and presented his case before the school board as if it had been a trial. The school board's decision resembled a legal verdict. Independent of Looney's actions, however, Spencer knew full well the power of the law.

Although Buchanan County appeared untouched by the modern world, attorneys had spent two decades burrowing into the jagged landscape. The county's hardwood forests and billions of tons of coal—the potential for millions of dollars from out-of-state investors—meant that land titles had to be clarified, competing claims resolved, and mineral rights bought and sold. Outsiders filed claims for hundreds of thousands of acres based on long-forgotten colonial land grants, leading to litigation that took upward of fifteen years to work through and subjected even the most obscure hollows to judicial scrutiny. Much of Chase and Daugherty's practice was devoted to title disputes. The litigation was all the more intense because the Grundy courthouse and all the county's property records had burned to cinders in 1885. Before there were loggers, there were lawyers. Before the railroads, before the mines—before modernity—there were lawyers.[23]

In laying the groundwork for industry, attorneys were altering what it meant to own land in Buchanan County. Land was becoming less of a means of survival, a guarantee of independence, a representation of kinship ties, an expression of honor and self. More than ever it was a commodity that could be cashed out. As George Spencer talked with his attorneys, they determined that George Looney's accusations and their consequences—the affront to Spencer's status and security and rights—could be distilled into a number. Spencer's vengeance had a price. He filed his complaint in Buchanan County Circuit Court, demanding $10,000 in damages.[24]

THE OLD MAN WOKE up early, while the air was still cool. Spring mornings had always been like this. Even before the first blinks of light over the hills, birds were warbling and roosters crowed, their songs damped by the rustle of leaves still new in early May. It was cloudy and calm as John Horn started riding through the Jordan Gap into Paintsville, Kentucky. The eighty-two-year-old would not be spending his Saturday doing chores around the farm, visiting with neighbors, or sitting on his porch.[25]

Behind Horn, above him, receding in the distance, was a steep clearing. Hand-knapped stones clustered like mushrooms on the hillside. All it would take was one year of neglect—one spring, summer, and fall—and no one would ever know that there was a graveyard on Horn's land. The man the Gap was named for—Horn's longtime neighbor—had been buried there some two years. Horn was heading to town because some men could not let Old Jordan Spencer rest in peace.[26]

After a short ride Paintsville started to spread out below. The surrounding hills were lush green, Paint Creek swollen with rain. The town was also swelling. Coal was starting to make many locals—and many more Yankee shareholders—rich. The coalfields extended several miles south into Van Lear, the town that had just risen along Miller's Creek, named for a director of the Maryland-based Consolidation Coal Company. The flood of cash had the curious effect of making the town appear newer and older at the same time. The buildings that were just being built evoked the architecture of older, more settled communities, suggesting that the mountains were no longer a perpetual frontier. At the edge of the business district, Horn passed by an enormous new colonnaded mansion that resembled a plantation house in the bluegrass country west of Lexington. Over the previous decade its owner, John C. Calhoun Mayo, had amassed a twenty-million-dollar fortune by selling hundreds of thousands of acres of coal rights to Northern partnerships and corporations. Next to his mansion was a vaulted and turreted Gothic church that Mayo had also built, hewn from local rock and adorned with exquisite stained-glass windows. The pipe organ inside was a token of appreciation from Andrew Carnegie.[27]

Past the church were a few sturdy blocks of businesses. Horn stopped under the shingle announcing Howes & Howes, attorneys at law, and entered the offices of Paintsville's most successful law practice. Frederick and Henry Howes did legal work for Mayo and represented the coal companies with the largest holdings in the area as well as local and national banks that did business in town. In May 1912 the firm had also been retained by George Spencer, the illiterate mountain farmer from Virginia, in matters relating to his slander case against George Looney.[28]

Horn was taken into a room that was already crowded with people. He recognized Old Jordan's son—had known Jordan Jr. since the day he was born. George Spencer, who looked just like his father and grandfather, was also a familiar face. In addition to a lawyer from Howes & Howes, George Spencer's two Virginia attorneys had accompanied him. George Looney was also there, as was his lawyer. A few other old men were waiting their turn to testify.[29]

Horn raised his right hand, and the shorthand stenographer administered an oath to tell the truth. Horn informed the lawyers that he had known Jordan Spencer fifty or sixty years, "ever since he came to this county, up to his death." For most of that time the two men had lived a quarter-mile apart. Horn said he could remember Old Jordan "when he was hot and when he was cold, when he was drunk and when he was sober."[30]

Because George Spencer's slander suit hinged on whether Looney's accusation was false, the lawyers had to gather evidence about Spencer's ancestry. While the Spencers were new people in Buchanan County, Virginia, they were well known across the line in Kentucky. Was George Spencer white in Johnson County? Was his father white? Or his grandfather? The case would turn on the memories of old men—and the lawyers' ability to get them talking.

George Spencer's lead attorney, Roland Chase, followed a simple script. He asked Horn and the dozen witnesses that followed about Old Jordan's skin color, hair, nose, lips, and eye color, and whether he had a "smell peculiar to the colored people." He also asked whether the Spencers had gone to white churches and schools and how they had been regarded by their neighbors. Whether someone was black or white was about how he or she looked, but not exclusively. It was also about how someone acted—character and reputation and the exercise of particular rights that had been reserved for the dominant race.[31]

Horn had no trouble answering Chase's questions in detail. Old Jordan had "tolerably straight" red hair, thin lips, a nose that was "a little fuller" than his son's, and blue eyes; he "smelled a little bit, when he was a little hot." "I did not see any negro about him," Horn said. Jordan's wife, Malinda, "was a very clever lady and as white a woman as you find anywhere." The Spencers prayed, ate, went to school, and visited with whites in the community. "I never heard of any objections to them," Horn declared. "There never was no racket in the neighborhood or school district."[32]

On cross-examination, Looney's lawyer Glenn Ratliff quickly established that Horn knew nothing about Spencer's ancestry. He asked whether Horn could say for sure whether Jordan "was a full blooded white man or not." When Horn said no, the lawyer subtly changed course: "Did you ever hear it questioned at any time in your life?"

Horn did not seem to understand. "There was nobody here that knew anything about it more than I did," he said.

Ratliff paused to rephrase the question. "I mean," said Ratliff, "did you ever hear it reported he had negro blood about him?"

"I might have heard it," Horn replied, "and I might not."

Ratliff was getting impatient with the old man. "Just answer the question," he said. "Did you at any time to your remembrance, hear it said that Jordan Spencer, Sr., was mixed blooded?"

"Well, I will tell you," Horn said, "I don't think a man has to swear over what he heard somebody else say."[33]

If Ratliff had expected Horn to be an unsophisticated witness, he was disabused of the notion. The eighty-two-year-old mountaineer understood the objection to hearsay testimony. The seductive rhythm of Ratliff's cross-examination—the string of easy yes-or-no questions designed to lure a witness into giving testimony that he was not planning on giving—had little effect on Horn. The old farmer was outwitting the young lawyer. Perhaps Horn was thinking back to being cross-examined once before, almost half a century earlier, in a congressional election contest involving allegations that disenfranchised rebels had illegally voted. Perhaps he had watched a trial or two over the years in the Paintsville courthouse, as had many a country farmer looking for entertainment in town. In any case, even in the hollows of eastern Kentucky, people knew how the law worked.[34]

The witnesses who followed Horn were equally cagey. J. Q. Horn, age sixty-five, declined to say whether Spencer was "a man of pure Caucasian blood": "That I don't know anything about, I don't bother with." Asked the same question—"Judging of what you have seen of Jordan Spencer, Sr. would you class him as a man of pure Caucasi[a]n blood?"—sixty-eight-year-old Tom Horn replied, "I don't know anything about anyone's blood, no matter who the man is." Despite admonitions not to evade Ratliff's questions, John Estep, Old Jordan's neighbor for forty years, also refused to comment on Spencer's "pedigree." "I have not formed any good opinion about it," Estep said. "It was none of my business." Even though racial purity was supposed to be everyone's business in 1912, Spencer's neighbors were determined to protect his family and, ultimately, to protect the community's decision to accept Old Jordan as one of their own.[35]

Only after repeated questions did the old men acknowledge the rumors that had long followed Jordan Spencer. John Horn remembered the time when Letcher Davis claimed that Spencer had "mixed blood." Another neighbor remembered when Jordan's sons tangled with a set of boys and their father went after Old Jordan with a gun, saying he was "going to kill a 'damn negro.'" Although in day-to-day life no one treated Old Jordan differently, the idea that he was black was never far below the surface. Asked whether "it was the general report that [Spencer] was not a man of pure white blood," seventy-one-year-old A. L. Rice had to admit, "No, I could not say, that it was. If him and anybody had any trouble, I have heard them call him a negro or a darkey on account of being mad at him." "I think there was something about him that was not pure white blood," Rice said. "He was of some other race, but I don't know what race."[36]

George Looney had seven of his own witnesses to depose in Paintsville. While the plaintiff called many of Old Jordan's neighbors to testify, the defense witnesses all lived in town. While just as plainspoken as the farmers from the hollows, they included some of Johnson County's leading men. They held official positions such as postmaster, county judge, circuit court clerk, member of the board of health, and public schools trustee. They had made money in timber. Two had been the coal baron John Mayo's business partners. They knew Jordan Spencer because he had worked for them. The witnesses had no trouble testifying that Spencer was "a little bit negro." His skin was dark. His hair was "kinky" and unconvincingly dyed. "When he was sweating," one remembered, "something red ran down over his temples."[37]

The reason his neighbors had accepted Jordan, a witness suggested, was that many of them were dark themselves. The people living along Rockhouse Creek could have been "the darkey race" or Indian or something else entirely, "neither black nor white." Although people in Johnson County "boasted and felt proud of the fact that they had a white county composed of white citizens," the area's leading men knew better. "It has a right smart sprinkle of African and Indian blood, or that is my opinion," said a seventy-six-year-old retired businessman. The witnesses claimed to remember Old Jordan as "a good man, a good worker, and he did good work." But that was not enough to gain him social acceptance. "We took from his looks, general appearance, and demeanor that he was mixed blooded," said Mayo's partner John Castle, "and we did not associate a great deal with that class of people." It was as if wealth and exposure to the world outside made a person more likely to care about the purity of a man's blood. In the mountains in 1912 disdain for black people did not signify backwardness. To the contrary, it was a measure of enlightenment.[38]

IT TAKES TIME FOR the August heat to seep into a county courthouse. For a judge on the bench or a spectator in the jury box or gallery, it can be hard to detect summer's grip until it is too late. One moment an onlooker might be following the testimony, objections, and rulings from the bench. The next, his collar is soggy and wilted, and he has to hold his head up, hand on cheek, to maintain any hope of staying awake. The fight for consciousness in the suddenly still air can be especially dire when depositions are read aloud in open court. Testimony that had been angry or heartbreaking or sly has a way of coming uncreased when repeated, word for word from the transcript, in halting monotone—a flat expanse of language, always on the verge of losing its meaning.

George Spencer took the witness stand in the Circuit Court of Buchanan County on August 1, 1912, after the depositions of seven of Old Jordan's Kentucky neighbors had been read into the record. On one side of the courtroom, George Looney sat flanked by four defense lawyers. On the other side were Spencer's two lawyers, as well as his parents, a sister, his wife, Arminda, and son Melvin. If the testimony from the old Kentucky men had revealed persistent rumors about Old Jordan even as he and his family participated fully in their community, his grandson held his ground. The jury watched George Spencer answer William Daugherty's questions politely—"yes, sir" and "no, sir"—but firmly. He and his brothers and sisters had gone to white schools. They prayed in white churches. "Did you ever hear the question raised that you and your father was colored until raised by the defendant?" asked his lawyer. "No sir," said Spencer. His whole family had had friendly relations with the Looneys for the better part of a decade, until Henderson Looney died.[39]

At the beginning and end of his direct examination, Spencer emphasized that Arminda, his wife, was Ray Justice's daughter. She was kin to much of the county. No one could have expected her to figure out her husband's hidden ancestry. Looney himself had freely and happily associated with the

Spencers. The prospect of an innocent victim of Looney's campaign—someone just as deeply rooted in Buchanan County as Looney—was a powerful point in Spencer's favor. If Arminda Spencer and George Looney could be fooled, anyone could be. If a "sprinkle" of African ancestry could turn a white man black—could turn Arminda Spencer's children black—then everyone had to worry about their bloodlines. All over the South lynch mobs were killing blacks with the stated purpose of protecting white women. George Spencer and his lawyers were suggesting to the jury that they could protect Arminda Spencer by finding that her husband was white.[40]

On cross-examination, nearly every question that Looney's lawyer asked included the word *Negro*. "Did you ever hear any one else call you negroes before George Looney?" "Did you ever hear your father say you were mixed with part negro?" George Spencer remained calm and polite.

Only once did he reveal a bit of temper. "Did not Will Short on Home Creek call you a negro to your face?" Looney's lawyer asked.

"No, sir," Spencer replied. "That would be a little dangerous." The very fact that the question offended him was evidence of his whiteness.[41]

THE DEFENSE CALLED SEVEN witnesses, mostly school board officials justifying their decision to expel Melvin Spencer, and read the depositions of seven more. Some witnesses alleged that the Spencers had been the subject of rumors about their race from the moment they moved into Buchanan County. Another witness suggested that George Spencer had been comfortable enough in his community that he could wear his race casually—that Home Creek was set apart from the rest of the South, that it did not subscribe to the same insistence on purity. "He told me they were mixed blooded," said Albert Stevenson, "he said he had negro blood in him, but he didn't object as it made him hardy."[42]

But George Looney's last witness brought the outside world, the rest of the South's obsession with racial purity, right back into the courtroom. Eugene Billisoly was different from everyone else who had testified. He was not from the mountains. He had attended the University of Virginia and made his living practicing law. He had crossed the state to testify, all the way from Norfolk, because he had a skill that no one else in the courtroom had. Billisoly informed the court that nearly half of Norfolk's eighty thousand residents were black, and he had personally supervised forty or fifty blacks while working as a city administrator. Based on that experience—and based on three years of medical training before he studied law—he suggested that he could tell at a glance if someone had more than "one-eighth negro blood in them."[43]

Supporters of segregation often spoke of blackness as a disastrous contaminant from which Jim Crow laws purported to protect whites. This sense of race and purity was premised on a belief that people could distinguish blacks from whites. Reflecting the growing authority of doctors and social scientists in a modernizing country, medicine and science provided the language, a method, and a basic confidence that segregation was right and could be maintained. In courtrooms all over the country experts were identifying people as black or white based on the whites of their eyes, the curve of their spines, the texture of their hair, the shape of their nostrils, and the tint of their fingernails. It was unclear whether scientific testimony would outweigh common sense in Buchanan County, but the very fact that Looney's lawyers would put Billisoly on the stand suggested that the new thinking about race—and the new authority of science—had some resonance for a mountain jury.[44]

Billisoly's testimony was brief. Looney's lawyer pointed to Melvin Spencer and asked, "Is there any negro blood in this boy?"

Billisoly looked at the nine-year-old and concentrated. "Well," he said, "he looks like there is negro blood in him. Has nose, lips, and chin very much like a negro. Very characteristic."

"Look at that man," the lawyer said, pointing at George Spencer, "and tell us what you think of him."

Again Billisoly leveled his gaze. "Well, sir, he has some of the features of a negro."

William Daugherty rose from his chair for cross-examination. He pointed to George Spencer's sister. "What do you think of her?"

The defense expert declared that he "would consider her of pure Caucasian blood."

Daugherty pointed to Spencer's mother. "Look at that lady," he said. "Do you think she has any negro blood in her?"

"No, sir," said Billisoly. "I do not. She is a white woman."

Daugherty pointed to Spencer's father. "Look at that man . . . what do you think of him?"

"Let me see his hair," the witness said. "His hair looks a little like a negro. I believe there is some negro there, I can't say how much."[45]

THE JUDGE INSTRUCTED THE jury that under Virginia law, Melvin Spencer was legally white unless he had "one-sixteenth or more . . . negro blood." By one-sixteenth, the judge clarified that if the boy's great-grandfather, Old Jordan Spencer, was "less than one-half negro . . . then the said Melvin Spencer had less than one-sixteenth of negro blood and is not a negro." Even if the jury believed that the Spencers had a reputation for being black in Johnson or Buchanan counties, it would still have to find for the plaintiffs if the child had less than the exact proportion of "negro blood" spelled out in the statute. Because it was nearly impossible to determine exactly how black Melvin and his father were—let alone determine the blood fraction of Melvin's dead great-grandfather—the instructions seemed to favor the Spencers.[46]

At the same time the judge also allowed the jury to excuse George Looney's "strong or violent language disproportioned to the occasion" if it believed "that the party using the language was engaged in a bona fide investigation for a lawful purpose." Given the importance of segregating the schools—"few things would . . . tend more toward social equality and the amalgamation of the races than to educate them together," Looney's lawyers would argue—the judge seemed to be giving Looney considerable leeway with even slanderous accusations, as long as they were meant to protect white children from contamination.[47]

The jury filed out of the courtroom to deliberate. They had to determine whether Looney's accusations were false and malicious, but also whether a Buchanan County native's word was worth more than a newcomer's, whether Arminda Spencer was worth protecting, and whether the color line had to be drawn no matter what the human consequences. It did not take them long to reach a decision. They returned to the jury box and delivered their verdict: judgment for the defendant. George Looney had not slandered George Spencer by referring to his family as "God damned negroes."

FACED WITH THE FINDINGS of a Buchanan County jury, the airing of his family's history in an open courtroom, and the triumph of an enemy whom he would regularly encounter along Home Creek, George Spencer and his father and brothers could have picked up their guns. More than one blood feud had started in the mountains after a jury verdict, particularly when one party believed the verdict had been biased. Spencer and his family also could have packed their belongings and left the area. Once it was generally known that they had been legally classified as "colored," what future did the Spencers have in an all-white county?[48]

But George Spencer stood his ground and appealed the verdict to the Virginia Supreme Court. Convincing a court to overturn a jury verdict was never easy, and Spencer's case was all the more difficult because on balance the evidence showed that Old Jordan had been widely regarded as racially different. Moreover, where race had yet to become an overwhelming obsession in the hills—regardless of their reputation, the Spencers had had little trouble finding a place in their community—Richmond was an epicenter of the movement for racial purity. Looney's justification for destroying the Spencers, "preserv[ing] the racial integrity and superiority of the white man," would resonate with a court that was fundamentally engaged with the task of enabling Virginia to segregate.[49]

Nevertheless Roland Chase and William Daugherty raised seventeen grounds for reversal. They objected to seven of the jury instructions and to seven rulings by the trial judge that admitted or excluded particular testimony or physical evidence. The lawyers emphasized Looney's foul mouth. Defense counsel would later complain that Chase and Daugherty's submission to the court "has the term, 'God damned negroes,' coming twelve times from the lips of this Appellee. It would be hard to find a coarser and more profane type of man than the Declaration attempts to make [Looney]." But Spencer's lawyers devoted most of their energy to arguing that the evidence failed to support the jury's verdict. Nothing proved that Melvin Spencer was more than one-sixteenth black, and any privilege that George Looney could claim for taking extreme action to keep the schools racially exclusive was undermined by his malice toward the Spencers. If the evidence did not exactly show that the Spencers were "of pure caucasian blood," neither did it prove that they were legally black. But even supposing that Spencer won on this argument, could his neighbors on Home Creek accept a family that was white on a technicality?[50]

In response, Looney's lawyers stated simply that Virginia's public policy "gives to the citizens of the state the right to have their children educated with children of their own race." "Now how can such policy be properly carried into effect and such right of the citizen be properly protected," they asked, "if the patrons of the school be not allowed, without fear of slander suits, to protest . . . against pupils who they do not consider under the laws entitled so to do, attending the same school attended by their children[?]" The defense lawyers implored the court not to let the fact that George Looney was "habitually profane" overshadow his laudable purpose in keeping blacks and whites separate.[51]

For two years and a month, the appeal was pending. For two years Melvin Spencer was shunned from school, and his family had to share their hollow with a sworn enemy. But there was no violence.

On September 7, 1914, just as news of the Battle of the Marne was reaching the United States, the Virginia Supreme Court set aside the jury verdict in *Spencer v. Looney* and ordered a new trial. The justices discounted the evidence of the Spencers' reputation, insisting instead on the nearly impossible proof of an exact blood quantum. "It is true that several witnesses . . . say that the grandfather of plaintiff . . . had some of the appearances of a negro," the opinion held, "but none were able to say what proportion of negro blood, if any, he had in him." Any privilege that Looney had to safeguard his children's segregated schooling was overcome for several reasons: first, Looney had used "the most profane, uncalled for, and violent language"; second, the two warring families had been friendly until the defendant's brother was killed; and finally, Looney had gone to a tremendous amount of trouble and expense to wage his war. By strictly interpreting the one-sixteenth rule and by inferring malice, in part, from

Looney's zealous investigation of the Spencers' race, the court made it difficult for anyone to raise questions about racial identity without fear of legal action.[52]

Despite the grounds for its ruling, the Virginia Supreme Court was not opposed to segregation. Yet no matter how compelling it was to "preserve the racial integrity and superiority of the white man," the court showed some sense that a judgment for Looney would portend a bleak future for the white South: the possibility that petty feuds would increasingly take the form of racial witch hunts, that government authorities would reflexively err on the side of purity and paranoia—and that a good number of allegations might be borne out with the proper investigation. White communities had to be secure in their racial status before they could commit to the politics of racial purity. By letting the Spencers remain white, by discouraging efforts to investigate and uncover individuals' racial backgrounds, the court was making the South safe for segregation.

After the court ruled, no one bothered the Spencers again. The case was probably never retried, and the Buchanan County courthouse was gutted in a 1915 fire that destroyed most of Grundy. The family remained on Home Creek. Years later Melvin Spencer would marry a local woman and had eleven children who survived him. Perhaps their neighbors regarded the judicial decision as the final word on the Spencers' race. Or maybe the case never mattered much at all—people knew Looney had a war to fight, but they never believed or cared about the accusation. There was too much work to do, hillsides to harvest, in the long-shadowed hours between sunup and sundown.[53]

As Melvin Spencer resumed his education, scientists from the Virginia Geological Survey were determining that there were coal deposits three feet thick opposite the schoolhouse and up and down Home Creek. The 1920 census declared Buchanan County to be entirely white, with all but four residents native-born Americans. It became a selling point to attract mining companies into the hills. "Among such a homogenous population," concluded one report, "industrialists need have little fear of labor disturbances."[54]

CHAPTER NINETEEN

GIBSON

Paris and Chicago, 1931–33

Paris, Summer 1931

S HE WAS PERFECT. Henry Field took one look and made his way through the gaping crowds. In the summer of 1931 the International Colonial Exposition was drawing thousands of visitors to the Bois de Vincennes on the eastern outskirts of Paris. Tourists, Parisians, and even the occasional Bolshevik packed the pavilions and plazas displaying the arts, industries, and cultures of France's global empire, from Algeria to Cambodia, Dahomey to Djibouti.[1]

The exposition was painstakingly designed to be ethnographic—sober and scientific, an authentic account of humankind in all its variation. At the same time there was no avoiding a carnival atmosphere. The exposition billed itself as a "Tour of the World in a Single Day," a sliding scale from civilization to savagery and all points in between. It promised "the seductions of the picturesque and the irresistible magic of art," offering at a glance "the thatch roofs of Togo, the red kasbahs of West Africa, and the circumflex, surprising, aerial accent of . . . Sumatra houses . . . the tom-tom of a Negro . . . the Melody of the World, and its History." Although Asians and Africans in native dress milled through the crowds and periodically performed traditional songs and dances, few visitors would have been shocked at the sight of them. For centuries, people from the remotest parts of the world had entertained the French, as caged curiosities and sideshow freaks.[2]

The pavilion representing French Equatorial Africa combined two tribal architectures. A low-slung story inspired by the Mangbetu people of the Congo was painted with geometrical designs, while a towering cupola rising in the center was reminiscent of a conical Mousgoum house of northern Cameroon. To critics, the combination of styles was too jarring. The cupola looked like a fat bunch of bananas. The building was overly mannered, contrived, even fake.[3]

Inside, though, Field saw someone more than authentic—she was ideal. The woman had come from Central Africa, an area the French called Oubangui-Chari. As a baby, her lips had been cut away from her face and enhanced with small wooden discs. As she grew older, larger and larger discs were inserted, stretching and beautifying her lips. As an adult, she looked to Western eyes as if she had a duck's bill or, as the sideshows of the time described Ubangi women, "crocodile lips" or "monster mouths."[4]

Field sought out the exposition's organizer, Marshal Hubert Lyautey, the elderly French general who had tamed Morocco and Madagascar, and asked if he could borrow the woman for the day. Although Lyautey was wary that anticolonial subversives were trying to infiltrate the Bois de Vincennes and sow dissent among the native workers, he gave his blessing without hesitation. Given Field's immense family wealth and status in the world of ethnography, Lyautey's decision to grant his request was an easy one; Field's interest in the woman was flattering.[5]

Field was not even thirty years old, but he was a man accustomed to deference. He traced his family to one Hubertus de la Feld, a ninth-century French chieftain. Field's visits to France sometimes included a trip to the Strasbourg cemetery, where a mossy stone marked a remote forefather's grave. One side of Henry Field's family had arrived in the United States among the first Puritans in seventeenth-century Massachusetts. The other side included Southerners of dignity and worth, most notably Field's grandfather, the Louisiana senator Randall Lee Gibson.

What impressed people most about Henry Field's pedigree, however, was his great-uncle, the department store magnate Marshall Field. As a student at Oxford, Henry Field had done extensive anthropological fieldwork in the Near East. In 1926, a year after graduating, he moved from England to Chicago. He assumed the position of Assistant Curator of Physical Anthropology at the Field Museum of Natural History, founded and run by his family.[6]

The young anthropologist escorted the woman from the Equatorial Africa pavilion to a taxi, waiting with its top down in the morning sun. They sat side by side in the backseat. Field was tall, tweedy, with a patrician's forehead and strong chin. The woman wore her hair in braids tightly woven along her head. With her left hand, she held up her lower lip, which extended ten inches from her mouth.

The taxi headed west, toward the center of Paris. The streets and sidewalks were crowded with summer traffic. At the Bastille they turned onto the rue de Rivoli and drove its length, with the Marais on their right, Notre Dame and the Île-de-France on their left. At every stoplight, there was pandemonium. In cars, on foot, Parisians cheered and saluted the Ubangi woman. She started jabbing Field with her right elbow and talking at a rapid clip. Field could not understand her but assumed that she was "chatter[ing] like a magpie" to express her pleasure. "Like all beautiful women," he wrote, "my companion did not remain oblivious to this attention." He was certainly enjoying the moment, something he would remember decades later with "mingled amusement and embarrassment." The great fashion designers of Paris might create distinctive and original looks, he thought, "but my companion had the biggest lips in France!"[7]

After the Louvre and Tuileries, they turned left, skirting the Champs-Élysées as they drove straight through the place de la Concorde and across the shimmering Seine. Past Bonaparte's tomb and the Eiffel Tower, they plunged into the Fifteenth Arrondissement, winding their way to the rue de Vouillé and the Villa Chauvelot. It was a humble neighborhood, and there was little commotion at the woman with lip plates. The neighbors had grown used to the procession of unusual people: Nepalese princes and princesses, a student from Shanghai, Malays, Hawaiians, a boy from Madura, off the Javanese coast.[8]

Field brought the woman to a quiet stone building. A fountain built into its outside wall was adorned with small North African tiles, black and turquoise. By design, one black tile was missing from the pattern; otherwise, perfection would attract the evil eye. They entered the building and went upstairs. They were greeted by a startled Siamese cat. Behind him was an open studio cluttered with clay models and plaster casts: heads, feet, legs, hands. A "haughty and extremely handsome" woman with long gray hair tied in an elaborate bun, flowing green smock, artfully draped scarf, and oversize black tam approached Field and his find. Her handshake was firm.[9]

While her assistants shaped approximations of full-length bodies around wire and wood frames, Malvina Hoffman—Auguste Rodin's disciple and Henry Field's protégée—was endowing the rough clay with life, proportion, and a sense of movement. A New Yorker, Hoffman had been based in Paris for the entirety of the Colonial Exposition. Nearly every day she would "kidnap" native workers from the Bois de Vincennes. The exposition provided a wealth of splendid subjects. The Ubangi woman was hardly the first Hoffman had met. The sculptor had spent years traveling through Africa; while in the Congo, she had drawn a portrait of a woman with lip plates. The sculptor may have offered her new subject a cigarette, having seen Ubangis smoke through long hollowed reeds. Hoffman agreed with her patron that the Ubangi he had chosen was ideal for the vast project that he had commissioned.[10]

WHEN FIELD STARTED WORK in Chicago in 1926, he had proposed to his curator an entire exhibition hall devoted to what he called "the principal racial types of the world." Alongside more traditional exhibits that "would illustrate the bases on which mankind may be divided," dozens of sculptures—full bodies, busts, heads—would populate the hall. It would represent the latest knowledge of physical anthropology through the work of "the finest artists in the world." The curator, Berthold Laufer, a German brought to the United States by the eminent anthropologist Franz Boas, embraced the idea, and the museum's president, Field's cousin, told him to plan it "without regard to space, time, or cost." It would open in time for the 1933 world's fair.[11]

In order to commence the project, Field first had to determine what he meant by the "principal racial types of the world." Of course, there were three principal groups—he could ask just about anyone walking down Lake

Shore Drive, and they would give the same answer: white, yellow, and black. Within those groups, Field knew there were important subgroups that could be determined by analyzing "the form, color, and quantity of the hair; the color of the skin; the shape of the head and face; and the character of the nose, eyes, mouth, and lips," as well as stature. For years Field covered "yards of paper" with notes, waking from sleep to write down ideas and interrupting his reveries at the Thursday-night symphony. He inspected more than a million pictures of representative types from galleries, photo services, and museum collections across the United States and in more than a dozen cities in Europe, creating a Library of Racial Photographs with twenty thousand prints. Consulting with Laufer, with anthropologists at the Smithsonian, Harvard, and the Museum of Natural History, and with leading scientists in England, France, and Germany, Field developed a list of 164 racial types, from Kalahari Bushmen to Basques to Blackfoot Indians.[12]

The next step was to find "one single artist with the talent and physical endurance" to travel the world and sculpt all 164 types. Field's cousin, Marshall Field III, suggested Hoffman. The anthropologist traveled to Hoffman's New York studio and was particularly struck by an "amazingly lifelike" sculpture of Anna Pavlova as well as two oversize heads of Nubians that showed "the most delicate realism combined with a strong dramatic sense."[13]

In February 1930 Field commissioned Hoffman for the years-long project. To keep costs in control after the stock market crash, he deleted some of the "less important types" from his list of races, culling it to an even one hundred. That summer the sculptor set up her Paris studio. Field and his colleagues helped her establish other studios around the world and provided her with dozens of letters of introduction for upcoming trips through Europe, India, Africa, Asia, and Australia. From the start she was working at "concert pitch," sculpting from live models all day and from memory at night. At a Paris foundry, sixty men were employed in creating plaster and sand molds and casting her statues in bronze. Hoffman supervised the patina work closely, "to suggest the variety of tones and textures of all the races."[14]

In September 1931, after several months of sculpting workers at the

Colonial Exposition, Hoffman left Paris and began traveling around the world, from New York to San Francisco, Honolulu and Yokohama, to Hong Kong and the Philippines, Bali and Batavia, Singapore and Calcutta and Ceylon. She sailed in forty types of ships, from ocean liners to outriggers, slept in castles and huts, donned pith helmets and crossed jungles and dosed with quinine. As she traveled around the world, she found models, sketched portraits, and shaped a mountain's worth of heads and bodies out of clay and plaster of Paris. Eight months later she was back in Paris, enjoying "spring blossoms . . . peace and fertility, balanced temperature and modern plumbing." By the end of 1932 the finished sculptures were in Chicago: twenty-seven life-size, twenty-seven busts, and fifty heads. When the Hall of the Races of Mankind opened in May 1933, the sculptures would make her famous, and they became one of the signal triumphs of Henry Field's long and distinguished career.[15]

HENRY FIELD HAD BEEN estranged from his father for years. His parents had divorced in 1907, before he turned five, and a year later his mother had married an Englishman. They moved from Washington, D.C., to Baggrave, his stepfather's country house in Leicestershire. Field enjoyed an aristocratic upbringing, digging up fossils on the family estate as a boy, then went on to Eton and Oxford. By the time he headed back to Chicago to take his job at the Field Museum, he had dropped his father's family name and assumed his mother's.[16]

Like Malvina Hoffman's sculptures, Field's father, Preston Gibson, was broadly representative of a certain type of man—dark and dashing, the quintessence of privilege in the first two decades of the twentieth century. Randall Lee Gibson's youngest son had been twelve when he was orphaned, a sad, lonely boy with an inheritance worth millions. According to the terms of his father's will, he had no guardian, just four trustees of his fortune. Preston moved a few doors down the street from his father's mansion in Washington to the house of his mother's sister Leita. Within months Leita had married Preston's trustee Edward Douglass White, who had been recently appointed a Supreme Court justice.[17]

Soon after his appointment Justice White cast his vote with the majority in *Plessy v. Ferguson*, upholding a Louisiana statute that required railroads to segregate their cars by race. When he was not addressing issues of national importance, Justice White tried to establish a home for his new wife and nephew that embraced simplicity and order. Preston and his uncle took silent afternoon walks through the city, nodding to passersby; spent late nights in their private library, reading about George Washington and John Marshall; and enjoyed frequent visits from the Roman Catholic archbishop of Baltimore. White often entertained his nephew with stories that featured "old colored m[e]n" he had run across in New Orleans and Washington. The justice assumed their accents and idiosyncratic diction for comic effect.[18]

Yet for all the love Preston Gibson claimed to feel for his aunt and uncle, the teenage boy brought constant disorder into their lives. Aunt Leita found him to be "unruly and disobedient . . . reckless . . . [and] unfortunately depraved." "It is impossible to compel him to tell the truth on any subject," she complained. "The exposure of one falsehood after the other seems only to excite a sense of amusement in his mind when spoken to on the subject." Preston's "tendency to dissipation" was matched only by his "irresistible tendency to theft," from which no family member, houseguest, or servant was safe.[19]

Instead of being sent to a reform school, as his aunt would have wished, Gibson wound up at Yale. He was popular on campus, a pitcher on the baseball team and a secret society inductee, idolized by classmates for his role on the football squad that held an undefeated Harvard to a zero–zero tie just before Thanksgiving in 1899. He gained national notoriety two months later when he eloped with Marshall Field's niece Minna, a seventeen-year-old debutante boarding at the Misses Masters' School in Dobbs Ferry, New York. Despite their scandalous union, the couple was embraced by her mother and stepfather, the prominent novelist Thomas Nelson Page, whose tales of "ole Virginia" reflected a national nostalgia for vast plantations, belles and gallants, and happy slaves. It was an attractive version of the past at a moment when legislatures were enacting Jim Crow laws and lynch mobs were murdering hundreds of men and women every year. Preston Gibson could certainly find common ground with Page in conversation. Typical of his generation, the rakish Yalie enjoyed nothing more than a minstrel show, and he was becoming an accomplished teller of "Kentucky Negro stories."[20]

From the time he married Minna Field, Preston Gibson became a fixture of high society. His life whirled among Chicago, Washington, and New York, a dozen exclusive clubs, and resort destinations from Georgia to Maine, Paris to Cairo. It was a world governed by elaborate rules and rituals, yet its denizens lived to flout conventional morality—smoking, drinking, gambling, engaging in all-night revels and love affairs. "A new scandal is like a Parisian model," Gibson would write. "It wants to air itself every afternoon."[21]

Gibson's life revolved around cotillions and turkey trots, roulette, bridge and mah-jongg, polo matches and baseball games. He socialized with Astors and Vanderbilts, presidents, senators, and Supreme Court justices, counts and princes and foreign ambassadors. When Theodore Roosevelt's daughter Alice visited Chicago, the iconic "New Woman" stayed with the Gibsons. Preston hosted balls that began at the stroke of midnight, was admired for swimming the Rhode Island Sound from Narragansett to Newport, and won a $500 bet when the catcher for the Washington Nationals, Gabby Street, caught a baseball that Preston had thrown from the top of the Washington Monument. Regarded by the society pages as one of the best dancers in his circle, he once revealed his secret to doing a successful Argentine tango: "the lifting of the body and holding it as the negroes do in the cake walk."[22]

After briefly working for his wife's family, Preston turned his attention to higher pursuits. By 1905 he was contributing pieces to newspapers and establishing himself as a playwright. His plays were a garish parade of socialites, bounders, frauds, thieves, and gold diggers. Unhappy husbands tried to hang themselves. Long-lost lovers were reunited. The embraces were always "passionate," the kisses unfailingly "violent." A pistol placed on the mantel on page six was fired by page thirteen.[23]

Some of his work was performed with amateur actors from his social circle, providing them an excuse to don fancy costumes and grope one another, but several plays were produced on Broadway. The reviews were never positive. His most successful play, *The Turning Point*, merged high-society comedy with Appalachian melodrama, as a member of the old Virginia gentry refuses to sell a railroad right-of-way to a Northern businessman intent on mining the area's coal, forms a competing company of his own, and then wins the heart of a fetching New York City heiress. The play also borrowed some of its best lines from Oscar Wilde's *An Ideal Husband*. As controversy raged, Gibson took the stage during one performance and addressed the audience, attributing any similarity in language to "the result of uniform human experiences" and comparing himself to Shakespeare and Rostand.[24]

Although his plays revealed some capacity for self-awareness, Gibson seemed unable to avoid becoming the kind of person he wrote about. He divorced Minna Field in 1907, moved back to Washington, and married another heiress in 1909. His best man was Reginald Vanderbilt, the Commodore's grandson, and among the notables in attendance were Justice White, Senator Elihu Root, and Admiral Dewey. After six years, two children, a dozen plays, hundreds of tea dances, and a series of publicly aired indiscretions involving a young woman in Baltimore, Gibson divorced again.[25]

As Gibson's second marriage dissolved, he found a new source of focus and meaning in his life: the war in Europe. He raised money for French and Serbian relief, and after a German U-boat sank the *Lusitania* in 1915, he underwent training in trench warfare at Plattsburgh, New York, with a group of prominent New York, Philadelphia, and Boston businessmen. In early 1917 Gibson headed to France, volunteered for the ambulance corps, and found himself on the Western Front in the Aisne Valley, sixty miles from Paris, just as the French were mounting a major offensive. Through the "stupendous disemboweling roar of the artillery," the "cauldron of blood and mud," Gibson worked ninety hours at a time without sleep, bringing the wounded to surgeons he described as "literally dripping." The soldiers he saw had holes in their heads, chests, guts, and limbs; they could not stop crying from the mustard bombs and were coughing and vomiting blood from other gas attacks that clouded the valley. The shelling knocked him down and dented his helmet. While Gibson and a French soldier watched a dogfight overhead, "a piece of shrapnel about as big as a saucer simply cut [the Frenchman's] head off as he stood facing me, just as though an axe had done it."[26]

Occasionally Gibson thought of his previous life. Firing antiaircraft guns at German spotter planes reminded him of "shooting quail in South Carolina." But most of his experiences were entirely new. Many of the soldiers participating in the offensive had come from Senegal and other African colonies, rushing from the trenches armed only with grenades and long knives. "It seemed so curious, in a way, to go up to one of these fellows, a black Algerian, covered with mud, who had fallen or slipped down and help him up and have him put his arm over your shoulder," Gibson wrote. "At the moment one only thought of him as one of your own."[27]

Like his father, Gibson returned from war a hero. The French awarded him the Croix de Guerre. Back in the United States, he refused an army captain's commission and in 1918 enlisted in the Marines as a thirty-eight-year-old private. Working as a recruiter, he broke records by convincing 3,200 men to enlist during a two-week drive; a speech he gave at a New York theater raised $163,000 in Liberty Loans. A major press published his war memoir, *Battering the Boche*, which received the best reviews of his literary career.[28]

Poised to leap from society to substance, Gibson instead reverted to form at war's end. In 1919 he eloped to Greenwich, Connecticut, with a Standard Oil heiress who dreamed of being a movie star. Two years later she sailed to Paris and divorced him, complaining that she had married a "flock of outstanding bills." Sued by creditors and auctioning his possessions, hair receding, mustache gray, Gibson spent years abroad, in Zurich and Deauville, cruising the Mediterranean. By his fourth marriage in 1925, he was a running joke in the society pages. "Preston Gibson gets his name in the headlines again," wrote one wag. "You guessed it—Boston girl. He knows beans!"[29]

Gibson and his wife announced their intention to live in Paris, but they worked their way around the world. Like a character in one of his plays, Gibson resorted to writing bad checks when he was short on cash in Shanghai. He and his wife fled China but were arrested in Vancouver. Over the next year Gibson's Shanghai fraud and the protracted legal battles that followed provided fodder for his last great burst of national publicity, at least until his fourth divorce in 1928.[30]

Gibson spent the next decade languishing in a furnished room in New York, old, sick, and poor. He had outlived his two older brothers, one of whom had suffered years of mental illness and the other a bankrupt. He did not know any of his children. Two sons, one of whom was Henry Field, changed their names. When his daughter married in 1934, her stepfather gave her away. In 1937, at age fifty-seven, Gibson died at a veterans hospital in the Bronx. He was remembered as someone who "packed ten lives into one," a "man with the fatal gift of charm." Gibson was not a wit, wrote one reporter, nor did he have a "mellifluous voice." What made him the embodiment of the Smart Set was simple: "Preston Gibson [was] never a bore." He was buried at Arlington National Cemetery.[31]

Chicago, May 1933

A S THE TWENTY-ONE-GUN SALUTE blasted and the Soldier Field crowd waved flags and cheered, Will Rogers cracked a wad of gum in his cheek. The gesture was slow, almost thoughtful—to Henry Field it sounded like a Bushman's clicks. The two men were braving a May morning in Chicago, sitting together on the podium at the opening ceremony of the 1933 world's fair. Just as a dignitary rose to address the crowd, the humorist turned to the anthropologist.

"Hear you work in that marble mausoleum over there," Rogers said. "Get any kick out of playing with mummies?"

"Sure," Field answered. "They never say no."[32]

All day a thick current of visitors flowed through the Hall of the Races of Mankind. For weeks it never stopped. Two long galleries—a procession of bronze statues resting on dark wood pedestals—met at an octagonal room, where a larger-than-life statue, the Unity of Mankind, celebrated the three central races, black, white, and yellow. In the diffused light of the galleries, the statues were warm and tactile. Although they bristled with life, they did not encourage viewers to see similarities between themselves and the figures. Rather, they presented incomplete stories that invited people to fill in the gaps with whatever they thought they knew about Africans, Asians, and Indians—from movies and newsreels, books and magazines, lectures and casual conversation. A "Shilluk Warrior" from the Sudan stood long and lean on one leg, contemplating something that museumgoers could only imagine, his spear stabbing the ground. A "Chinese Jinriksha Coolie" strained at an invisible load. A "Kalahari Bushman" peered off in the distance, pulling back his bow, his prey eternally unseen.[33]

Visitors bought postcards of the sculptures by the thousands, and they paged through a leaflet that Henry Field had prepared with his curator Berthold Laufer. On paper Laufer sought to distinguish "the physical traits acquired by heredity" from "experience and the total complex of habits and thoughts acquired from the group to which we belong." Laufer spoke of cultural assimilation, something he believed in deeply as an educated German Jew, even four months after Adolf Hitler had taken his oath as chancellor. It was possible for blacks to assimilate in America, he wrote, as long as the "social and legal restriction and segregation that [keep] their race consciousness alive" were eliminated. The only difference would be physical. "Our Negroes belong to the African or 'black' race and will always remain within this division," he wrote. "Even intermarriage with whites will not modify their racial characteristics to any marked degree." The exhibition, however, undermined Laufer's premise: the statues suggested it was impossible to separate physical from cultural traits. The physicality of the sculptures—the narratives inspired by every furrowed brow and flexing muscle—implied character, culture, and difference. The images, reproduced in encyclopedias, atlases, and textbooks, would supply a generation of schoolchildren across the United States with their first introduction to the concept of race. Henry Field's vision rooted race in art and imagination but gave it the authority of science.[34]

Day after day Henry Field spent hours giving personal tours of the exhibition to visiting dignitaries. He took special care to show them materials at the end of the hall that illustrated how anthropologists measured racial difference; it could be discerned in the shape and size of the skull, "variations in the outlines and proportions of the body; variations in the shapes of the eyes, nose, chin, and lips; and age changes in dentition." A series of transparencies "indicate[d] the true skin colors of the human races." But the sculptures were what everyone had come to see.[35]

Field took his time guiding his guests through the exhibition, past the "tiny African Pygmies portray[ing] the seriousness of family life . . . , the African dancing girl, . . . a jungle Pavlova . . . the merchant from Lhasa, Tibet, wear[ing] the look of the philosopher." And then, among the busts and heads, Field would see someone familiar: the "Ubangi Woman," his "gay acquaintance of the Paris boulevards." Her face was tilted upward, eyes narrowed to a squint, mouth opened wide. "The urge to touch her elongated lower lip has proven irresistible to many visitors," Field wrote. In time thousands of fingers wore through the bronze patina. "Reminiscent of St. Peter's toe kissed by the faithful in Rome," it began to shine.[36]

CHAPTER TWENTY

WALL

Freeport, Long Island, 1946

T HE LITTLE GIRL WAS exhausted. The drive had seemed endless, hours upon hours through small towns on small roads all the way up from Texas. She had gone south with her parents during the war. Her father's employer, the Hudson Mohair Company, had sent him from Massachusetts to train workers at a new mill fifty miles north of San Antonio in the Texas hill country. When the Germans surrendered, the girl stood on her father's shoes and danced. Soon afterward her father finished his job. They bought a Model A Ford that had been on blocks when gasoline was being rationed, and they headed back to New England. They took their time driving up the East Coast, visiting what family they had.[1]

Alone in the backseat, the girl passed the time staring out the window and talking to her teddy bear. They spent a month in central Florida, staying with her mother's sister and her family while the girl finished third grade. They stopped in Washington, D.C., where her mother had grown up; her father tried to get a job with the government, but nothing worked out. The next day they turned off Route 1 and headed into New York City. After staring up at Manhattan's skyscrapers, they crossed the East River and meandered for two hours through Queens. City suburbs gave way to quiet villages along the south shore of Long Island. In Freeport, just shy of Jones Beach and the Atlantic Ocean, they finally reached the house on Cottage Court.

The house was tall and narrow, a relic of the early part of the century when New York's actors would retreat to Freeport when the theaters closed for the summer. As the girl walked inside, her eyes adjusted to the gloom. She could tell something was wrong. It was getting hard to breathe. The air was heavy with the smell of smoke—charred wood. The house seemed to be crumbling from the inside out. After days of boredom, she felt jolted, almost queasy with fear.[2]

The girl's mother guided her into a room. Someone was sitting in there—her mother's aunt, the girl knew. Stepping closer, she saw a very old woman in an old-fashioned dress, one of the oldest people she had ever seen. The woman was skeletal, her papery skin crumpled up and smoothed out again. The girl startled when her great-aunt looked at her. Framed by white hair, the woman's eyes were blazing blue, enormous, almost pushing out of her head. They softened as she attempted a smile. It was not every day that three generations of Isabel Walls gathered together in one place.[3]

The oldest, Isabel Elterich—Aunt Bel—was O.S.B. and Amanda Wall's daughter, born during the Civil War and still alive at the end of World War II. Elterich's niece Isabel Winward was in her forties, still beautiful, though no longer the "pretty little miss" in blond ringlets once celebrated by newspapers across the country. Winward's young daughter, Isabel, was almost the same age her mother had been, nearly thirty-seven years before, when the Brookland School kicked her out of the first grade.

THE LITTLE GIRL WANDERED around the house while her parents talked with Aunt Bel. Aside from her husband, daughter, and sister Ethel, Isabel Winward only had her aunt left. Her parents were long dead. In the years after they lost their lawsuit against the District of Columbia school board, the Walls never stayed in one place. They shuttled from one neighborhood to another, west across the city. Although they disappeared from colored Washington, Winward's father, Stephen Wall, never lost touch with his brother and sisters. Stephen was the only one of O.S.B. Wall's sons and daughters to have children of his own. They knew they had aunts and uncles, and their aunts and uncles knew about them. As Isabel grew up, she heard their names mentioned: Aunt Bel, Aunt Helen, Uncle Edward.[4]

Stephen Wall worked at the Government Printing Office until the day before his sixty-fifth birthday in 1922. He tried to extend his job two years past the mandatory retirement date—his foreman agreed that he was "quite efficient and a willing worker and appears to be in vigorous physical condition"—but the public printer denied the request without explanation. Outside of work, the Walls had changed their names, so after he retired, no one knew him as Stephen Wall again. To all the world, he had become Steven Russell Gates. Until he dropped dead in the spring of 1934, he moved whenever he noticed a black family living nearby. He told his children that black neighbors made property values go down.[5]

As Stephen's government service was ending, his wife, Lillie, took a job as a clerk in the War Department and then moved to Treasury. At the office and at home, she was known as Elizabeth Jane Gates. Leaving work on a December evening in 1930, she fell down the steps outside the Treasury Building. She spent more than six months in the hospital but never fully recovered, lingering until 1936.[6]

Isabel Irene Wall took her mother's name, Lillian. Everyone called her Lillie, including her brother and sister. As Lillian Isabel Gates, she went through the District's white public schools and, eight years after her court case, went on to the city's Business High School. After briefly working as a secretary in her twenties, she married Frank McGowan, a scientist who worked at the Department of Agriculture, and settled into a gracious brick house across the Potomac River in Alexandria, Virginia. There were moments when it seemed to Lillian Gates McGowan that she had found a comfortable life, but she soon realized that she too had to keep moving. Her husband started beating her. When she dyed her hair to match a dress that she was wearing to a party, he expressed his disapproval by throwing a glass of beer in her face. By 1933 she had left him, and that April he jumped fifty feet from a bridge, shattering his skull.[7]

Isabel went north. Her sister Ethel had married someone from Bristol, Rhode Island, and moved there to live with his family. In Bristol a quiet man Isabel's age named Charles Winward was boarding with them. Isabel and Charles fell in love and married in November 1933. Winward's parents had died when he was seven, and he grew up in an orphanage with his six brothers and sisters. Although he had left school after the eighth grade, he was an avid reader and taught himself trigonometry. A jack-of-all-trades, he did everything from repairing refrigerators to writing calligraphy for a Providence greeting card company. Mostly, though, he worked as a wool-sorter, one of the only skilled jobs in a textile mill. He spent his days surrounded by sacks of just-sheared fleece shipped straight from the farm. He pulled apart the wool, slowly separating and categorizing the fleece into fourteen grades. It was a job that experienced sorters, in time, could do just with their hands, intuiting from feel alone the different qualities of wool. After years of combing through the lanolin-coated bales, Winward's hands were as soft as a child's.[8]

Together the couple went from Rhode Island to New York and back, and then to Hudson, Massachusetts, west of Boston, where Charles worked as a sorter for a mohair mill. Isabel had long been accustomed to a nomadic life, but now it was life on a humbler scale than what she had known as a child. When there was no work, her husband would put on waders and boots and rake for scallops in shallow water on the coast. They shucked the shells together, sold what they could, and ate the rest. She fried scallops, stewed them, fricasseed and baked them. She performed so many miracles with scallops that her daughter could not look at them for years.[9]

To her daughter, Isabel would make occasional remarks about her childhood, hints of a different existence: a cook, a big house with a dumbwaiter, dates with college boys. When Isabel showed her daughter fading sepia pictures of herself as a child, the girl admired the intricately stitched dresses and the beautiful white ribbons in her hair. Every night Isabel set the table with linens and china. She would never live in a city like Washington again, go to grand parties, or live in a fine home. But she did not seem to mind. The Winwards' life revolved around wool, not fine clothes.[10]

Early on in their relationship Charles Winward learned that his wife's real name was Isabel Wall, not Lillian Gates. Perhaps she told him the truth about her childhood, and the wool-sorter refused to classify her differently. Years later she explained the name change as a decision her family made after nasty property litigation between her father and his sisters. While her sister Ethel and her husband's family called her Lillie for the rest of her life, Charles took to calling her Isabel. When their daughter was born in 1937, they put down "Gates" as the mother's maiden name on the girl's birth certificate. But they named her Isabel Wall Winward.[11]

The girl did not like her middle name. "Isabel Wall Winward was not . . . feminine . . . in my estimation," she later said. At school, when her full name was announced at attendance or listed in the yearbook, her classmates would call her "Stonewall Jackson." She once asked her mother, "Where did I get the Wall from? Why couldn't it be Irene like yours?" Her mother said, "Your father named you because there were no more Walls to carry the name on." "And I said, 'Thank you very much,'" the daughter remembered, "with tongue in cheek."[12]

Isabel doted on her girl. She tried but could not have other children. To her husband's occasional distress, she "spent money like water" on her daughter. She raised her strictly—good manners, proper dress. A bar of soap in the mouth washed away bad words. Above all, in Isabel's house, there would be no lying. "Her famous saying was, 'Oh what tangled webs we weave once we practice to deceive,'" her daughter recalled. "I was brought up, you do not lie, you do not fib. No matter what it is, you tell the truth."[13]

THE OLD WOMAN, Aunt Bel, opened her eyes wide, like the star of a silent film. Every word she spoke was meticulously chosen and enunciated, each sentence long and ornate, baroquely phrased, with peaks of high inflection. Instead of asking, "Would you get me a cup of coffee?" Aunt Bel might say, "Isabel, do you think that you could possibly get me a cup of coffee?" To her grand-niece, she sounded "so very old English . . . , what I call putting on airs." It was as if everyday life were high performance.[14]

Bel always had a flair for the dramatic, having trained at elocution school in the art of "personal magnetism," "by which a person is enabled to control those within reach of his voice, eye, or touch." In even the most mundane interactions, she enjoyed using what she called "my best theatrical voice, smile and manner." When a peddler once asked if she wanted to buy perfume, Bel brought a busy commercial area to a standstill with a resounding "No!" Shaking her head, staring straight at the peddler, she added, "I never use perfume. I use soap and water! I *prefer* soap and water!"[15]

In the 1890s Bel headed with her sister Sallie to the larger stage of New York. While the two sisters initially lived together on the Upper West Side, they soon went in different directions. Sallie changed her name to Helen Easton and moved uptown, renting rooms in her apartment on Harlem's southern fringe to a generation of Columbia University students, laboratory assistants, and teachers, all white. In 1897 Bel married a German engineer who built railroads in the American West and was fluent in five languages. Assuming the role of Mrs. Gotthold Otto Elterich, she lived in Greenwich Village and summered in Freeport. Like every one of her siblings except Stephen, she had no children. Her husband sailed frequently to Europe to raise money for new projects.[16]

In May 1907 Bel's husband went to Paris to promote a railroad in Vancouver, British Columbia, to French financiers. On his way home a month later, he stopped in London and met a wealthy American widow who had been touring Cairo and the Holy Land, with a detour to Monte Carlo. On her thirty-fifth birthday, the two of them took a day trip to the scenic town of Maidenhead, west of London. They rented a boat and rowed out on the Thames toward Cliveden, an estate with formal gardens often visited by Queen Victoria, famous for its Fountain of Love. A boatman noticed that Elterich was an unskilled oarsman and could not avoid the thickets banking the river. The boat ran against the roots of a tree and started taking on water. Panicking, Elterich and his companion jumped. She sank ten feet to the river's bottom, and he was swept away by the current.[17]

Newspapers across the United States could not resist what appeared to be a perfect summer story: wealthy characters, romantic Old World setting, gruesome deaths, a hint of scandal. In New York and Washington and coast-to-coast, the dailies reported details of the accident, the detective work that helped identify the bodies, the "handsome and charming" appearance of the "millionaire widow," and the findings of the coroner's inquest. *The Washington Post* noted that Elterich's wife was the former "Miss Isabel Irene Wall." Although the newspaper had published dozens of stories about her father, fifteen years after O.S.B. Wall's death there was no mention of his race. Instead, Bel was described only as the "daughter of a successful lawyer," a woman "well known in diplomatic and social circles in Washington." It was as if, in the context of her husband's death, it was impossible to imagine that she was not white. Racial passing was one scandal too many for the story. Bel played the part of the "prostrated" widow so well that she could use her real name in her hometown, and no one questioned her status.[18]

Childless and alone, with enough money to live comfortably, Bel devoted her days to inventions, some tangible and others less so. Six months after her husband's death, she patented a "shield for ladies' drawers" that promised easy removal for washing. At a time when many women were immobilized by their menstrual periods, Bel saw her shield of overlapping triangles of fabric as a first step toward freeing women to join the world as equals to men. Fashioning herself as a feminist thinker, she advertised herself as a lecturer to women's groups on subjects ranging from "Are we fair to our children?" to "What is and who gave us etiquette?" "No one today need be poor, unsuccessful, unhealthy or unhappy," she wrote. "We live in a wonderful age—reach out and take what you will!"[19]

A strong supporter of women's rights, Bel published in 1918 a florid manifesto called *The Girl of the Golden Future*, which declared to men, "I am your peer! My birthright came as yours did with the first draw of breath . . . We'll hear no more talk of woman's sphere. Unhand us, gentlemen! gently, gently! Thank you, sirs!" Much of her "Message-Appeal to Girlies Everywhere" was eccentric, the product of a lonely mind. She advocated feminine strength in modesty, but her language was anything but demure. She urged young women to embrace "bodily cleanliness, clothes-crispiness and simplicity" over "jewels, dingles, [and] gimcracks that scream 'look at me!'" "Fringes, dangles, impediments, cumbersome useless ornaments; too big hats trimmed in feathers, spears, swords and bowie-knives that tickle or inflict injuries on innocent unwary passers-by—let's wave them aside," she wrote. She had created a voice that was too conspicuous, too self-contained, and too singular to afford any question or suspicious thought about her race. People would fixate on the wide shock of her blue eyes, not on her skin.[20]

Bel was so confident in her voice that in the course of her manifesto she repeatedly invoked civil rights for blacks. "Since the beginning of time Girlies have been treated unfairly. They have been discriminated against," she wrote. "There was a difference made between brother and sister. There was Liberty and Freedom for brother; for his sister a chain." It was rhetoric that women's advocates had been using since before the Civil War. Bel, however, was channeling her parents' activism, which had viewed the struggle for full citizenship of blacks and women as one and the same fight. Alongside her suggestion that young women eat only five ounces of food, three times a day, Bel described how "in my dressing-room by the side of my mirror is pinned a picture of Lincoln, the Liberator." She wrote that the picture inspired her to work for "Independence, Freedom, Justice and Liberty" for "one half of the world." Her readership understood that she meant women; few outside her family could have imagined that she meant anything else.[21]

Bel's essays contained even more specific calls for racial equality and justice. When an "ebony-hued" woman spoke to Bel one day on the streets of Freeport, it was occasion for more drama. The very sight of the woman made Bel swell with indignation at the way blacks were held in "scorn, opprobrium, stigma, discrimination." "I wanted to purge the black of its stigma," she wrote. "I wanted us both to begin a new way of thinking—to ignore the past unjust placement of her inferiority. All that my soul felt of altruism shone through my eyes as I looked in hers." Bel advertised her sympathy with blacks, but it was a sentiment that seemed to affirm her position as a white woman more than anything else. To feel for another only reinforced their difference. It was as if she wanted to connect with her past and her heritage but always had to stay in character. In New York, as in Washington and other points south, blacks lived apart from whites, were shut out of all but the most menial jobs, were brutalized by police, and were denied service at hotels and restaurants. After decades of living in a way that constantly foreclosed the issue of her race, she could only drift further away.[22]

When Bel's niece and her family drove to her house, she was in her eighties, a solitary woman who craved an audience. To see two other Isabels, two younger generations named for her—happy and beautiful—must have delighted her. They had gone out of their way to visit and did not have any particular place they had to be. Bel asked if they would like to stay the night.[23]

The little girl did not want to spend another minute in Aunt Bel's house, let alone sleep there. She had been walking around, looking for the source of the horrible smell that burned her throat and saturated her dress and hair. It did not take long to find. The stairway was scorched and charred, leading up to a second floor where no one seemed to go. There had been a big fire. She did not know how long ago, but the damage had never been fixed. The house was worse than haunted; it was blackened. It might suffocate them. It might fall on their heads.[24]

To the girl's relief, her parents declined Aunt Bel's invitation, and they drove back to New York as the sun set. While in the city, they went to a Horn & Hardart's Automat for dinner. Compared with the house in Freeport, it was hard to imagine a place so bright. Around them were all kinds of people, rich and poor, young and old, happy and despondent, but the Winwards did not have to talk to anyone. The restaurant was self-service, no waiters, and the hum of voices and report of silverware on plates and bowls insulated the family from other conversations. The girl marveled at the hundreds of little windows framed in gleaming chrome, each holding a dish—Salisbury steak, creamed spinach, a slice of pie—each catching a bit of light, a glimpse of the ceiling, a reflection of herself.[25]

After dinner the Winwards walked out into Times Square. The sidewalks on Broadway swarmed with people. Barkers announced the attractions at clubs and theaters. Pinball arcades rang and flashed. Overhead, billboards shined and bellowed, making up for time lost during wartime blackouts. At the Claridge's Hotel, a giant face blew five-foot-wide smoke rings next to a neon pack of cigarettes one story high. Headlines angled along the "news zipper" around the Times Building. Tourists stood dazzled by spectacular advertisements: a giant steaming cup of coffee and a cascading Pepsi bottle. Young Isabel Winward held her parents' hands. She never forgot what she saw—lightbulbs, hundreds of thousands of them. They turned night into day.[26]

BEFORE THEY LEFT NEW YORK, the Winwards made one more stop at a small Manhattan apartment where a divorced mother and her son, Ruth and Patrick Gates, lived. Patrick was a few years older than the Winwards' daughter, his first cousin. Model airplanes, the fighters and bombers that had leveled Germany and Japan, dangled from the ceiling of his room. Patrick's father was Isabel Winward's brother, Stephen Wall's youngest child. Born Roscoe Wall, he grew up as Russell Gates but died Patrick Murphy.[27]

Isabel had known her brother as Russell and told her daughter stories about him. He was handsome, slightly built with intense dark eyes, black hair in tight waves coming to a widow's peak. Isabel, Ethel, and Russell had gotten along well as children. "He could always get out of trouble with his parents because of his smile," Isabel's daughter was told. "He'd give this grin, and it melted them right then and there."[28]

Russell had died just shy of his fortieth birthday, a matter of months before the Winwards visited Ruth Gates and her son. Isabel told her daughter that it was pneumonia that killed Uncle Russell. She was not telling the truth.

Russell was three years old when his sister was kicked out of the Brookland School. He never knew a time when the family was not moving, changing neighborhoods and friends, shedding names and identities and pasts. While his older sisters looked for solid ground, going to school and finding jobs and getting married, Russell relished the drift. In 1923, when he was seventeen, he and a friend stole a truck, packed it with camping equipment, and drove to North Carolina. The boys spent months on the road before they were arrested in Durham for beating up a black man. After serving jail time in North Carolina, they were escorted back to the District to face charges for the theft.[29]

Russell's first arrests were not his last. When he was twenty-two, he fled the scene of a car crash. At the time he was under indictment for passing bad checks. The police already knew him under the aliases Steven Russell Gates, Stephen Russell, and C. E. Murphy. Three years later, in 1931, when a woman was murdered in her home after a struggle, the police rounded up Russell as one of the usual suspects. It was a sign that he was graduating from low-level grifts to more violent crimes.[30]

Meanwhile Russell met and married women. He learned how to fix cars and opened a garage in downtown Baltimore. But he remained unmoored. He wed Ruth in 1930, but when his father died four years later, Russell played no role in the probate—he was too busy hiding from process servers in the divorce dispute.[31]

By 1937 Russell Gates had become Patrick Murphy. One night he met a young waitress at a coffee shop named Charlotte Doster. Slight and dark-haired, she had moved from South Carolina to the District. A week later they were married. Still drifting, he spent the next five years moving north, south, east, and west, from Miami to New Orleans to Washington, D.C., to Knoxville, and back. In 1938 he was convicted in Miami of having sex with a minor. Within a few years his rap sheet included a series of rape and assault charges.[32]

Charlotte stayed with her husband the entire time. He gave her a list of aliases that he used when he was arrested: Russell or Stephen Russell Gates, F. S. Lee, and Roscoe Orin Wall. She never knew that the first alias was what he had been called as a child; the second, a play on his mother's maiden name, Slee; and the third, the name he had been born with. Between 1939 and 1943 Charlotte had three boys and a girl, the youngest named Thomas, but she never met any of her husband's family. Once, while she was taking care of the babies, he shouted to her that his sister Ethel was visiting. By the time Charlotte made it downstairs, just minutes later, Ethel was gone. Charlotte's family was convinced that the man they knew as Patrick Murphy would kill her one day. He was a small man, but he terrified them. They had him arrested for beating her, but she insisted that the police drop the charges. He always seemed to talk his way out of his other arrests, collecting suspended sentences like so much pocket change.[33]

Charlotte was spared her husband's most notorious act of violence. On April 19, 1942, while his wife was pregnant with their third child, he went on a double date with a sailor and two women who worked as attendants at St. Elizabeth's Hospital. After they spent some time at a club, one of the women had to leave to work the night shift. Murphy offered to give her a ride to the hospital, but instead of driving there, he headed out into Maryland. She told him to turn around, so he stopped the car and tried to have sex with her. When she resisted, he choked her. She fled the car but stumbled. He followed. People at a house nearby heard her screaming. They found her weeping, bloody, filthy, neck bruised, cheek scratched. She had been raped.[34]

Two years passed between Patrick Murphy's arrest and his trial. During that time he was arrested for rape in Knoxville and was indicted for raping his secretary in Baltimore. Charlotte attended the trial in Prince George's County Circuit Court, as did Murphy's secretary. The proceedings lasted a day. Charlotte sat through testimony from the victim, the people who had found her, and the doctor who treated her. It took twenty minutes for the jury to return a guilty verdict.[35]

The judge proceeded straight to sentencing. "You are the kind of man who has no regard for the chastity of women," he told Murphy. "You violate them in the most despicable manner whenever you get the chance. While you feel that every woman is fair game, the Court must inform you that this is not the conception in this county or in this country generally."

The defendant interrupted the judge and told him the victim had been lying. Take her into chambers, Murphy said, and get the "whole truth" from her. The judge cut him off. "There was no doubt in the mind of the [C]ourt that the young woman involved in this case told the truth," he said. "It is difficult to conce[iv]e of a more brutal crime." He sentenced Murphy to death. Charlotte started wailing and had to be restrained.[36]

The defendant's arrest record and his long list of aliases were proof to the prosecutors and the judge of an incorrigible criminal mind. No one ever linked the names to the Wall family's passing from black to white. Although Patrick Murphy could not escape the law, he succeeded in outrunning race. Thirty-five years after a District of Columbia court held that his sister was black, Murphy would await execution as a white prisoner.[37]

After a year of appeals and clemency hearings and psychiatric evaluations, Patrick Murphy was taken from his cell in the Maryland Penitentiary in downtown Baltimore. It was midnight, deepest summer, two weeks before the atomic bomb was dropped on Hiroshima. The heat did not penetrate the prison's thick stone walls. Murphy was escorted into a narrow room. He stood on a walkway with two guards, about twenty feet above the ground. The room below was almost bare, furnished with little besides the mechanism that extended a long length of rope to the ceiling and down again. The glare of floodlights softened and dimmed as the guards placed a hood over his head.[38]

FROM NEW YORK CITY, the Winwards continued north. They stopped in Rhode Island to visit Charles's family, and from there they headed to Cape Cod to see friends. Isabel and the girl stayed on the Cape, and Charles returned to the mill at Hudson, visiting them on weekends. Although he had the hands of an experienced wool-sorter, Charles tired of being apart from his family. He joined them on the Cape and found work as a landscape gardener, a contractor building homes, and finally as a skilled finish carpenter. In his spare time he did calligraphy for plaques and certificates for the police and the Masons; he always kept vials of India ink and gold leaf around the house. He created an elaborate, illuminated May- flower Compact for a local historical society. With their daughter in school, Isabel went back to work. She was a bank teller, then a drugstore clerk. But the first job she took on the Cape was in the art room at the Colonial Candle Company. She painted by hand specialty candles for the tourist trade: Miles Standish and Priscilla Mullens, George and Martha Washing- ton, people and legends that had made America.[39]

TOWARD THE END OF his life, Hart Gibson sat down in his turreted castle on the outskirts of Lexington, Kentucky, and began composing a long essay entitled "The Race Problem." Some forty years after watching George Fitzhugh and Wendell Phillips debate the slavery question in New Haven, Gibson promised a "Graphic Review of the American Negro's Condition as a Slave, a Freedman and Citizen." Looking back, he admitted that slavery had been a poisonous force in the American Republic, and he expressed relief that the Civil War had destroyed the institution in a "sharp and summary" fashion. But Reconstruction had been a "tremendous leap in the dark," he wrote, an unholy experiment with "African supremacy" ended only by "the courage, intelligence and sagacity of the Anglo-Saxon that have made it the heroic race of history." With Jim Crow now the law of the land, Gibson felt compelled to consider "the final destiny" of blacks in the United States. Would the race "remain an unsightly excres[c]ence, disfiguring the fair proportions of our public and social life," he asked, "or shall it under the subtle influence of that wonderful solvent, political freedom, become an integral, effective and beneficent force in the body-politic?"[1]

For Gibson the question had an easy answer: blacks were congenitally incapable of having a place in American society. The Constitution might guarantee them some legal rights, and in Gibson's view the segregation statutes then being enacted by Southern legislatures actually protected

blacks from ruinous competition with a superior race. But "positive legislation" alone, Gibson wrote, stood no chance against a different set of rules
"to which all classes and races, in all circumstances, must finally succumb.
There is no court of equity in Nature's jurisprudence. The law is unbend-
ing, universal, relentless, and supreme." As a matter of natural fact, blacks
were "sprung from a savage ancestry . . . whose fierce war cries alone dis-
turbed the awful silence of a sleeping continent." They would always be a
blight on American life. As the United States prepared to enter the twentieth century, Gibson proposed forcibly removing citizens of African descent to "the magnificent valley of the Congo."[2]

Gibson's views were nothing if not typical of his time and place. In
the 1890s legions of amateur and professional race theorists were contemplating the moral and physical degradation of blacks and the imperative of
keeping them absolutely separate from whites. Gibson drew his hard line
on the future of blacks in the United States in part because the nation was
at that very moment rapidly absorbing "vast multitudes" of newcomers.
While "a single generation makes Americans of the children of the im-
migrant and all trace of their alien origin is lost," he wrote, blacks "recline
upon a dead level of hopeless uniformity, aliens upon the very soil of their
nativity." However common the sentiment, it was a curious position for
Gibson to be taking little more than a decade after his brother Randall had
faced unsettling accusations about their own family tree.[3]

In fact, the Gibsons' family history was evidence that, like the recent
immigrants from Southern and Eastern Europe, descendants of African
slaves could assimilate completely into the larger world around them. This
migration from black to white had been happening for centuries and
continued to occur on a daily basis. While late-nineteenth-century essays such as Gibson's may have reinforced the idea that the color line was
impregnable—reflecting a landscape littered with "whites only" signs and
smoldering from near-daily lynchings—the physical and intellectual brutality of Jim Crow wound up encouraging many racially ambiguous people
to establish themselves as white. As Gibson surmised, other codes did operate alongside "positive legislation" to give meaning to the categories of
black and white in the United States—but as often as not they undermined
the idea of natural, blood-borne differences between immutable races. In-

stead individuals, families, and communities applied their own rules and logic to the law of racial segregation as it affected their daily lives.

In a society in constant motion—where people were continually defining themselves anew—migrating from black to white did not have to be much of a leap. Individuals could make the move; communities could accept them; and government officials and the courts could deliberately decide not to intervene. They knew and could even say aloud that race was a legal and social fiction. At the same time, this abiding sense that the color line was easily crossed did not force people to question its powerful hold over American life. While everyday tolerance enabled people to establish themselves as white, it also allowed them to assert their new identities in ways that hardened racial categories to murderous extremes. Communities that conceived of themselves as white could subscribe to the idea of purity of blood without ever having to worry that any of their members' race would be questioned. If Hart Gibson felt insecure about his place in the world, his claim to elite status grew stronger with each comment he penned championing the "splendid traditions and hereditary aptitude" of the Anglo-Saxon over the "paralyzing and remorseless barbarism" of blacks.[4]

The Gibsons, Spencers, and Walls lived through events that defined America. They fought in the struggles of their times, great and small. Their histories reveal how the color line ran through the heart of the nation's experience. From the colonial era well into the twentieth century, the idea of race—the notion that blood transmitted moral character and social fitness—provided a central reason why American democracy exalted some people at the enduring expense of others.

The journeys of the Gibsons, Spencers, and Walls are significant not for how they were classified and whether those categories accurately reflected their ancestry. Rather, they reveal how the very existence of racial categories altered people's expectations and behavior—how these categories were at once undermined and strengthened by the steady stream of Americans migrating from black to white. The family histories reflect how blackness became a proxy for inequality. People could escape the category because it was not real, but the inequality persisted, growing only stronger with emancipation, as the promise of liberty bred new, potent forms of discrimination. The Gibsons, Spencers, and Walls embody fundamental tragedies of our past—the vexed relationship between liberty and equality, the possibility of tolerance alongside the choice to hate. At the same time their histories offer some reason for hope. They provide an occasion to understand race in a different way and an opportunity to acknowledge our enduring, if at times hidden, capacity to privilege the particular over the abstract, and everyday experience over what we have been told to believe.

TODAY'S DESCENDANTS OF THE Gibsons, Spencers, and Walls are spread out across the United States, north, south, east, and west. They are rich and poor and getting by. They live in the country and in the city, are more and less educated, healthy and ailing, Democrats and Republicans, devout and secular, happy and sad. Gibson descendants still live in and around Lexington, Kentucky—one lives a block away from the mansion that Randall Gibson's father built before the Civil War, which still stands as a monument to classical plantation and New Orleans architecture. Many of Jordan Spencer's descendants are a stone's throw from the slopes that the old man tilled. The Walls are scattered throughout the country. Some descendants live with the same prominent status—and alternatively, the same anonymity—that their ancestors had one hundred years ago. Some have moved up in the world, and some down. They are indistinguishable from any number of Americans who regard themselves as white in the early twenty-first century.

Despite the passage of centuries and the accretion of new identities, most of the descendants interviewed for this book already knew the broad contours of their family histories by the time I contacted them. The secrets of prior generations, it seems, are no match for the Internet. In just the past decade, historical and genealogical databases have reduced searches that used to take years—scrolling frame by frame through entire volumes of newspapers on microfilm—to mere days or even hours. Popular ancestry Web sites and vast communities of online researchers have allowed millions of Americans to learn previously inconceivable truths about their roots. All it takes is one genealogy buff in the family. Far from big cities and major archives, people like Freda Spencer Goble have gone to their local public library to search census records. When Goble found her great-great-grandfather—Jordan Spencer—in the 1850 census, she slowly deciphered the handwriting on the census-taker's original enumeration sheet. Then she called over the librarian to explain the meaning of the abbreviation scrawled by Spencer's name: "mul," for mulatto.[5]

If descendants of the Gibsons, Spencers, and Walls have uncovered their family histories with relative ease, their responses to evidence that their ancestors were people of color have been more complicated. Some have found it interesting but irrelevant to their lives—as meaningful, say, as finding out that a great-grandfather was a furrier—but many describe the discovery as a visceral experience and cause for soul searching, releasing a spectrum of emotions from elation to anguish. It can be a delicate matter, something to avoid in conversation with older relatives. While it has become increasingly common for white descendants of slaveowners to hold reunions with descendants of slaves and acknowledge and celebrate black kin, black ancestry is something different altogether, inverting rather than affirming old hierarchies and forcing people to examine hard-wrought views of themselves, their families, and their worlds. Even in today's "postracial" society, race still functions as a remarkably fixed set of rules and expectations. As in centuries past, however, today's Gibsons, Spencers, and Walls have accommodated the rules to their own lived experience, pushing and shaping the meaning of race in the process.[6]

Denial is a common and understandable reaction. Members of these families have identified so closely with the mainstream of white America— and the line between black and white has appeared to be so solid—that an alternative account of their origins seems outlandish. Given the vagaries of the historical record and the well-documented shortcomings of DNA ancestry testing when it comes to measuring remote African ancestry, it is not difficult to conceive of other reasons that a family was categorized as black or reputed to be dark. After all, for centuries people migrating across the color line drew liberally on that same universe of explanations.[7]

Living descendants of the Gibsons, for example, have encountered public discussions of their family's "extraordinary career" ever since a 1962 article by the historian Winthrop Jordan described Gideon Gibson's "successful hurdling of the barrier" between black and white in colonial South

Carolina. In the decades that have followed, Gibson genealogy hobbyists have spent countless hours attempting to prove that the family is not descended from African slaves. William LaBach, the great-great-grandson of Randall Gibson's sister Sarah and an avid genealogist, has heard just about every account of why the Gibsons were regarded as people of color: they were Gypsies, Portuguese Huguenots, Seneca Indians, Sephardic Jews, Moroccans, Turks. "Then there's the story where we [descended] from the Bishop of London," said LaBach, a Kentucky lawyer with a Ph.D. in mathematics and a master's degree in history. "It couldn't all be right . . . There's not a lot of certain answers in some genealogy. I tend to disbelieve all of it."[8]

For others the discovery has been harder to explain away. When Thomas Murphy learned that his great-grandparents were O.S.B. and Amanda Wall, he said, he marched into the Atlanta airport rent-a-car where he was employed and told his black coworkers, "You can't call me a racist because I *is* one of you." As if to prove to himself that he could not be black, he started harboring and expressing more racist feelings than he had ever felt before. There was a time when he could barely sit in a restaurant near an African American. He approached his minister with the question "Am I black?" but found little solace in the answer he got: that according to the Bible, Murphy's African ancestry was too remote to change how he classified himself. He loathed the way his grandparents and their children lied about their backgrounds. He attributed O.S.B. Wall's success in the world to his white father, the plantation owner Stephen Wall. "The way I see it, I don't descend from a black man," Murphy said. "I descend from a white man who couldn't keep his genes in his pants."[9]

Yet Thomas has worked tirelessly to learn as much as he can about O.S.B. and Amanda Wall and their children, reveling in every new piece of information. In reconstructing his family tree, he has contacted distant cousins repeatedly and posted his findings on the Web for the world to see. As much as he resisted defining himself as black, his ancestry has given him a place in the world, a claim to some of the central events in American history. For most of his life, he had heard little about his father other than that Patrick Murphy terrorized his wife and had hanged for rape. In recent years Thomas's research has given him a different, richer set of stories—preserved in newspaper articles, government records, and child-hood pictures—about his ancestors and a father he never knew. Ultimately, the pull of family, the balm of knowing, drew him past the issue of race.

For some descendants, their family history provided answers to lifelong questions. When Freda Goble began researching her genealogy, her findings about Jordan Spencer became an occasion to reflect on her family's hard-fought path to the middle class. Her father was one of ten children who grew up during the Depression on a small mountain farm in Johnson County. They lived much like Jordan Spencer had, sleeping in a two-room house, raising everything they ate, and sewing their own clothes and quilts. The children were worked too hard to stay in school past the eighth grade. Despite day after day of grueling labor and horizons bounded by their mountain hollow, "every one of them wanted to be somebody and do something with their lives," Goble said. Several went north in the 1950s, got factory jobs, and educated themselves. Her father found religion and pastored a neighborhood church in Johnson County for decades.[10]

Goble, who started and owned a local candle-making business, grew up surrounded by Spencers who "had to be the strongest," she said. "They worked harder, could lift more, could do more in a day than anyone else." Though poor and uneducated, they always wanted to be recognized as "pillars of the community." "They demanded respect was how they got it," she said. "They just demanded respect. There was something about it. Even my father, when he walked, he walked with his shoulders back, head in the air, he had a proud look about him." As Freda thought about how her family kept their heads up despite daunting odds, Jordan Spencer's migration across the color line—his determination to make a place for himself and put down roots in Johnson County's rocky soil—suggested an answer. "They were a very proud people—yes they were," Freda said. "My grandfather was one of the proudest men I ever met in my life. And they said his father was the same way. So I assume they got this from somewhere. I don't know how or where or why, but they were very, very proud."[11]

What mattered most to Freda was not Jordan Spencer's race. Rather, it was how racial categories—the rules of race—pushed the man and his descendants, and how they pushed back. In researching her genealogy, she learned that "you don't have to be rich to pick up all of the Southern charm and ideas." When she informed her mother about Jordan Spencer, the elderly woman got very upset. "She said, 'Your daddy would roll over in his grave if he knew that you said something like that,'" Freda remembered. "Allegedly, someone in the neighborhood must have called him 'negro' or something like that, and I think he bloodied their nose for it." As a boy, Freda's father intuitively understood that the Spencers would always be accepted as white as long as they regarded any suggestion otherwise as an insult. Freda Goble has begun to understand the color line as it has always functioned—in terms of racism, not race; hierarchy as opposed to heredity; barriers instead of blood.[12]

Other descendants of the Gibsons, Spencers, and Walls have shared Goble's insight, as revelations about African ancestry opened up a world that might have been. Isabel Wall Whittemore, Thomas Murphy's first cousin, was sixty-five when her daughter called nearly ten years ago with exciting news about a genealogy project and a man named O.S.B. Wall. "My kids all thought it was cool—they were ecstatic," Whittemore recalled, but she found herself inexplicably dumbstruck. "The only ancestry I knew supposedly came from England and Ireland and Scotland," she said. She did not tell her husband because, in her words, "I thought he would lose love for me." But almost immediately she asked herself, "What's it to be ashamed about, Isabel?"[13]

It is a question that Isabel continues to ponder. Knowing full well that she had no reason to feel ashamed, she wondered instead why such feelings came so reflexively. Now in her mid-seventies, slowed by illness and the pain of her husband's death, she has contemplated her life and family and everything her mother ever said about her childhood. "Most families have one skeleton in the closet. My family has more skeletons than they have living bodies," Isabel said. "It's amazing . . . I don't know whether *enigma* is the correct [word], but there is mystery to it. There's mystery, there's lies, there's violence . . . It's a big, big, big, big thing to chew over and swallow and try to understand."[14]

Isabel grew up on Cape Cod and speaks with a gentle Massachusetts accent. Until 2009 she lived in central New Hampshire in a white clapboard house, with a front room converted into a shop where a daughter sold tea to summer tourists who strayed from Lake Winnipesaukee. Sitting at her kitchen table in August 2008 and gazing out on the yard—regularly crossed by moose until a neighbor built a fence—she expressed pride in the accomplishments of O.S.B. and Amanda Wall, fascination with their world, and anguish about its rupture. For the first time in her life, Isabel felt pity for her mother, who was the little girl kicked out of the first grade in Washington, D.C., in 1909.

Isabel Whittemore also has thought about the lingering effects of her grandfather Stephen Wall's decision to pass for white. Beyond the downward social mobility—his white descendants have lived with less money, education, and influence than their black ancestors did—Isabel focuses most on the loss of a large, close-knit family. In nineteenth-century Washington the Walls and the Langstons lived next door to each other, siblings and cousins growing up together in a community that they had built. By comparison, Isabel's life has been marked by an abiding solitude. "When you're an only child, you feel very much alone . . . When I was small, I played by myself. You get hurt a lot as you get older, because you want to have friends," she said. "I've always wanted family. I always envied large families, and that's why . . . I want to know more and more and more. I want to know all there is to know. I want to know I have a family back there. Wherever."[15]

"Wherever" can feel very far away, and to Whittemore the past has at times seemed impossibly remote. If anything, though, her story reveals its proximity. Isabel Wall Whittemore's name is not her only link to her family's history. She has O.S.B. Wall's strong chin as well as the same striking blue eyes, flair for the dramatic, and wry sense of humor as her forebears. She grew up with people who directly experienced the ordeal of passing for white. Her own mother could have explained what it was like to be expelled from school for being black, or to play with a doll on the witness stand while the District of Columbia school board scrutinized her appearance. As a young girl visiting Long Island in 1946, Isabel met her great-aunt, O.S.B. Wall's daughter, a woman who had grown up in the heart of black Washington during and after Reconstruction, lived in a home where Frederick Douglass and Susan B. Anthony called, and received words of wisdom and encouragement from her uncle John Mercer Langston. Ulti-mately what makes Whittemore's family history so fascinating to her is not how alien it is to her experience but rather how tantalizingly close it is.

Other descendants have also felt history's insistent reach. It speaks to them directly, through dozens upon dozens of letters by Randall Gibson, his parents, and siblings that have remained in family hands for generations, stuffed into manila folders and envelopes. It survives in memory. Freda Goble grew up listening to her grandfather talk about living as a young boy with Jordan and Malinda Spencer in their mountain cabin, and several other Spencer descendants and Johnson County residents still repeat stories from people who knew Old Jordan, a man who has been dead one hundred years. Though the past may appear to be long gone, it continues to echo and haunt, intruding into the present and subtly shaping how people see themselves, their families, and communities. But the Gibsons, Spencers, and Walls never entirely accepted what the past demanded for them. Their histories reveal constant questioning, acts of interpretation and reinterpre-tation, stubborn assertions of will, and outright escape. More than any-thing, this is their legacy. They help us understand the rules of the past while insisting that we make our own.

ACKNOWLEDGMENTS

I started thinking about the issues at the heart of this book nearly twenty years ago, and expressing my gratitude to all of the friends, family, teachers, colleagues, mentors, and organizations that have contributed to this project during that time is almost like writing another work of history. This book began with the aid of several generous fellowships. In 2003, when I was about to embark on a life of legal practice, the National Endowment for the Humanities awarded me a fellowship to work on this project full-time as an independent scholar. I thank Jane Aikin at the NEH for her support and the scholars who evaluated my fellowship application for changing the course of my life. The project was nurtured at crucial moments by the inaugural Raoul Berger–Mark DeWolfe Howe Fellowship in Legal History at Harvard Law School and the Samuel I. Golieb Fellowship in Legal History at New York University School of Law. I also benefited enormously from fellowships from the William Nelson Cromwell Foundation, the Southern Historical Collection at the University of North Carolina at Chapel Hill, the W.E.B. DuBois Institute for African and African American Research at Harvard, and Yale Law School. I presented portions of this book and received invaluable feedback at Vanderbilt, Boston University, NYU, Stanford, the American Bar Foundation/Illinois Legal History Seminar, and the annual conference of the American Society for Legal History.

Patient librarians and archivists at a number of institutions enabled me to research this book thoughtfully and thoroughly. I am indebted to the staffs of the Southern Historical Collection; Louisiana State; Tulane and the Amistad Research Center; the University of Mississippi; Duke; Virginia State; the University of Kentucky; Bowdoin College; the Moorland-Spingarn Research Center at Howard University; the South Caroliniana Library at the University of South Carolina; the Freedmen and Southern Society Project at the University of Maryland; Harvard's Law Library, Widener Library, Houghton Library, and Peabody Museum Archives; Manuscripts and Archives at Yale; the Filson Club Historical Society; the Gilder Lehrman Institute of American History; Old Courthouse Museum in Vicksburg; the Library of Congress; the National Archives and Records Administration; the Maryland State Archives; the Mississippi Department of Archives & History; the North Carolina Office of Archives & History; the South Carolina Department of Archives & History; the Washingtoni-ana Collection at the D.C. Public Library; the Louisiana Division of the New Orleans Public Library; the Schomburg Center for Research in Black Culture in New York; the Buchanan County Public Library in Grundy, Virginia; the Johnson County Public Library in Paintsville, Kentucky; and the Terrebonne Parish Main Library in Houma, Louisiana.

As I traveled north and south, the people and places in this book came to life through conversations I had and friendships I made with a group of people whose thoughtfulness, generosity, candor, and trust I will never forget. Understanding O.S.B. Wall, Jordan Spencer, and Randall and Hart Gibson, among others, would not have been possible without Linda Alexander, Calvin Beale, Danny Blevins, Lisa Colby, Gordon Cotton, Robert Denton Jr., Robert Denton Sr., Freda Spencer Goble, Thelma Denton Hancock, Ed Hazelett, Paul Heinegg, Jan Horne, Ginger Hunley, William LaBach, Val McKenzie, Sarah B. Morrison, Sir Thomas L. Murphy, Joe Pearce, H. Foster Pettit, Walter Preston, Hewey Purvis, Tommy Ratliff, Lowell Ed Spencer, Manuel Spencer, Ed Talbott, Valentine Van Zee, and last but certainly not least, Isabel Wall Whittemore.

At Vanderbilt University Law School, my home since 2007, I have been blessed with brilliant colleagues and a warm, welcoming community. In addition to generous funding from the Law and Human Behavior Program, the Constitutional Law Program, and the Dean's Office, I have had a wealth of superb readers, mentors, and friends. Without their support, this book would not have been written. Special thanks go to Mark Brandon, Ed Rubin, Gary Gerstle, Sarah Igo, Chris Guthrie, Kevin Stack, Lisa Bressman, and John Goldberg, as well as Frank Bloch, Rebecca Brown, Jon Bruce, Chris Brummer, Jim Ely, Tracey George, Nancy King, Liz Lunbeck, Alistair Newbern, Erin O'Hara, Bob Rasmussen, Jeff Schoenblum, Mike Vandenbergh, and Ingrid Wuerth. Vanderbilt's librarians and library staff have spent nearly four years helping me track down hundreds of books, statutes, and hearing transcripts, as well as the weather in eastern Kentucky on May 4, 1912. My sincere thanks go to Jo Bilyeu, Peter Brush, Martin Cerjan, Michael Jackson, Stephen Jordan, Jim Kelly, Linda Tesar, Bill Walker, and especially Mary Miles Prince. For terrific research assistance, I thank Benjamin Berlin, Kathleen Gilchrist, William Hardin, Shaina Jones, Matthew Koreiwo, Lauren Lowe, Jacob Neu, and Steven Riley. For miraculous feats of administrative assistance, I thank Brandy Drinnon, and I am also grateful for the work of Christie Bishop, Marita Bush, and Sue Ann Scott. Grace Renshaw has been very helpful with publicity and communications. Stephen McElroy and Scott Nelson provided crucial technical support.

Before this project was a project, I had teachers who opened up new worlds to me. I thank Steve Biel, Larry Buell, Henry Louis Gates Jr., Karl Guthke, Jeff Melnick, Peggy Pfeiffer, Tom Siegel, and Werner Sollors. My first sustained encounter with the complexity of the color line occurred in 1993 in South Africa, where I volunteered on a voter education project before the country's first "nonracial" election. It was an intense introduction to apartheid-era classifications, and my conversations there—especially with Thabo Manyoni, Cinque Henderson, and Natosha Reid—put me on a path that led to this book. Howard French, Jesus Sanchez, Janette Williams, Larry Wilson, and Dave Zahniser are dear friends who helped shape how I see the world and write about it.

At Yale I had incomparable mentors and untiring advocates in Bob Gordon, Harold Koh, Carol Rose, and Peter Schuck. I also thank Emily Bazelon, Lincoln Caplan, Crystal Feimster, Glenda Gilmore, and Mark

Templeton for their guidance and support. My conversations with Daniel Markovits, absurd and profound, have been a great joy these last thirteen years. As a lawyer, I had the privilege of working with extraordinary judges and attorneys, including Dorothy Nelson and Rya Zobel, Michael Strumwasser, Fred Woocher, Kevin Reed, and Johanna Shargel, all of whom deepened my understanding of law and the lives lived in its shadow. In Boston I became a legal historian with the help of Charlie Donahue, Mort Horwitz, Christine Desan, Mary Dudziak, Pnina Lahav, David Seipp, Jed Shugerman, Michael Stein, and especially Ken Mack, who has been a friend and a reader of my work without equal. I was also lucky enough to belong to a writing group with Steve Biel, Jona Hansen, Jane Kamensky, John Plotz, Jennifer Roberts, Seth Rockman, Conevery Valenčius, and Michael Willrich, whose comments and suggestions from the start of the project to its completion were unfailingly insightful. I am particularly grateful to Jane for reading and commenting on the entire manuscript. At NYU I learned from some of the best readers and writers of legal history, including Richard Bernstein, Harold Forsythe, Dan Hulsebosch, John Phillip Reid, and especially Bill Nelson, who has been a mentor of boundless generosity to more than a generation of scholars. George Barnum, Randall Burkett, Vernon Burton, Rachel Cohen, Jane Dailey, Doug DeMay and Nell Ma'luf, Adam Feibelman and Cindy Gardner, Crystal Feimster and Dani Botsman, George Flautau, Laura Freidenfelds, Matthew Gilmore, Andrew Kent, Morgan Kousser, Brian Kraft, Joe Mathews, Mary Gorton McBride, Seth Mnookin, Nick Parrillo, Matthew Pearl, Zach Schrag, and Diana Williams were all helpful with research and publishing questions at various stages of the project. Chris Capozzola, Kristin Collins, Dan Hamilton, Alison LaCroix, and Brad Snyder are friends and colleagues who read portions of the book and have long been sources of ideas and advice; Matthew Lindsay read the entire manuscript and had excellent suggestions. John Donahue, Jeremy Hockenstein, and Ira Stoll have been my friends for more than twenty years, and it was always a pleasure to talk with them after a day of research or writing.

I am grateful to Wendy Strothman and Dan O'Connell at the Strothman Agency for believing in and shepherding the book before a single word had been committed to paper. At The Penguin Press, Vanessa Mobley had the vision to see what this project could become, and Janie Fleming was a careful reader with a keen sense of narrative. Janet Biehl and Bruce Giffords provided elegant and meticulous copyediting and production support. I owe special thanks to my editor, Ginny Smith, whose incisive comments and infectious enthusiasm improved the book in countless ways.

Writing about big families across generations often reminded me of my own loving extended family. My grandparents, Sidney and Beverly Sharfstein and Reuben and Pearl Shiling, loved stories and jokes and ideas and books, but most of all they loved me. I wish they were alive to see this book. I am grateful for the love, support, and friendship of my sister Sarah and Brian and baby Sydney, Yngvild and Sam and Isak, Howard and Jill, David and Claire, my in-laws Curt and Mary Mikkelsen, and Erika and Mike and Katherine. My brother Josh read the entire manuscript in one weekend during a blizzard in Baltimore in December 2009, and as always his comments were spot on, medically sound, and in the public interest. For as long as I can remember, he has been my friend and champion. I thank my father, Steven Sharfstein, not only because there was a copy of *Black Skin, White Masks* in the house when I was growing up, and not only because he told stories about what it was like to meet Martin Luther King Jr. and attend the March on Washington as a young man. My father has shown me how to live a socially engaged life of ideas and action. He has always put family first. And it is always fun to watch baseball with him—even when the Orioles are playing. My mother, Margaret Sharfstein, has the most acute observational skills and best sense of humor of anyone I have ever met. She has kept our family together with the kind of strength and abiding love that has its own gravitational force. I am who I am because of her.

Since I began this project, my immediate family has doubled in size. My two boys, Saul and Abe, make every day wonderful. I see the world with new eyes because of them. That said, any inadvertent mentions in this book of dinosaurs, spiders, robots, spaceships, skeletons, pirates, and dogs that talk are entirely my own.

When there was no end in sight, Ann Mikkelsen's advice and encouragement, patience and unfailing support, kept this project going. She has read every word that I have written many times, and I would be lost without her wise counsel and brilliant editing. Every day for eighteen years we have spent hours talking, and every day I am inspired by her ideas and intellect and empathy, her way of reading the world closely. I understand love and family, truth and beauty, happiness and home, because of her. My gratitude is indescribable. This book is dedicated to her.

NOTES

ARCHIVES CITED

American Missionary Association Archives, Amistad Research Center, Tulane University, New Orleans

Mrs. Mason Barrett Collection of the papers of Albert Sidney Johnston and William Preston Johnston, Louisiana Research Collection, Tulane University, New Orleans

Sayles Jenks Bowen Papers, Manuscript Division, Library of Congress, Washington, D.C.

John E. Bruce Papers, Manuscripts, Archives, and Rare Books Division, Schomburg Center for Research in Black Culture, New York Public Library, New York

Calliopean Society Papers, Manuscripts and Archives, Yale University Library, New Haven, Connecticut

J.F.H. Claiborne Papers, Mississippi Department of Archives and History, Jackson

Anna Julia Cooper Papers, Collection 23-1, Moorland-Spingarn Research Center, Howard University, Washington, D.C.

Charles Nunnally Dean Papers, Special Collections, J. D. Williams Library, University of Mississippi, Oxford

District of Columbia Public School Records, Charles Sumner School Museum and Archives, Washington, D.C.

Randall Lee Gibson Papers, Louisiana and Lower Mississippi Valley Collections, Louisiana State University Libraries, Baton Rouge

Randall Lee Gibson Papers, Louisiana Research Collection, Tulane University, New Orleans

Gibson and Humphreys Family Papers, Southern Historical Collection, Wilson Library, University of North Carolina, Chapel Hill

Randall Lee Gibson and Family Archive, Gilder Lehrman Institute of American History, New York

Hart Gibson Alumni Records, Manuscripts and Archives, Sterling Memorial Library, Yale University, New Haven, Connecticut

Grigsby Collection, Filson Historical Society, Louisville, Kentucky

Edmund T. Halsey Papers, Filson Historical Society, Louisville, Kentucky

Oliver Otis Howard Papers, George J. Mitchell Department of Special Collections and Archives, Bowdoin College Library, Brunswick, Maine

Josiah Stoddard Johnston Papers, Filson Historical Society, Louisville, Kentucky

John Mercer Langston Papers, Special Collections, John Hope and Aurelia E. Franklin Library, Fisk University, Nashville, Tennessee

Leak and Wall Family Papers, 1785–1897, Southern Historical Collection, Wilson Library, University of North Carolina at Chapel Hill

Liddell (Moses, St. John R., and Family) Papers, Louisiana and Lower Mississippi Valley Collections, Louisiana State University Libraries, Baton Rouge

McConnell Family Papers, Louisiana Research Collection, Tulane University, New Orleans

Whitefield McKinlay Papers, Carter G. Woodson Collection, Manuscripts Division, Library of Congress, Washington, D.C.

Kelly Miller Papers, Manuscripts Collection, Moorland-Spingarn Research Center, Howard University, Washington, D.C.

Mrs. William and H. Foster Pettit Family Collection, University of Kentucky Archives, Lexington

Rufus and S. Willard Saxton Papers, Yale University Library, New Haven, Connecticut

Robert H. Terrell Papers, Manuscript Division, Library of Congress, Washington, D.C.

Washingtoniana Collection, District of Columbia Public Library, Washington, D.C.

David Weeks and Family Papers, Louisiana and Lower Mississippi Valley Collections, Louisiana State University Libraries, Baton Rouge

INTRODUCTION: THE HOUSE BEHIND THE CEDARS

1 Thomas L. Murphy, interview by author, October 28, 2005, Hampton, Ga.

2 See Willard B. Gatewood, *Aristocrats of Color: The Black Elite, 1880–1920* (Bloomington: Indiana University Press, 1990), pp. 166–67, 176, 178.

3 For nearly a century, sociologists and others have attempted to estimate the percentage of whites in the United States who have some recent African ancestry; speculation ranges from 1 to 20 percent. See, e.g., Hornell M. Hart, *Selective Migration as a Factor in Child Welfare in the United States, With Special Reference to Iowa* (Iowa City: University of Iowa Press, 1921); Caroline Bond Day, *A Study of Some Negro-White Families in the United States* (Cambridge, Mass.: Harvard University Press, 1932); John H. Burma, "The Measurement of Negro Passing," *American Journal of Sociology* 52 (1946), p. 18; E. W. Eckard, "How Many Negroes 'Pass'?" *American Journal of Sociology* 52 (1947), p. 498; Roi Ottley, "Five Million White Negroes," *Ebony*, March 1948, pp. 22–28; Robert P. Stuckert, "African Ancestry of the White American Population," *Ohio Journal of Science* 58 (1958), pp. 155, 160 ("Over twenty-eight million white persons are descendants of persons of African origin"); James Ernest Conyers, "Selected Aspects of the Phenomenon of Negro Passing" (unpublished Ph.D. diss., Washington State University, 1962), pp. 23–27, summarizing and critiquing sociological studies; Werner Sollors, *Neither Black Nor White Yet Both: Thematic Explorations of Interracial Literature* (New York: Oxford University Press, 1997), pp. 280–84; and Brent Staples, "A Hemings Family Turns from Black, to White, to Black," *New York Times*, December 17, 2001, p. A20. On assertions of newly white status, see Linda J. Alexander's account of discovering her family's origins as free people of color in Louisiana, "The 'White' House," *Sunday Advocate Magazine* (Baton Rouge), April 30, 2000, p. 18, online at http://www.authorsden.com/visit/viewarticle.asp?AuthorID=9014&id=5920.

4 See generally Winthrop D. Jordan, *White Over Black: American Attitudes Toward the Negro, 1550–1812* (Chapel Hill: University of North Carolina Press, 1968); and Kathleen M. Brown, *Good Wives, Nasty Wenches, and Anxious Patriarchs: Gender, Race, and Power in Colonial Virginia* (Chapel Hill: University of North Carolina Press, 1996). On migration as a central theme of African American history, see Ira Berlin, *The Making of African America: Four Great Migrations* (New York: Viking Press, 2010). The journey from black to white arguably constitutes a fifth migration.

5 See generally Ira Berlin, *Slaves Without Masters: The Free Negro in the Antebellum South* (New York: Random House, 1974); Leon F. Litwack, *North of Slavery: The Negro in the Free States, 1790–1860* (Chicago: University of Chicago Press, 1961); and Leon F. Litwack, *Trouble in Mind: Black Southerners in the Age of Jim Crow* (New York: Knopf, 1998).

6 "The problem of evidence is insurmountable," observes Winthrop Jordan. "The success of

the passing mechanism depended upon its operating in silence." See Jordan, *White Over Black*, p. 174. Nevertheless, historians have punctuated their accounts of the evolution of race in the United States and the prevalence of interracial sex with anecdotes in which African Americans refashioned themselves as white. See, e.g., Joel Williamson, *New People: Miscegenation and Mulattoes in the United States* (New York: Free Press, 1980), pp. 100–106; Berlin, *Slaves Without Masters*, pp. 160–64; James Hugo Johnston, *Race Relations in Virginia and Miscegenation in the South, 1776–1860* (Amherst: University of Massachusetts Press, 1970), pp. 191–216; Martha Hodes, *White Women, Black Men: Illicit Sex in the 19th-Century South* (New Haven, Conn.: Yale University Press, 1997), pp. 96–122; Joshua D. Rothman, *Notorious in the Neighborhood: Sex and Families Across the Color Line in Virginia, 1787–1861* (Chapel Hill: University of North Carolina Press, 2003), pp. 212–15; and Annette Gordon-Reed, *The Hemingses of Monticello: An American Family* (New York: W. W. Norton, 2008), p. 601. For reverse-passing stories, in which whites chose to live with and as blacks, see, e.g., Martha Hodes, *The Sea Captain's Wife: A True Story of Love, Race, and War in the Nineteenth Century* (New York: W. W. Norton, 2006); and Martha Sandweiss, *Passing Strange: A Gilded Age Tale of Love and Deception Across the Color Line* (New York: Penguin, 2009). On conventional passing narratives, see Sollors, *Neither Black Nor White Yet Both*, pp. 246–84.

7 See, e.g., "Desdemona After a Divorce," *New York Times*, December 23, 1883, p. 6; "Drafted Man, Classed as Colored, Commits Suicide in an Ohio Camp," *Washington Post*, September 29, 1917, p. 4; "Colored Girl at Vassar," *New York Times*, August 16, 1897, p. 1; "Negro Passing as White Reveals Ole Miss Career," *Washington Post*, September 26, 1962, p. A4; Mitchell Owens, "Surprises in the Family Tree," *New York Times*, January 8, 2004, p. F1; Pauli Murray, *The Autobiography of a Black Activist, Feminist, Lawyer, Priest, and Poet* (Knoxville: University of Tennessee Press, 1990), pp. 34–35; Shirlee Taylor Haizlip, *The Sweeter the Juice: A Family Memoir in Black and White* (New York: Simon and Schuster, 1994); Gregory Howard Williams, *Life on the Color Line: The True Story of a White Boy Who Discovered He Was Black* (New York: Penguin, 1996); Adele Logan Alexander, *Homelands and Waterways: The American Journey of the Bond Family, 1846–1926* (New York: Vintage, 2000); Bliss Broyard, *One Drop: My Father's Hidden Life—A Story of Race and Family Secrets* (Boston: Little, Brown, 2008); Ariela J. Gross, *What Blood Won't Tell: A History of Race on Trial in America* (Cambridge, Mass.: Harvard University Press, 2008).

8 See generally George M. Fredrickson, *The Black Image in the White Mind: The Debate on Afro-American Character and Destiny, 1817–1914* (New York: Harper & Row, 1971); Berlin, *Slaves Without Masters*; Leon F. Litwack, *Been in the Storm So Long: The Aftermath of Slavery* (New York: Knopf, 1979).

9 On the strong link between race and the law, see, e.g., Peggy Pascoe, *What Comes Naturally: Miscegenation Law and the Making of Race in America* (New York: Oxford University Press, 2009); and Gross, *What Blood Won't Tell*. The vision of law as a continuous struggle over meaning has been given powerful expression by, among others, Sally Falk Moore, *Law as Process: An Anthropological Approach* (New York: Oxford University Press, 1978); Hendrik Hartog, "Pigs and Positivism," *Wisconsin Law Review* (1985), p. 899; and Robert W. Gordon, "Critical Legal Histories," *Stanford Law Review* 36 (1984), p. 57.

10 For a thorough introduction to "racial identity trials," see Gross, *What Blood Won't Tell*. For evidentiary rulings that required proof of "pure African blood," see, e.g., *Ferrall v. Ferrall*, 69 S.E. 60, 61–62 (N.C. 1910); and Daniel J. Sharfstein, "The Secret History of Race in the United States," *Yale Law Journal* 112 (2003), pp. 1473, 1502–3, 1506.

11 See Robert M. Cover, "Foreword: Nomos and Narrative," *Harvard Law Review* 97 (1983), p. 4.

CHAPTER 1: GIBSON: MARS BLUFF, SOUTH CAROLINA, 1768

1 George Gabriel Powell to William Bull, August 19, 1768, in *South Carolina Council Journal*, August 26, 1768, South Carolina Department of Archives and History (hereafter SCDAH),

Columbia. The description of the physical setting is based on the Reverend Charles Woodmason's diaries of his travels in the Pee Dee area and elsewhere in the South Carolina backcountry in the mid-1760s. See Charles Woodmason, *The Carolina Backcountry on the Eve of the Revolution*, ed. Richard J. Hooker (Chapel Hill: University of North Carolina Press, 1953).

2 See Richard Maxwell Brown, *The South Carolina Regulators* (Cambridge, Mass.: Harvard University Press, 1963), p. 56; George C. Rogers Jr., *The History of Georgetown County, South Carolina* (Columbia: University of South Carolina Press, 1970), pp. 63, 105; Suzanne Cameron Linder and Marta Leslie Thacker, *Historical Atlas of the Rice Plantations of Georgetown County and the Santee River* (Columbia: South Carolina Department of Archives and History, 2001), pp. 281–83; Winthrop D. Jordan, *White Over Black: American Attitudes Toward the Negro, 1550–1812* (Chapel Hill: University of North Carolina Press, 1968), pp. 172–73; and Rachel N. Klein, *Unification of a Slave State: The Rise of the Planter Class in the South Carolina Backcountry, 1760–1808* (Chapel Hill: University of North Carolina Press, 1990), pp. 69–71.

3 Brown, *South Carolina Regulators*, p. 55; Woodmason, *Carolina Backcountry*, pp. 7, 13, 15, 18, 25, 31, 52; and *South Carolina Gazette*, August 15, 1768. Accompanying Powell on the journey upcountry was Roger Pinckney, South Carolina's highest law enforcement official, the deputy provost marshal.

4 Powell to Bull, August 19, 1768; Brown, *South Carolina Regulators*, pp. 56–57.

5 Powell to Bull, August 19, 1768; Jordan, *White Over Black*, p. 172; Brown, *South Carolina Regulators*, p. 192n8; Klein, *Unification*, p. 69; Robert L. Meriwether, *The Expansion of South Carolina, 1729–1765* (Kingsport, Tenn.: Southern Publishers, 1940), pp. 90, 96; Alexander Gregg, *History of the Old Cheraws* (1867; reprint, Columbia, S.C.: State Co., 1905), pp. 73–74; Paul Heinegg, "Gibson Family," in *Free African Americans of Virginia, North Carolina and South Carolina*, online at http://www.freeafricanamericans.com/Gibson_Gowen.htm; and *Supplement to South Carolina and American General Gazette*, April 18, 1764, transcript available from South Carolina Newspaper Collection, Accessible Archives.

6 Brown, *South Carolina Regulators*, pp. 1–12; Klein, *Unification*, pp. 37–38.

7 Brown, *South Carolina Regulators*, pp. 29–37; Klein, *Unification*, pp. 57–60; "America," *St. James's Chronicle or, The British Evening Post*, October 25–27, 1768, p. 3.

8 Woodmason, "The Remonstrance," in *Carolina Backcountry*, pp. 213, 226; "America," *St. James's Chronicle*, October 25–27, 1768; Klein, *Unification*, pp. 63, 68; Brown, *South Carolina Regulators*, pp. 41–43, 70–73; Edward McCrady, *The History of South Carolina Under the Royal Government, 1719–1776* (New York: Macmillan, 1899), pp. 627–34; and Richard Cumberland to Roger Pinckney, July 31, 1765, in *Documents Connected with the History of South Carolina*, ed. Plowden Charles Jennett Weston (London, 1856), p. 115. King George had awarded the offices of Provost Marshal, Clerk of the Peace, and Clerk of the Crown to Richard Cumberland, a well-born civil servant just beginning a career as a London playwright, who in turn leased the office to Roger Pinckney, another Londoner seeking his fortune. From London, Cumberland resisted efforts to end his monopoly on legal process in South Carolina.

9 Brown, *South Carolina Regulators*, pp. 38–39, 40, 45–46, 49; Klein, *Unification*, p. 47; "America," *St. James's Chronicle*, October 25–27, 1768.

10 *South Carolina Gazette*, August 15, 1768; Brown, *South Carolina Regulators*, p. 54; "America," *St. James's Chronicle*, October 25–27, 1768.

11 Brown, *South Carolina Regulators*, pp. 54–55; George Lloyd Johnson, *The Frontier in the Colonial South: South Carolina Backcountry, 1736–1800* (Westport, Conn.: Greenwood Press, 1997), pp. 56, 135n47; *Robert Weaver v. Gideon Gibson* (1764), judgment roll, SCDAH.

12 The account that follows is drawn primarily from a petition one of the militiamen presented to the colonial legislature two years after the events at Mars Bluff: Petition of William White, *Commons House Journal*, August 15, 1770, SCDAH. See also Brown, *South*

Carolina Regulators, pp. 54–58; Johnson, *Frontier in Colonial South*, pp. 122–26; Jordan, *White Over Black*, p. 173; Klein, *Unification*, pp. 69–71; and *South Carolina Gazette*, August 15, 1768.

13 Petition of William White.

14 Ibid.

15 *South Carolina Gazette*, August 15, 1768; Petition of William White; "A Proclamation," *South Carolina Gazette*, August 8, 1768; Brown, *South Carolina Regulators*, p. 58.

16 Powell to Bull, August 19, 1768.

17 Ibid.; Philip Gosse, *St. Helena, 1502–1938* (Shropshire, U.K.: Anthony Nelson, 1938), pp. 181–82; *Extracts from the St. Helena Records*, comp. Hudson Ralph Janisch (St. Helena, 1908), pp. 136, 181–83; A. S. Salley, ed., "Diary of William Dillwyn During a Visit to Charles Town in 1772," *South Carolina History and General Magazine* 36 (1935), pp. 29, 34–35; Woodmason, *Carolina Backcountry*, p. 270.

18 *Extracts from St. Helena Records*, pp. 74, 183; Gosse, *St. Helena*, p. 182.

19 See generally Jordan, *White Over Black*; Ira Berlin, *Many Thousands Gone: The First Two Centuries of Slavery in North America* (Cambridge, Mass.: Harvard University Press, 1998), pp. 29–46; Edmund Morgan, *American Slavery, American Freedom: The Ordeal of Colonial Virginia* (New York: W. W. Norton, 1975), pp. 134–35, 185–86; Kathleen M. Brown, *Good Wives, Nasty Wenches, and Anxious Patriarchs: Gender, Race, and Power in Colonial Virginia* (Chapel Hill: University of North Carolina Press, 1996), pp. 109–16, 223–25.

20 Brown, *South Carolina Regulators*, pp. 212–41; Thomas D. Morris, *Southern Slavery and the Law, 1619–1860* (Chapel Hill: University of North Carolina Press, 1996), pp. 43–49; Heinegg, introduction to *Free African Americans*, online at http://www.freeafrican americans.com/introduction.htm; Daniel J. Sharfstein, "Crossing the Color Line: Racial Migration and the One-Drop Rule, 1600–1860," *Minnesota Law Review* 91 (2007), pp. 592, 604–5, 614–16.

21 Brown, *Good Wives*, pp. 213–22; Ira Berlin, *Slaves Without Masters: The Free Negro in the Antebellum South* (New York: Random House, 1974), pp. 7–9.

22 Sharfstein, "Crossing the Color Line," p. 616; Heinegg, introduction to *Free African Americans*; Jordan, *White Over Black*, pp. 171–72; Peter Wood, *Black Majority: Negroes in Colonial South Carolina from 1670 Through the Stono Rebellion* (New York: Knopf, 1974), pp. 97–101.

23 Wood, *Black Majority*, pp. 150, 220–21; "Extracts of Mr. Von Reck's Journal," in Peter Force, *Tracts and Other Papers Principally Relating to the Origin, Settlement and Progress of the North American Colonies* (Washington, D.C., 1846), p. 4:9; Jordan, *White Over Black*, p. 172.

24 Jordan, *White Over Black*, p. 172.

25 Klein, *Unification*, pp. 11, 44; Meriwether, *Expansion of South Carolina*, pp. 90–91; Donald G. Mathews, *Religion in the Old South* (Chicago: University of Chicago Press, 1977), pp. 25–26; Gregg, *History of Old Cheraws*, p. 67.

26 Robert Mills, *Statistics of South Carolina* (Charleston: Hurlbut and Lloyd, 1826), p. 625; Michael Trinkley and Natalie Adams, *Archaeological, Historical, and Architectural Survey of the Gibson Plantation Tract, Florence County, South Carolina* (Columbia: Chicora Foundation, 1992), pp. 22–24; Meriwether, *Expansion of South Carolina*, p. 94; Amelia Wallace Vernon, *African Americans at Mars Bluff, South Carolina* (Baton Rouge: Louisiana State University Press, 1993), p. 125; Wood, *Black Majority*, p. 324; Woodmason, *Carolina Backcountry*, p. 228.

27 Klein, *Unification*, pp. 62–63, 71; Brown, *South Carolina Regulators*, pp. 31–32.

28 Powell to Bull, August 19, 1768; Brown, *South Carolina Regulators*, pp. 56–57.

29 Powell to Bull, August 19, 1768.

30 Ibid.

31 Ibid.

32 Jordan, *White Over Black*, p. 173; Henry Laurens to William Drayton, February 23, 1783, *Papers of Henry Laurens*, ed. Philip M. Hamer et al. (Columbia: University of South Carolina

Press, 2003), pp. 16:155–56; Wood, *Black Majority*, p. 324; An Act of the Better Ordering and Governing Negroes and Other Slaves in this Province, May 10, 1740, in *Statutes at Large of South Carolina*, ed. David J. McCord (Columbia: A. S. Johnston, 1840), sec. 56, pp. 7:416–17.

33 Heinegg, introduction to *Free African Americans*; Larry Koger, *Black Slaveowners: Free Black Slave Masters in South Carolina, 1790–1860* (Columbia: University of South Carolina Press, 1985), pp. 12–16.

34 Laurens to Drayton, pp. 16:155–56.

35 Brown, *South Carolina Regulators*, pp. 96–104; Klein, *Unification*, pp. 74–77; McCrady, *History of South Carolina*, pp. 638–43, 716.

36 Klein, *Unification*, pp. 78–108. In 1867 Gregg, in *History of Old Cheraws*, reported that Gibson was murdered for his Tory sympathies during the Revolution, but there is no independent corroboration of the anecdote.

CHAPTER TWO: WALL: ROCKINGHAM, NORTH CAROLINA, 1838

1 See, e.g., Emory Washburn, *A Treatise on the American Law of Real Property* (Boston: Little Brown, 1860–62), pp. 2:451–53.

2 Thomas Jefferson to John Randolph, August 25, 1775, in *Memoir, Correspondence, and Miscellanies: From the Papers of Thomas Jefferson*, ed. Thomas Jefferson Randolph (Boston: Gray & Bowen, 1829), pp. 150, 151; Washburn, *Treatise on American Law*, pp. 2:452–53.

3 State Board of Agriculture, *North Carolina and its Resources* (Winston, N.C.: M. I. & J. C. Stewart, 1896), pp. 304, 388. *Wall v. Wall*, 55 S.E. 283 (N.C. 1906), contains a discussion of Stephen Wall's landholdings.

4 Anne Wall Thomas, *The Walls of Walltown* (1969; reprint by author), pp. 21–25, 31–33; *Wall v. Wall*, 55 S.E. 283; "General Assembly: In the Senate," *Raleigh Register and North Carolina Gazette*, December 22, 1820; classified advertisement, *Carolina Observer*, June 19, 1832 (Wall was a commissioner for the Cape Fear & Yadkin Railroad); "Communications," *Fayetteville Observer*, July 29, 1834 (on the internal improvement committee of Richmond County); and classified advertisement, *Raleigh Register*, February 14, 1837 (on Raleigh & Columbia Railroad stock). On the Whig Party generally and in the South, see Arthur C. Cole, *The Whig Party in the South* (Washington, D.C.: American Historical Association, 1914); and Sean Wilentz, *The Rise of American Democracy: From Jefferson to Lincoln* (New York: W. W. Norton, 2006), p. 431. On Wall's involvement in the party, see "Communications," *Fayetteville Observer*, June 12, 1839; he was a delegate at a meeting that declared the Van Buren administration "corrupt and tyrannical." See also "Communications," *Fayetteville Observer*, April 24, 1839; *Fayetteville Observer*, March 17, 1836; and "District Convention," *Raleigh Register*, May 10, 1836.

5 *Fayetteville Observer*, October 8, 1845. This description is based on a photograph of Wall in Dean Papers.

6 Thomas, *Walls of Walltown*, p. 32; *Fayetteville Observer*, October 8, 1845.

7 Early Accounts of Stephen Wall, Leak and Wall Papers; William Cheek and Aimee Lee Cheek, *John Mercer Langston and the Fight for Black Freedom, 1829–65* (Urbana-Champaign: University of Illinois, 1989), pp. 250, 273n27; and Mial Wall to Caroline Wall, March 16, 1853, Langston Papers. See also miscellaneous documents relating to the estate of Sara K. Fidler in Langston Papers. On Caroline Matilda of Denmark, see C. F. Lascelles Wraxall, *Life and Times of Her Majesty Caroline Matilda* (London: W. H. Allen & Co., 1864).

8 See John C. Inscoe, "Carolina Slave Names: An Index to Acculturation," *Journal of Southern History* 49 (1983), pp. 527, 541–43; Simón Bolívar, "The Angostura Address" (February 15, 1819), in *El Libertador: Writings of Simón Bolívar*, ed. David Bushnell, trans. Frederick H. Fornoff (New York: Oxford University Press, 2003), pp. 31, 38.

9 See Ira Berlin, *Slaves Without Masters: The Free Negro in the Antebellum South* (New York: Random House, 1974); John Hope Franklin, *The Free Negro in North Carolina, 1790–1860*

(Chapel Hill: University of North Carolina Press, 1943, 1995); Eva Sheppard Wolf, *Race and Liberty in the New Nation: Emancipation in Virginia from the Revolution to Nat Turner's Rebellion* (Baton Rouge: Louisiana State University Press, 2006), p. 14; Barbara Jeanne Fields, *Slavery and Freedom on the Middle Ground: Maryland During the Nineteenth Century* (New Haven, Conn.: Yale University Press, 1985), pp. 1, 4–5.

10 Ira Berlin has referred to this migration as the "Second Middle Passage" in *Generations of Captivity: A History of African-American Slaves* (Cambridge, Mass.: Harvard University Press, 2003), pp. 161–230. See also Steven F. Miller, "Plantation Labor Organization and Slave Life on the Cotton Frontier: The Alabama-Mississippi Black Belt, 1815–1840," in *Cultivation and Culture: Labor and the Shaping of Slave Life in the Americas*, ed. Ira Berlin and Philip D. Morgan (Charlottesville: University of Virginia Press, 1993), p. 155; Susan Eva O'Donovan, *Becoming Free in the Cotton South* (Cambridge, Mass.: Harvard University Press, 2007), pp. 10–58.

11 Berlin, *Slaves Without Masters*, pp. 188–91, 368–72; Wilentz, *Rise of American Democracy*, pp. 403, 451–52; Bertram Wyatt-Brown, "The Abolitionists' Postal Campaign of 1835," *Journal of Negro History* 50 (1965), pp. 227–38. In 1836 the House of Representatives responded to the overwhelming number of petitions by banning floor debates on them, a "gag rule" that lasted until 1844.

12 See, e.g., George M. Fredrickson, *The Black Image in the White Mind: The Debate on Afro-American Character and Destiny, 1817–1914* (1971; New York: Harper and Row, 1987), pp. 43–96.

13 Early Accounts of Stephen Wall, Leak and Wall Papers.

14 See Berlin, *Generations of Captivity*, pp. 214–20.

15 Early Accounts of Stephen Wall, Leak and Wall Papers; Berlin, *Generations of Captivity*, pp. 174–75.

16 Early Accounts of Stephen Wall, Leak and Wall Papers. Gunter is likely Charles Grandison Gunter, who was originally from North Carolina and was married to a Richmond County woman. See Thomas McAdory Owen III, *History of Alabama and Dictionary of Alabama Biography* (Chicago: S. J. Clarke, 1921), pp. 715–16. Gunter had a large plantation on Pintlala Creek ten miles west of Montgomery. According to the slave schedules for the 1850 U.S. Census, he owned eighty-one slaves, ages one to ninety. Instrumental in enacting Alabama's married women's property law, Gunter served as a captain in the Confederate army during the Civil War and afterward moved to Brazil rather than take an oath of allegiance to the Union. See also Miller, "Plantation Labor Organization," p. 157; Wilentz, *Rise of American Democracy*, pp. 439–45; and Charles Sellers, *The Market Revolution: Jacksonian America, 1815–1846* (New York: Oxford University Press, 1991).

17 Miller, "Plantation Labor Organization," p. 157; Berlin, *Generations of Captivity*, p. 172.

18 Miller, "Plantation Labor Organization," p. 159; Berlin, *Generations of Captivity*, pp. 176–77.

19 Berlin, *Generations of Captivity*, pp. 176–77, 188–93; William E. Wiethoff, *Crafting the Overseer's Image* (Columbia: University of South Carolina Press, 2006); William K. Scarborough, *The Overseer: Plantation Management in the Old South* (Baton Rouge: Louisiana State University Press, 1966).

20 See Berlin, *Generations of Captivity*, pp. 214–20.

21 Thomas, *Walls of Walltown*, pp. 30–31.

22 For details on a typical journey west, see Miller, "Plantation Labor Organization"; Berlin, *Generations of Captivity*.

23 Will of Stephen Wall, June 23, 1845, North Carolina Office of Archives and History, Raleigh; "Friends in Indiana," *Liberator*, November 30, 1838, p. 190.

24 "Friends in Indiana," *Liberator*, November 30, 1838, p. 190; John T. Plummer, "Suburban Geology, or Rocks, Soil, and Water, about Richmond, Wayne County, Indiana," *American Journal of Science and the Arts* 44 (1843), pp. 281, 283; Levi Coffin, *Reminiscences of Levi Coffin*, 2nd ed. (Cincinnati: Robert Clarke & Co., 1880), pp. 76–77, 106–07.

25 "Friends in Indiana," *Liberator*, November 30, 1838, p. 190; *The Discipline of the Society of Friends, of Indiana Yearly Meeting* (Cincinnati: A. Pugh, 1839), pp. 60–61.

26 Coffin, *Reminiscences*, pp. 106–10; Ryan P. Jordan, *Slavery and the Meetinghouse: The Quakers and the Abolitionist Dilemma, 1820–1865* (Bloomington: Indiana University Press, 2007), pp. 20, 48–49; "Friends in Indiana," *Liberator*, November 30, 1838, p. 190; *Discipline of Society of Friends*.

27 "Friends in Indiana," *Liberator*, November 30, 1838, p. 190.

28 Ibid.; see also 1840 U.S. Census, Kemper County, Miss.

29 Willard J. Wright, ed., "The Story of Warren County," in *Memoirs of the Miami River Valley*, ed. John Calvin Hover et al. (Chicago: Robert O. Law Co., 1919), pp. 2:247, 420.

30 A. W. Brayton, "A Sketch of the Life of the Late Dr. Thomas B. Harvey, of Indianapolis, Indiana," *Medical Mirror* 1 (1890), p. 76.

31 Coffin, *Reminiscences*, p. 581; Cheek and Cheek, *Langston and the Fight*, p. 250.

32 Will of Stephen Wall, North Carolina State Archives.

33 Ibid.; Mial Wall to Caroline Wall, March 16, 1853, Langston Papers.

CHAPTER THREE: SPENCER: CLAY COUNTY, KENTUCKY, 1848

1 On use of the spring pole, see R. B. Woodworth, "The Evolution of Drilling Rigs," *Bulletin of the American Institute of Mining Engineers*, November 1915, pp. 2247, 2250–55.

2 John Adams Bownocker, "Salt Deposits and the Salt Industry in Ohio," in *Ohio Geological Survey*, 4th ser., bull. 8 (1906), p. 15; John F. Smith, "The Salt-Making Industry of Clay County, Kentucky," *Filson Club History Quarterly* 1 (1927), pp. 134, 136; John E. Stealey III, *The Antebellum Kanawha Salt Business and Western Markets* (Lexington: University Press of Kentucky, 1993), p. 15; Augustus Beauchamp Northcote, "On the Brine-springs of Cheshire," *London, Edinburgh and Dublin Philosophical Magazine and Journal of Science*, 4th ser., vol. 14 (1857), pp. 457, 462; Dwight B. Billings and Kathleen M. Blee, *The Road to Poverty: The Making of Wealth and Hardship in Appalachia* (New York: Cambridge University Press, 2000), pp. 61–78.

3 Billings and Blee, *Road to Poverty*, pp. 65–70.

4 Ibid., p. 209.

5 Ibid., p. 77. John F. Smith recalled, "Some years ago I talked with an ancient African whose task, when a young man, was to clean the furnaces at one of the principal works. He told me of the darkness, the cramped working space, the constant fear that he might get hung in a tight place"; in "Salt-Making Industry," pp. 138–39.

6 Stealey, *Antebellum Kanawha Salt Business*, pp. 142–44; Billings and Blee, *Road to Poverty*, pp. 210–11.

7 "Color in Kentucky is generally considered prima facie evidence of slavery": *Commonwealth v. Johnson*, Mason Circuit Court, Order 32, p. 129 (October Term 1837), quoted in J. Winston Coleman, *Slavery Times in Kentucky* (Chapel Hill: University of North Carolina Press, 1940), pp. 201, 205. On the lives of subsistence farmers in Clay County, see Billings and Blee, *Road to Poverty*, pp. 157–84.

8 Deed Book 3, p. 20, Lee County, Va., quoted in Manuel Ray Spencer, comp., *The Descendants of Joseph Spencer, 1735–1836* (self-published, 1996), pp. 7–8, 325. For a description of free blacks jailed or sold as slaves, see Coleman, *Slavery Times*, pp. 206–7. See also Billings and Blee, *Road to Poverty*, p. 211; and James B. Murphy, "Slavery and Freedom in Appalachia: Kentucky as a Demographic Case Study," *Register of the Kentucky Historical Society* 80 (1980), pp. 151, 162.

9 See Juliet E. K. Walker, "The Legal Status of Free Blacks in Kentucky, 1792–1825," *Filson Club History Quarterly* 57 (1983), pp. 382–95.

10 Winthrop Jordan, *White Over Black: American Attitudes Toward the Negro, 1550–1812* (Chapel Hill: University of North Carolina Press, 1968), pp. 544–45; Daniel J. Sharfstein, "Crossing the Color Line: Racial Migration and the One-Drop Rule, 1600–1860," *Minnesota Law Review* 91 (2007), pp. 592, 644.

11 Walker, "Legal Status of Free Blacks."

12 Billings and Blee, *Road to Poverty*, pp. 219–23, 226 and table 6.5.

13 Ibid., pp. 213–14.

14 Spencer, *Descendants of Joseph Spencer*; see also Wilma A. Dunaway, *Slavery in the American Mountain South* (New York: Cambridge University Press, 2003), pp. 60–62.

15 1820 U.S. Census, Clay County, Ky.; see also James S. Brown, *Beech Creek: A Study of a Kentucky Mountain Neighborhood* (1950; reprint Berea, Ky.: Berea College Press, 1988), pp. 5–6. Years later descendants of the family recalled leading similar lives. Freda Spencer Goble, interview by author, August 29, 2005, Paintsville, Ky.

16 Billings and Blee, *Road to Poverty*, pp. 82–86.

17 Ibid., p. 229.

18 See George Spencer Death Certificate, April 1, 1912, Johnson County Death Certificate No. 10477, Kentucky Bureau of Vital Statistics, Ancestry.com; Lydia Margaret Ratliff Death Certificate, September 1, 1938, Johnson County Death Certificate No. 20096, Kentucky Bureau of Vital Statistics; *Spencer v. Looney* (Va. 1912), No. 2012, Virginia State Law Library, Richmond, trial transcript, pp. 61, 66, 73, 77, 81; Goble interview.

19 *Acts Passed at the First Session of the Thirty-Fourth General Assembly for the Commonwealth of Kentucky* (Frankfort, Ky.: Holeman, 1825), chap. 146, pp. 137–38; and Walker, "Legal Status of Free Blacks," p. 392. Victoria Bynum, *Unruly Women: The Politics of Social and Sexual Control in the Old South* (Chapel Hill: University of North Carolina Press, 1992), pp. 99–103; Bynum describes how North Carolina courts' apprenticeship rulings "sometimes crippled the tenuous economic base of a fatherless or free black family" (p. 101) and how apprenticeship was "an instrument of racial control" (p. 99).

20 *Freeman v. Strong*, 6 Dana 282 (Ky. 1838); Billings and Blee, *Road to Poverty*, pp. 110, 376n23.

21 Billings and Blee, *Road to Poverty*, pp. 108–9.

22 Brown, *Beech Creek*, pp. 72–73.

23 On Henderson, see 1840 U.S. Census, Rockcastle County, Ky.; *Kentucky State Register for the Year 1847*, ed. Taliaferro P. Shaffner (Louisville: Morton & Griswold, 1847), p. 15; An Act to Authorise the Establishment of a Library in Rockcastle County, *Acts Passed at the First Session of the Forty-First General Assembly for the Commonwealth of Kentucky* (1833), c. 137, pp. 115–16.

24 *Freeman v. Strong*, 6 Dana 282 (Ky. 1838).

25 Ellen Churchill Semple, "The Anglo-Saxons of the Kentucky Mountains: A Study in Anthropogeography," *Geographical Journal* 17 (1901), pp. 588, 594, 596. See also Wilma A. Dunaway, *Women, Work, and Family in the Antebellum Mountain South* (New York: Cambridge University Press, 2008), pp. 140–46.

26 Semple, "Anglo-Saxons," p. 591. Information on Clarissa Centers has been compiled online by a descendant at http://freepages.genealogy.rootsweb.ancestry.com/~jude/index.htm.

27 Contemporaneous accounts are quoted in John C. Campbell, *The Southern Highlander and His Homeland* (1921; reprint, Lexington: University Press of Kentucky, 1973), pp. 35, 47–48. On westward expansion generally, see D. W. Meinig, *The Shaping of America: A Geographical Perspective on 500 Years of History*, vol. 2, *Continental America, 1800–1867* (New Haven, Conn.: Yale University Press, 1993).

28 Dunaway, *Women, Work*, p. 249.

29 1850 U.S. Census, Clay County, Ky.

30 Billings and Blee, *Road to Poverty*, pp. 214–15; see also Martha Hodes, *White Women, Black Men: Illicit Sex in the 19th-Century South* (New Haven, Conn.: Yale University Press, 1997), p. 4.

31 Hodes, *White Women, Black Men*, pp. 62–63. See also Amy Dru Stanley, *From Bondage to Contract: Wage Labor, Marriage, and the Market in the Age of Emancipation* (New York: Cambridge University Press, 1998); and Billings and Blee, *Road to Poverty*, pp. 51–52.

32 Hodes, *White Women, Black Men*, p. 3.

33 1850 U.S. Census, Clay County, Ky.; Semple, "Anglo-Saxons," p. 594; *Spencer v. Looney*, trial transcript, p. 151.
34 *State v. Cantey*, 20 S.C.L. (2 Hill) 614 (S.C. Ct. App. 1835). On skin complexion in frontier America, see Conevery Bolton Valenčius, *The Health of the Country: How American Settlers Understood Themselves and Their Land* (New York: Basic Books, 2002), pp. 230, 244; and Martha Hodes, "The Mercurial Nature and Abiding Power of Race: A Transnational Family Story," *American Historical Review* 108 (2003), pp. 84, 99.
35 1850 U.S. Census, Clay County and Knox County, Ky.
36 1850 U.S. Census, Johnson County, Ky.
37 On overpopulation in Clay County and its effect on agricultural production, see Billings and Blee, *Road to Poverty*, pp. 194-99.
38 Ibid., p. 229.
39 See *Spencer v. Looney*, trial transcript.

CHAPTER FOUR: GIBSON: NEW HAVEN, CONNECTICUT, 1850-55

1 Douglas W. Rae, *City: Urbanism and Its End* (New Haven, Conn.: Yale University Press, 2005), pp. 44-45, 57; Chauncey Jerome, *History of the American Clock Business for the Past Sixty Years* (New Haven, Conn.: F. C. Dayton, 1860), pp. 134-39.
2 Rollin G. Osterweis, *Three Centuries of New Haven* (New Haven, Conn.: Yale University Press, 1953), p. 243.
3 Randall Lee Gibson to Tobias Gibson, May 25, 1850, box 1, folder 1, Gibson Papers, Tulane; Hart Gibson to William Preston Gibson, October 10, 1850, box 29, folder 10, Pettit Collection.
4 Randall Lee Gibson to Tobias Gibson, December 13, 1848, box 1, folder 1, Gibson Papers, Tulane; Tobias Gibson to Randall Lee Gibson, November 15, 1849, box 18, folder 128, Weeks Papers; Samuel L. Cartwright, Treatment Instructions, May 10, 1850, ser. 2, folder 2, Gibson and Humphreys Papers; Sarah Thompson Gibson to Randall Lee Gibson, January 1850, Grigsby Collection.
5 Osterweis, *Three Centuries of New Haven*, pp. 313-16; Randall Lee Gibson to Tobias Gibson, September 19, 1848, box 1, folder 1, Gibson Papers, Tulane; Randall Lee Gibson to Tobias Gibson, November 20, 1850, Gibson Papers, LSU.
6 Lyman Hotchkiss Bagg, *Four Years at Yale* (New Haven, Conn.: Charles C. Chatfield & Co., 1871), pp. 298-99; Osterweis, *Three Centuries of New Haven*, p. 255. Randall Gibson's Yale career is detailed in Mary Gorton McBride with Ann Mathison McLaurin, *Randall Lee Gibson of Louisiana: Confederate General and New South Reformer* (Baton Rouge: Louisiana State University Press, 2007), pp. 27-44.
7 "Cattle Show and Fair," *Connecticut Herald*, August 31, 1850, p. 3; Andrew Dickson White, *Autobiography of Andrew Dickson White* (New York: Century, 1905), pp. 1:27-29.
8 Osterweis, *Three Centuries of New Haven*, p. 268; Charlton Thomas Lewis, "Poem," in *Poem by Charlton Thomas Lewis; and Valedictory Address, by Randall Lee Gibson, Pronounced Before the Senior Class in Yale College, June 16, 1853*, p. 8, Manuscripts and Archives, Yale University Library; Arthur Marvin Shaw, *William Preston Johnston: A Transitional Figure of the Confederacy* (Baton Rouge: Louisiana State University Press, 1943), pp. 35-36, 42; Brooks Mather Kelley, *Yale: A History* (New Haven, Conn.: Yale University Press, 1974), p. 215; Randall Lee Gibson to Tobias Gibson, October 7, 1849, Gibson Papers, LSU.
9 Calliopean Society Papers; *Diary, 1843-1852, of James Hadley, Tutor and Professor of Greek in Yale College, 1845-1872*, ed. Laura Hadley Moseley (New Haven, Conn.: Yale University Press, 1951), p. 266.
10 Josiah Stoddard Johnston, Yale Diary, p. 1:59, Johnston Papers; Randall Lee Gibson to Tobias Gibson, October 7, 1849, Gibson Papers, LSU; McBride, *Gibson of Louisiana*, pp. 43-44; George W. Smalley, "Randall Gibson," *Deke Quarterly* 11 (1893), pp. 26, 27.

11 Smalley, "Randall Gibson," p. 27.
12 White, *Autobiography*, p. 30; Calliopean Society Papers.
13 Smalley, "Randall Gibson," p. 26; Moncure Daniel Conway, *Autobiography* (Boston: Houghton Mifflin, 1905), p. 1:71; Henry Hughes, *Treatise on Sociology* (Philadelphia: Lippincott, Grambo & Co., 1854), pp. 239–40. On Southern proslavery ideology, see Michael O'Brien, *Conjectures of Order: Intellectual Life and the American South, 1810–1860* (Chapel Hill: University of North Carolina Press, 2004), pp. 2:938–92.
14 Smalley, "Randall Gibson," pp. 26–27; Bagg, *Four Years at Yale*, pp. 221–23; Calliopean Society Papers; McBride, *Gibson of Louisiana*, p. 41.
15 Smalley, "Randall Gibson," p. 28; White, *Autobiography*, p. 68; McBride, *Gibson of Louisiana*, p. 38; Randall Lee Gibson, "Valedictory Address," in *Poem*, pp. 33–34.
16 John Albert Granger, "Col. Hart Gibson," p. 5, Hart Gibson Alumni Records; Tobias Gibson to Randall Lee Gibson, December 26, 1848, box 17, folder 121, Weeks Papers; Tobias Gibson to Randall Lee Gibson, April 16, 1854, box 29, folder 216, Weeks Papers; Tobias Gibson to Randall Lee Gibson, January 5, 185[4], box 25, folder 179, Weeks Papers. See also McBride, *Gibson of Louisiana*, pp. 29–30.
17 Randall Lee Gibson to Tobias Gibson, October 10, 1852, Gibson Papers, LSU; Randall Lee Gibson to Tobias Gibson, July 22, 1850, Gibson Papers, LSU.
18 See McBride, *Gibson of Louisiana*, p. 9.
19 Ibid., pp. 13–15; *Brabston v. Gibson*, 50 U.S. 263 (1850); Tobias Gibson to Alfred Shelby, July 3, 1830, Grigsby Collection; "Terrebonne Parish, Louisiana," *Commercial Review of the South and West* 2 (February 1850), pp. 146, 149; Clay Lancaster, *Antebellum Architecture of Kentucky* (1991), pp. 209–10. See also J. Carlyle Sitterson, *Sugar Country: The Cane Sugar Industry in the South, 1753–1950* (Lexington: University Press of Kentucky, 1953).
20 McBride, *Gibson of Louisiana*, pp. 19–21; "Terrebonne Parish, Louisiana," *Commercial Review of the South and West* 2 (February 1850), pp. 146, 150.
21 McBride, *Gibson of Louisiana*, p. 25. Randall Lee Gibson's Yale valedictory address echoes his father's sensibility; see Gibson, "Valedictory Address," in *Poem*, p. 26: "Not that educated men are expected to embrace every new-fangled notion, simply because recommended by novelty; and so on the other hand they are expected not to adhere to every old custom and notion on the ground merely that they are venerable with the dust of antiquity, but while subjecting every theory to the closest analysis, they are required to hold to what is true and discard what is false . . . The true and the good are at least as likely to be found in the present, as in the past."
22 William Winans, *Funeral Sermons of Rev. Randal Gibson and Mrs. Harriet Gibson* (1838), pp. 13–14, 20, Houghton Library, Harvard.
23 J. M. Gibson, *Memoirs of J. M. Gibson: Terrors of the Civil War and Reconstruction Days*, ed. James Gibson Alverson and James Gibson Alverson Jr. (n.p., 1929, 1966), p. 6; see also Christopher Morris, *Becoming Southern: The Evolution of a Way of Life, Warren County and Vicksburg, Mississippi, 1770–1860* (New York: Oxford University Press, 1995), p. 95; McBride, *Gibson of Louisiana*, pp. 10–12.
24 Hart Gibson to Tobias Gibson, March 26, 1855, ser. 2, folder 3, Gibson and Humphreys Papers.
25 Ibid.
26 Granger, "Col. Hart Gibson."
27 Calliopean Society Papers; McBride, *Gibson of Louisiana*, p. 41; W. P. Bacon, comp., *First, or Septennial Meeting of the Class of Fifty Eight, Yale College* (New Haven, Conn.: Tuttle, Morehouse & Taylor, 1865), p. 89; Randall Lee Gibson to Hart Gibson, April 22, 1854, Gibson and Humphreys Papers; Shaw, *William Preston Johnston*, p. 41; Granger, "Col. Hart Gibson." On Hart Gibson's fashion sense, see Hart Gibson to William Preston Gibson, October 10, 1850, box 29, folder 10, Pettit Collection: "They have some of the strangest fashions I ever heard of at N.Y. Every little fellow that can walk alone wears a standing collar up to his ears & a gold watch with a chain almost to his knees. I of course have to conform in

some degree to the fashion. I should think I would look quite strange in Lex[ington] with a collar about a foot long, nevertheless I wear these here & think nothing about it."

28 Randall Lee Gibson to Hart Gibson, April 22, 1854, Gibson and Humphreys Papers.

29 Ralph Waldo Emerson, "Self-Reliance," in *Self-Reliance and Other Essays* (1841; reprinted Mineola, N.Y.: Dover, 1993), pp. 19, 26; Hart Gibson to Tobias Gibson, March 26, 1855, Gibson and Humphreys Papers.

30 Hart Gibson to Tobias Gibson, March 26, 1855, Gibson and Humphreys Papers.

31 Ibid.; Randall Lee Gibson to Hart Gibson, October 21, 1853, Gibson and Humphreys Papers.

32 Hart Gibson to Tobias Gibson, March 26, 1855, Gibson and Humphreys Papers; Edward E. Atwater, ed., *History of the City of New Haven to the Present Time* (New York: W. W. Munsell & Co., 1887), p. 251; Eric Foner, *Free Soil, Free Labor, Free Men: The Ideology of the Republican Party Before the Civil War* (1970; reprint, New York: Oxford University Press, 1995), p. 281; Theodore Parker, *The Nebraska Question* (Boston: Benjamin B. Mussey & Co., 1854), pp. 50, 65; Debby Applegate, *The Most Famous Man in America: The Biography of Henry Ward Beecher* (New York: Doubleday, 2006), pp. 226–29; Cassius Marcellus Clay, *The Life of Cassius Marcellus Clay* (Cincinnati: J. Fletcher Brennan & Co., 1886), p. 209.

33 Appendix to *Congressional Globe*, April 20, 1848, 30th Cong., 1st sess., p. 502; Hart Gibson to Tobias Gibson, March 26, 1855, Gibson and Humphreys Papers.

34 Hart Gibson to Tobias Gibson, March 26, 1855, Gibson and Humphreys Papers; "New Publications," *Liberator*, March 6, 1857, p. 38; see also Harvey Wish, *George Fitzhugh: Propagandist of the Old South* (Baton Rouge: Louisiana State University Press, 1943), pp. 200–201; C. Vann Woodward, "George Fitzhugh, Sui Generis," introduction to George Fitzhugh, *Cannibals All! Or, Slaves Without Masters* (1857; Woodward ed., 1960; reprint, Cambridge, Mass.: Harvard University Press, 1988); Eugene Genovese, *The World the Slaveholders Made: Two Essays in Interpretation* (1969; reprint, Hanover, N.H.: University Press of New England, 1988).

35 O'Brien, *Conjectures of Order*; George Fitzhugh to George Frederick Holmes, March 27, 1855, Holmes Letterbook, Special Collections, Duke University; George Fitzhugh, *Sociology for the South* (Richmond, Va.: A. Morris Publisher, 1854), pp. vi, 21, 88, 253–54, 257.

36 Hart Gibson to Tobias Gibson, March 26, 1855, Gibson and Humphreys Papers; Osterweis, *Three Centuries of New Haven*, pp. 280, 317.

37 Thomas A. Kinney, *The Carriage Trade: Making Horse-Drawn Vehicles in America* (Baltimore: Johns Hopkins University Press, 2004), p. 174; "People's Lectures," *New Haven Daily Palladium*, March 15, 1855, p. 2; Hart Gibson to Tobias Gibson, March 26, 1855, Gibson and Humphreys Papers.

38 *New Haven Daily Palladium*, March 22, 1855, p. 2; see also Wish, *George Fitzhugh*, pp. 132–35.

39 *New Haven Daily Palladium*, March 22, 1855, p. 2.

40 Ibid.; Conway, *Autobiography*, pp. 224–25; Fitzhugh to Holmes, March 27, 1855, Holmes Letterbook, Special Collections, Duke University.

41 Hart Gibson to Tobias Gibson, March 26, 1855, Gibson and Humphreys Papers.

42 *New Haven Daily Palladium*, March 23, 1855, p. 2.

43 Ibid.; Wish, *George Fitzhugh*, p. 140; Hart Gibson to Tobias Gibson, March 26, 1855, Gibson and Humphreys Papers; Robert M. Cover, *Justice Accused: Antislavery and the Judicial Process* (New Haven, Conn.: Yale University Press, 1975), pp. 150–54.

44 *New Haven Daily Palladium*, March 23, 1855, p. 2.

45 Hart Gibson to Tobias Gibson, March 26, 1855, Gibson and Humphreys Papers.

46 Wish, *George Fitzhugh*, pp. 140–42; Moncure D. Conway, *Addresses and Reprints, 1850–1907* (Boston: Houghton Mifflin, 1909), p. 113; George Fitzhugh, "Wealth of the North and the South," *DeBow's Review* 23 (1857), pp. 587, 592, 593.

47 Charles Sumner, *Freedom National; Slavery Sectional: Speech of Hon. Charles Sumner, of Massachusetts, on His Motion to Repeal the Fugitive Slave Bill, in the Senate of the United States, August 26, 1852* (Boston: Ticknor, Reed & Fields, 1852), p. 15; Randall Lee Gibson to Hart Gibson, April 22, 1854, Gibson and Humphreys Papers.

CHAPTER FIVE: SPENCER: JORDAN GAP, JOHNSON COUNTY, KENTUCKY, 1855

1 William Elsey Connelley, *Eastern Kentucky Papers: The Founding of Harman's Station* (New York: Torch Press, 1910), pp. 51–52; Fred E. Coy et al., *Rock Art of Kentucky* (Lexington: University Press of Kentucky, 2003), pp. 143–44.
2 Connelley, *Eastern Kentucky Papers*, pp. 51–52.
3 Ibid., pp. 81–86.
4 *Spencer v. Looney* (Va. 1912), No. 2012, Virginia State Law Library, Richmond, trial transcript, pp. 62, 66.
5 Ibid., pp. 65, 116; Tommy Ratliff, interview by author, October 25, 2005, Paintsville, Ky.
6 See 1860 U.S. Census, Johnson County, Ky.; 1870 U.S. Census, Johnson County; 1880 U.S. Census, Johnson County.
7 On cornhusking in eastern Kentucky in the early nineteenth century, see Daniel Drake, *Pioneer Life in Kentucky* (Cincinnati: Robert Clarke & Co., 1870), p. 54.
8 Ratliff interview; Drake, *Pioneer Life*; Donald Edward Davis, *Where There Are Mountains: An Environmental History of the Southern Appalachians* (Athens: University of Georgia Press, 2000), p. 137; John Alexander Williams, *Appalachia: A History* (Chapel Hill: University of North Carolina Press, 2002), pp. 118–19; Nicholas P. Hardeman and Linda M. Steele, *Shucks, Shocks, and Hominy Blocks: Corn as a Way of Life in Pioneer America* (Baton Rouge: Louisiana State University Press, 1981), pp. 174, 212.
9 C. Mitchel Hall, *Johnson County: The Heart of Eastern Kentucky* (self-published, 1928), p. 1:130; Davis, *Mountains*, pp. 137–38; Roger D. Abrahams, *Singing the Master: The Emergence of African American Culture in the Plantation South* (New York: Pantheon, 1992), pp. 77–79.
10 See Abrahams, *Singing the Master*.
11 Fletcher Douglas Srygley, *Seventy Years in Dixie* (Nashville, Tenn.: Gospel Advocate Publishing Co., 1893), p. 152.
12 Deed Book B, August 9, 1854, pp. 435–36, Johnson County Courthouse, Paintsville, Ky.; 1850 U.S. Census, Johnson County, Ky.
13 On women's labor on Appalachian farms, see Wilma A. Dunaway, *Women, Work, and Family in the Antebellum Mountain South* (New York: Cambridge University Press, 2008), pp. 142–43. Dunaway disputes the "myth of male farming." See also *Spencer v. Looney*, trial transcript, p. 64; "Clever," *Dictionary of American Regional English*, ed. Frederic G. Cassidy (Cambridge, Mass.: Harvard University Press, 1985), p. 1:684.
14 1860 U.S. Census, Johnson County, Ky. The Spencers lost two baby boys to scarlet fever almost exactly a year apart, in September 1853 and 1854. Both were named James. Kentucky Death Records, 1852–1953, Ancestry.com.
15 Johnson County Historical Society, *Johnson County, Kentucky: History and Families* (Paducah, Ky.: Turner Publishing Co., 2001), p. 10.
16 *Spencer v. Looney*, trial transcript, p. 123; William Ely, *The Big Sandy Valley* (Catlettsburg, Ky.: Central Methodist, 1887), pp. 76–79.
17 Ely, *Big Sandy Valley*; J. K. Wells, *A Short History of Paintsville and Johnson County* (Paintsville Herald for the Johnson County Historical Society, 1962), p. 14 (map of Paintsville, 1850); 1850 U.S. Census, Johnson County, Ky.; 1860 U.S. Census, Johnson County; 1850 U.S. Census Slave Schedules, Johnson County; 1860 U.S. Census Slave Schedules, Johnson County.
18 Wilma A. Dunaway, *Slavery in the American Mountain South* (New York: Cambridge University Press, 2003), p. 151; J. Winston Coleman, *Slavery Times in Kentucky* (Chapel Hill: University of North Carolina Press, 1940), pp. 206, 208, and n31.
19 Coleman, *Slavery Times*, pp. 196ff and 321–22; see also Harold D. Tallant, *Evil Necessity: Slavery and Political Culture in Antebellum Kentucky* (Lexington: University Press of Kentucky, 2003).
20 Tallant, *Evil Necessity*.
21 H. B. Bascom, *Methodism and Slavery* (Frankfort, Ky.: Hodges, Todd & Pruett, 1845), p. 46; *Congressional Globe*, 33rd Cong., 1st sess. (1854), p. 73; Coleman, *Slavery Times*, pp. 302ff; Tallant, *Evil Necessity*.

22 Quoted in David L. Smiley, *Lion of White Hall: The Life of Cassius M. Clay* (Madison: University of Wisconsin Press, 1962), p. 56.

23 Lowell H. Harrison and James C. Klotter, *A New History of Kentucky* (Lexington: University Press of Kentucky, 1997), p. 176; Coleman, *Slavery Times*, pp. 318–19; Ely, *Big Sandy Valley*, p. 294.

24 See, e.g., Deed Book D, p. 191, Johnson County Courthouse, Paintsville, Ky.

25 Ibid.; *Spencer v. Looney*, trial transcript, pp. 115–16.

26 *Spencer v. Looney*, trial transcript, p. 78; Williams, *Appalachia*, pp. 98–99. See also Deborah Vansau McCauley, *Appalachian Mountain Religion: A History* (Urbana-Champaign: University of Illinois Press, 1995).

27 *Spencer v. Looney*, trial transcript, pp. 60, 121.

28 Ibid., pp. 71, 137; Ariela J. Gross, *What Blood Won't Tell: A History of Race on Trial in America* (Cambridge, Mass.: Harvard University Press, 2008), pp. 111–39; William Harlen Gilbert Jr., "Memorandum Concerning the Characteristics of the Larger Mixed-Blood Racial Islands of the Eastern United States," *Social Forces* 24 (1946), p. 438; Edward T. Price, "The Mixed-Blood Racial Strain of Carmel, Ohio, and Magoffin County, Kentucky," *Ohio Journal of Science* 50 (1950), pp. 281–90; Calvin L. Beale, "An Overview of the Phenomenon of Mixed-Racial Isolates in the United States," in *A Taste of the Country: A Collection of Calvin Beale's Writings*, ed. Peter A. Morrison (University Park: Penn State Press, 1990), pp. 33–41.

29 Lewis Shepherd, "Romantic Account of the Celebrated 'Melungeon' Case," *Watson's Magazine* 17 (1913), pp. 34, 39, quoted in David Henige, "Origin Traditions of American Racial Isolates: A Case of Something Borrowed," *Appalachian Journal* 11 (1984), pp. 201, 202; Gross, *What Blood Won't Tell*; see also N. Brent Kennedy with Robyn Vaughan Kennedy, *The Melungeons: The Resurrection of a Proud People*, rev. ed. (Macon, Ga.: Mercer University Press, 1997); John Shelton Reed, "Mixing in the Mountains," *Southern Cultures* 3 (1997), p. 25; William Byrd, *The Commonplace Book of William Byrd II of Westover*, ed. Kevin Berland et al. (Chapel Hill: University of North Carolina Press, 2001), sec. 173, pp. 139–40; Daniel J. Sharfstein, "Crossing the Color Line: Racial Migration and the One-Drop Rule, 1600–1860," *Minnesota Law Review* 91 (2007), pp. 592, 610, and n72.

30 On the phenomenon of millions of Americans claiming to have "Cherokee grandmothers," see Russell Thornton, *The Cherokees: A Population History* (Lincoln: University of Nebraska Press, 1990), pp. 172–74. Many Americans "without an actual Cherokee grandmother claim one," says Thornton. "There are also explanations for this. Such 'lineage' might be from another, non-Cherokee tribe or it might be totally non-Indian." See also Calvin Beale, "Notes on a Visit to Hancock County, Tennessee," in Beale, *Taste of the Country*, pp. 42–52; 1860 U.S. Census, Johnson County, Ky.

31 James Weir, *Lonz Powers* (Philadelphia: Lippincott, Grambo & Co., 1850), p. 1:242, quoted in Otto A. Rothert, *A History of Muhlenberg County* (Louisville, Ky.: John P. Morton & Co., 1913), p. 171. Although *Lonz Powers* is a novel, its author was a frequent participant in muster-day activities in Muhlenberg County in south-central Kentucky; Rothert describes his fictional account as accurate (p. 170).

32 Daniel Walker Howe, *What Hath God Wrought: The Transformation of America, 1815–1848* (New York: Oxford University Press, 2007), p. 18; "The Hunters of Kentucky, or Half Horse and Half Alligator" (n.d), a song published in Boston and popular in the 1820s; Hall, *Johnson County*, pp. 90, 93–94.

33 Rothert, *History of Muhlenberg County*, pp. 165, 168.

34 *Spencer v. Looney*, trial transcript, p. 139.

35 Ibid., p. 127.

36 Weir, *Lonz Powers*, pp. 243–44, quoted in Rothert, *History of Muhlenberg County*, pp. 172–73.

CHAPTER SIX: WALL: OBERLIN, OHIO, SEPTEMBER 1858

1 Jacob R. Shipherd, comp., *History of the Oberlin-Wellington Rescue* (Boston: John P. Jewett & Co., 1859), quotes from the testimony of Anderson Jennings and closing argument of Rufus Spaulding on pp. 19, 20, 77. See also Nat Brandt, *The Town That Started the Civil War* (New York: Dell, 1990), p. 54.

2 In 1850 Jennings owned seven people: an old man, a baby girl and boy, and two boys and two girls in their teens. Over the course of the decade, six more children were born on Jennings's property, including two mixed-race babies. 1850 U.S. Census, Mason County, Ky.; 1850 U.S. Census Slave Schedule, Mason County; 1860 U.S. Census Slave Schedule, Mason County. See also Shipherd, *Oberlin-Wellington Rescue*, pp. 17, 101. According to the Consumer Price Index, $1,500 in 1858 is the equivalent of approximately $40,000 today. For that calculation as well as ones using other economic indicators, see http://www.measuringworth.com.

3 James Harris Fairchild, *Oberlin: Its Origin, Progress, and Results* (Oberlin, Ohio: R. Butler, 1871), pp. 4–5, 29; James Harris Fairchild, *Oberlin: The Colony and the College, 1833–1883* (Oberlin, Ohio: E. J. Goodrich, 1883), pp. 21–22, 25–27.

4 Fairchild, *Oberlin: Its Origin*, p. 30.

5 See generally Act of September 18, 1850, 9 Stat. 462–65; *Dred Scott v. Sandford*, 60 U.S. (19 How.) 393 (1857).

6 See Brandt, *Town That Started*, pp. 122–23; William E. Bigglestone, *They Stopped at Oberlin: Black Residents and Visitors of the Nineteenth Century* (Oberlin College, 2002), pp. 206–10; Shipherd, *Oberlin-Wellington Rescue*, p. 42.

7 Bigglestone, *Stopped at Oberlin*, p. 207; see also E. J. Hobsbawm and Joan Wallach Scott, "Political Shoemakers," *Past and Present* 89 (1980), pp. 86–114.

8 1850 U.S. Census, Warren County, Ohio; 1850 U.S. Census, Clinton County, Ohio.

9 See Hobsbawm and Scott, "Political Shoemakers."

10 William Cheek and Aimee Lee Cheek, *John Mercer Langston and the Fight for Black Freedom, 1829–1865* (Urbana-Champaign: University of Illinois Press, 1989), pp. 170, 176; *Minutes of the State Convention, of the Colored Citizens of Ohio* (Columbus, Ohio: E. Glover, 1851), pp. 6, 11.

11 Cheek and Cheek, *Langston and the Fight*, pp. 251–54.

12 John Mercer Langston, *From the Virginia Plantation to the National Capitol* (Hartford, Conn.: American Publishing Co., 1894), p. 158; Cheek and Cheek, *Langston and the Fight*, pp. 254, 278.

13 Carol Lasser, "Enacting Emancipation: African American Women Abolitionists at Oberlin College and the Quest for Empowerment, Equality, and Respectability," in *Women's Rights and Transatlantic Antislavery in the Era of Emancipation*, ed. Kathryn Kish Sklar and James Brewer Steward (New Haven, Conn.: Yale University Press, 2007), pp. 319–45; Frank U. Quillin, *The Color Line in Ohio: A History of Race Prejudice in a Typical Northern State* (Ann Arbor: George Wahr, 1913), p. 32; 1850 U.S. Census, Hamilton County, Ohio; Amanda Wall, September 18, 1867, U.S. Freedmen Bank Records, 1865–1874, Ancestry.com.

14 Cheek and Cheek, *Langston and the Fight*, pp. 260, 296; Brandt, *Town That Started*, pp. 45–46.

15 Cheek and Cheek, *Langston and the Fight*, p. 278; Langston, *From Virginia Plantation*, pp. 126–27, 158–59; 1860 U.S. Census, Lorain County, Ohio.

16 Albert J. Von Frank, *The Trials of Anthony Burns: Freedom and Slavery in Emerson's Boston* (Cambridge, Mass.: Harvard University Press, 1998), pp. 302–5; James M. McPherson, *Battle Cry of Freedom: The Civil War Era* (New York: Oxford University Press, 1988), pp. 120–21; Brandt, *Town That Started*, p. 75.

17 Brandt, *Town That Started*, pp. 52, 54; William C. Cochran, *The Western Reserve and the Fugitive Slave Law: A Prelude to the Civil War* (Cleveland, Ohio: Western Reserve Historical Society, 1920), pp. 118–57.

18 Cochran, *Western Reserve*, p. 121; Shipherd, *Oberlin-Wellington Rescue*, p. 242; Brandt, *Town That Started*, pp. 51–52, 113–14.

19 Brandt, *Town That Started*, p. 51; Cheek and Cheek, *Langston and the Fight*, p. 283.

20 Brandt, *Town That Started*, p. 54.

21 Shipherd, *Oberlin-Wellington Rescue*, pp. 16–17; Brandt, *Town That Started*, pp. 6–7.

22 Shipherd, *Oberlin-Wellington Rescue*, pp. 101, 242; Brandt, *Town That Started*, p. 55.

23 Shipherd, *Oberlin-Wellington Rescue*, p. 21.

24 Ibid., pp. 19, 35.

25 On drapetomania, see Samuel Cartwright, "Diseases and Peculiarities of the Negro Race," *DeBow's Review of the Southern and Western States* 1 (1851), pp. 331ff; George Fredrickson, *The Black Image in the White Mind: The Debate on Afro-American Character and Destiny, 1817–1914* (New York: Harper and Row, 1971), p. 57.

26 Shipherd, *Oberlin-Wellington Rescue*, p. 16; Loren Schweninger, "Counting the Costs: Southern Planters and the Problem of Runaway Slaves, 1790–1860," *Business and Economic History* 28 (1999), pp. 267, 272.

27 See, e.g., "The Captured Slaver—Three Hundred and Eighteen Africans On Board," *Daily Ohio Statesman*, September 1, 1858, p. 3; Hobsbawm and Scott, "Political Shoemakers"; 1860 U.S. Census, Lorain County, Ohio.

28 Cheek and Cheek, *Langston and the Fight*, pp. 278, 297.

29 *Minutes of the State Convention, of the Colored Citizens of Ohio*, p. 11; Cheek and Cheek, *Langston and the Fight*.

30 Cochran, *Western Reserve*, p. 123.

31 Brandt, *Town That Started*, p. 50; Cheek and Cheek, *Langston and the Fight*, p. 317.

32 Shipherd, *Oberlin-Wellington Rescue*, p. 35.

33 Ibid., p. 99; Brandt, *Town That Started*, pp. 57–58.

34 Brandt, *Town That Started*, p. 58.

35 Ibid.; Shipherd, *Oberlin-Wellington Rescue*, p. 19.

36 Shipherd, *Oberlin-Wellington Rescue*, p. 22; Brandt, *Town That Started*, p. 65.

37 Brandt, *Town That Started*, pp. 65–66.

38 Shipherd, *Oberlin-Wellington Rescue*, p. 29.

39 Brandt, *Town That Started*, p. 67. The other young man walking with Lyman by the Pittsfield graveyard, Seth Bartholomew, had little interest in helping John Price. Shipherd, *Oberlin-Wellington Rescue*, p. 22.

40 Brandt, *Town That Started*, p. 65.

41 Ibid., p. 79.

42 Richard Winsor, "How John Price Was Rescued," in *The Oberlin Jubilee, 1833–1883*, ed. W. G. Ballantine (Oberlin, Ohio: E. J. Goodrich, 1883), p. 251.

43 Shipherd, *Oberlin-Wellington Rescue*, p. 22.

44 Ibid., p. 20.

45 Ibid., p. 18.

46 Ibid., p. 24.

47 Ibid., pp. 23, 121–22.

48 Ibid., p. 177.

49 Ibid., p. 100.

50 Ibid., p. 102; Cheek and Cheek, *Langston and the Fight*, p. 132.

51 Shipherd, *Oberlin-Wellington Rescue*, p. 24.

52 Ibid., p. 100.

53 Winsor, "How John Price," pp. 251–55.

54 Ibid.; Shipherd, *Oberlin-Wellington Rescue*, p. 18.

55 Langston, *From Virginia Plantation*, p. 185.

CHAPTER SEVEN: CIVIL WAR: WALL, GIBSON, AND SPENCER, 1859–63

1 Jacob R. Shipherd, comp., *History of the Oberlin-Wellington Rescue* (Boston: John P. Jewett & Co., 1859), p. 89; Nat Brandt, *The Town That Started the Civil War* (New York: Dell, 1990),

pp. 160–61. See also William Cheek and Aimee Lee Cheek, *John Mercer Langston and the Fight for Black Freedom, 1829–65* (Urbana-Champaign: University of Illinois, 1989), pp. 329–35.

2 "The Politics of the Jury," *Daily Cleveland Herald,* April 19, 1859; Brandt, *Town That Started,* pp. 140–41.

3 Shipherd, *Oberlin-Wellington Rescue,* pp. 113, 175. After the Civil War, misnomer provided frequent grounds for dismissing charges against newly freed slaves in the South. See Christopher Waldrep, "Substituting Law for the Lash: Emancipation and Legal Formalism in a Mississippi County Court," *Journal of American History* 82 (1996), pp. 1425, 1445–46.

4 Shipherd, *Oberlin-Wellington Rescue,* p. 42; "The Rescue Cases: Sixth and Seventh Days," *Daily Cleveland Herald,* April 12, 1859.

5 Cheek and Cheek, *Langston and the Fight,* p. 329; Brandt, *Town That Started,* pp. 132–33, 196–99.

6 Brandt, *Town That Started,* pp. 199–200.

7 Ibid., pp. 191–92. A version of the image appeared on the front page of *Frank Leslie's Illustrated Newspaper,* May 7, 1859.

8 Randall Lee Gibson to Tobias Gibson, December 9, 1861, GLC 4501.013, Gibson Archive, Gilder Lehrman; James McPherson, *Battle Cry of Freedom: The Civil War Era* (New York: Oxford University Press, 1988, 2003), p. 393. See also Federal Writers' Project, *Kentucky: A Guide to the Bluegrass State* (New York: Harcourt Brace, 1939), p. 325; Ulysses S. Grant, *Personal Memoirs of U.S. Grant* (New York: Charles L. Webster & Co., 1885), vol. 1, in *Ulysses S. Grant: Memoirs and Selected Letters* (New York: Library of America, 1990), pp. 1:187ff; and Mary Gorton McBride with Ann McLaurin, *Randall Lee Gibson of Louisiana: Confederate General and New South Reformer* (Baton Rouge: Louisiana State University Press, 2007), p. 73.

9 Randall Lee Gibson to Tobias Gibson, December 9, 1861, Gibson Archive, Gilder Lehrman. Among those traveling with Gibson were Gen. Benjamin Franklin Cheatham, a Nashville planter; Col. James Camp Tappan, an Arkansas lawyer and Yale graduate; and Capt. George Norton, a New Orleans cotton merchant.

10 R. L. Gibson, "Our Federal Union," *DeBow's Review* 29 (July 1860), pp. 31–42; see also McBride, *Gibson of Louisiana,* p. 61.

11 See Mary G. McBride and Ann M. McLaurin, "Sarah G. Humphreys: Antebellum Belle to Equal Rights Activist, 1830–1907," *Filson Club History Quarterly* 65 (1991), pp. 231, 238; McBride, *Gibson of Louisiana,* pp. 52–60, 66.

12 McBride, *Gibson of Louisiana,* pp. 68, 91.

13 *New Orleans Picayune,* August 2, 9, September 6, 1903, quoted in John McGrath, "In a Louisiana Regiment," *Southern Historical Society Papers* 31 (1903), p. 103; McBride, *Gibson of Louisiana,* pp. 68–72; Randall Lee Gibson to Tobias Gibson, December 2, 1861, GLC 4501.012, Gibson Archive, Gilder Lehrman; Randall Lee Gibson to Tobias Gibson, December 19, 1861, GLC 4501.014, Gibson Archive, Gilder Lehrman.

14 Randall Lee Gibson to Tobias Gibson, December 9, 1861, Gibson Archive, Gilder Lehrman; Grant, *Personal Memoirs,* pp. 185, 187; McBride, *Gibson of Louisiana,* p. 73; William S. McFeely, *Grant: A Biography* (New York: W. W. Norton, 2002), pp. 62–63.

15 Randall Lee Gibson to Tobias Gibson, December 9, 1861, Gibson Archive, Gilder Lehrman; McBride, *Gibson of Louisiana,* p. 72; Grant, *Personal Memoirs,* pp. 177–86.

16 Randall Lee Gibson to Tobias Gibson, December 9, 1861, Gibson Archive, Gilder Lehrman.

17 Ibid.

18 Ibid.

19 George Washington Noble, *Behold He Cometh in the Clouds* (Hazel Green, Ky.: Spencer Cooper, 1912), p. 11; Robert Perry, *Jack May's War: Colonel Andrew Jackson May and the Civil War in Eastern Kentucky, Eastern Tennessee, and Southwest Virginia* (Johnson City, Tenn.: Overmountain Press, 1998), pp. 14–15; John David Preston, *The Civil War in the Big Sandy Valley of Kentucky,* 2nd ed. (Baltimore: Gateway Press, 2008), pp. 52–71; James M. Perry, *Touched With Fire: Five Presidents and the Civil War Battle That Made Them* (New York: Public Affairs, 2003), p. 75.

20 On the "family cycle" of life on an Appalachian farm, see James S. Brown, *Beech Creek: A Study of a Kentucky Mountain Neighborhood* (1950; reprint, Berea, Ky.: Berea College Press, 1988), pp. 72–73. On wartime life in Johnson County, see J. K. Wells, *The Gathering of the Trades People: The Early and Pre-History of Paintsville and Johnson County, Kentucky* (Baltimore: Gateway Press, 1992), pp. 92–94; 1870 U.S. Census, Johnson County, Ky.

21 Noble, *Behold He Cometh*, pp. 11–13; Perry, *Jack May's War*, p. 16; and J. K. Wells, *A Short History of Paintsville and Johnson County* (Paintsville Herald for the Johnson County Historical Society, 1962), p. 34. Spencer's service record is summarized in Preston, *Civil War in the Big Sandy Valley*, p. 289. Describing his own family history, Johnson County historian Edward R. Hazelett mentioned *Uncle Tom's Cabin's* conspicuous place next to the Bible. Edward R. Hazelett, interview by author, August 29, 2005, Paintsville, Ky.

22 Perry, *Jack May's War*, pp. 3, 13–14; Preston, *Civil War in Big Sandy Valley*, p. 32.

23 State of Kentucky, *Report of the Adjutant General of the State of Kentucky: Confederate Kentucky Volunteers, War 1861–1865* (Frankfort, Ky.: State Journal Co., 1915), p. 260, Ancestry.com; Perry, *Touched With Fire*, pp. 62, 72–73; Noble, *Behold He Cometh*, p. 12; Dorothy Denneen Volo and James M. Volo, *Daily Life in Civil War America* (Westport, Conn.: Greenwood Press, 1998), p. 167 (drummers served as stretcher bearers); Eileen Southern, *The Music of Black Americans: A History*, 3rd ed. (New York: W. W. Norton, 1997), p. 206 (blacks were musicians in the Confederate army too); State of Kentucky, *Report of the Adjutant General of the State of Kentucky: Union Kentucky Volunteers* (Frankfort, Ky.: John H. Harney, Public Printer, 1866), p. 2:498, Ancestry.com; see also the Centers family history at http://freepages.genealogy.rootsweb.ancestry.com/~jude/webdoc5.htm.

24 H. Marshall to A. Sidney Johnston, January 3, 1862, in *The War of the Rebellion: A Compilation of the Official Records of the Union and Confederate Armies*, ed. George W. Davis et al. (Washington, D.C.: Government Printing Office, 1897), ser. 2, p. 2:1410; James A. Garfield, "My Campaign in Eastern Kentucky," *North American Review* 143 (1886), pp. 525, 527, 529.

25 Preston, *Civil War in the Big Sandy Valley*, pp. 64–70; Perry, *Touched With Fire*, p. 78.

26 Preston, *Civil War in the Big Sandy Valley*, p. 68; Perry, *Touched With Fire*, pp. 94–95.

27 Preston, *Civil War in the Big Sandy Valley*, p. 68; Noble, *Behold He Cometh*, p. 14; Perry, *Jack May's War*, p. 21.

28 Preston, *Civil War in the Big Sandy Valley*, p. 128; Perry, *Jack May's War*, pp. 43–44; Freda Spencer Goble, interview by author, August 29, 2005, Paintsville, Ky.

29 Preston, *Civil War in the Big Sandy Valley*, p. 128; Perry, *Jack May's War*, pp. 43–44.

30 See Basil W. Duke, *History of Morgan's Cavalry* (Cincinnati: Miami Printing and Publishing Co., 1867), pp. 429–45.

31 Ibid., p. 29.

32 Ibid., pp. 396–400.

33 James A. Ramage, *Rebel Raider: The Life of General John Hunt Morgan* (Lexington: University Press of Kentucky, 2005), pp. 162–66; Duke, *Morgan's Cavalry*, pp. 423–24.

34 Duke, *Morgan's Cavalry*, pp. 168–69, 437–38, 456–57; S. B. McGavran, *A Brief History of Harrison County, Ohio* (1894), pp. 52–55, quoted in Susan G. Hall, *Appalachian Ohio and the Civil War, 1862–1863* (Jefferson, N.C.: McFarland & Co., 2000), p. 233.

35 Ramage, *Rebel Raider*, p. 172.

36 Hart Gibson to David Tod, December 10, 1863, in *The War of the Rebellion: A Compilation of the Official Records of the Union and Confederate Armies*, ed. Fred C. Ainsworth and Joseph W. Kirkley (Washington, D.C.: Government Printing Office, 1899), ser. 2, pp. 6:684–85; Duke, *Morgan's Cavalry*, pp. 468–74.

CHAPTER EIGHT: CIVIL WAR: WALL AND GIBSON, 1863–66

1 Susan G. Hall, *Appalachian Ohio and the Civil War, 1862–1863* (Jefferson, N.C.: McFarland & Co., 2000), p. 216.

2 Ibid., pp. 231–39.

3 Daniel J. Sharfstein, "Crossing the Color Line: Racial Migration and the One-Drop Rule," *Minnesota Law Review* 91 (2007), pp. 592, 646–47, and nn648.

4 William Cheek and Aimee Lee Cheek, *John Mercer Langston and the Fight for Black Freedom, 1829–65* (Urbana-Champaign: University of Illinois, 1989), p. 385; Jennifer L. Weber, *Copperheads: The Rise and Fall of Lincoln's Opponents in the North* (New York: Oxford University Press, 2006); Hall, *Appalachian Ohio*, pp. 212–14.

5 *Douglass's Monthly*, August 1863, quoted in Versalle F. Washington, *Eagles on Their Buttons: A Black Infantry Regiment in the Civil War* (Columbia: University of Missouri Press, 1999), p. xi.

6 Luis F. Emilio, *History of the Fifty-Fourth Regiment of the Massachusetts Volunteer Infantry, 1863–1865*, 2nd rev. ed. (Boston: Boston Book Co., 1894), pp. 6–7; John Mercer Langston, *From the Virginia Plantation to the National Capitol* (Hartford, Conn.: American Publishing Co., 1894), p. 206.

7 Cheek and Cheek, *Langston and the Fight*, pp. 393–96.

8 George W. Williams, *A History of the Negro Troops in the War of the Rebellion, 1861–1865* (New York: Harper & Bros., 1888), pp. 133–34.

9 *Cleveland Herald*, July 24, 1863, quoted in Washington, *Eagles on Their Buttons*, p. 13.

10 Wiley Sword, *Embrace an Angry Wind: The Confederacy's Last Hurrah: Spring Hill, Franklin, and Nashville* (New York: HarperCollins, 1992), p. 373.

11 Ibid., p. 381; James McPherson, *Battle Cry of Freedom: The Civil War Era* (New York: Oxford University Press, 1988), p. 815.

12 Mary Gorton McBride with Ann Mathison McLaurin, *Randall Lee Gibson of Louisiana: Confederate General and New South Reformer* (Baton Rouge: Louisiana State University Press, 2007), p. 108; Randall Lee Gibson to McKinley Gibson, September 25, 1864, GLC04501.027, Gibson Archive, Gilder Lehrman.

13 McBride, *Gibson of Louisiana*, pp. 95–96.

14 W. J. Minor et al. to Maj. Gen. Banks, January 14, 186[3], in *Wartime Genesis of Free Labor: The Lower South*, ed. Ira Berlin et al. (New York: Cambridge University Press, 1990), pp. 408, 409.

15 Tobias Gibson to Sarah Gibson Humphreys, August 3, 1864, GLC04501.097, Gibson Archive, Gilder Lehrman; Tobias Gibson to Louly Gibson, April 14, 1864, GLC04501.095, Gibson Archive, Gilder Lehrman.

16 Randall Lee Gibson to Tobias Gibson, October 31, 1862, GLC04501.019, Gibson Archive, Gilder Lehrman; McBride, *Gibson of Louisiana*, pp. 105, 108.

17 Ibid.; McKinley Gibson to Tobias Gibson, December 17, 1864, box 1, folder 2, Gibson Papers, Tulane.

18 McBride, *Gibson of Louisiana*, pp. 109–10.

19 Sword, *Embrace an Angry Wind*, p. 361; "Report of Brig. Gen. Randall L. Gibson," January 11, 1865, in *The War of the Rebellion: A Compilation of the Official Records of the Union and Confederate Armies*, ed. George B. Davis et al. (Washington, D.C.: Government Printing Office, 1894), ser. 1, vol. 45, pt. 1, p. 702.

20 Report of Brig. Gen. James T. Holtzclaw, January 12, 1865, in Davis et al., *War of the Rebellion*, ser. 1, vol. 45, pt. 1, p. 702; Anne J. Bailey, "The USCT in the Confederate Heartland, 1864," in *Black Soldiers in Blue: African American Troops in the Civil War Era*, ed. John David Smith (Chapel Hill: University of North Carolina Press, 2002), pp. 227, 237–39.

21 Sword, *Embrace an Angry Wind*, p. 386.

22 "Official Report of General R. L. Gibson of the Defence and Fall of the Spanish Fort," *Southern Historical Society Papers* 4 (November 1877), pp. 215–23.

23 "Farewell Address of Brigadier-General R. L. Gibson," *Southern Historical Society Papers* 4 (November 1877), pp. 223–24.

24 *Scioto Gazette* (Chillicothe, Ohio), April 18, 1865.

25 S. Willard Saxton Journal, vol. 26, pp. 96–100, Saxton Papers; Eric Foner, *Reconstruction: America's Unfinished Revolution, 1863–1877* (1988; reprint, New York: Perennial Classics, 2002), p. 72.

26 Willie Lee Rose, *Rehearsal for Reconstruction: The Port Royal Experiment* (Athens: University of Georgia Press, 1964), pp. 153–54; O.S.B. Wall to George Whipple, December 11, 1865, American Missionary Association Archives.

27 "Colored Men Engaged in the Profession of Law," *Daily Evening Bulletin* (San Francisco), June 13, 1885; Wall to Whipple, December 11, 1865; Amy Dru Stanley, *From Bondage to Contract: Wage Labor, Marriage, and the Market in the Age of Emancipation* (New York: Cambridge University Press, 1998), pp. 20–21; O.S.B. Wall to J. W. Alvord, January 24, 1866, National Archives, Washington, D.C., Record Group 105, Records of the Bureau of Refugees, Freedmen, and Abandoned Lands, Records of the Commissioner, Education Division, 1865–71, Unregistered Letters Received and Miscellaneous Documents Relating to the Freedmen's Bank (ser. 157), Document A-10521, photocopied from the Freedmen and Southern Society Project, University of Maryland.

28 S. Willard Saxton Journal, November 22, 1865, vol. 27, pp. 6–7, Saxton Papers; Foner, *Reconstruction*, pp. 208–9.

29 Wall to Alvord, January 24, 1866; O.S.B. Wall to Rufus Saxton, August 9, 1865, National Archives, Washington, D.C., Record Group 105, Records of the Bureau of Refugees, Freedmen, and Abandoned Lands, Office of the Assistant Commissioner for South Carolina, Registered Letters Received (ser. 2922), Box W-20, Document A-7330, photocopied from the Freedmen and Southern Society Project, University of Maryland.

30 Amanda Wall to Samuel Hunt, January 5, 1866, American Missionary Association Archives.

31 Wall to Whipple, December 11, 1865; Wall to Alvord, January 24, 1866.

32 Wall to Alvord, January 24, 1866.

33 O.S.B. Wall to J. W. Alvord, February 12, 1866, National Archives, Washington, D.C., Record Group 105, Records of the Bureau of Refugees, Freedmen, and Abandoned Lands, Records of the Commissioner, Education Division, 1865–71, Unregistered Letters Received and Miscellaneous Documents Relating to the Freedmen's Bank (ser. 157), Document A-10521, photocopied from the Freedmen and Southern Society Project, University of Maryland; Wall to Alvord, January 24, 1866.

CHAPTER NINE: GIBSON: MISSISSIPPI, NEW ORLEANS, AND NEW YORK, 1866–68

1 Randall Lee Gibson to Louly Gibson, June 29, 1865, box 15, folder 26, Pettit Collection.

2 Ibid. See also Mary Gorton McBride with Ann M. McLaurin, *Randall Lee Gibson of Louisiana: Confederate General and New South Reformer* (Baton Rouge: Louisiana State University Press, 2007), pp. 115–18; McSwain to Gibson, October 4, 1865, quoted in "From Brazil," *Daily Picayune*, March 8, 1866, p. 3. See also Eugene C. Harter, *The Lost Colony of the Confederacy* (College Station: Texas A&M University Press, 2000), pp. 64–65.

3 William Preston Hart to Letitia Wallace, November 20, 1865, MSS A.H196 58, Halsey Papers; Randall Lee Gibson to Louly Gibson, n.d. [1866], ser. 8, folder 21, Gibson and Humphreys Papers; W. P. Hart to Letitia Wallace, September 24, 1865, MSS A.H196 58, Halsey Papers (describing Randall Gibson's plans to practice law with Sue Grigsby's husband); "Reminiscences of Mrs. Hart Gibson," pp. 18–20, Pettit Collection. Special thanks to Mary Gorton McBride for her help in locating this document. McBride's account of the steamboat trip appears in *Gibson of Louisiana*, pp. 121–22.

4 Randall Lee Gibson to Louly Gibson, n.d. [1866], Gibson and Humphreys Papers; "The Disaster to the 'W. R. Carter,'" *Philadelphia Inquirer*, February 28, 1866, p. 2 (reprinting a letter from Randall Lee Gibson in Pettit Collection).

5 Randall Lee Gibson to Louly Gibson, n.d. [1866], Gibson and Humphreys Papers; "The Disaster"; McBride, *Gibson of Louisiana*, pp. 120–21.

6 Randall Lee Gibson to Louly Gibson, n.d. [1866], Gibson and Humphreys Papers.

7 "The Disaster."

8 Ibid.

9 Ibid.

10 Ibid.

11 Ibid.

12 J. T. Trowbridge, *The South: A Tour of Its Battle-Fields and Ruined Cities* (Hartford, Conn.: L. Stebbins, 1866), pp. 399–400; W. J. Minor et al. to Maj. Gen. Banks, January 14, 186[3], in *Wartime Genesis of Free Labor: The Lower South*, ed. Ira Berlin et al. (New York: Cambridge University Press, 1990), pp. 408, 409; Tobias Gibson to Sarah [Gibson] Humphreys, August 3, 1864, GLC04501.097, Gibson Archive, Gilder Lehrman.

13 Advertisements, *New Orleans Bee*, March 24, 1866, p. 1; Randall Lee Gibson to William Preston Johnston, April 2, 1866, box 13, folder 10, Barrett Collection; McBride, *Gibson of Louisiana*, pp. 122–23.

14 William Preston Johnston to Randall Lee Gibson, March 1, 1867, box 1, folder 3, Gibson Papers, Tulane; Randall Lee Gibson to St. John Liddell, January 20, 1870, box 20, folder 8, Liddell Papers.

15 Randall Lee Gibson to J. S. Preston, May 13, 1867, box 60, folder 464, Weeks Papers; J. M. Steger to Gibson and Austin, January 19, 1871, box 1, folder 4, Gibson Papers, Tulane.

16 Gibson to Johnston, April 2, 1866; "The Uncertainty of Human Life," *Sunday Star (Daily Southern Star)*, February 4, 1866, p. 4; "Testimony by a Louisiana Planter [Tobias Gibson] before the Smith Brady Commission," April 25, 1865, in Berlin, *Wartime Genesis*, pp. 607, 609; Randall Lee Gibson to Louly Gibson, June 29, 1865, Pettit Collection.

17 William Cohen, *At Freedom's Edge: Black Mobility and the Southern White Quest for Racial Control, 1861–1915* (Baton Rouge: Louisiana State University Press, 2001), pp. 30, 32; Ted Tunnell, *Crucible of Reconstruction: War, Radicalism, and Race in Louisiana, 1862–1877* (Baton Rouge: Louisiana State University Press, 1984), pp. 95–96, 101–2; McBride, *Gibson of Louisiana*, p. 124; "The Appalling Calamities," *Daily True Delta*, February 4, 1866, p. 1. Steamboat regulation on a comprehensive national scale predates the Civil War. See Jerry L. Mashaw, "Administration and 'The Democracy': Administrative Law from Jackson to Lincoln, 1829–1861," *Yale Law Journal* 117 (2008), p. 1568.

18 John Fabian Witt, *The Accidental Republic: Crippled Workingmen, Destitute Widows, and the Remaking of American Law* (Cambridge, Mass.: Harvard University Press, 2004), pp. 47–50, 134–35, 142, 146; Gibson to Johnston, April 2, 1866. On Louisiana's civil law tradition, see generally Vernon Valentine Palmer, *The Louisiana Civilian Experience: Critiques of Codification in a Mixed Jurisdiction* (Durham, N.C.: Carolina Academic Press, 2005); Shael Herman, "Under My Wings, Everything Prospers: Reflections Upon Vernon Palmer's *The Louisiana Civilian Experience*," *Tulane Law Review* 80 (2006), p. 1491.

19 Gibson to Johnston, April 2, 1866.

20 Gibson to Preston, May 13, 1867; Gibson to Johnston, April 2, 1866; "A New Accession to the N.O. Bar," *New Orleans Bee*, March 24, 1866, p. 1; "Gen. R. L. Gibson," *Daily Crescent*, March 29, 1866, p. 4.

21 Gibson to Johnston, April 2, 1866; James K. Hogue, *Uncivil War: Five New Orleans Street Battles and the Rise and Fall of Radical Reconstruction* (Baton Rouge: Louisiana State University Press, 2006), pp. 31–44.

22 See testimony of William Carson, Governor James Madison Wells, and John Ackley, *New Orleans Riots*, H. Exec. Doc. 39–68 (January 29, 1867), pp. 156, 166, 273; Gibson to Johnston, April 2, 1866; "Benevolent Association of Gibson's Brigade," *Daily Crescent*, June 2, 1866, p. 1.

23 Charlton T. Lewis to Randall Lee Gibson, April 22, 1867, box 60, folder 464, Weeks Papers.

24 "A New York Crowd," *Independent*, July 9, 1868, p. 4.

25 Ibid.; "The New York Convention: First Day's Proceedings," *Daily National Intelligencer*, July 6, 1868.

26 Ashcan School painter John Sloan, quoted in Ellen Wiley Todd, *The "New Woman" Revised: Painting and Gender Politics on Fourteenth Street* (Berkeley and Los Angeles: University of California Press, 1993), p. 108.

27 "The Democratic Convention," *New York Times*, July 1, 1868, p. 8; "Tammany Hall," *Harper's Weekly*, July 11, 1868, p. 439.

28 Eric Foner, *Reconstruction: America's Unfinished Revolution, 1863–1877* (1988; reprint, New York: Perennial Classics, 2002), pp. 338–40; Ida Husted Harper, *The Life and Work of Susan B. Anthony* (Indianapolis: Hollenbeck Press, 1898), pp. 1:305–6; Gustavus Myers, *The History of Tammany Hall* (New York: Boni & Liveright, 1917), p. 216.

29 "A New York Crowd," *Independent*, July 9, 1868, p. 4; William Preston Johnston to Rosa Duncan Johnston, July 2, 1868, box 14, folder 6, Barrett Collection.

30 Randall Lee Gibson to William Preston Johnston, June 9, 1868, box 14, folder 5, Barrett Collection; Gibson to Johnston, March 10, 1868, box 14, folder 3, Barrett Collection.

31 Gibson to Johnston, March 10, 1868; McBride, *Gibson of Louisiana*, pp. 128–29.

32 "Obituary Notes," *New York Times*, August 19, 1892, p. 4; John Thomas Scharf, *History of Westchester County* (Philadelphia: L. E. Preston & Co., 1886), vol. 1, pt. 2, p. 803; "Address of Mr. [Clifton] Breckinridge, of Arkansas," in *Memorial Addresses on the Life and Character of Randall Lee Gibson* (Washington, D.C.: Government Printing Office, 1894), pp. 102, 104. New York City annexed High Bridge in 1874. It is now part of the Bronx.

33 William Preston Johnston to Rosa Duncan Johnston, July 10, 1868, box 14, folder 6, Barrett Collection. See also "Alex. H. Stephens on States' Rights," *New York Times*, July 13, 1868, p. 4. Gibson continued to subscribe to antebellum theories of states' rights and to believe in the legality of secession. See Gibson to Johnston, June 9, 1868, Barrett Collection. The 1868 Democratic Party Platform appears in Edward McPherson, *The Political History of the United States of America During the Period of Reconstruction* (Washington, D.C.: Philip & Solomons, 1871), p. 367.

34 Francis P. Blair to James O. Broadhead, June 30, 1868, in James D. McCabe Jr., *The Life and Public Services of Horatio Seymour, Together with a Complete and Authentic Life of Francis P. Blair, Jr.* (New York: W. E. Turner, 1868), p. 463; "A New York Crowd," *Independent*, July 9, 1868, p. 4.

35 "A Look at the Convention," *Nation*, July 16, 1868, p. 49; Foner, *Reconstruction*, pp. 340–43.

36 Gibson to Johnston, January 17, 1867, box 13, folder 18, Barrett Collection; Gibson to Johnston, June 9, 1868, Barrett Collection.

37 Quoted in Kinsley Twining, *The Class of 'Fifty-Three in Yale College: A Supplementary History* (New Haven, Conn.: Yale University Press, 1894), p. 32.

38 Ibid.; see also McBride, *Gibson of Louisiana*, pp. 132–33.

39 Rollin G. Osterweis, *Three Centuries of New Haven, 1638–1938* (New Haven, Conn.: Yale University Press, 1953), pp. 329–50, 363.

40 "Yale Commencement," *Boston Daily Journal*, July 24, 1868, p. 4.

41 Ibid.; Twining, *Class of 'Fifty-Three*, p. 33.

42 "Yale Commencement"; Twining, *Class of 'Fifty-Three*, p. 33.

CHAPTER TEN: WALL: WASHINGTON, D.C., JUNE 14, 1871

1 "Shooting of Justice Wall," *New National Era*, June 15, 1871, p. 3.

2 Ibid.

3 Ibid.

4 *Congressional Globe*, 41st Cong., 3d sess. (January 23, 1871), p. 687; William Tindall, "A Sketch of Alexander Robey Shepherd," *Records of the Columbia Historical Society* 14 (1911), pp. 49, 56; John Burroughs, *Wake-Robin* (Boston and New York: Houghton Mifflin, 1871), p. 144. See also Wilhelmus Bogart Bryan, *A History of the National Capital* (New York: Macmillan, 1916), pp. 2:496–506.

5 See *Special Report of the Commissioner of Education on the Improvement of Colored Schools in the District of Columbia* (1871), reprinted as *History of Schools for the Colored Population* (New York: Arno Press, 1969), p. 242.

6 Affairs in the District of Columbia, H. Rep. 42–72 (1872), pp. 89, 90.

7 Henry Latham, *Black and White: A Journal of Three Months' Tour of the United States* (Carlisle, Mass.: Applewood Books, 1867), p. 87; Gath, "Washington: Kasson on Things; The Rough Side of Washington Society," *Chicago Tribune*, November 17, 1873, p. 7.

8 On Reyburn and Glennan, see Daniel Smith Lamb, ed., *Howard University Medical Department: A Historical, Biographical and Statistical Souvenir* (Washington, D.C.: R. Beresford, 1900), pp. 109–10, 114. On the treatment of abdominal wounds at this time, see George A. Otis, *The Medical and Surgical History of the War of the Rebellion* (Washington, D.C.: Government Printing Office, 1876), p. 2:2.

9 "Shooting of Justice Wall," *New National Era*, June 15, 1871, p. 3.

10 Lt. A. F. Higgs to Maj. Gen. J. M. Schofield, February 28, 1867, "Reports of Operations Received, Assistant Commissioner, Virginia, Bureau of Refugees, Freedmen and Abandoned Lands," quoted in James Edmund Stealey III, "The Freedmen's Bureau in West Virginia," *West Virginia History* 39 (1978), pp. 99, 106.

11 O.S.B. Wall to C. H. Howard, April 20, 1867, National Archives, Washington, D.C., Record Group 105, Records of the Bureau of Refugees, Freedmen, and Abandoned Lands, Office of the Assistant Commissioner for the District of Columbia, Letters Received (ser. 456), #1801, Document A-9838, photocopied from the Freedmen and Southern Society Project, University of Maryland.

12 Higgs quoted in Stealey, "Freedmen's Bureau"; Wall to Howard, April 20, 1867.

13 John Mercer Langston, *From the Virginia Plantation to the National Capitol* (Hartford, Conn.: American Publishing Co., 1894), p. 260.

14 John Mercer Langston, *A Speech on Equality Before the Law* (St. Louis, Mo.: Democrat Book and Job Printing House, 1866), p. 9.

15 Leon Litwack, *Been in the Storm So Long: The Aftermath of Slavery* (New York: Vintage, 1979), pp. 297, 316–18, 323; *Evening Critic*, July 20, 1881, p. 2.

16 Rayford W. Logan, *Howard University: The First Hundred Years, 1867–1967* (Washington, D.C.: Howard University, 1968), p. 38; Amanda Wall to Oliver Otis Howard, September 4, 1895, Howard Papers.

17 "On the Road: The Trotters of the District," *Daily Critic*, July 16, 1873, p. 1; "Congregationalist Church, Washington," *Christian Recorder*, July 13, 1867; "Editorial Items," *Christian Recorder*, February 9, 1867; Everett O. Alldredge, *Centennial History of the First Congregational United Church of Christ, Washington, D.C., 1865–1965* (Pikesville, Md.: Port City Press, 1965), pp. 23–26.

18 O.S.B. Wall to C. H. Howard, April 13, 1867, National Archives, Washington, D.C., Record Group 105, Records of the Bureau of Refugees, Freedmen, and Abandoned Lands, Office of the Assistant Commissioner for the District of Columbia, Letters Received (ser. 456), #1629, Document A-9835, photocopied from Freedmen and Southern Society Project, University of Maryland; Amanda Wall to Edward P. Smith, May 31, 1870, American Missionary Association Archives.

19 See Letters Received by Employment Agents, Records Relating to Employment of Freedmen, Records of the Field Offices for the District of Columbia, Bureau of Refugees, Freedmen, and Abandoned Lands, 1865–1870, Roll 18, M 1902, National Archives, Washington, D.C.; F. A. James to O.S.B. Wall, February 4, 1867, Letters Received by Employment Agents, Roll 18, M 1902, National Archives. See generally Amy Dru Stanley, *From Bondage to Contract: Wage Labor, Marriage, and the Market in the Age of Emancipation* (New York: Cambridge University Press, 1998).

20 1870 U.S. Census, Washington, D.C.; Lamb, *Howard Medical Department*.

21 "Washington News: Justice Wall Given Over by his Doctors," *Philadelphia Inquirer*, June 17, 1871, p. 1; 1870 U.S. Census, Washington, D.C.

22 "A Fox-Chase Extraordinary, and Almost a Riot," *Daily National Intelligencer*, September 25, 1869, p. 3.

23 Ibid.

24 Ibid.

25 *Daily Patriot*, September 26, 1872, quoted in Thomas R. Johnson, "Reconstruction Politics in Washington: 'An Experimental Garden for Radical Plants,'" *Records of the Columbia Historical Society* 50 (1980), p. 180.

26 "City News: National Equal Rights League of Colored Men," *Daily National Intelligencer*, January 11, 1867; *U.S. Senate Journal*, 39th Cong., 2nd sess. (January 18, 1867), pp. 112–13; O.S.B. Wall to J. W. Alvord, January 24, 1866, National Archives, Washington, D.C., Record Group 105, Records of the Bureau of Refugees, Freedmen, and Abandoned Lands, Records of the Commissioner, Education Division, 1865–71, Unregistered Letters Received and Miscellaneous Documents Relating to the Freedmen's Bank (ser. 157), Document A-10521, photocopied from Freedmen and Southern Society Project, University of Maryland (discussing a bill that eventually passed over President Johnson's veto); Kate Masur, *An Example for All the Land: Emancipation and the Struggle Over Equality in Washington, D.C.* (Chapel Hill: University of North Carolina Press, 2010), pp. 185–87; Elizabeth Cady Stanton et al., eds., *History of Woman Suffrage* (Rochester, N.Y.: Charles Mann, 1887), p. 3:813 and n; see also Ellen Carol DuBois, *Woman Suffrage and Women's Rights* (New York: New York University Press, 1998), pp. 99–100.

27 Katherine Masur, "Reconstructing the Nation's Capital: The Politics of Race and Citizenship in the District of Columbia, 1862–1878" (Ph.D. diss., University of Michigan, 2001), pp. 207–9, 217. "At least two thirds of the colored men in the District had been slaves only three or four years before," according to Constance McLaughlin Green, in *The Secret City: A History of Race Relations in the Nation's Capital* (Princeton, N.J.: Princeton University Press, 1967), p. 80. On Bowen, see generally William Tindall, "A Sketch of Mayor Sayles J. Bowen," *Records of the Columbia Historical Society* 18 (1915), pp. 25, 28.

28 Affairs in the District of Columbia, H. Rep. 42–72 (1872), p. 473.

29 A. G. Riddle, *Law Students and Lawyers* (Washington, D.C.: W. H. and O. H. Morrison, 1873), pp. 13, 30, 41. Wall had been acquainted with his professor for more than a decade. Riddle, a former Ohio congressman, had served as one of the defense attorneys in the Oberlin-Wellington Rescue trials.

30 "A Disorderly Character," *Daily National Intelligencer*, October 6, 1869, p. 4; "Disorderly," *Daily National Intelligencer*, October 27, 1869, p. 4; "Assault and Battery With Intent to Kill," *Daily National Intelligencer*, October 8, 1869, p. 4; "Police Items," *Daily National Intelligencer*, December 30, 1869, p. 2; "Petit Larceny," *Daily National Intelligencer*, November 2, 1869, p. 4; "Items," *Daily National Intelligencer*, December 24, 1869, p. 2; "Police Items," *Daily National Intelligencer*, December 11, 1869, p. 2; "Police Items," *Daily National Intelligencer*, December 14, 1869, p. 2. On the climate of race relations in the District at this time, see Masur, "Reconstructing," pp. 125–29; see also Masur, *Example for All the Land*, p. 123.

31 *Evening Critic*, July 20, 1881, p. 2; Bryan, *History of National Capital*, p. 558.

32 Green, *Secret City*, p. 94.

33 James H. Whyte, *The Uncivil War: Washington During Reconstruction, 1865–1878* (New York: Twayne, 1958), p. 128.

34 Tindall, "Sketch of Shepherd," pp. 54–55.

35 Ibid., p. 55; Affairs in the District of Columbia, H. Rep. 42–72 (1872), pp. 176, 184.

36 Whyte, *Uncivil War*, pp. 111–12.

37 "District Matters," *New National Era*, June 22, 1871, p. 3. "The colored Justice of the Peace, O.S.B. Wall, is somewhat better to-day, and his surgeons have slight hopes of his final recovery," reported "Jottings About Town," *Critic*, June 20, 1871, p. 3. See also "Capt. O.S.B. Wall," *New National Era*, June 29, 1871, p. 3; "By Telegraph: Domestic News," *Leavenworth Bulletin*, July 1, 1871, p. 1; "Jottings About Town," *Critic*, August 25, 1871, p. 3.

38 Affairs in the District of Columbia, H. Rep. 42–72 (1872), pp. 93–94.

39 Ibid., pp. 460–61, 474.

40 Ibid., pp. 462, 466.
41 Ibid., pp. 460, 461, 474.
42 Ibid., p. 474.
43 See generally Matthew Pinsker, *Lincoln's Sanctuary: Abraham Lincoln and the Soldiers' Home* (New York: Oxford University Press, 2003), pp. 25, 63, 65–66.
44 Affairs in the District of Columbia, H. Rep. 42–72 (1872), p. 474.
45 Ibid., p. 467.

CHAPTER ELEVEN: SPENCER: JORDAN GAP, JOHNSON COUNTY, KENTUCKY, 1870S

1 This account is drawn primarily from John David Preston's deposition testimony that he played poker with Jordan Spencer, in *Spencer v. Looney* (Va. 1912), No. 2012, Virginia State Law Library, Richmond, trial transcript, pp. 115–16; Johnson County historian Edward Hazelett's account of a regular game of poker in the Jordan Gap after the Civil War, Edward Hazelett, interview by author, August 29, 2005, Paintsville, Ky.; and other accounts in court testimony and interviews of Jordan Spencer's habits and personality.
2 *Spencer v. Looney*, trial transcript, pp. 115–16; 1880 U.S. Census, Johnson County, Ky.; Magoffin County Historical Society, *The Conley/Connelley Clan of Eastern Kentucky: The Descendants of Captain Henry Connelly and Related Conley Families* (Saylersville, Ky.: Magoffin County Historical Society, 1984), pp. 326–27.
3 *Spencer v. Looney*, trial transcript, p. 80; Harry K. Schwarzweller et al., *Mountain Families in Transition: A Case Study of Appalachian Migration* (University Park: Penn State University Press, 1971), pp. 26–27; 1880 U.S. Census, Johnson County, Ky.
4 See John David Preston, *The Civil War in the Big Sandy Valley of Kentucky*, 2nd ed. (Baltimore: Gateway Press, 2008), pp. 289–90, 338, 351.
5 Papers in the Case of Samuel McKee Against John D. Young, Ninth Congressional District of Kentucky, H. Misc. Doc. No. 40-13 (1868), pp. 80–81; Preston, *Civil War in Big Sandy Valley*, pp. 243, 246–47; Carolyn Clay Turner and Carolyn Hay Traum, *John C. C. Mayo: Cumberland Capitalist* (Pikeville, Ky.: Pikeville College Press, 1983), pp. 9–10.
6 Preston, *Civil War in Big Sandy Valley*, pp. 232, 239, 288; see also Gordon B. McKinney, *Southern Mountain Republicans, 1865–1900: Politics and the Appalachian Community* (Chapel Hill: University of North Carolina Press, 1978), pp. 52–55; and Edward R. Hazelett's account in Magoffin County Historical Society, *Conley/Connelley Clan*, pp. 326–27.
7 Robert C. Schenck, *Draw: Rules for Playing Poker* (Brooklyn, N.Y., 1880), p. 6.
8 J. K. Wells, *A Short History of Paintsville and Johnson County* (Paintsville Herald for the Johnson County Historical Society, 1962), p. 22. "I went up the Sandy river into Johnson county that day, and laid that night in a house. It was warm—in July. I came to Paintsville, in Johnson county, that day. For the first time I saw a derrick. They were drilling for oil there": George W. Noble, *Behold He Cometh in the Clouds* (Hazel Green, Ky.: Spencer Cooper, 1912), p. 74. See also C. Mitchel Hall, *Johnson County: The Heart of Eastern Kentucky* (self-published, 1928), pp. 357–58, 361.
9 This is the origin of the phrase "passing the buck." *Dictionary of American Regional English*, ed. Frederic G. Cassidy (Cambridge, Mass.: Harvard University Press, 1985), p. 1:407.
10 *Spencer v. Looney*, trial transcript, p. 116.
11 Ibid. "A '*buck* nigger' is a term often vulgarly applied to a negro man . . . During the discussion preceding the Presidential election, in 1860, one argument against the Republican ticket was, 'Should you like to have your sister marry a big *buck nigger?*' ": *Bartlett's Dictionary of Americanisms*, 4th ed. (Boston: Little, Brown, 1877), p. 71.
12 Eric Foner, *Reconstruction: America's Unfinished Revolution, 1863–1877* (1988; reprint, New York: Perennial Classics, 2002), pp. 37–38; Leon Litwack, *Been in the Storm So Long: The Aftermath of Slavery* (New York: Knopf, 1979), pp. 261–67, 274–82, 517; E. Merton Coulter, *The Civil War and Readjustment in Kentucky* (Chapel Hill: University of North Carolina Press, 1926), pp. 360–61.

13 Marion B. Lucas, *A History of Blacks in Kentucky* (Frankfort: Kentucky Historical Society, 1992), pp. 1:292–93; *Bowlin v. Commonwealth*, 65 Ky. 5 (1867). On violence and rigid racial ideology in the post–Civil War South, see generally Litwack, *Been in the Storm*.

14 Lucas, *Blacks in Kentucky*, pp. 187–88; see also George C. Wright, *Racial Violence in Kentucky, 1865–1940: Lynchings, Mob Rule, and "Legal Lynchings"* (Baton Rouge: Louisiana State University Press, 1996); 1865–66 Laws, *Public Statutes of the State of Tennessee Since the Year 1858*, 2nd ed. (1872), ch. 40, sec. 1, p. 177; Ariela J. Gross, *What Blood Won't Tell: A History of Race on Trial in America* (Cambridge, Mass.: Harvard University Press, 2008), p. 116; 1870 U.S. Census, Johnson County, Ky.; 1880 U.S. Census, Johnson County.

15 John W. Keller, *The Game of Draw Poker* (New York: Frederick Stokes & Brother, 1889), p. 56. Keller warns of the player who "loses all patience, becomes enraged at the dire misfortune that so steadily besets him, strives to change affairs by bluffing and playing recklessly otherwise, and finally rushes on headlong to destruction. Cultivate patience if you would succeed at Poker."

16 "He claimed he strayed from Clay County," Horn said: *Spencer v. Looney*, trial transcript, p. 64.

17 Manuel Ray Spencer, who is related to Davis, has compiled extensive information about Davis's criminal record and reputation, based on criminal court records in Clay County, Kentucky, and local newspaper accounts. These materials are on file with the author.

18 See generally Altina L. Waller, *Feud: Hatfields, McCoys, and Social Change in Appalachia, 1860–1900* (Chapel Hill: University of North Carolina Press, 1988); Noble, *Behold He Cometh*.

19 Hambleton Tapp and James C. Klotter, *Kentucky: Decades of Discord, 1865–1900* (Frankfort: Kentucky Historical Society, 1977), p. 400. One cabin was full of "guns and guns—the deadly Winchesters and shotguns of the vendetta—on the wall and standing in the corners": Dwight B. Billings and Kathleen M. Blee, *The Road to Poverty: The Making of Wealth and Hardship in Appalachia* (New York: Cambridge University Press, 2000), pp. 282–85. See also John Ed Pearce, *Days of Darkness: The Feuds of Eastern Kentucky* (Lexington: University Press of Kentucky, 1994), pp. 32–40.

20 Manuel Ray Spencer materials. Letcher Davis was involved in a 1905 shoot-out when "Hades broke loose in Wolfe County": *Interior Journal* (Stanford, Ky.), June 9, 1905, p. 2. Years earlier, Davis brawled in the aftermath of a school trustee election: see *Hazel Green (Ky.) Herald*, June 9, 1886, p. 3.

21 Manuel Ray Spencer materials.

22 *Spencer v. Looney*, trial transcript, p. 70.

23 Ibid., p. 65. "Some things about the relations between the races had been established quickly after emancipation. Schools, poor houses, orphanages, and hospitals, founded to help people who had once been slaves, were usually separated by race at their inception": see Edward L. Ayers, *The Promise of the New South: Life After Reconstruction* (New York: Oxford University Press, 1992), p. 136. "Even the Radical legislatures in which blacks played a prominent role made no concerted effort to force integration on unwilling and resisting whites, especially in the public schools; constitutional or legislative provisions mandating integration were almost impossible to enforce": see Leon F. Litwack, *Trouble in Mind: Black Southerners in the Age of Jim Crow* (New York: Knopf, 1998), pp. 229–30.

24 *Spencer v. Looney*, trial transcript, p. 63.

25 William Roscoe Thomas, *Life Among the Hills and Mountains of Kentucky* (Louisa, Ky.: Big Sandy Valley Historical Society, 1926, 1983), p. 165; Hall, *Johnson County*, pp. 131–32, 135.

26 Wilma A. Dunaway, *Women, Work, and Family in the Antebellum Mountain South* (New York: Cambridge University Press, 2008), p. 204; Jesse Stuart, *Men of the Mountains* (New York: Dutton, 1941), pp. 106–7; James Watt Raine, *The Land of Saddle-Bags* (1924; reprint, Lexington: University Press of Kentucky, 1997), p. 83; Thomas, *Life Among Hills*, pp. 165–66; Hall, *Johnson County*.

27 *Spencer v. Looney*, trial transcript, p. 151.

28 Martha Hodes, *White Women, Black Men: Illicit Sex in the 19th-Century South* (New Haven, Conn.: Yale University Press, 1997), pp. 147, 174; George C. Wright, "By the Book: The

Legal Execution of Kentucky Blacks," in *Under Sentence of Death*, ed. W. Fitzhugh Brundage (Chapel Hill: University of North Carolina Press, 1997), p. 250. Wright notes that while there were 117 documented lynchings, many bodies were buried or burned. He distinguishes these numbers from "legal lynchings," in which death sentences were foregone conclusions for blacks tried for serious crimes, regardless of the strength of the evidence against them (p. 251).

29 Hodes, *White Women, Black Men*, p. 149.

30 1880 U.S. Census, Johnson County, Ky.; *Spencer v. Looney*, trial transcript, p. 151.

31 1880 U.S. Census, Johnson County.

32 Schwarzweller, in *Mountain Families*, describes the power of "family and kin" in the Beech Creek neighborhood of Clay County (pp. 43–44). On hog killing in eastern Kentucky as an annual winter rite, see Lynwood Montell, "Hog-Killing in the Kentucky Hill Country: The Initial Phases," *Kentucky Folklore Record* 18 (1972), pp. 61–67.

CHAPTER TWELVE: GIBSON: WASHINGTON, D.C., 1878

1 Benjamin P. Thomas and Harold M. Hyman, *Stanton: The Life and Times of Lincoln's Secretary of War* (New York: Knopf, 1962), p. 392; Frank A. Flower, *Edwin McMasters Stanton: The Autocrat of Rebellion, Emancipation, and Reconstruction* (Akron, Ohio: Saalfield, 1905), p. 79.

2 Randall Lee Gibson to William Preston Johnston, March 26, 1878, box 17, folder 6, Barrett Collection.

3 "Really a Mad. Wells," *Washington Post*, February 20, 1878, p. 1.

4 Randall Lee Gibson to William Preston Johnston, November 26, 1872, box 15, folder 28, Barrett Collection; Randall Lee Gibson to William Preston Johnston, September 11, 1875, box 16, folder 33, Barrett Collection.

5 Gibson to Johnston, November 26, 1872; Randall Lee Gibson to William Preston Johnston, February 6, 1876, box 17, folder 3, Barrett Collection.

6 Randall Lee Gibson, "Counting the Electoral Vote—Louisiana," January 25, 1877, in *Select Speeches of the Hon. Randall Lee Gibson of Louisiana* (Washington, D.C.: Government Printing Office, 1887), pp. 5, 30; and "Address of Mr. Sherman of Ohio," *Memorial Addresses on the Life and Character of Randall Lee Gibson* (Washington, D.C.: Government Printing Office, 1894), p. 47. One newspaper described Gibson as "the representative of a very large class of the best white people in the Southern States—people who are in perfect sympathy with the best men in the Republican party of the North, and have been kept from joining its ranks only by the Southern policy of the Administration": see "Gov. Hayes and the South," *New York Tribune*, December 27, 1876, p. 1. See also *Congressional Record* 4 (1876), pp. 2715–16, 2771–72.

7 "Address of Mr. Sherman," 47; Michael O'Brien, *Henry Adams and the Southern Question* (Athens: University of Georgia Press, 2005), p. 69; Matthew Arnold, quoted in Mary Gorton McBride with Ann Mathison McLaurin, *Randall Lee Gibson of Louisiana: Confederate General and New South Reformer* (Baton Rouge: Louisiana State University Press, 2007), p. 191; Arnold was describing to William Gladstone a December 1883 dinner at historian George Bancroft's house.

8 Eric Foner, *Reconstruction: America's Unfinished Revolution, 1863–1877* (1988; reprint, New York: Perennial Classics, 2002), pp. 575–80.

9 *Congressional Record* 4 (1875–76), pp. 206, 720; "Nicholls: Senator R. L. Gibson's Speech at Monroe," *Daily Picayune*, November 14, 1887, pp. 2, 3.

10 Ella Lonn, *Reconstruction in Louisiana After 1868* (New York: Putnam, 1918), p. 500 and n3; Presidential Election Investigation, House Misc. Doc. 31, 45th Cong., 3d sess. (1879), pp. 1008–9.

11 Lonn, *Reconstruction in Louisiana*, p. 496; Presidential Election Investigation, p. 1009; McBride, *Gibson of Louisiana*, p. 156; "Nicholls: Senator R. L. Gibson's Speech at Monroe," *Daily Picayune*, November 14, 1887, pp. 2, 3.

12 Gibson, "Counting the Electoral Vote," pp. 30–31.
13 Ibid., p. 30; Presidential Election Investigation, p. 964; Foner, *Reconstruction*, pp. 580–81; David W. Blight, *Race and Reunion: The Civil War in American Memory* (Cambridge, Mass.: Harvard University Press, 2001), pp. 137–38.
14 "Nicholls: Senator R. L. Gibson's Speech at Monroe," *Daily Picayune*, November 14, 1887, p. 2. To be sure, the Stalwart faction of the Republican Party remained committed to a Radical Southern policy. See, e.g., Heather Cox Richardson, *The Death of Reconstruction: Race, Labor, and Politics in the Post–Civil War North, 1865–1901* (Cambridge, Mass.: Harvard University Press, 2001), pp. xv, 154.
15 Randall Lee Gibson to John McGrath, May 25, 1877, box 1, folder 6, Gibson Papers, Tulane.
16 See generally Walter McGehee Lowrey, "The Political Career of James Madison Wells," *Louisiana History Quarterly* 31 (1948), p. 995.
17 *Congressional Record* 7 (1878), p. 1031.
18 "The Louisiana Officials," *New York Times*, February 19, 1878, p. 1.
19 Ibid.; "Instead of being reckless and extremist, as they imagined, . . . we were really men of equal moderation and firmness, devoted to the peace, the prosperity, and the honor of our whole country": see *Congressional Record* 7 (1878), p. 1030.
20 "The Louisiana Officials," *New York Times*, February 19, 1878, p. 1; see also McBride, *Gibson of Louisiana*, pp. 173–74.
21 "Really a Mad. Wells," *Washington Post*, February 20, 1878, p. 1.
22 Ibid.
23 Ibid.
24 Randall Lee Gibson to William Preston Johnston, March 23, 1872, box 15, folder 21, Barrett Collection; Randall Lee Gibson to William Preston Johnston, June 1, 1874, box 16, folder 20, Barrett Collection; Mary Montgomery Gibson to Sarah Gibson Humphreys, February 16, 1877, ser. 5, folder 9, Gibson and Humphreys Papers.
25 Randall Lee Gibson to McKinley Gibson, August 4, 1879, ser. 5, folder 10, Gibson and Humphreys Papers; McBride, *Gibson of Louisiana*, p. 179; Randall Lee Gibson to H. T. Duncan, January 13, 1874, Letterbook 6, p. 71, Weeks Papers; Randolph Hollingsworth, *Lexington: Queen of the Bluegrass* (Charleston, S.C.: Arcadia, 2004), p. 126; Randall Lee Gibson to Sarah Gibson Humphreys, August 20, 1878, ser. 5, folder 9, Gibson and Humphreys Papers; Mary G. McBride and Ann M. McLaurin, "Sarah G. Humphreys: Antebellum Belle to Equal Rights Activist, 1830–1907," *Filson Club History Quarterly* 65 (1991), pp. 231, 241–42.
26 *Congressional Record* 7 (1878), pp. 1030–31.
27 Randall Lee Gibson to William Preston Johnston, November 26, 1872, box 15, folder 28, Barrett Collection; James K. Hogue, *Uncivil War: Five New Orleans Street Battles and the Rise and Fall of Radical Reconstruction* (Baton Rouge: Louisiana State University Press, 2006), pp. 116–43; McBride, *Gibson of Louisiana*, pp. 146–47; Randall Lee Gibson to William Preston Johnston, October 21, 1878, box 18, folder 23, Barrett Collection.
28 Editorial, *Washington Post*, February 20, 1878, p. 2; *Eden v. Legare*, 1 S.C.L. (1 Bay) 171 (S.C. Com. Pleas Gen. Sess. 1791); *Boullemet v. Phillips*, 2 Rob. 365 (La. 1842); *Toye v. McMahon*, 21 La. Ann. 308 (1869). On the legal doctrine of racial defamation, see generally Samuel Brenner, " 'Negro Blood in his Veins': The Development and Disappearance of the Doctrine of Defamation Per Se by Racial Misidentification in the American South," *Santa Clara Law Review* 50 (2010), p. 233.
29 "Louisiana Legislature," *Daily Picayune*, February 20, 1857, p. 7. See also Daniel J. Sharfstein, "Crossing the Color Line: Racial Migration and the One-Drop Rule," *Minnesota Law Review* 91 (2007), pp. 592, 631, 643; *Richmond Enquirer*, January 3, 1854, and December 31, 1853, quoted in Ira Berlin, *Slaves Without Masters: The Free Negro in the Antebellum South* (New York: Random House, 1974), pp. 365–66.
30 Randall Lee Gibson to J.F.H. Claiborne, April 20, 1878, Claiborne Papers.
31 Ibid.; J.F.H. Claiborne to Randall Lee Gibson, May 15, 1878, box 1, folder 6, Gibson

Papers, Tulane; John G. Jones to McKinley Gibson, May 17, 1878, reprinted in William Winans, *Funeral Sermons of Rev. Randal Gibson and Mrs. Harriet Gibson* (Lexington, Ky., n.d.), pp. 40–43. The letter appeared in a later edition of Winans's 1837 funeral sermons that was published for the Gibson family in Lexington, Kentucky.

32 Jones to Gibson, May 17, 1878.

33 *Congressional Record* 7 (1878), p. 1346; McBride, *Gibson of Louisiana*, pp. 173–74.

34 "Madison Wells Retracts," *Daily Picayune*, April 7, 1878, p. 6; Sarah Gibson Humphreys to Hart Gibson, April 22, 1895, Pettit Collection.

35 Randall Lee Gibson to William Preston Johnston, September 14, 1878, box 18, folder 19, Barrett Collection; Randall Lee Gibson to McKinley Gibson, August 4, 1879, ser. 5, folder 10, Gibson and Humphreys Papers.

CHAPTER THIRTEEN: WALL: WASHINGTON, D.C., JANUARY 21, 1880

1 See generally Robert C. Byrd, *The Senate, 1789–1989: Addresses on the History of the United States Senate* (Washington, D.C.: Government Printing Office, 1991), p. 222; Donald A. Ritchie, *Press Gallery: Congress and the Washington Correspondents* (Cambridge, Mass.: Harvard University Press, 1991).

2 *Report and Testimony of the Select Committee of the United States Senate to Investigate the Causes of the Removal of the Negroes from the Southern States to the Northern States*, S. Rep. 46–693 (1880), p. 20; and "The Negro Exodus in Congress," *Indianapolis Daily Sentinel*, December 18, 1879, p. 4. For overviews of the Negro Exodus, see Steven Hahn, *A Nation Under Our Feet: Black Political Struggles in the Rural South from Slavery to the Great Migration* (Cambridge, Mass.: Harvard University Press, 2003), pp. 317–63; Heather Cox Richardson, *The Death of Reconstruction: Race, Labor, and Politics in the Post–Civil War North, 1865–1901* (Cambridge, Mass.: Harvard University Press, 2001), pp. 156–82; and Nell Irvin Painter, *Exodusters: Black Migration to Kansas After Reconstruction* (New York: Knopf, 1976).

3 F. C. Adams, *Our Little Monarchy: Who Runs It, and What It Costs* (Washington, D.C.: F. A. Fills, 1873), p. 6; Eric Foner, *Reconstruction: America's Unfinished Revolution, 1863–1877* (1988; reprint, New York: Perennial Classics, 2002), pp. 461–62, 512; Contract with Robert J. Fleming for the Construction of Hillside Cottage, box 3, folder 22, Langston Papers.

4 Amanda Wall to Edward P. Smith, May 31, 1870, American Missionary Association Archives; Amanda Wall to O. O. Howard, February 11, 1872, Howard Papers.

5 Foner, *Reconstruction*, p. 512; Rayford W. Logan, *Howard University: The First Hundred Years, 1867–1967* (Washington, D.C.: Howard University, 1969), pp. 42, 64; Constance McLaughlin Green, *The Secret City: A History of Race Relations in the Nation's Capital* (Princeton, N.J.: Princeton University Press, 1967), p. 113.

6 Foner, *Reconstruction*, pp. 553–63; *United States v. Cruikshank*, 92 U.S. 542 (1876).

7 Green, *Secret City*; Kate Masur, *An Example for All the Land: Emancipation and the Struggle Over Equality in Washington, D.C.* (Chapel Hill: University of North Carolina Press, 2010), pp. 134–38, 197, 217–21, 256; Thomas R. Johnson, "The City on the Hill: Race Relations in Washington, D.C., 1865–1885" (Ph.D. diss., University of Maryland, 1975), p. 247.

8 Green, *Secret City*, pp. 112, 115; James H. Whyte, *The Uncivil War: Washington During Reconstruction, 1865–1878* (New York: Twayne, 1958), pp. 233–34; Masur, *Example for All the Land*, pp. 250–51.

9 "The Case of Dr. C. B. Purvis and Prof. J. M. Langston vs. Messrs. Harvey and Holden," *Daily Critic*, September 29, 1874, p. 4. See also Green, *Secret City*, pp. 119–23.

10 "The District Commissionership," *Daily Critic*, May 2, 1877, p. 1; "Seeking for Suffrage," *Washington Post*, October 22, 1878, p. 4; "The Mount Pleasant Meeting," *Daily Critic*, April 27, 1877, p. 4; *Congressional Record* 4 (1876), p. 5138; "The Lincoln Monument," *Daily Critic*, March 21, 1876, p. 4.

11 "A Justice of the Peace and an Attorney," *Daily Critic*, October 30, 1873, p. 4; *Wall v. Murtagh*, Law #12,492 (1874), Record Group 21, Records of the District Courts of the United States, District of Columbia, Law Case Files, National Archives, Washington, D.C. See also "Absent but Not Forgotten," *Daily Critic*, April 21, 1874, p. 4; "O.S.B. Wall Speaks," *Daily Critic*, June 16, 1877, p. 1; "Those Colored Justices," letter to the editor, *Washington Post*, June 17, 1878, p. 2; "Jottings About Town," *Daily Critic*, May 2, 1874, p. 4.

12 *Report on the Management of the Freedmen's Hospital*, S. Rep. 45-209 (1878), pp. 162, 168.

13 Ibid., p. 288.

14 Ibid., pp. 191, 239, 241, 288.

15 Ibid., p. 239.

16 Ibid., pp. 219–20, 225; "The Cincinnati Convention: Electing District Delegates," *Daily Critic*, March 27, 1876, p. 4.

17 "Those Colored Justices," *Washington Post*, June 17, 1878, p. 2; "Concerning Mr. Wall," letter to the editor, *Washington Post*, June 18, 1878, p. 2; *Report on Freedmen's Hospital*, p. 217.

18 *Congressional Record* 7 (1878), p. 3503; O.S.B. Wall to O. O. Howard, September 13, 1878, Howard Papers; Richard T. Greener to John E. Bruce, September 16, 1885, box 2, item 390, Bruce Papers; O.S.B. Wall to John Mercer Langston, September 16, 1879: Langston, "The Exodus," in *Freedom and Citizenship: Selected Lectures and Addresses of Hon. John Mercer Langston* (1883; reprint, Miami, Ohio: Mnemosyne, 1969), p. 232.

19 Hahn, *Nation Under Our Feet*, pp. 319–28; *Congressional Record* 8 (1879), p. 483.

20 "Bad for St. Louis," *Daily Constitution*, April 22, 1879, p. 2; Painter, *Exodusters*, pp. 184–201.

21 Wall to Langston, September 16, 1879; "To Aid the Exodus of the Negroes from the South," *New Haven Evening Register*, April 7, 1879, p. 1; *Report of the Select Committee to Investigate*, pp. 3, 35, 77; "Encouraging the Emigrants," *Washington Post*, December 9, 1879, p. 1 (describing Purvis as a speaker at a mass meeting organized by Wall); and "The Negro Exodus Mass-Meeting," *Washington Post*, May 6, 1879, p. 1.

22 John Mercer Langston, "The Exodus," in *Freedom and Citizenship*, pp. 232, 249–50.

23 *Report of the Select Committee to Investigate*, p. 166.

24 Ibid., pp. 32–33, 36, 72–73.

25 *Report of the Select Committee to Investigate*, pp. 33, 90–91, 106–7; Frederick Douglass, "The Negro Exodus from the Gulf States" (September 12, 1879), in *Negro Orators and Their Orations*, ed. Carter G. Woodson (Washington, D.C.: Associated Publishers, 1925), pp. 453, 466; "Exposing the Exodus," *Washington Post*, December 20, 1879, p. 1.

26 "Senator Voorhees: His Views on the Negro Exodus," *Indianapolis Daily Sentinel*, December 23, 1879, p. 4; "City Talk and Chatter," *Washington Post*, March 1, 1880, p. 4.

27 *Report of the Select Committee to Investigate*, pp. 21–22.

28 Ibid., p. 26.

29 Ibid.

30 Ibid.

31 Ibid.

32 Ibid., p. 27.

33 Ibid., p. 28.

34 Ibid.

35 Ibid., pp. 28–29.

36 Ibid., p. 29.

37 Ibid.

38 Ibid.

39 Ibid., pp. 39, 42–43.

40 Ibid., pp. iv, vi–vii.

41 Ibid., pp. 130, 412–13.

42 Ibid., p. 129 (quoting an editorial from the *Argus* dated December 6, 1879); "Sunday's Subscriptions," *Washington Post*, January 3, 1881, p. 4; "Emancipation Day Appropriately Celebrated by the Colored People of the District," *Evening Critic*, April 17, 1882, p. 1; "The Emancipation Celebration," *Evening Critic*, March 25, 1882, p. 3; "The Emancipation

Celebration," *Evening Critic*, April 4, 1882, p. 3; "The Emancipation Celebration," *Evening Critic*, April 6, 1882, p. 3; "Capt. O.S.B. Wall," *Washington Bee*, November 22, 1884, p. 2; "The Color Line Again Drawn in the Public Schools: Colored Children Admitted to White Schools," *Evening Critic*, September 22, 1882, p. 1; and "The Color Line in Schools," *Washington Post*, September 23, 1882, p. 4.

43 "City Talk and Chatter," *Washington Post*, March 1, 1880, p. 4; *Indianapolis Daily Sentinel*, April 22, 1879, p. 4; and "With the President: Some of the Callers at the White House To-day," *Daily Critic*, June 8, 1881, p. 3. See also O.S.B. Wall to Sayles J. Bowen, June 8, 1881, box 4, Bowen Papers.

44 *Report of the Select Committee to Investigate*, p. 30.

45 Ibid., p. 45.

CHAPTER FOURTEEN: GIBSON: WASHINGTON, D.C., NEW ORLEANS, AND HOT SPRINGS, ARKANSAS, 1888–92

1 Ray Hanley and Steven Hanley, *Hot Springs, Arkansas* (Charleston, S.C.: Arcadia, 2000), p. 84.

2 Sarah Gibson Humphreys to Hart Gibson, November 28, 1892, Pettit Collection; see also "The Sick Statesman," *Daily Picayune*, December 1, 1892, p. 3; and Mary Gorton McBride with Ann Mathison McLaurin, *Randall Lee Gibson of Louisiana: Confederate General and New South Reformer* (Baton Rouge: Louisiana State University Press, 2007), pp. 253–55.

3 Randall Lee Gibson to William Preston Johnston, May 8, 1886, Barrett Collection; "Gen. Gibson's Will," *Daily Picayune*, April 5, 1893, p. 3; "Randall Lee Gibson," *Daily Picayune*, December 16, 1892, p. 1.

4 McBride, *Gibson of Louisiana*, pp. 248–49.

5 Gibson to Johnston, May 8, 1886, box 25, folder 10; Gibson to Johnston, February 21, 1886, box 25, folder 4, Barrett Collection; McBride, *Gibson of Louisiana*, p. 208.

6 McBride, *Gibson of Louisiana*, p. 249.

7 Preston Gibson to Randall Lee Gibson, March 15, 1892, box 1, folder 11, Gibson Papers, Tulane.

8 McBride, *Gibson of Louisiana*, pp. 237ff.

9 See, e.g., *Congressional Record* 19 (1888), pp. 7865–66.

10 Ibid., pp. 3574–75.

11 Ibid., p. 8985; *Congressional Record* 20 (1889), p. 921.

12 *Congressional Record* 20 (1889), p. 922.

13 Ibid., pp. 921–22.

14 Stephen Crane, "Seen at Hot Springs," *Macon Telegraph*, March 3, 1895.

15 McBride, *Gibson of Louisiana*, p. 254.

16 Crane, "Seen at Hot Springs."

17 Ibid.

18 See generally Arthur Marvin Shaw, *William Preston Johnston: A Transitional Figure of the Confederacy* (Baton Rouge: Louisiana State University Press, 1943); McBride, *Gibson of Louisiana*, p. 187; Randall Lee Gibson to William Preston Johnston, January 17, 1867, box 13, folder 18, Barrett Collection.

19 McBride, *Gibson of Louisiana*, pp. 194–207.

20 Ibid., pp. 189–90, 196–98; State ex rel. *Board of Administrators of Tulane Education Fund v. Board of Assessors*, 35 La. Ann. 668 (1883); *Administrators of Tulane Education Fund v. Board of Assessors*, 38 La. Ann. 292 (1886).

21 McBride, *Gibson of Louisiana*, p. 196; Mary G. McBride, "Senator Randall Lee Gibson and the Establishment of Tulane University," *Louisiana History* 28 (1987), pp. 245, 259.

22 Randall Lee Gibson to Board of Administrators of the Tulane Education Fund, February 20, 1884, 156–13–17, Legal Papers: Tulane Incorporation, McConnell Papers.

23 McBride, *Gibson of Louisiana*, p. 202.

24 Sarah Gibson Humphreys to Hart Gibson, November 28, 1892, Pettit Collection.

25 Mary G. McBride and Ann M. McLaurin, "Sarah G. Humphreys: Antebellum Belle to Equal Rights Activist, 1830–1907," *Filson Club History Quarterly* 65 (1991), pp. 231, 241.

26 Ibid.

27 Sarah Gibson Humphreys to Joseph A. Humphreys, June 10, 1883, Gibson and Humphreys Papers, quoted ibid.

28 McBride and McLaurin, "Sarah G. Humphreys," p. 248.

29 Sarah Gibson Humphreys to Hart Gibson, December 13, 1892, Pettit Collection; McBride and McLaurin, "Antebellum Belle," p. 254.

30 "Sudden Was Col. Gibson's Death," *Lexington Morning Herald*, January 5, 1904, p. 5; "Noted Horse Breeder Dead," *Philadelphia Inquirer*, January 5, 1904, p. 10.

31 Humphreys to Gibson, November 28, 1892; "Advertisement of Partition Sale," *Daily Picayune*, March 10, 1894, p. 13; "The Courts," *Daily Picayune*, June 2, 1891, p. 6; "College Escapade," *Dallas Morning News*, October 26, 1888, p. 1; "Montgomery Gibson Found," *New Haven (Conn.) Register*, October 26, 1888, p. 1.

32 Humphreys to Gibson, November 28, 1892.

33 "Gen. Gibson's Will," *Daily Picayune*, April 5, 1893, p. 3.

34 Ibid.

35 Ibid. See also McBride, *Gibson of Louisiana*, p. 256.

36 "Senator Gibson's Condition Unchanged," *Wilkes-Barre Times*, December 7, 1892, p. 2; Humphreys to Gibson, December 13, 1892; "Randall Lee Gibson," *Daily Picayune*, December 16, 1892, p. 1.

CHAPTER FIFTEEN: WALL: WASHINGTON, D.C., 1890–91

1 See, e.g., "Life at Washington," *New York Freeman*, March 20, 1886; "Ex-Liberian Minister Smythe," *New York Freeman*, February 13, 1886; "The National Capital," *New York Freeman*, January 30, 1886; "The National Capital," *New York Globe*, September 13, 1884; and "The National Capital," *New York Globe*, October 20, 1883. See also "The National Capital," *New York Freeman*, February 7, 1885; *Washington Bee*, January 31, 1885, p. 3 (Richard Greener and Robert Terrell blackballed from the District's Harvard Club); and Willard B. Gatewood, *Aristocrats of Color: The Black Elite, 1880–1920* (Bloomington: Indiana University Press, 1990), pp. 163–64 passim.

2 "The National Capital," *New York Globe*, January 12, 1884, p. 1; "Colored Men Engaged in the Profession of the Law," *Daily Evening Bulletin* (San Francisco), June 13, 1885, p. 4; Jane Dailey, *Before Jim Crow: The Politics of Race in Post-Emancipation Virginia* (Chapel Hill: University of North Carolina Press, 2000), p. 158; John Mercer Langston, *From the Virginia Plantation to the National Capitol* (Hartford, Conn.: American Publishing Co., 1894), pp. 495–503.

3 See, e.g., "Mr. Fortune in the South," *New York Freeman*, October 3, 1885; "Mr. Douglass' Great Speech," *New York Freeman*, May 2, 1885; and "A White Wife," *St. Louis Globe-Democrat*, January 26, 1884, p. 3.

4 See, e.g., "Mr. Douglass' Great Speech," *New York Freeman*, May 2, 1885.

5 "The National Capital," *New York Globe*, January 12, 1884, p. 1.

6 "The National Capital," *New York Freeman*, February 7, 1885; "The National Capital," *New York Globe*, January 12, 1884, p. 1. The conversation with Susan B. Anthony was likely animated. Among the guests at the party was O.S.B. Wall's sister Sara Fidler, an outspoken opponent of women's suffrage, "claiming that woman was not made for the rough conditions of life, in political or professional efforts and struggles, or hard, severe, straining physical labors, as evidenced in her peculiar mental conformation and endowments, and her delicate, unique, physical organism." John Mercer Langston, "A Representative Woman: Mrs. Sara K. Fidler," *A.M.E. Church Review*, July 1887, pp. 461, 471–72. On Henry Wall's visit, see Anne Wall Thomas, *The Walls of Walltown* (1969; reprint by author, 2007), p. 33; Thomas quotes a letter from Charles N. Dean that is now among the Dean Papers.

7 Amanda A. Wall to O. O. Howard, August 13, 1890, Howard Papers.

8 "A Deserved Compliment," *Washington Critic*, May 16, 1888, p. 1; "Judge Snell Denounces Impudent Questions by Counsel," *Evening Critic*, January 13, 1885, p. 4; "No Hearsay Evidence for Snell," *Evening Critic*, June 28, 1884, p. 1.

9 "Defending His Reputation," *Washington Post*, June 10, 1888, p. 8.

10 "Christmas in Court," *Washington Post*, December 26, 1884, p. 4; "Not Much of an Imbecile," *Washington Post*, September 29, 1885, p. 4; "A Sensational Story Denied," *Washington Critic*, October 17, 1885, p. 4; "An Unfounded Story," *Washington Critic*, December 2, 1885, p. 4; and "Bits of Local News," *Washington Post*, December 3, 1885, p. 4. Wall's letter of recommendation survives in Benjamin Rhodes's personnel file, Record Group 351, Personnel Case Files, National Archives, Washington, D.C.

11 Constance McLaughlin Green, *The Secret City: A History of Race Relations in the Nation's Capital* (Princeton, N.J.: Princeton University Press, 1967), p. 131; Affidavit of A. C. Richards, *In re: Estate of O.S.B. Wall*, No. 4523 (1891), Washingtoniana Collection; "A Disgusting Exhibition," *Evening Critic*, September 2, 1884, p. 1.

12 "A Disgusting Exhibition," *Evening Critic*, September 2, 1884, p. 1.

13 "Mr. Douglass' Great Speech," *New York Freeman*, May 2, 1885, p. 3.

14 Ibid.

15 "A Fatal Street Brawl," *Washington Post*, March 5, 1884, p. 1.

16 "The National Capital," *New York Globe*, March 15, 1884. "On cross-examination Captain Wall admitted doing all that he could to get Langston out of the country, and keeping him there until his father reached home": "Frank Langston's Defense," *Evening Critic*, May 31, 1884, p. 2. See also "National Capital," *New York Globe*, May 10, 1884; "Frank Langston Here," *Evening Critic*, May 5, 1884, p. 1; "Langston Acquitted," *Washington Post*, June 4, 1884, p. 3; "Ex-Minister Langston's Son," *Washington Post*, April 5, 1887, p. 1; "Frank M. Langston at Liberty," *Washington Post*, December 30, 1891, p. 1; O.S.B. Wall to John Mercer Langston, April 12, 1887, box 1, folder 7, Langston Papers.

17 Judge's notes and testimony of William Colbert, *District of Columbia v. Stephen R. Wall*, Crim. Case #17014 (1888), Record Group 21, Records of the District Courts of the United States, District of Columbia, Criminal Case Files, 1863–1946, National Archives, Washington, D.C.

18 Ibid., p. 9; "More Liquor Cases Tried," *Washington Post*, February 9, 1888, p. 3; "More Barroom Licenses," *Washington Post*, November 14, 1888, p. 8; "War on Gambling Dens," *Washington Post*, August 27, 1890, p. 2; and "A Blow at Poker Clubs," *Washington Post*, August 24, 1890, p. 2.

19 "The Trustees Feel Bold," *Washington Post*, December 15, 1886, p. 2; "Teachers for Next Year," *Washington Post*, June 25, 1884, p. 2; "Amateur Actors on the Stage," *Washington Post*, June 4, 1889, p. 4; "Graduates of Martyn College," *Washington Post*, June 5, 1889, p. 7; classified advertisement, *Washington Post*, June 16, 1889, p. 2 ("Miss Bel Irene Wall will appear in Junior Excelsior's Ovation, June 19, at the Metropolitan Church"); Edmund Shaftesbury, *Lessons in the Mechanics of Personal Magnetism* (Washington, D.C.: Martyn College Press, 1888), title page; and classified advertisement, *Washington Post*, March 5, 1889, p. 15.

20 "Unprofessional Conduct," *Washington Critic*, June 22, 1886, p. 4; "A Falling Out," *Washington Critic*, April 8, 1889, p. 1; William S. McFeely, *Frederick Douglass* (1991), p. 365; "Lawyers at Fisticuffs," *Washington Critic*, March 15, 1887, p. 4; and "Two Colored Lawyers Come to Blows," *Washington Post*, March 16, 1887, p. 3.

21 O.S.B. Wall to John Mercer Langston, April 4, 1887, and March 8, 1887, both in box 1, folder 7, Langston Papers.

22 "Stricken With Paralysis," *Washington Post*, April 13, 1890, p. 1.

23 Ibid.; "The Weather," *Washington Post*, April 12, 1890, p. 1; Ronald M. Johnson, "From Romantic Suburb to Racial Enclave: LeDroit Park, Washington, D.C., 1880–1920," *Phylon* 45 (1984), pp. 264, 265.

24 William Tindall, "Homes of the Local Government," *Records of the Columbia Historical Society* 3 (1900), pp. 279, 295. According to Tindall, the courthouse had previously been used as a church where "Daniel Webster attended divine worship when he wasn't worshipping the Constitution or himself."

25 "Stricken with Paralysis," *Washington Post*, April 13, 1890, p. 1.
26 Ibid.
27 Ibid.
28 Amanda A. Wall to O. O. Howard, August 13, 1890, Howard Papers.
29 Ibid.; O. O. Howard to William Windom, August 15, 1890, Correspondence of O. O. Howard, 1833–1912, Roll 22: June 17, 1890–December 8, 1890, pp. 290–91, Howard Papers.
30 A. A. Wall to O. O. Howard, November 7, 1890, Howard Papers; Stephen Wall Personnel File, National Archives, National Personnel Records Center, St. Louis.
31 "Capt. O.S.B. Wall," *Washington Post*, April 28, 1891, p. 7.

CHAPTER SIXTEEN: SPENCER: JORDAN GAP, JOHNSON COUNTY, KENTUCKY, CA. 1900

1 On ghosts in the Appalachian fog, see, e.g., Charles Edwin Price, "The Face in the Fog," in *Haints, Witches, and Boogers: Tales from Upper East Tennessee* (Winston-Salem, N.C.: John F. Blair, 1992), pp. 75–77.
2 C. Mitchel Hall, *Johnson County: Heart of Eastern Kentucky* (self-published, 1928), pp. 381–82; James C. Hower, "Uncertain and Treacherous: The Cannel Coal Industry in Kentucky," *Natural Resources Research* 4 (1995), pp. 310, 318.
3 Harry M. Caudill, *Theirs Be the Power: The Moguls of Eastern Kentucky* (Urbana-Champaign: University of Illinois Press, 1983), pp. 71–72; Carolyn Clay Turner and Carolyn Hay Traum, *John C. C. Mayo: Cumberland Capitalist* (Pikeville, Ky.: Pikeville College Press, 1983), pp. 10–12; Ronald D. Eller, *Miners, Millhands, and Mountaineers: Industrialization of the Appalachian South, 1880–1930* (Knoxville: University of Tennessee Press, 1982), pp. 65–85, 142, and maps 2, 3, 4, 5, 8.
4 Hall, *Johnson County*, p. 135; Edward L. Ayers, *The Promise of a New South: Life After Reconstruction* (New York: Oxford University Press, 1992), pp. 7, 12–13, 22.
5 Ayers, *Promise of New South*; Barbara Young Welke, *Recasting American Liberty: Gender, Race, Law, and the Railroad Revolution, 1865–1920* (New York: Cambridge University Press, 2001), pp. 249–79.
6 See Marion B. Lucas, *A History of Blacks in Kentucky* (Frankfort: Kentucky Historical Society, 1992), pp. 1:295–98, 384n9; Welke, *Recasting American Liberty*, pp. 296–97; Kenneth W. Mack, "Law, Society, Identity, and the Making of the Jim Crow South: Travel and Segregation on Tennessee Railroads, 1875–1905," *Law and Social Inquiry* 24 (1999), pp. 377, 401; Pauli Murray, comp., *States' Laws on Race and Color* (1951; reprint, Athens: University of Georgia Press, 1997), p. 169; *Plessy v. Ferguson*, 163 U.S. 537 (1896); Leon Litwack, *Trouble in Mind: Black Southerners in the Age of Jim Crow* (New York: Knopf, 1998), pp. 233, 246.
7 See Welke, *Recasting American Liberty*, pp. 357–58; Daniel J. Sharfstein, "The Secret History of Race in the United States," *Yale Law Journal* 112 (2003), pp. 1473, 1498–501; *Southern Railway Co. v. Thurman*, 90 S.W. 240, 241 (Ky. 1906).
8 Lowell Ed Spencer, interview by author, August 29, 2005, Paintsville, Ky.
9 Ibid.; Tommy Ratliff, interview by author, October 25, 2005, Paintsville, Ky.; Thomas Whitehead, *Virginia: A Hand-Book* (1893), p. 90.
10 Spencer interview.
11 1900 U.S. Census, Johnson County, Ky.; James S. Brown, *Beech Creek: A Study of a Kentucky Mountain Neighborhood* (1950; reprint, Berea, Ky.: Berea College Press, 1988), pp. 74–75 (describing how elderly couples lived in an Appalachian hollow); Deed Book 11, p. 510, Johnson County Courthouse, Paintsville, Ky.; Deed Book 20, pp. 340–41; Deed Book 23, pp. 628–29; Deed Book 55, pp. 369–71.
12 1900 U.S. Census, Johnson County, Ky.
13 Edward R. Hazelett, interview by author, August 29, 2005, Paintsville, Ky.
14 1900 U.S. Census, Johnson County, Ky.

15 Freda Spencer Goble, interview by author, August 29, 2005, Paintsville, Ky.

16 S. Monzon et al., "Airborne Occupational Allergic Contact Dermatitis from Coal Dust," *Allergy* 62 (2007), p. 1346; Anthony Cavender, *Folk Medicine in Southern Appalachia* (Chapel Hill: University of North Carolina Press, 2003), pp. 71, 98; Henry C. Sheafer, "Hygiene of Coal-Mines," in *A Treatise on Hygiene and Public Health*, ed. Albert H. Buck (New York: W. Wood, 1879), p. 2:229.

17 Miners developed "accidental tattoos" made of coal dust, typically on their shoulders and upper backs, from repeatedly scraping against tunnel walls; see O. Braun Falco et al., *Dermatology*, 2nd ed. (Berlin: Springer-Verlag, 2000), p. 1048. See also Alan Derickson, *Black Lung: Anatomy of a Public Health Disaster* (Ithaca, N.Y.: Cornell University Press, 1998), pp. 1–21.

18 Ayers, *Promise of New South*, p. 119; Eller, *Miners, Millhands*, pp. 128–29, 140.

19 Turner and Traum, *John Mayo*, pp. 16, 20; Hower, "Uncertain and Treacherous," pp. 318–19; Johnson County Deed Book 55, p. 350, Johnson County Courthouse, Paintsville, Ky.

20 Charles E. Martin, *Hollybush: Folk Building and Social Change in an Appalachian Community* (Knoxville: University of Tennessee Press, 1984), a study of a community two counties south of Johnson County, cited in Ayers, *Promise of New South*, p. 118.

21 Ratliff interview; Eller, *Miners, Millhands*, pp. 176–78; Ayers, *Promise of New South*, pp. 121–22; Sheafer, "Hygiene of Coal-Mines," pp. 233–34; E. N. Clopper, "Child Labor in Coal Mines, West Virginia," *Railroad Trainman* 27 (1910), pp. 103, 106; and Keith Dix, *Work Relations in the Coal Industry: The Hand-Loading Era, 1880–1930* (Morgantown: West Virginia University, Institute for Labor Studies, 1977), pp. 4–12.

22 Eller, *Miners, Millhands*, pp. 176–78; Ayers, *Promise of New South*, pp. 121–22; and Dix, *Work Relations*, pp. 8–12.

23 Eller, *Miners, Millhands*, p. 178; see also Mike Yarrow, "Capitalism, Patriarchy and 'Mens Work': The System of Control of Production in Coal Mining," in *The Impact of Institutions in Appalachia*, ed. Jim Lloyd and Anne G. Campbell (Boone, Ky.: Appalachian Consortium Press, 1986), pp. 29, 31–32; Jean Thomas, *Big Sandy* (New York: Henry Holt, 1940), p. 135; Sheafer, "Hygiene of Coal-Mines," p. 232.

24 Eller, *Miners, Millhands*, pp. 161–62; George Korson, *Coal Dust on the Fiddle: Songs and Stories of the Bituminous Industry* (Philadelphia: University of Pennsylvania Press, 1943), p. 31.

25 Van Lear, the mining community at Miller's Creek, was named after Consolidation Coal executive Van Lear Black; see Danny K. Blevins, *Van Lear* (Charleston, S.C.: Arcadia, 2008), p. 19. See also Eller, *Miners, Millhands*, p. 70. Rand Dotson, in *Roanoke, Virginia, 1882–1912: Magic City of the New South* (Knoxville: University of Tennessee Press, 2007), p. 4, notes that the town of Big Lick was near the Roanoke River in Roanoke County, making the name change an obvious one.

26 Eller, in *Miners, Millhands*, pp. 171, 182–98, describes mine personnel policies that created a "judicious mixture" of locals and outsiders, blacks and native whites and foreigners. See also Ronald L. Lewis, *Black Coal Miners in America: Race, Class, and Community Conflict, 1780–1980* (Lexington: University Press of Kentucky, 1987), p. 134.

27 Eller, *Miners, Millhands*, pp. 169–72; Lewis, *Black Coal Miners*, pp. 128, 143, 148; and Blevins, *Van Lear*, p. 87.

28 *Spencer v. Looney* (Va. 1912), No. 2012, Virginia State Law Library, Richmond, trial transcript, pp. 59ff; 1900 U.S. Census, Buchanan County, Va. On the necessity of horseback travel in the mountains, see Ellen Churchill Semple, "The Anglo-Saxons of the Kentucky Mountains: A Study in Anthropogeography," *Geographical Journal* 17 (1901), pp. 588, 590–91.

29 See Turner and Traum, *John Mayo*, p. 17; and Semple, "Anglo-Saxons," pp. 590–91. Jasper Spencer lived in Floyd County, just below Johnson County: 1900 U.S. Census, Floyd County, Ky.

30 See Dwight B. Billings and Kathleen M. Blee, *The Road to Poverty: The Making of Wealth and Hardship in Appalachia* (New York: Cambridge University Press, 2000), pp. 198–99. A Johnson County survey conducted in 1941 found that "small farms and poor land" were cited as frequent reasons for out-migration. Robin M. Williams and Howard W.

Beers, "Attitudes Towards Rural Migration and Family Life in Johnson and Robertson Counties, 1941," *Kentucky Agricultural Experiment Station Bulletin* 452 (June 1943), pp. 35-36. Nevertheless, researchers in the 1940s also found that low mobility rates correlated with high fertility in Johnson County, because of "traditions of fixed residence and of strong family life." Irving A. Spaulding and Howard W. Beers, "Mobility and Fertility Rates of Rural Families in Robertson and Johnson Counties, Kentucky, 1918-1941," *Kentucky Agricultural Experiment Station Bulletin* 451 (June 1943), p. 19.

31 W. G. Schwab, *The Forests of Buchanan County* (Charlottesville, Va., 1918), p. 9; and Alan J. Banks, "Land and Capital in Eastern Kentucky, 1890-1915," *Appalachian Journal* 8 (1980), pp. 8-18, cited in Altina L. Waller, *Feud: Hatfields, McCoys, and Social Change in Appalachia, 1860-1900* (Chapel Hill: University of North Carolina Press, 1988), p. 152.

32 The wave of Hatfield-McCoy violence in the late 1880s came after years of peace between the families and had, in fact, been sparked by the insistence of local merchants and politicians on bringing Hatfields to justice for earlier crimes. Waller, *Feud*, pp. 195, 200-201, 233.

33 John Fox Jr., "To the Breaks of the Sandy," *Scribner's Magazine* 28 (1900), pp. 340-41.

CHAPTER SEVENTEEN: WALL: WASHINGTON, D.C., 1909

1 On the rural character of Brookland, see Merrill Lavine and Sarah Lightner, "Establishment of the Brookland Community, 1887-1920," in *Images of Brookland: The History and Architecture of a Washington Suburb*, ed. George W. McDaniel (Washington, D.C.: George Washington University, 1979), pp. 9, 24-26.

2 Contemporaneous photographs of compositors at the Government Printing Office—the position Wall held for decades—show everyone wearing three-piece suits. See also Stephen R. Wall Personnel File, National Archives, National Personnel Records Center, St. Louis; Lavine and Lightner, "Establishment of Brookland Community," p. 27. Regarding the neighborhood's social status, one early resident said, "For a time we thought we were going to have a nabob neighborhood. We had about 8 families of social prominence. But they discovered their mistake about 1910 and moved elsewhere." Ibid., p. 26.

3 See *Report on Site for Government Printing Office*, S. Rep. 51-2494 (1891), pp. 67, 98.

4 Daniel R. MacGilvray, "Age of Electricity," in *A Short History of GPO* (1986), online at http://www.access.gpo.gov/su_docs/fdlp/history/macgilvray.html#5.

5 Ibid.

6 "City Bulletins: Printers Must Be Neat," *Washington Post*, April 23, 1909, p. 14.

7 Wall Personnel File; "Printers' Two Camps," *Washington Post*, July 17, 1905, p. 2; Public Printer Donnelly in *Richmond Reformer*, November 11, 1911, quoted in MacGilvray, "Age of Electricity"; see also Booker T. Washington, "The Negro and the Labor Unions" (June 1913), in *The Booker T. Washington Papers*, ed. Louis R. Harlan and Raymond W. Smock (Urbana-Champaign: University of Illinois Press, 1982), p. 12:208.

8 See Daniel J. Sharfstein, "The Secret History of Race in the United States," *Yale Law Journal* 112 (2003), pp. 1473, 1486, and nn62-68.

9 Fragment of a letter to the *Washington Post*, n.d., box 23-1, folder 8, Cooper Papers; "What It Means to Be Colored in the Capital of the United States," *Independent*, January 24, 1907, p. 181. The anonymous author was Mary Church Terrell, who reprinted the piece in her 1940 autobiography, *A Colored Woman in a White World* (1940; reprint, New York: Arno Press, 1980). See also "Color Line Drawn," *Washington Post*, February 23, 1908, p. 6; "Heflin Shoots Two," *Washington Post*, March 28, 1908, p. 1.

10 "Dig Deep at Printery," *Washington Post*, February 9, 1908, p. 3. "Very Slow to Strike," *Washington Post*, October 5, 1903, p. 5, describes complaints about black workers dating back to the 1860s. According to Terrell, in *Colored Woman*, "Colored women know all too

well if they make themselves conspicuous or objectionable, either to their fellow clerks or to their superior officers, they are courting disaster and ruin. The few colored women who are assigned to rooms in which white women work are constantly in a state of suspense and apprehension, not knowing the day or the hour when the awful summons of removal or dismissal will come. They know they are there either by mistake or sufferance, and they would as soon think of 'creating a disturbance' as they would plot to dynamite the White House. All they ask is to be let alone and be allowed to do their work in peace" (p. 253). See also Stephen R. Wall to Charles A. Stillings, June 27, 1906, Wall Personnel File. "Having married a little late in life, six years ago," he wrote, "I feel keenly the responsibility of the future welfare of my family, and as my years for active service are limited, I am making every effort to finish paying for my home and then to the education of my children that they may be self supporting in early life, and not be unfortunate as I have been."

11 Wall to Stillings, June 27, 1906; Stillings to Wall, June 28, 1906, Wall Personnel File.

12 "Remains of Mrs. Wall Laid to Rest," *Washington Post*, November 17, 1902, p. 14; "Weather," *Washington Post*, November 13, 1902, p. 1.

13 "Capt. O.S.B. Wall," *Washington Post*, April 28, 1891, p. 7; "Funeral of Captain Wall," *Washington Post*, April 30, 1891, p. 4; Everett O. Alldredge, *The Centennial History of the First Congregational United Church of Christ, Washington, D.C., 1865–1965* (Pikesville, Md.: Port City Press, 1965), pp. 23–24.

14 "Remains of Mrs. Wall Laid to Rest," *Washington Post*, November 17, 1902, p. 14; *Wall v. Oyster*, No. 2203 (1910), record transcript, p. 23, Record Group 21, Records of the Supreme Court of the District of Columbia, National Archives, Washington, D.C. Writes Jenny Carson, "In 1955, after a protracted legal struggle, two porters were promoted to conducting jobs, becoming the first Black men in North America to be hired as sleeping car conductors." See Carson, "Riding the Rails: Black Railroad Workers in Canada and the United States," *Labour/Le Travail* 50 (Fall 2002), online at http://www.historycooperative .org/journals/llt/50/carson.html. I thank Donald Fyson for suggesting this source, as well as the Lovell's Montreal directories, online at http://bibnum2.bnquebec.ca/bna/lovell/. See also 1900 U.S. Census, Washington, D.C., New York, N.Y., Queens County, N.Y.; 1910 U.S. Census, Washington, D.C., New York, N.Y., Queens County, N.Y.

15 Kelly Miller, *As to the Leopard's Spots: An Open Letter to Thomas Dixon, Jr.* (Washington, D.C.: Howard University, 1905), p. 16; "Young Langston Wanted," *Washington Post*, June 26, 1891, p. 1. Langston never ventured over the color line again, although people continued to cluck over another transgression: he became a Democrat. See "Negro Democrats," *Washington Bee*, September 10, 1904, p. 4. See also Heidi Ardizzone, *An Illuminated Life: Belle da Costa Greene's Journey from Prejudice to Privilege* (New York: W. W. Norton, 2007); Lawrence Otis Graham, *The Senator and the Socialite: The True Story of America's First Black Dynasty* (New York: HarperCollins, 2006), p. 182.

16 See, e.g., "Avers Taint in Blood: White Woman Says She Unknowingly Married Negro," *Washington Post*, August 29, 1908, p. 14; "Court Declares Her White," *Washington Post*, August 6, 1907, p. 5; "White, Said Courts," *Washington Post*, July 25, 1907, p. 1; "Old Dominion Stirred," *Washington Post*, February 25, 1907, p. 5; "Miscreants Wreck House: Race Issue Supposed Cause of Outrage in Frederick County: Victim's Son Reinstated in School After Allegation of Negro Blood Had Been Disproved by Physicians," *Washington Post*, May 24, 1906, p. 12; "Woman Ejected from Hotel," *Washington Post*, July 28, 1904, p. 9; "Taint of Negro Blood: Charge Against a Wife Leads to Suit for Damages," *Washington Post*, March 10, 1900, p. 9; "Wife of Negro Blood," *Washington Post*, July 7, 1899, p. 2; "Her Children Expelled: A Washington Woman Protests Against Charge of Having Negro Blood," *Washington Post*, April 15, 1899, p. 1; and "Charged with Miscegenation: An Apparently White Woman Who Insists She Is of Negro Descent," *Washington Post*, December 15, 1898, p. 3. Chase and Wall were both involved in Republican Party politics, albeit in opposing factions, in the 1880s. See, e.g., "Perry Carson's Victory,"

Washington Post, January 11, 1888, p. 1. See also "The White Fever," *Washington Bee*, June 6, 1908, p. 4; and advertisement, *Washington Bee*, July 17, 1909, p. 5. The phenomenon of passively passing for white is depicted simply and powerfully in Caroline Bond Day's short story "The Pink Hat," which appeared in the December 1926 issue of *Opportunity*. See also Adrian Piper, "Passing for White, Passing for Black," *Transition* 58 (2002), p. 4.

17 Caroline Langston's annual reception "signaled the opening of the social season among aristocrats of color in the nation's capital." Willard B. Gatewood, *Aristocrats of Color: The Black Elite, 1880–1920* (Bloomington: Indiana University Press, 1990), p. 336. See also John Mercer Langston, *From the Virginia Plantation to the National Capitol* (Hartford, Conn.: American Publishing Co., 1894), pp. 522–23; Kelly Miller, unpublished autobiography, chap. 21, p. 2, box 71-1, folder 59, Miller Papers.

18 Wall to F. W. Palmer, August 18, 1899, Wall Personnel File; Personal Question Sheet, signed August 22, 1906, Wall Personnel File.

19 For an example of a contemporaneous passing narrative, see James Weldon Johnson, *The Autobiography of an Ex-Colored Man* (New York: Sherman French, 1912). See also 1880 U.S. Census, Essex County, Mass.; *Wall v. Oyster*, trial transcript, p. 21. White marriages met with a certain amount of disapproval in colored Washington, but they were hardly unheard of. In addition to Frederick Douglass, Charles Purvis, the physician who cared for Stephen's father in his final illness and a friend from their Oberlin days, had a white wife but remained a leader of the race. See Gatewood, *Aristocrats of Color*, p. 178.

20 *Wall v. Oyster*, trial transcript, p. 22; 1910 U.S. Census.

21 Inventory of Money of Deceased and List of Debts Due Her, *In the Matter of Amanda A. Wall*, No. 11,202 (1903), Washingtoniana Collection; "Remains of Mrs. Wall Laid to Rest," *Washington Post*, November 17, 1902, p. 14. Amanda Wall's contemporaries took pains to distinguish upbringing and ancestry from material wealth. Gatewood, in *Aristocrats of Color*, pp. 336–37, cites Caroline Wall Langston and others quoted by an English journalist in the *Washington Bee*, December 26, 1914.

22 *Wall v. Easton*, Case No. 23,642 (1902), Record Group 21, Records of the District Courts of the United States, District of Columbia, Equity Case Files, 1863–1938, National Archives, Washington, D.C.; *Douglass v. Wall*, Case No. 17,607 (1896), Record Group 21, Records of the District Courts of the United States, District of Columbia, Equity Case Files, 1863–1938. Amanda Wall eventually settled this case in 1900. See also Complaint, *Wall v. Easton*, No. 23,642, Record Group 21, Records of the District Courts of the United States, District of Columbia, Equity Case Files, 1863–1938: "The consideration named in this deed is $3000; but the complainant avers that there was no consideration actually passed between the grantor and the grantee to said deed; . . . Amanda A. Wall was at that time . . . indebted to certain persons in the District of Columbia, who threatened to bring suit, and . . . she made the conveyance for her own convenience, and in order to obtain time to pay her creditors, which she subsequently did."

23 *Wall v. Easton*; *In the Matter of the Estate of Amanda Wall*, answer of Stephen R. Wall; *Wall v. Elterich*, Case No. 23,789 (1903), Record Group 21, Records of the District Courts of the United States, District of Columbia, Equity Case Files, 1863–1938, National Archives, Washington, D.C.

24 *Wall v. Elterich*, Case No. 27,256 (1907), Record Group 21, Records of the District Courts of the United States, District of Columbia, Equity Case Files, 1863–1938, National Archives, Washington, D.C.; "Mott School Dedicated," *Washington Post*, May 18, 1909, p. 16.

25 "Legal Record: Real Estate Transfers," *Washington Post*, July 3, 1908, p. 13; Wall Personnel File; Stephen R. Wall to Whitefield McKinlay, January 27, 1909, McKinlay Papers. McKinlay was Booker T. Washington's "most trusted ally" in the District. A successful real estate agent, he was appointed customs collector of the Port of Georgetown by Theodore Roosevelt. He lived in Frederick Douglass's old home in Anacostia. See Gatewood, *Aristocrats of Color*, p. 304; "Collector Is Named," *Washington Post*, July 20, 1910, p. 4.

26 The house was large enough that the next owner advertised for four to six male boarders

in *The Washington Post.* Advertisement, *Washington Post*, June 12, 1913, p. 12; "May Bar Young Girl from School," *Washington Herald*, October 10, 1909, pp. 1, 11.

27 "May Bar Young Girl from School," *Washington Herald*, October 10, 1909, p. 1.

28 1910 U.S. Census, Washington, D.C.; "D. H. Oertly Dies; Retired Engineer," *Washington Post*, December 24, 1956, p. B2; "Brookland Brotherhood Title to 'Reds,'" *Washington Post*, July 5, 1911, p. 5; "Growers Get Prizes," *Washington Post*, October 6, 1909, p. 2.

29 "May Bar Young Girl from School," *Washington Herald*, October 10, 1909, p. 11; *Wall v. Oyster*, record transcript, p. 23.

30 "May Bar Young Girl from School," *Washington Herald*, October 10, 1909, p. 1. Terrell, in *Colored Woman*, describes one girl's "bitter disappointment and keen humiliation" after being rejected by a series of elite boarding schools on racial grounds (p. 288). See "Brookland Colored School," *Washington Post*, April 6, 1901, p. 12. "Discuss Road Extension," *Washington Post*, May 5, 1906, notes objections to the proposal on the ground that streetcar service was already poor and that very few blacks rode streetcars through Brookland (p. 9). See also *Index to the Applications to the Manassas Chapter of the United Daughters of the Confederacy in Virginia, July 21, 1896–June 1928*, Ruth E. Lloyd Information Center (RELIC), Prince William Public Library System, Manassas; "Virginia Obituary," *Washington Post*, June 15, 1902, p. 11.

31 "Court Must Draw School Color Line," *New York Times*, June 3, 1910, p. 3. See also Terrell, "Colored Woman," p. 131; "May Bar Young Girl from School," *Washington Herald*, October 10, 1909, p. 1; *Wall v. Oyster*, record transcript, p. 23.

32 "May Bar Young Girl from School," *Washington Herald*, October 10, 1909, p. 1.

33 "Court Must Draw School Color Line," *New York Times*, June 3, 1910, p. 3.

34 The first openly black families moved into Brookland some twenty-five years later and never forgot the hateful reaction of local whites. Poet and Howard University professor Sterling Brown recalled the experience of moving in 1935 to a house one block from where Stephen Wall had lived: "A less friendly white—I believe he was Irish from his pronunciation—for several weeks drove past in his rickety car, yelling 'Naygur, Naygur' at us, louder than the rattling of his jalopy. The word was frequently painted on our steps near the street. Once it was spelled 'NIGER,' though my only connection with that country that I know of is my friendship with our former ambassador there, W. Mercer Cook. But what is a single G among friends?" Sterling A. Brown, "Blacks in Brookland," *Washington Star*, April 18, 1979, online at http://www.bawadc.com/brown.html.

35 "May Bar Young Girl from School," *Washington Herald*, October 10, 1909, p. 1.

36 Ibid.

37 Ibid.

38 Ibid.

39 Board of Education Meeting Minutes, January 28, 1910, D.C. Public School Records.

40 C. B. Purvis to Whitefield McKinlay, October 13, 1909, McKinlay Papers.

41 Ibid.

42 Ibid.

43 Wall Personnel File.

44 Lillie A. Wall to Board of Education of District of Columbia, October 29, 1909, in *Wall v. Oyster*, record transcript, pp. 19–20; John Ridout to Board of Education, December 15, 1909, in *Wall v. Oyster*, record transcript, p. 20; and Board of Education Meeting Minutes, January 28, 1910. Mary Terrell socialized with Amanda and Gertrude Wall, and Robert Terrell participated with O.S.B. Wall in the District's Colored Cadets; see Scrapbooks, Terrell Papers. "Votes Blaine Cannot Poll," *New York Age*, December 12, 1891. When Robert T. Douglass sued Amanda Wall in 1896 over outstanding debts, he was represented by Robert H. Terrell. *Douglass v. Wall*, Case No. 17,607 (1896), Record Group 21, Records of the District Courts of the United States, District of Columbia, Equity Case Files, 1863–1938, National Archives. See also Terrell, *Colored Woman*, pp. 131–32.

45 *Wall v. Oyster*, mandamus petition para. 9; *Wall v. Oyster*, answer of James F. Oyster para. X;

Stanton C. Peelle to Government Printing Office, May 18, 1910, Wall Personnel File. Wall's petition misrepresented his mother's ancestry. Amanda Thomas Wall regarded herself, and was widely known, as a person of color.

46 *Wall v. Oyster,* record transcript, pp. 23-24.

47 Ibid., pp. 21-22. Daniel R. Ernst has memorably described the impeachment proceedings against Judge Wright: "It was said [Wright] never paid his bills, safe in the knowledge that no merchant would risk his enmity. (One banker who tried to collect on Wright's $500 note found himself on jury duty in the judge's court for weeks at a time.) He was known to frequent some of the city's most notorious establishments ... Wright, it was said, participated in a late-night interrogation of a young woman who apparently stole $1,500 from a bedroom bureau when [Justice] Gould brought her to his home while his wife was away." See Daniel R. Ernst, *Lawyers Against Labor: From Individual Rights to Corporate Liberalism* (Urbana-Champaign: University of Illinois, 1995), p. 138.

48 "Affirms His Action," *Washington Herald,* May 27, 1910, p. 2; *Wall v. Oyster,* transcript, p. 7; District of Columbia Board of Education, May 26, 1910, D.C. Public School Records.

49 *Wall v. Oyster,* transcript, p. 3; "Affirms His Action," *Washington Herald,* May 27, 1910, p. 2; "Court Must Draw School Color Line," *New York Times,* June 3, 1910, p. 3.

50 *Wall v. Oyster,* transcript, pp. 9-11.

51 "Old Dominion Stirred," *Washington Post,* February 25, 1907, p. 5; "Ovation from Crowds for B. T. Washington," *New York Times,* March 6, 1905, p. 7; and "The Nigger Acted at the New Theatre," *New York Times,* December 5, 1909, p. C12. See also Frederick Douglass, "The Color Line," *North American Review* 132 (June 1881), pp. 567, 569: "One drop of negro blood, though in the veins of a man of Teutonic whiteness, is enough of which to predicate all offensive and ignoble qualities." The use of the one-drop rule by post-Reconstruction civil rights leaders echoed abolitionist rhetoric that invoked the rule to illustrate the cruelty and arbitrariness of slavery. See Daniel J. Sharfstein, "Crossing the Color Line: Racial Migration and the One-Drop Rule, 1600-1860," *Minnesota Law Review* 91 (2007), pp. 592, 649-54.

52 See Gilbert Thomas Stephenson, *Race Distinctions in American Law* (New York: D. Appleton, 1910), p. 15. In addition to Maryland, Florida, Georgia, Indiana, Kentucky, Mississippi, Missouri, North Carolina, South Carolina, Tennessee, and Texas had one-eighth rules. Tennessee's black codes of 1865-66 defined "persons of color" as anyone "having any African blood in their veins," but an 1870 miscegenation statute prohibited intermarriage with "negroes, mulattoes or persons of mixed blood descended from a negro to the third generation inclusive." Act of 1870, c. 39. See also Sharfstein, "Crossing the Color Line."

53 *Wall v. Oyster,* transcript, pp. 13-14. William Calvin Chase, whose weekly newspaper *The Washington Bee* promised "honey for its friends and stings for its enemies," had only stings for Wall. Comparing him unfavorably with his father and uncle, who "always defended the race to which they were identified," Chase "suggest[ed] to all colored Americans to be satisfied with our own schools, and never attempt to go where they are not wanted. It is no disgrace to associate with colored children or to attend colored schools." "She Is Colored," *Washington Bee,* June 10, 1910, p. 4.

54 *Wall v. Oyster,* record transcript, pp. 16-17.

55 *Wall v. Oyster,* brief for appellant, p. 9. On legal arguments about race, see generally Ariela J. Gross, *What Blood Won't Tell: A History of Race on Trial in America* (Cambridge, Mass.: Harvard University Press, 2008); Sharfstein, "Crossing the Color Line"; Sharfstein, "Secret History of Race."

56 See, e.g., "Negroes Are Barred from White Schools," *Atlanta Constitution,* December 6, 1910, p. 5; "Must Bear the Brand," *Boston Globe,* December 6, 1910, p. 11; "Can't Go to White School," *Chicago Defender,* December 10, 1910, p. 1; "Sixteenth Negro Blood Is Colored," *Grand Forks (N.D.) Daily Herald,* December 6, 1910, p. 1; "Girl With a Sixteenth Negro Blood Barred," *Hartford Courant,* December 6, 1910, p. 1; "Classification of Negro," *Idaho Daily Statesman,* December 6, 1910, p. 1; "Half-Octoroon Is a Negro, Says Court," *Lexington (Ky.) Herald,* December 6, 1910, p. 1; "Little Negro Blood Counts," *Los*

Angeles Times, December 6, 1910, p. 1-4; "Justice Shepard Finds Wall Girl Ranks as Negro," *Washington Bee*, December 10, 1910, p. 1; and "Pupil Is Declared a Negro," *Washington Post*, December 6, 1910, p. 12.

57 Washington City Directories 1917-21, 1923-25, Washingtoniana Collection; 1920 U.S. Census, Washington, D.C. Ethel Ada Gates is listed at Western High School in "1,822 High School Pupils Registered for Summer Study," *Washington Post*, August 24, 1923, p. 15. The Western High School yearbook lists Ethel Ada Gates as a freshman girl: *The Westerner 1924*, pp. 88-89, Charles Sumner School Museum and Archives, Washington, D.C. See also Wall Personnel File. After much difficulty finding a house, Mary Church Terrell lived for many years at 326 T Street in the LaDroit Park subdivision, a property that her father had purchased for her. In her autobiography, Terrell claimed not to know what became of the Walls, except to suggest, falsely, that Isabel had become an actress and died young. Terrell, *Colored Woman*, p. 132.

CHAPTER EIGHTEEN: SPENCER: HOME CREEK, BUCHANAN COUNTY, VIRGINIA, 1912

1 Henry Hinds, *The Geology and Coal Resources of Buchanan County, Virginia* (Charlottesville, Va., 1918), p. 5; W. G. Schwab, *The Forests of Buchanan County* (Charlottesville, Va., 1918), pp. 4-6.

2 "Virginia Stores Destroyed," *Washington Post*, December 22, 1907, p. 6. "Buchanan county is about forty miles from the railroad and as the returns have to be sent to Grundy, the county seat, the result will probably not be known before to-morrow afternoon": see "Third Senatorial District," *Richmond Times*, November 8, 1901, p. 1. See also "Fight With Moonshiners," *Alexandria Gazette and Virginia Advertiser*, May 4, 1904, p. 2; and "Avoided Capture for Many Years," *Richmond Times-Dispatch*, December 1, 1910, p. 5.

3 See, e.g., Ellen Churchill Semple, "The Anglo-Saxons of the Kentucky Mountains: A Study in Anthropogeography," *Geographical Journal* 17 (1901), pp. 588, 621; N. S. Shaler, "The Transplantation of a Race," *Appletons' Popular Science Monthly* 56 (March 1900), pp. 513, 519.

4 "Anchored Post-Office to Trunk of Great Tree," *Richmond Times-Dispatch*, September 6, 1908, p. 9; Helen Ruth Henderson, *A Curriculum Study in a Mountain District* (New York: Teachers College, Columbia University, 1937), pp. 12-13; *Spencer v. Looney* (Va. 1912), No. 2012, Virginia State Law Library, Richmond, trial transcript, pp. 56, 58; 1910 U.S. Census, Buchanan County, Va.; George Looney, World War I Selective Service System Draft Registration Card, World War I Draft Registration Cards, 1917-18, Ancestry .com; *O'Quinn v. Looney*, 74 S.E.2d 157, 157-58 (Va. 1953).

5 Schwab, *Forests of Buchanan County*, pp. 7, 9; George W. Hilton, *American Narrow Gauge Railroads* (Stanford, Calif.: Stanford University Press,1990), pp. 540-41; Ronald D. Eller, *Miners, Millhands, and Mountaineers: Industrialization of the Appalachian South, 1880-1930* (Knoxville: University of Tennessee Press, 1982), pp. 104-5; Brenda S. Baldwin, *Buchanan County* (Charleston, S.C.: Arcadia, 2007), pp. 8, 91.

6 Hinds, *Geology and Coal Resources*, p. 2; *O'Quinn v. Looney*, 74 S.E.2d 157, 157-58 (Va. 1953); "Anchored Post-Office to Trunk of Great Tree," *Richmond Times-Dispatch*, September 6, 1908, p. 9.

7 *Spencer v. Looney*, trial transcript, p. 93; 1910 U.S. Census, Buchanan County, Va.; Semple, "Anglo-Saxons," pp. 594-95.

8 *Spencer v. Looney*, trial transcript, pp. 49, 93-94.

9 1900 U.S. Census, Buchanan County, Va.; 1910 U.S. Census, Buchanan County, Va.; 1920 U.S. Census, Buchanan County, Va.; Jack Spencer, World War I Selective Service System Draft Registration Card, World War I Draft Registration Cards, 1917-18, Ancestry.com; *Spencer v. Looney*, trial transcript, pp. 94-95; *Tester v. Commonwealth*, 160 S.E. 62, 62 (Va. 1931), where Spencer is described as "a member of the officer's party and a witness for the Commonwealth."

10 See, e.g., "The Murder of Bud McCoy," *Baltimore Sun*, November 13, 1890, supp. 2. On the Hatfield-McCoy feud, see Altina L. Waller, *Feud: Hatfields, McCoys, and Social Change in Appalachia, 1860–1900* (Chapel Hill: University of North Carolina Press, 1988).

11 Semple, "Anglo-Saxons," p. 618; "Father and Sons Held for Murder; May Be Lynched," *Richmond Times-Dispatch*, September 24, 1909, p. 1; "News Items," *Virginia Citizen*, February 3, 1905; "Killed in Quarrel," *Washington Post*, September 12, 1903, p. 4; "Charles Convicted of Manslaughter," *Washington Post*, June 7, 1903, p. 6; "Testament Saved His Life," *Atlanta Constitution*, April 29, 1901, p. 3.

12 Henry D. Shapiro, *Appalachia on Our Mind: The Southern Mountains and Mountaineers in the American Consciousness, 1870–1920* (Chapel Hill: University of North Carolina Press, 1978), pp. 102–6, 138–39; J. W. Williamson, *Southern Mountaineers in Silent Films: Plot Synopses of Movies About Moonshining, Feuding, and Other Mountain Topics, 1904–1929* (Jefferson, N.C.: McFarland, 1994); *Spencer v. Looney*, 82 S.E. 745 (Va. 1914), No. 2012, Virginia State Law Library, Richmond, brief of counsel for appellee, pp. 5–9. See also Daniel J. Sharfstein, "The Secret History of Race in the United States," *Yale Law Journal* 112 (2003), pp. 1473, 1474–75.

13 See *Acts and Joint Resolutions (Amending the Constitution) of the General Assembly of the State of Virginia* (1910), ch. 357, p. 581; see also Gilbert Thomas Stephenson, *Race Distinctions in American Law* (New York: D. Appleton, 1910), pp. 12–20; Peter Wallenstein, *Tell the Court I Love My Wife: Race, Marriage, and Law—An American History* (New York: Palgrave Macmillan, 2004), pp. 4, 137–41; and Leon Litwack, *Trouble in Mind: Black Southerners in the Age of Jim Crow* (New York: Knopf, 1998), pp. 217–18, 238–43, 280–83.

14 Semple, "Anglo-Saxons," p. 594.

15 Eric Foner, *Reconstruction: America's Unfinished Revolution, 1863–1877* (1988; reprint, New York: Perennial Classics, 2002), pp. 11–18, 186–88, 300–303; and Shaler, "Transplantation of a Race," p. 519. Shaler's observations were undoubtedly colored by decades of theorizing black racial inferiority. See John S. Haller Jr., *Outcasts from Evolution: Scientific Attitudes of Racial Inferiority, 1859–1900* (Urbana-Champaign: Illinois University Press, 1971), pp. 166–87.

16 W. Fitzhugh Brundage, *Lynching in the New South: Georgia and Virginia, 1880–1930* (Urbana-Champaign: Illinois University Press, 1993), pp. 143, 146, 282; "Four Negroes Lynched," *Columbia State*, February 2, 1893, p. 1.

17 *Spencer v. Looney*, 82 S.E. 745 (Va. 1914), No. 2012, Virginia State Law Library, Richmond, brief of counsel for the plaintiff in error, p. 6; *Spencer v. Looney*, trial transcript, pp. 59, 107–8, 120, 128–29; 1920 U.S. Census, Buchanan County, Va.; Glenn Ratliff, World War I Selective Service System Draft Registration Card, World War I Draft Registration Cards, 1917–18, Ancestry.com.

18 *Spencer v. Looney*, trial transcript, pp. 51–52.

19 Although the 1910 U.S. Census listed George Spencer as literate and Arminda as illiterate, George Spencer signed his World War I draft registration card with an X. The 1920 Census listed both George and Arminda Spencer as illiterate. On the place of schools in rural society during this period, see generally William A. Link, *A Hard Country and a Lonely Place: Schooling, Society, and Reform in Rural Virginia, 1870–1920* (Chapel Hill: University of North Carolina Press, 1986). On Looney's conduct upon returning from Kentucky, see *Spencer v. Looney*, trial transcript, pp. 50–51, 99–100, 103–9.

20 1910 U.S. Census, Buchanan County, Va.; *Spencer v. Looney*, trial transcript, pp. 93–98; Williamson, *Southern Mountaineers*.

21 1900 U.S. Census, Pike County, Ky.; 1910 U.S. Census, Buchanan County, Va.

22 William Annan Daugherty, World War I Selective Service System Draft Registration Card, World War I Draft Registration Cards, 1917–18, Ancestry.com; Elihu Jasper Sutherland, *"Meet Virginia's Baby": A Brief Pictorial History of Dickenson County, Virginia* (Clintwood, Va., 1955), p. 279; and *Report of the Eighteenth Annual Meeting of the Virginia State Bar Association* (1906), p. 49. The "fabled W. A. Daugherty" in the 1940s was "the best and

most experienced criminal lawyer in [Pike County,] Kentucky," according to Harry M. Caudill, *Slender Is the Thread: Tales from a Country Law Office* (Lexington: University Press of Kentucky, 1987), pp. 54, 171. See also "Roland E. Chase," *Washington Post*, September 15, 1948, p. B2; "Official Visitation," *Alexandria Gazette*, November 26, 1906, p. 3; and Victoria L. Osborne, *Dickenson County* (Charleston, S.C.: Arcadia, 2007), p. 122.

23 See, e.g., *Watkins v. King*, 188 F. 524 (4th Cir. 1902); "Busy Term Before Court of Appeals," *Richmond Times*, November 7, 1901, p. 8; "Sues for Vast Estate," *Washington Post*, September 8, 1899, p. 4. In a suit regarding ownership of fifty thousand white oak trees in Dickenson County, Roland Chase represented the defendants: "Big Timber Suit," *Richmond Times*, June 13, 1901, p. 1. See also Baldwin, *Buchanan County*, p. 11.

24 *Spencer v. Looney* (Va. 1914), record, p. 41.

25 *Spencer v. Looney*, trial transcript, pp. 58–59, 91, deposition taken May 4, 1912; R. E. Horsey, "Bird Distribution in Eastern Kentucky," *Auk* 39 (1922), pp. 79–84. Records for weather stations near Paintsville describe a calm and cloudy day with no precipitation. See, e.g., Pikeville, Ky., Precipitation Report, May 1912, available from the National Climatic Data Center, U.S. Department of Commerce.

26 "W.P.A. Graves Registration Part 6," *Highland Echo* 15 (March 1998), online at http://www.rootsweb.ancestry.com/~kyjchs/highlandecho.html; *Spencer v. Looney*, trial transcript, p. 60.

27 Carolyn Clay Turner and Carolyn Hay Traum, *John C. C. Mayo: Cumberland Capitalist* (Pikeville, Ky.: Pikeville College Press, 1983), pp. 75–86; Danny K. Blevins, *Van Lear* (Charleston, S.C.: Arcadia, 2008).

28 *Spencer v. Looney*, trial transcript, p. 59; William Elsey Connelly and E. M. Coulter, *History of Kentucky* (Chicago, 1922), pp. 4:560–61; J. Favill Capron, *American Bank Attorneys*, 2nd ed. (Boston, 1922), p. 149; *Consolidated Coal Co. v. Baldridge*, 179 S.W. 18 (Ky. 1915) (H. S. Howes for Consolidated); *Millers Creek R. Co. v. Blevins*, 167 S.W. 886 (Ky. 1914) (H. S. Howes for the railroad); *Fluehart Collieries Co. v. Elam*, 151 S.W. 34 (Ky. 1912) (Howes and Howes for the coal company).

29 *Spencer v. Looney*, trial transcript, pp. 59, 61, 114.

30 Ibid., pp. 59–60, 66.

31 Ibid., pp. 59–62. See also Ariela J. Gross, *What Blood Won't Tell: A History of Race on Trial in America* (Cambridge, Mass.: Harvard University Press, 2008), pp. 58–72.

32 *Spencer v. Looney*, trial transcript, pp. 61–62, 64.

33 Ibid., p. 63.

34 *Papers in the Case of Samuel McKee Against John D. Young, Ninth Congressional District of Kentucky*, H. Misc. Doc. No. 40–13 (1868), p. 82.

35 *Spencer v. Looney*, trial transcript, pp. 75–76, 78, 82; Sharfstein, "Secret History of Race," p. 1485.

36 *Spencer v. Looney*, trial transcript, pp. 63–64, 74, 89, 91.

37 William Ely, *The Big Sandy Valley* (Catlettsburg, Ky.: Central Methodist, 1887), p. 90; *Spencer v. Looney*, trial transcript, pp. 121, 132, 136, 139; Kentucky State Board of Health, *Official Register, Medical Laws and Court Decisions, 1896–97* (1897), p. x; Laurel Shackelford and Bill Weinberg, eds., *Our Appalachia: An Oral History* (1977; reprint, Lexington: University Press of Kentucky, 1988), pp. 138–39; Turner and Traum, *John Mayo*, p. 11.

38 *Spencer v. Looney*, trial transcript, pp. 126, 131, 141, 145. One witness thought the Spencers were "Black Dutch" (transcript, p. 136), a designation for racially ambiguous groups that was interchangeable with terms such as Melungeon, Ramps, and Brass Ankles. See the discussion of triracial groups in chapter 5; see also Gross, *What Blood Won't Tell*, pp. 132–35.

39 Spencer's testimony appears in *Spencer v. Looney*, trial transcript, pp. 93–98.

40 Ibid., pp. 93, 97.

41 Ibid., pp. 96–97.

42 Ibid., p. 113.

43 Ibid., pp. 149–50.

44 A Baltimore case involved a six-pronged physical examination by a team of Johns Hopkins

doctors, an example of the growing prevalence of expert scientific testimony: see "Girl Held Not White," *Washington Post*, February 28, 1911, p. 9. See also Gross, *What Blood Won't Tell*, pp. 211ff.

45 *Spencer v. Looney*, trial transcript, pp. 149–50.

46 Ibid., pp. 158–59.

47 Ibid.; *Spencer v. Looney*, brief of counsel for appellee, p. 13.

48 The celebrated Hatfield-McCoy feud, for example, had its roots in litigation over timber rights. See Waller, *Feud*, pp. 41–49.

49 *Spencer v. Looney*, brief of counsel for appellee, p. 13. On the "racial integrity" movement in Virginia, see Wallenstein, *Tell the Court I Love My Wife*, pp. 139–41; Paul A. Lombardo, "Miscegenation, Eugenics, and Racism: Historical Footnotes to *Loving v. Virginia*," *U.C. Davis Law Review* 21 (1988), p. 421.

50 *Spencer v. Looney* (Va. 1914), petition, pp. 2–4, 14–31; brief of counsel for appellee, p. 9; trial transcript, p. 33.

51 *Spencer v. Looney*, brief of counsel for appellee, pp. 9, 13–14.

52 *Spencer v. Looney* (Va. 1914).

53 1930 U.S. Census, Buchanan County, Va.; "Melvin Spencer," *Virginia Mountaineer*, May 6, 1982.

54 Hinds, *Geology and Coal Resources*, p. 193; R. L. Humbert, *Industrial Survey: Buchanan County, Virginia* (Blacksburg: Virginia Polytechnic Institute, 1930), p. 36.

CHAPTER NINETEEN: GIBSON: PARIS AND CHICAGO, 1931–33

1 Henry Field, *The Track of Man: Adventures of an Anthropologist* (Garden City, N.Y.: Doubleday, 1955), pp. 199–200; see generally Patricia A. Morton, *Hybrid Modernities: Architecture and Representation at the 1931 Colonial Exposition, Paris* (Cambridge, Mass.: MIT Press, 2000).

2 Morton quotes two French writers describing the Exposition in 1931 in *Hybrid Modernities*, p. 5.

3 Ibid., pp. 43, 45.

4 Field, *Track of Man*, p. 199; Joe Nickell, *Secrets of the Sideshows* (Lexington: University Press of Kentucky, 2005), pp. 189–90.

5 Field, *Track of Man*, p. 199; Morton, *Hybrid Modernities*, pp. 97–129.

6 Field, *Track of Man*, pp. 113–14; Ed Yastrow and Stephen E. Nash, "Henry Field: Collections, and Exhibit Development, 1926–1941," in *Curators, Collections, and Contexts: Anthropology at the Field Museum, 1893–2002*, ed. Stephen E. Nash and Gary M. Feinman (Chicago: Field Museum, 2003), pp. 127–28.

7 Field, *Track of Man*, pp. 199–200.

8 Malvina Hoffman, *Heads and Tales* (New York: Scribner's, 1936), pp. 172, 174.

9 Field, *Track of Man*, pp. 191, 194. See also Hoffman, *Heads and Tales*.

10 Hoffman, *Heads and Tales*, p. 150.

11 Field, *Track of Man*, pp. 132–33.

12 Ibid., p. 134.

13 Ibid., pp. 190–91.

14 Hoffman, *Heads and Tales*, p. 177.

15 Ibid., pp. 182, 332; Pamela Hibbs Decoteau, "Malvina Hoffman and the 'Races of Man,'" *Women's Art Journal* 10 (1989–1990), p. 7; Field, *Track of Man*, p. 198.

16 Field, *Track of Man*, pp. 14–15; "Henry Field Comes from London to Take Up His Abode Here," *Chicago Tribune*, October 8, 1926, p. 35; Philip J. Funigiello, *Florence Lathrop Page: A Biography* (Charlottesville, Va.: University Press of Virginia, 1994), p. 272n44.

17 "Gen. Gibson's Will," *Daily Picayune*, April 5, 1893, p. 3; Mary Gorton McBride with Ann Mathison McLaurin, *Randall Lee Gibson of Louisiana: Confederate General and New South Reformer* (Baton Rouge: Louisiana State University Press, 2007), p. 257.

18 Preston Gibson, "The Human Side of the Late Chief Justice White," *New York Times*, May 22, 1921, sec. 7, p. 2.

19 Leita Montgomery Kent to Hart Gibson, September 19, 1894, Pettit Collection.

20 "Baseball and Negro Minstrels were among his early delights, and the writer remembers him as a slim lad, playing ball all afternoon and being treated to Dockstader's Minstrels . . . in the evening": see "In Town and Country," *Town and Country*, August 17, 1912, p. 17. See also Robert Neville, "He's Lieutenant Preston Gibson of the Marines 'For Life!'" *New York World*, October 12, 1918, which notes, "His Kentucky Negro stories have gained great popularity."

21 Preston Gibson, *The Turning Point: A Play in Three Acts* (New York: Samuel French, 1910), p. 53.

22 "'Castles' 'Half-and-Half Dance Ugly,' Says Preston Gibson, Giving Opinions of the True Stepping Art in the Ballroom," *Washington Post*, February 24, 1914, p. 4.

23 See generally Preston Gibson, *S.O.S. and Five One Act Plays* (New York: Samuel French, 1912).

24 "Gibson Admits He Took from Wilde," *New York Times*, March 1, 1910, p. 7.

25 Karl K. Kitchen, "He Has Achieved a Notable Record in Wedding a Procession of Wealthy and Beautiful Women, Who Subsequently Divorced Him, Yet His Popularity Is Unabated and His Re-engagement Is Rumored—The Story of a Man With the Fatal Gift of Charm," *World Magazine*, July 20, 1924, in Preston Gibson Alumni File, Manuscripts and Archives, Yale University.

26 Preston Gibson, *Battering the Boche* (New York: Century, 1918).

27 Ibid., p. 64.

28 "Preston Gibson, 57, Yale Athlete, Dies," *New York Times*, February 16, 1937.

29 "Wife of Preston Gibson Starts Divorce Action," *Chicago Tribune*, July 4, 1921, p. 10; Kitchen, "He Has Achieved."

30 John Powell, "Preston Gibson, Social Lion, Faces Jail on Fraud Charge," *Chicago Daily Tribune*, February 11, 1928, p. 3; "Free Preston Gibson, Charges Dropped," *New York Times*, February 19, 1928, p. 23; "Fourth Wife Freed From Gibson," *New York Times*, December 20, 1928, p. 17; "Preston Gibson Held in New York on Check Charge," *Chicago Daily Tribune*, January 30, 1929, p. 3.

31 "Preston Gibson, Who Packed Ten Lives Into One, Dies at 57," *Washington Post*, February 16, 1937, p. 1; Kitchen, "He Has Achieved."

32 "Chicago Fair Opened by Farley," *New York Times*, May 28, 1933, p. 1; Field, *Track of Man*, p. 211.

33 See Marianne Beatrice Kinkel, "Circulating Race: Malvina Hoffman and the Field Museum's Races of Mankind Sculptures" (Ph.D. diss., University of Texas at Austin, 2001), pp. 146–59.

34 Berthold Laufer, introduction, *The Races of Mankind: An Introduction to Chauncey Keep Memorial Hall* (Chicago: Field Museum of Natural History, 1933), pp. 5–6; Kinkel, *Circulating Race*.

35 Field, *Track of Man*, pp. 227–28.

36 Ibid., pp. 226–27.

CHAPTER TWENTY: WALL: FREEPORT, LONG ISLAND, 1946

1 Isabel Wall Whittemore, interview by author, August 24, 2008, South Tamworth, N.H.

2 Ibid.

3 Ibid.

4 1920 U.S. Census, Washington, D.C.; Whittemore interview.

5 Stephen R. Wall Personnel File, National Archives, National Personnel Records Center, St. Louis; Whittemore interview.

6 Elizabeth J. Gates Personnel File, National Archives, National Personnel Records Center, St. Louis.

7 "Pupils in Eighth Grade Win Promotions to High Schools," *Washington Post*, January 27, 1918, p. 13; "Man Tries Suicide by Bridge Plunge," *Washington Post*, April 25, 1933, p. 1; Whittemore interview.

8 Whittemore interview; "Wages and Hours of Labor in the Lumber, Millwork, and Furniture Industries, 1915," *Bulletin of the U.S. Bureau of Labor Statistics*, No. 225, Wages and Hours of Labor Series No. 26 (1918), pp. 88–89.

9 Hudson [Mass.] City Directory (1941), p. 35; Whittemore interview.

10 Whittemore interview.

11 Ibid.

12 Ibid.

13 Ibid.

14 Ibid.

15 See "Amateur Actors on the Stage," *Washington Post*, June 4, 1889, p. 4; "Graduates of Martyn College," *Washington Post*, June 5, 1889, p. 7. "Miss Bel Irene Wall will appear in Junior Excelsior's Ovation, June 19, at the Metropolitan Church," classified advertisement, *Washington Post*, June 16, 1889, p. 2; Edmund Shaftesbury, *Lessons in the Mechanics of Personal Magnetism* (Washington, D.C.: Martyn College Press, 1888), title page; and Isabel Irene Elterich, "Ebony, Ivory and Cologne," *Roycroft* 1 (1917), p. 121.

16 1900 U.S. Census, Queens County, N.Y. According to immigration records, G. Otto Elterich completed six trips to Europe between 1904 and 1906. See New York Passenger Lists, 1820–1957, Ancestry.com.

17 "Drown in the Thames," *Washington Post*, June 8, 1907, p. 3.

18 Ibid.

19 Isabel I. Elterich, Shield for Ladies Drawers, Patent No. 872,172; Isabel Wall Elterich, *The Girl of the Golden Future* (East Aurora, N.Y.: The Roycrofters, 1918), p. 45; see also Lara Freidenfelds, *The Modern Period: Menstruation in Twentieth-Century America* (Baltimore: Johns Hopkins University Press, 2009).

20 Elterich, *Girl of Golden Future*, pp. 13, 21, 23, 29–30, 44.

21 Ibid., pp. 5, 32, 34.

22 Elterich, "Ebony, Ivory and Cologne," pp. 121–22; see also Ann Mikkelsen, "From Sympathy to Empathy: Anzia Yezierska and the Transformation of the American Subject," *American Literature* 82 (2010), pp. 361ff.

23 Whittemore interview.

24 Ibid.

25 Ibid.; see generally Lorraine B. Diehl and Marianne Hardart, *The Automat: The History, Recipes, and Allure of Horn & Hardart's Masterpiece* (New York: Clarkson Potter, 2002).

26 Whittemore interview; Marshall Berman, *On the Town: One Hundred Years of Spectacle in Times Square* (New York: Random House, 2006), pp. 204–5; Darcy Tell, *Times Square Spectacular* (New York: HarperCollins, 2007), pp. 119–21.

27 Whittemore interview.

28 Ibid.

29 "Return District Boys to Face Theft Charge," *Washington Post*, September 2, 1923, p. 6.

30 "Hit-and-Run Charge Nets 45 Days in Jail," *Washington Post*, July 7, 1928, p. 16; "Langdon Held, Denies Part in Girl's Slaying," *Washington Post*, January 4, 1931, p. M1.

31 "Roscoe Orin Wall . . . , who also goes under the name of Stephen Roscoe Gates, has been sued by his wife for limited divorce and maintenance, . . . and he is apparently avoiding service of process in that suit": see Wilson L. Townsend to Register of Wills, Washington, D.C., August 25, 1934, *In re: Estate of Stephen Roscoe Wall*, No. 47085, photocopy courtesy of Thomas L. Murphy.

32 Record in *Murphy v. State*, 184 Md. 70 (Md. 1944) (No. 52), Maryland State Archives, Annapolis.

33 Thomas L. Murphy, interview by author, October 28, 2005, Hampton, Ga.; *Murphy v. State*, p. 80.

34 *Murphy v. State*, p. 75; "Maryland Garage Operator Sentenced to Die for Rape," *Washing-*

ton Post, April 29, 1944, p. 1; "Death Sentence in Rape Upheld by Md. Court," *Washington Post*, December 14, 1944, p. 9.
35 "Maryland Garage Operator Sentenced to Die for Rape," *Washington Post*, April 29, 1944, p. 1.
36 Ibid.
37 Ibid.
38 "Convicted Rapist Hanged in State Penitentiary," *Baltimore Sun*, July 20, 1945, p. 22.
39 Whittemore interview.

EPILOGUE

1 Hart Gibson, "The Race Problem," Pettit Collection.
2 Ibid.
3 Ibid.; George M. Fredrickson, *The Black Image in the White Mind: The Debate on Afro-American Character and Destiny, 1817–1914* (New York: Harper and Row, 1971), pp. 228–55.
4 Gibson, "Race Problem."
5 Freda Spencer Goble, interview by author, August 29, 2005, Paintsville, Ky.
6 See, e.g., Edward Ball, *Slaves in the Family* (New York: Farrar, Straus and Giroux, 1998).
7 For critiques of DNA ancestry testing, see Duana Fullwiley, "The Biologistical Construction of Race: 'Admixture' Technology and the New Genetic Medicine," *Social Studies of Science* 38 (2008), pp. 695ff; Deborah A. Bolnick et al., "The Science and Business of Ancestry Testing," *Science* 318 (2007), pp. 399–400.
8 Winthrop D. Jordan, "American Chiaroscuro: The Status and Definition of Mulattoes in the British Colonies," *William and Mary Quarterly*, 3d ser., 19 (1962), pp. 183, 189–91; William LaBach, interview by author, March 4, 2009, Georgetown, Ky.
9 Thomas Murphy, interview by author, October 28, 2005, Hampton, Ga.
10 Goble interview.
11 Ibid.
12 Ibid.
13 Isabel Wall Whittemore, interview by author, August 24, 2008, South Tamworth, N.H.
14 Ibid.
15 Ibid.